Lecture Notes in Artificial Int

Subseries of Lecture Notes in Computer ⟨
Edited by J. G. Carbonell and J. Siekmann

Lecture Notes in Computer Science
Edited by G. Goos, J. Hartmanis, and J. van Leeuwen

Springer
Berlin
Heidelberg
New York
Hong Kong
London
Milan
Paris
Tokyo

Ralph Bergmann

Experience Management

Foundations, Development Methodology,
and Internet-Based Applications

Springer

Series Editors

Jaime G. Carbonell, Carnegie Mellon University, Pittsburgh, PA, USA
Jörg Siekmann, University of Saarland, Saarbrücken, Germany

Author

Ralph Bergmann
University of Hildesheim
Mathematics and Applied Computer Science
Data and Knowledge Management Group
P.O. Box 101363, 31113 Hildesheim, Germany
E-mail: bergmann@dwm.uni-hildesheim.de

Cataloging-in-Publication Data applied for

Die Deutsche Bibliothek - CIP-Einheitsaufnahme

Bergmann, Ralph:
Experience management : foundations, development methodology, and Internet
based applications / Ralph Bergmann. - Berlin ; Heidelberg ; New York ; Hong
Kong ; London ; Milan ; Paris ; Tokyo : Springer, 2002
  (Lecture notes in computer science ; 2432 : Lecture notes in artificial
intelligence)
  ISBN 3-540-44191-3

CR Subject Classification (1998): I.2.4, I.2.8, I.2, H.4, H.5.3, J.1

ISSN 0302-9743
ISBN 3-540-44191-3 Springer-Verlag Berlin Heidelberg New York

Springer-Verlag Berlin Heidelberg New York,
a member of BertelsmannSpringer Science+Business Media GmbH

http://www.springer.de

© Springer-Verlag Berlin Heidelberg 2002
Printed in Germany

Typesetting: Camera-ready by author, data conversion by Boller Mediendesign
Printed on acid-free paper   SPIN: 10870114   06/3142   5 4 3 2 1 0

Preface

Human problem solving in many fields is based on extensive experience. A long time ago, business organizations recognized the concrete value of knowledge, but only recently have they started to systematically introduce measures to grow, capture, explore, and maintain their knowledge. The interdisciplinary research field that deals with these issues is called *knowledge management.*

Experience management is a special kind of knowledge management that is limited to the management of *experience.* Experience is valuable, stored, *specific knowledge* that was acquired by a problem-solving agent in a problem-solving situation. Today it is recognized that experience covers large portions of the knowledge in an organization that need to be managed and reused in a systematic manner.

From the computer science point of view, artificial intelligence provides methods for experience representation and experience processing. Case-based reasoning, which has been an active research and application field for the past 20 years, addresses these issues in particular. With the recently growing importance of knowledge-management applications, the case-based reasoning branch providing appropriate methods is raising increasing attention. At the same time the former frontiers to related areas such as machine learning, information theory, organizational learning, or process modeling have started to vanish. Moreover, Web technologies are playing an important role in experience management. They provide the connectivity that is required to share experiences. Although the Internet is primarily a new medium, it enables the development of new applications implementing services that support humans during different kinds of complex problem solving.

Content of This Book

This book primarily addresses the computer science view of experience management and presents methods for building experience-management software systems. However, managerial and organizational issues involved when implementing an experience-management system in an organization are also touched on.

Starting from the requirements of complex problem solving the main conceptual questions for experience management are identified and an experience-management framework is proposed. Following the structure of this framework, the theoretical foundations for experience management are laid down. To this end, a large body of principal methods for experience representation and reasoning with experience are analyzed and presented for the first time in a unified and concise terminology. This can be considered the theory of experience-management technology.

Furthermore, the process of application development is highlighted, pointing out successful practically proven ways of obtaining and operating experience-management applications. In this way the theory is put into industrial practice. Three divergent and significant application areas are discussed in detail in this book: *electronic commerce*, *diagnosis of complex technical equipment*, and *electronic design reuse*. For each area, a specialized architecture for implementing experience-management applications is described and assessments of the effectiveness of fielded example applications are presented.

Acknowledgements

Many colleagues and friends significantly supported the work reported in this book, which is based on the Habilitation thesis I presented at the University of Kaiserslautern. My first thanks goes to my former supervisor Prof. Dr. Michael M. Richter, who gave me the opportunity to conduct very freely my own research work and projects in his group at the University of Kaiserslautern. Based on his longstanding experience, he always provided extremely valuable advice when I had to master this or that difficulty. I also thank him very much for a lot of inspiring discussions we had, which significantly influenced my way of thinking about experience management. I also want to thank Prof. Dr. Pádraig Cunningham and Prof. Dr. David Leake for many discussions at various locations and particularly for acting as external reviewers for the Habilitation thesis and for providing valuable feedback on the manuscript.

Many of the results presented in this book emerged in the context of the funded projects I was involved in or for which I was responsible. Funding for these projects came from the European Commission, the German "Federal Ministry for Education and Research" (BMBF) and from the "Stiftung Rheinland-Pfalz für Innovation". I want to thank the former members of the project teams at the University of Kaiserslautern, particularly PD Dr. Klaus-Dieter Althoff, Dr. Peter Oehler, Sascha Schmitt, Armin Stahl, Ivo Vollrath, Dr. Stefan Wess, and Dr. Wolfgang Wilke. For recent results in the current projects, I want to thank the members of my research group at the University of Hildesheim, particularly Kerstin Maximini, Rainer Maximini, Martin Schaaf, Marco Spinelli, and Alexander Tartakovski.

Several people from the commercial and academic project partners DaimlerChrysler, empolis (formerly known as tec:inno), IMS MAXIMS (formerly known as IMS), Kaidara (formerly known as Acknosoft), Trinity College Dublin, and University College Dublin also contributed important ideas during numerous workshops and conferences, project meetings, and informal events. Some of the results collected in this book (particularly those from the reported applications) were achieved by the commercial partners, doing the hard work of application development and evaluation. In particular, I want to thank Dr. Eric Auriol, Martin Bräuer, Sean Breen, Prof. Dr. Pádraig Cunningham, Dr. Mehmet Göker, Dr. Roy Johnston, Dr. Michel Manago, Bénédicte Minguy, Thomas Roth-Berghofer, Jürgen Schumacher, Dr. Reinhard Skuppin, Dr. Barry Smyth, Emmanuelle Tartarin-Fayol, Ralph Traphöner, Dr. Stefan Wess, and Max Wolf.

For many inspiring discussions, for a lot of practical help in various occasions, and for the pleasant and collaborative atmosphere I want to thank everyone involved in Kaiserslautern and Hildesheim, and very particularly I want to thank the secretaries Edith Hüttel, Petra Homm, and Martina Rosemeyer.

Last but not least I want to thank my wife Manuela for giving me the necessary encouragement and help during some laborious and difficult periods in my scientific life so far, as well as for showing me many inspiring things outside the world of computer science. Very special thanks are devoted to my son Julian for the very refreshing smiles on his face during the time I did the final editing of this book. My final thanks goes to my parents Irene and Robert Bergmann for their permanent support that paved the way that led to the work presented in this book.

Enjoy reading!

Hildesheim, June 2002   *Ralph Bergmann*

Contents

Part I. Knowledge Representation for Experience Management

Part II. Methods for Experience Management

List of Figures

List of Tables

1. Introduction

> *"What makes an expert's behavior so peculiar is the knowledge, not anything peculiar about his or her brain. We're betting that the process underlying thinking is actually very straightforward: selective search and recognition."*

> Herbert A. Simon,
> Nobel Price Laureate,
> 1916 – 2001

Business organizations have started to give more attention to their knowledge; they are looking for ways to grow, capture, explore, and maintain their knowledge. This is what is called *knowledge management. Experience management* is a special kind of knowledge management that is restricted to the management of experience knowledge, i.e., specific knowledge situated in a particular problem solving context. Experience management deals with collecting, modeling, storing, reusing, evaluating, and maintaining experience. For experience management, Web technologies for the Inter- and Intranet play an important role. They provide the connectivity that is required to share experience.

This chapter motivates this work and gives a first introduction to experience reuse and management. The three application areas addressed in this book are briefly characterized. Each of them requires Internet or Intranet-based approach to experience management. This chapter ends with an outline of this book, which provides further guidance for the reader.

1.1 Complex Problem Solving in the Internet Age

In this book we systematically explore methods for experience management through intelligent Internet-based applications. We restrict the scope of this investigation to applications that are designed to support human users during complex problem solving. The focus is on complex problem solving tasks in specialized, well-defined domains with clear boarders, rather then general problem solving (Ernst and Newell 1969) as studied, for example, in the early days of artificial intelligence research. The tasks of interest are complex in the sense that there is no well-defined problem solving process, there is no complete model of the domain, and there are no problem solving algorithms available. Hence problem solving cannot be fully automated. Such problem solving performed by the human experts relies very much on experience. In particular, the tasks we are looking at require very specific expert knowledge from the respective field rather than large amounts of common sense knowledge.

1.1.1 Knowledge Intensive Problem Solving

Human problem solving in many field is based on extensive experience. This is true for business problem solving, problem solving in administrations, and even for solving problems that occur in everyday life. Experience knowledge has now generally been recognized as a very important resource and factor of success. Business organizations have started to give more attention to their knowledge; they are looking for ways to grow, capture, explore, and maintain their knowledge like they do with other resources, too. *Knowledge management* (O'Leary 1998; Davenport and Prusak 1997; Davenport et al. 1996; Nonaka et al. 1995) recently appeared as a new discipline that addresses the problems related to this intention. It aims at systematically investigating organizational processes, socio-cultural aspects, and supporting technologies to improve the way knowledge is created, structured, shared, maintained, and accessed within an organization. Closely related to knowledge management are the areas of *learning organizations* and *organizational* or *corporate memory* (Borghoff and Pareschi 1997; Abecker et al. 1998), and *experience factory* (Basili et al. 1994a; Basili et al. 1994b).

Also, state-of-the art electronic commerce requires providing customers directly with electronic services for product recommendation, purchasing, and after-sales support. *Customer Relationship Management* (Newell 1999; Plattner 1999; Martin 1999; CRM Forum 1999) has become a recent topic in the business world that stands for the observation that all kinds of business, including electronic commerce, must become more customer-centric, providing knowledge asked for by the customer via a single communication point. All such services rely on large amounts of experience, for example about products, specifications, application scenarios, trouble-shooting, etc.

1.1.2 Complexity Issues

There are typical complexity characteristics of these problem solving types, which are dominant to different degrees. The problems to be solved can be complex because of the following reasons:

- *High problem solving effort:* Problem solving requires a lot of effort, e.g. in terms of time, money, or consumed resources.
- *Knowledge intensive:* Problem solving requires a large amount of knowledge and experience.
- *Involves several people:* Several people are involved in the problem solving process, each of which may have a different role or may act in a different task.
- *Large solution space:* The space of possible solutions is very huge and a single solution can be very complex in terms of size or structure.
- *Vague Problem descriptions:* The problems to be solved are typically incompletely specified or imprecise. Problems may only become more precisely while being solved.
- *Highly dynamic:* Problem solving is situated in a highly dynamic and rapidly changing world. Such changes affect the knowledge, the people involved, the problems to be solved, the potential solutions, and the processes involved.

1.1.3 Internet-Based Applications

Although the Internet is primarily only a new medium, it enables the development of new applications implementing services that support humans during such complex problem solving. This includes services that were previously only available in non-electronic form where the communication is performed directly between humans. The most important advantages of Internet-based applications compared to traditional, non-electronic services are that they

- can be made available around the clock,
- can reach a much large group of users than comparable non-electronic counter-parts
- can be used without physically moving to the service provider's location,
- provide the user with up-to-date information,
- cost less for providing the service.

The quality of a service strongly depends on how experienced the service provider is and how much of this experience reaches the user. For a traditional non-electronic service this experience and other knowledge is in the head of the human expert who is in charge of providing the service; for an Internet-based service, such experience must be captured, represented, and (re-)used automatically.

1.2 Example Application Scenarios

Some example areas of such complex problem solving are now discussed to illustrate the previously mentioned characteristics and to make them more concrete. Part III of this book elaborates these areas in depth.

1.2.1 Electronic Commerce

Electronic Commerce is the exchange of information, goods, or services via electronic networks (Klein and Szyperski 1998). If we have a closer look at the problem solving involved in electronic commerce, we can identify three consecutive phases (Klein 1997; Wilke et al. 1998). During *pre-sales* a potential customer is provided with all possible and necessary marketing information s/he is interested in about certain products. A mix of marketing tools is used to serve customers with product information. In the consecutive *sales* phase a customer and a sales agent negotiate about products, their desired costs, terms, and conditions of sale, etc. The task is to discover the customer's demands and to find an appropriate product for her/him. Unlike pre-sales which is often a one-step or even one-way communication, sales is a complex process with many interactions between the seller and the buyer. *After-sales* refers to situations in which a customer had already bought a product and needs additional support for the use of it. Searching for information s/he may contact a sales assistant, the manufacturer of the product, or any other institution who may provide her/him this kind of service.

We briefly characterize problem solving in electronic commerce with respect to the aforementioned complexity characteristics.

- *Knowledge intensive:* Corporate knowledge, e.g., about products (e.g. product specifications, application range, product compatibility, troubleshooting, etc.), competitors, and customers (customer classes, typical customer requirements and preferences, etc.) plays an important role in all phases.
- *Involves several people:* There are several people with different roles involved: the clients, the sales agents, the product experts. Clients typically have different kinds of requirements and preferences. They can be experts in the product area or they can be complete novices. Sales agents and product experts are typically specialized for a particular product category.
- *Large solution space:* There is typically a large spectrum of products that are offered. There is a spectrum of products ranging from simple fixed products to complex configurable products. Due to the large number of products with different variants, there is a large solution space that must be handled during problem solving.
- *Vague problem descriptions:* The requirements or queries stated by customers are often vague, incompletely specified, or even contradictory. Customers often mix their wish with its fulfillment.

- *Highly dynamic:* Since the market demands shorter product development cycles and customer-tailored products, the product spectrum and the related knowledge changes rapidly.

1.2.2 Diagnosis of Complex Technical Equipment

The ever-increasing complexity of technical equipment makes it difficult for the users of these systems to operate and maintain them. While the probability that technical systems will fail grows exponentially with their complexity, the expertise needed to be able to control every feature of such complex systems usually exceeds the resources available to end-users.

Help-desks support end-users of complex technical equipment. When end-users have problems, they count on help-desks to provide emergency services. Help-desk operators provide guidance on how to use the system and keep the system operational by performing necessary maintenance tasks. They are expected to be able to solve problems on very short notice, in a very short time, and to be knowledgeable in all areas that are related to the technical system at hand.

Help-desk operators use their own experiences to solve most of the problems that are relayed to them. However, as systems become more complex, the areas help-desk operators are experts in tend to diverge, i.e., problem solving experience is distributed among experts and the areas of expertise do not necessarily overlap. Nevertheless, when an end-user has a problem, s/he wants it to be solved as soon as possible. If that expert is not available, the user has to wait, which is annoying and not acceptable in a commercial environment. The problem-solving experience must be available to every help-desk operator at all times.

The diagnosis of complex technical equipment has the following characteristics of complex problem solving:

- *Knowledge intensive:* Diagnosis is based on extensive troubleshooting experience and on general knowledge about the structure and the function of the equipment and its sub-components.
- *Involves several people:* For complex equipment, the diagnosis experience is very often distributed among different experts.
- *Large solution space:* Here, solution space refers to the set of possible faults and related remedy operations. The more complex the equipment is, the larger is the solution space.
- *Vague Problem descriptions:* Descriptions of the observed symptoms are very often imprecise; the characteristics of a symptoms can only be vaguely defined, or the certain values cannot be measured exactly. Also, problem descriptions are typically incomplete, since only a few observations have been made up to a certain point in the diagnosis process; important symptoms may not have been observed.

- *Highly dynamic:* New technical equipment is developed, installed, or updated continuously; regularly, new faults occur that have not been observed
before.

1.2.3 Electronics Design

The design of electronic circuits is a discipline in which two contrasting tendencies can be observed: On the one hand, modern circuit designs get more
and more complex and difficult to handle by electronic engineers. On the
other hand, global competition requires a continuous reduction of development times. The correctness and reliability of the designs should, of course,
not suffer from shorter development cycles.

These requirements have become so dominant that they cannot be met
anymore without extensive utilization of design reuse. It is getting vitally
important for an electronic engineer to reuse old designs (or parts of them)
and not to redesign a new application entirely from scratch. Reusing designs
from the past requires that the engineer has enough experience and knowledge about existing designs, in order to be able to find candidates that are
suitable for reuse in his specific new situation. The idea of design reuse is
not new, but until recently, reusable components in electronic designs have
been limited in complexity and were conceivable by application designers.
Nowadays, reusable designs are growing ever more complex and difficult to
understand by designers reusing them. In the electronic design scenario we
find the following properties of complex problem solving:

- *High problem solving effort:* The design of an electronic circuit is a very
time consuming task for engineers since today's components are getting
more and more complex.
- *Knowledge intensive:* General design knowledge is required, knowledge
about existing reusable designs, as well as knowledge about how designs
can be adapted to the current needs.
- *Large solution space:* Here, the solution space refers to the space of all possible electronics designs, which is obviously extremely large and typically
only limited by the available space on the chip. Each design itself is also
very complex.
- *Highly dynamic:* New reusable designs become available continuously. Also,
old designs will become outdated, for example, when the technology advances.

1.3 Experience Reuse

Complex problem solving in situations like those sketched before heavily depend on experience. Sharing experience enables to get access to experience

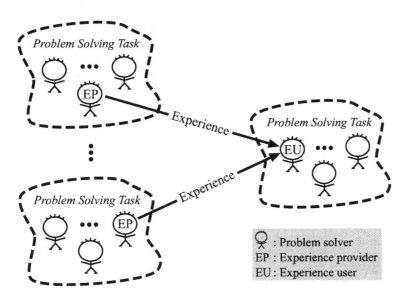

Fig. 1.1. Scenario of One-Directional Experience Distribution.

from different people, and avoids making mistakes that other people did already. Reusing experience avoids problem solving from scratch, i.e., already solved problems don't need to be solved over and over again.

1.3.1 Basic Scenarios of Experience Reuse

Figure 1.1 shows a first, very simple scenario for experience reuse. The experience that a human *problem solver* gains during previous problem solving situations is made available by her/him. Thereby this problem solver plays the role of an *experience provider*. A (usually different) problem solver responsible for solving a new problem is supported by experience from some of the experience providers. Thereby s/he becomes an *experience user*. To solve the new problem, the obtained experience must be interpreted in the context of the new problem solving task, which is likely to be different from the task from which the experience emerges.

This first scenario can be characterized as one-directional transfer of experience. The roles experience provider and experience user are clearly distinguished. The experience users are the ones who benefit from the experience. However, the experience providers can get or should get reimbursed for giving away their experience. By such a model, experience can become a tradable good, for which new specialized business models can emerge. Hence experience reuse by itself, if supported by the Internet, can be regarded as a special kind of electronic commerce.

An alternative scenario shown in Fig. 1.2 is that of sharing experience for the mutual benefit of a group of people, e.g., people working in a company, user groups, or common-interest groups. Here, there is no explicit distinction between experience providers and experience users. For one experience item, one person can be an experience provider, while the same person can become a user of an experience in another problem solving context. The experience is exchanged via a common experience pool or experience bus. If realized as a common pool within a corporation, this pool is the core of a corporate memory, that is continuously extended. Also this scenario can be regarded from the viewpoint of electronic commerce. Experience can be traded on some kind of market place, where people are offering and requesting experience.

1.3.2 Expected Benefits of Experience Reuse

Experience reuse is expected to lead to improvements during problem solving. These improvements can be substantiated as follows:

Shorter Problem Solving Time

Reuse leads to a reduction of the problem solving time, because problems don't need to be solved over and over again. A reduced problem solving time leads to the following benefits:

- The cost of problem solving is reduced.
- The time-to-market (in product development) is reduced and competitive advantage can be gained thereby.
- The time during which the problem to be solved exists and during which it possibly causes a loss or other harms is reduced.

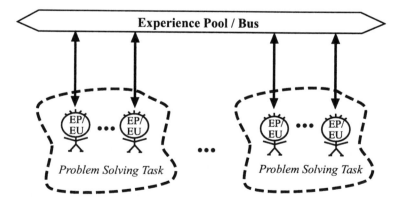

Fig. 1.2. Scenario of Experience Sharing.

Improved Solution Quality

The quality of the solution can be improved, because experience (hopefully) helps to find good solutions. It reduces the probability of wrong or harmful solutions. An improved solution quality leads to the following benefits:

- A better solution has usually a higher (commercial) value.
- It improves the general reputation of the problem solver.

Less Skills Are Required

The problem solvers need less skills and less own experience, because access to the other's experience is available. This leads to the following benefits:

- The problem solvers can be supported to solve problems they could not solve themselves otherwise.
- The cost of problem solving is reduced.
- The training cost for the problem solvers is reduced.

1.4 Experience Management

In order to enable the ultimate goal of efficient experience reuse, several enabling activities must be considered. The experience knowledge must be *managed*, i.e., it must be captured, modeled, stored, retrieved, adapted, evaluated, and maintained. This embeds experience reuse into the broader perspective of knowledge management.

1.4.1 Knowledge Management

Knowledge management deals with the process of creating value from an organization or a company's knowledge. Valuable knowledge can be available in different forms and media, such as in the mind of the employees, in working procedures, in documents, databases, Intranets, etc. Knowledge management aims at systematically collecting and sharing this knowledge by making use of the connectivity provided by Web-based and Inter- and Intranet technologies.

The term knowledge management (Abecker et al. 1998; Wolf et al. 1999; Studer et al. 1999; Liebowitz 1999) is more than 10 years old, during which different researchers and practitioners came up with several definitions (The Knowledge Management Forum 1996; Liebowitz 1999). These definitions don't differ in their core idea, but focus on different aspects and viewpoints. One such definition is the following:

Clarification of Terms 1.1 (Knowledge Management) Knowledge Management is the systematic, explicit, and deliberate building, renewal, and application of knowledge to maximize an enterprise's knowledge-related effectiveness and returns from its knowledge assets (Wiig 1997).

There is still an ongoing discussion about what activities are required for knowledge management. Different frameworks have been proposed so. For example, Beckman (1997) proposes the following briefly described steps:

- *Identify:* Determine the core competencies, sourcing strategies, and knowledge domains.
- *Capture:* Formalize existing knowledge.
- *Select:* Assess knowledge relevance, value, and accuracy.
- *Store:* Represent corporate memory in knowledge repository with various knowledge schema.
- *Share:* Distribute knowledge automatically to users based on interest and work.
- *Apply:* Retrieve and use knowledge in making decisions, solving problems, automating or supporting work, job aids, and training.
- *Create:* Discover new knowledge through research, experimenting, and creative thinking.
- *Sell:* Develop and market new knowledge-based products and services.

Although these activities interact and partially depend on each other, they may not be executed sequentially.

Knowledge management as a scientific discipline can be seen as a combination of methods and concepts from different areas such as computer science (in particular artificial intelligence and knowledge-based systems), business process re-engineering, human resource management, and organizational behavior analysis. The focus of this book is clearly on computer science methods; hence we primarily address the question of how IT technology can support efficient knowledge management. From this point of view, we can basically distinguish two areas which contribute methods: groupware and repositories.

Groupware

Groupware methods aim at enabling groups of people working together efficiently by organizing the distribution of knowledge among a group that can be geographically dispersed. Knowledge is exchanged in the context of the specific task in which the individual group member is involved, taking into account her/his specific needs. Examples of methods are Computer Supported Collaborative Work (CSCW) and Workflow Management.

Repositories

Organizational and Corporate Memory approaches focus on methods for managing knowledge repositories. Such repositories are collections of a companies knowledge that are integrated across different sources and which are online accessible.

For experience reuse, the repository-oriented approach is in the center of interest. However, access to knowledge must be integrated into the workflow and the task-specific context. Internet technologies must be integrated to enable organization-wide or world-wide access.

1.4.2 Experience Management versus Knowledge Management

Experience management can be considered a special kind of knowledge management. It is restricted to managing experience, which is a special kind of knowledge. Experience is valuable, stored, *specific knowledge* that was acquired by a problem solving agent in a problem solving situation. Thereby, experience is in contrast to *general knowledge*, which has a broader scope and which is discovered inductively from large bodies of experience, e.g. through scientific research (see also Sect. 2.1). This restriction has several important implications for the knowledge management activities:

Capture and Store

Capturing and storing experience is much easier than capturing and storing general knowledge. Since experience is situated in a concrete problem solving context, it is more easily observable or it is more easily describable by humans. Acquisition of general knowledge from humans is known to be very difficult, because it is more abstract and often only implicitly available. Capturing experience is also much easier because it is easier to formalize and to represent and can sometimes even be automated. Experience is much like fact knowledge whose formalization does not require logic-based knowledge representation formalisms which are hard to handle for non experts in artificial intelligence. Due to the lower requirements on knowledge representation, a smaller number of knowledge schemes is required than for general knowledge.

Select

Selecting relevant knowledge items is also much easier for experience than for general knowledge, because experience is situated in a specific problem solving context. Hence, relevance can be assessed by comparing the current problem solving context with the previous one. General knowledge by its nature abstracts from the specific problem solving context.

Share

Sharing of experience is easier than sharing general knowledge. This is due to the fact that experience due to its context specific nature is more understandable for humans than general knowledge. To understand general knowledge a person must first integrate it into her/his pre-existing knowledge, which can require significant cognitive work. Experience is more like examples which are much easier to understand.

Apply

When applying experience in decision making and problem solving a different kind of reasoning is required than for reasoning with general knowledge. Applying general knowledge requires logic-based inference mechanisms for deriving a particular conclusion. Experience, however, is already present in a specific form. It may need to be adapted in order to be applicable, which requires a different kind of reasoning.

Create

Discovering general knowledge from experience is outside the primary scope of experience management. Experience management deals with specific knowledge and hence, generalization is not necessary. Experience is not created but captured by recording problem solving episodes.

Maintain

The maintenance effort for the knowledge repository is lower for experience than for general knowledge. During maintenance, the experience items can be regarded mostly independent; changing a single experience item usually does not affect the behavior of the whole systems. However, changing a single piece of general knowledge might influence significantly the reasoning process for a large set of problems.

Sell

Due to the above mentioned reasons, experience management systems can be developed with less cost and can be deployed with a higher profit than systems that deal with general knowledge. This is particularly true if compared with systems that process highly formalized general knowledge.

1.4.3 Experience Management Activities

From the general activities related to knowledge management, we now derive specific activities for experience management.

Collecting Experience

The experience to be shared must be collected. Experience may be already available in documented form, for example, as text documents or as database entries. However, experience may also be only available in the memories of the experts. This experience must first be collected for reuse. Further, new experience arises continuously. It typically arises in the context of a certain problem solving situation. Mechanisms are required to collect such new experience at the time it becomes available.

Modeling Experience

In order to manage experience, it must be modeled. Modeling is the core for selecting reusable experience and for reusing it. Modeling experience means finding appropriate ways for representing it and for formalizing it, if necessary. Different kinds of experiences and different problem solving tasks may require tailored ways for experience modeling.

Storing Experience

The collected experience must be stored for future reuse. Such an experience memory can be either centralized or distributed.

Reusing Experience

Experience reuse is the ultimate goal of experience management. This requires

1. to get access to experience and to select appropriate experience for reuse,
2. to assess the utility of the selected experience in the context of the new problem to be solved,
3. if necessary, to adapt experience to new context, and
4. finally, to solve the new problem (or to support the user to solve the new problem) by reusing the experience.

Evaluating Experience

During problem solving by experience reuse, the reused experience can be evaluated in the context of the new problem to be solved. The evaluation can be in terms of the appropriateness of the selected experience, or in terms of the accuracy and actuality of the retrieved experience. Such evaluation is important to continuously improve the process of experience reuse.

Maintaining Experience

Finally, the available experience must be updated continuously. Due to the rapidly changing environment, experience may have only a limited life-time. Invalid experience must be identified and removed or updated. Also, the way the existing experience is modeled may be subject to changes. Experience maintenance can be triggered by a negative experience evaluation or can be performed precautionary.

1.4.4 Experience Management Definition

From the above considerations we can now summarize the idea of experience management in the following clarification of terms.

Clarification of Terms 1.2 (Experience   Management)   Experience management is a special kind of knowledge management that is restricted to managing experience knowledge, i.e., specific knowledge situated in a particular problem solving context. Experience management deals with collecting, modeling, storing, reusing, evaluating, and maintaining of experience.

The term experience management has recently also been used by other authors (Tautz 2000; Nick et al. 2002; Althoff and Nick forthcomming) in the spirit of this definition. On the first German workshop on Experience Management[1] Nick et al. (2002) suggest that experience management is a knowledge management subfield that provides an environment for research in various fields, such as knowledge management, case-based reasoning, experience factory, machine learning and knowledge discovery, cognitive science, software engineering, information retrieval, etc. Thus, experience management is a research field being concerned with all aspects of processing a continuous stream of knowledge and enabling sustained usage.

1.5 Web Technologies for Experience Management

For efficient experience management today, Web technologies for the Inter- and Intranet play an important role. Web technologies provide the connectivity that is required to share experience. While Intranets enable the communication between experience providers and experience users (possibly through an experience base), the Internet provides world-wide access to an experience base, for example for a customer within an electronic shop or service.

1.5.1 Representing and Storing Experience on the Web

Already today, the World-Wide-Web (WWW) is considered the largest collection of information and knowledge from nearly all areas. Some even view it as the largest knowledge-based system ever built (Fensel et al. 1997).

On the Web, information and knowledge can be represented in a multimedia form such as texts, graphics, hypertext, or even as video or audio sequences. Depending on the type, this information is coded in a respective data format (e.g. HTML, gif, avi, mpeg, ...) and stored on the file system

---

[1] The First workshop on experience management took place 2002 and is the first official event of the new Special Interest Group on Knowledge Management of the German Informatics Society (GI) after merging with the former Case-Based Reasoning Special Interest Group. See www.experience-management.org .

or database of a Web server which gives company-wide or world-wide access. There is no restriction or predefined representation structure; complete freedom is given about how to present some piece of information. This high degree of freedom has obvious advantages, because the presentation form which is most appropriate for the user can be chosen. Of course, experience can also be represented on the Web. In fact, the WWW contains already today lots of experience collections in various forms. Examples are FAQ lists, product evaluations, company profiles or even parts of personal home pages. However, the high degree of freedom does not only have positive effects. The big disadvantage is that there is no predefined structure which urge experience providers to represent experience in a way that they can be efficiently retrieved and reused. Hence, often the results are chaotic, unstructured and inhomogeneous pieces of experience that are far away from being useful for systematic experience management.

1.5.2 Accessing Experience from the Web

Being able to retrieve appropriate experience is one important task for experience reuse. Current Web technologies provide different ways to get access to Web documents.

Navigation

The most widely used way to find information on the Web is through navigation in some hyperlink structure. Information services or electronic shops often provide specialized structures for information access such as site maps or topical directories (e.g. as provided by Yahoo). To get some information, the user must navigate through the hyperlink structure. At each point in this navigation process s/he must chose one of the links of the current web page to follow, hopefully ending up in the desired content.

Keyword Queries

Keyword search is the most popular technique in current search engines (for the whole internet or for limited local searches). The Web documents that can be accessed by the search engine are indexed by selected keywords or by the whole set of occurring words (e.g. as provided by Altavista). The user must chose a combination of keywords to describe the documents s/he is looking for. The keywords can be combined with logical operators such as AND, OR and NOT. Keyword search results in a list of documents that exactly match the given query. Most keyword searches cannot deal with synonyms and often not even with morphological variations of words. Hence, the selection of the documents is based on the exact occurrence of the keywords in the query.

Database Queries

The access to large volumes of equally structured Web documents can be organized via a database (e.g. for last-minute-travels). For this purpose, each document is characterized as a record in a database. The record describes the document by a set of attribute values for a fixed set of attributes. To access a document, the user must describe the searched content by a combination of values for some of these attributes. The database search results in a list of documents which exactly match the given query.

1.5.3 Limitations of Information Access Approaches for Experience Reuse

Unfortunately, the previously sketched approaches have serious limitations if they are applied for experience reuse for complex problem solving. First, they can only support the retrieval sub-task. There is no support for evaluating a Web document that contains an experience item in the context of the new problem. There is also no support for adapting experience. Even for experience retrieval, the current approaches have serious shortcomings.

Navigation

To realize the navigation approach, it is difficult to create and maintain a hyperlink logic that appropriately reflects different user's problem solving tasks. Due to the fact that problem descriptions are only vaguely and incompletely known, it is difficult to decide which link to follow. To index a large experience base it would be necessary to build up a complex hyperlink structure (e.g. a taxonomy) that takes care of each piece of experience. Such a structure is very difficult and expensive to maintain, particularly in highly dynamic problem solving situations.

Keyword Queries

The keyword query approach does not cause big maintenance efforts since documents are indexed automatically, but leads to a bad retrieval accuracy. Documents are selected based on a purely syntactic criterion: the occurrence of a word in an arbitrary part of the document. Only exact word matches are considered and domain knowledge about the semantics of the current problem and the experience cannot be used. This causes problems with vague problem descriptions which are naturally expressed with different keywords than the experience that relates to the problem. As a consequence, many irrelevant documents are retrieved and the many relevant documents are overlooked. In information retrieval terms we speak about bad recall and precision values.

Database Queries

The shortcomings of database queries for experience retrieval is similar to those of keyword matching. Databases are also limited to exact queries[2] and domain knowledge can hardly be considered during retrieval. Hence, vague queries cannot be handled and experience which does not fit exactly but which is still useful is overlooked.

1.5.4 Internet Technologies as Infrastructure for Experience Management

Despite of these shortcomings of technologies for accessing Web content, Internet technologies play an important role for experience management. Although they don't contribute to conceptual aspects of knowledge processing and management, they provide the infrastructure and the connectivity that is necessary to establish intelligent services for experience management as follows:

- Standards are provided for the communication between agents and to realize client-server architectures in general.
- The "Internet languages" HTML, Java-Script, and Java are the basis for developing client interfaces to experience bases that are world-wide or organization-wide accessible.
- XML and related developments can be used as a means to represent experience items and to attach semantic information to them useful for accurate retrieval.
- The integration of experience management with other existing Internet-based applications, e.g., for electronic commerce or support is necessary.

1.6 Methods for Experience Management on the Conceptual Level

Besides the previously discussed contribution of Internet technologies to building the technical infrastructure for experience management, significant contributions for solving the conceptual problems involved in realizing the experience management activities are required. These methods are the core interest of this book.

---

[2] There are some exceptions from this general statement, e.g. spatial databases, but such extensions don't help much in the context of experience retrieval. See also Chap. 7.

Knowledge Management

As already discussed in Sect. 1.4.1 Knowledge Management as a multi-disciplinary approach combining organizational, technical, and socio-economical views is of course important for experience management as well. It provides the general frame into which experience management is inserted.

Knowledge-Based Systems

The field of *knowledge-based systems* (also called *expert systems*) has a long tradition in representing and processing knowledge. Most of the traditional work in this field deals with knowledge representation using logical formalisms and investigates logical inferences for knowledge processing. In recent years specialized knowledge representation and reasoning approaches have been developed, for example for diagnostic reasoning, planning, configuration, etc. Most of them, however, focus on representing and processing general knowledge, mostly neglecting experience knowledge. However, such methods may are also required for experience adaptation and when the problem solving step itself should be (partially) automatically performed.

Case-Based Reasoning

Case-based reasoning (CBR), as a sub-area of the field of knowledge-based systems, focuses primarily on problem solving by experience. It provides techniques for representing, storing, indexing, and adapting experience. CBR contributes a rich set of techniques which are highly relevant for experience management, particularly for the activities modeling, storing, reusing, and evaluating. However, the large variety of methods from CBR has never been comprehensively analyzed and presented under the unified view of experience management as it is the aim of this book.

Machine Learning

Machine learning is an artificial intelligence discipline which focuses on the generation of new general knowledge from examples. Although, knowledge generation is not in the center of experience management (since experience management deals with capturing existing or emerging experience, but not general knowledge) it is important to create knowledge that helps to assess the appropriateness of a piece of experience for a new problem and to create knowledge to support experience adaptation to a new context.

Process Modeling

In order to support the development and maintenance of an experience base as well as the whole experience management application itself, several processes (technical, organizational, and managerial) are required. These processes can usually not be automated but only supported by software tools. Important is the modeling of these processes, including their interactions. Process modeling provides the means for this purpose.

1.7 Overview of This Book

Before digging into the details, we will now provide an overview that should help the reader through this book.

1.7.1 The Topic in a Nutshell

This book deals with *experience management* in the sense of clarification 1.2. A particular focus is given by the requirements that arise in complex problem solving (see Sect. 1.1.2) and by the fact that modern experience management must be implemented as Internet-based applications. Concrete application areas that are discussed in this book are electronic commerce, diagnosis of complex technical equipment, and electronic design reuse (see Sect. 1.2).

This book explores how experience management can be supported by information technology (IT), especially by techniques that stem from the knowledge-based systems, case-based reasoning, machine learning, and process modeling. It surveys different methods in a unified terminology and investigates them with respect to application requirements. Further the process of application development and maintenance is highlighted, pointing out successful practically proven ways for obtaining and operating experience management applications.

1.7.2 Contributions from Recent Projects

This book is the condensed result from several publicly funded research projects, briefly sketched below.

INRECA: Induction and Reasoning from Cases

In the ESPRIT III project INRECA[3] (Althoff et al. 1995; Bergmann 2001), funded by the European Commission from 5/1992 till 10/1995, the initial foundations for object-oriented experience representations (see Sect. 3.3.2

---

[3] Project 6322, Partners: AcknoSoft (France), IMS Ltd.(Ireland), tec:inno GmbH (Germany), and University of Kaiserslautern (Germany).

and efficient retrieval of experience with index structures (see Sect. 7.3) have been laid. Inreca's basic technologies are inductive and case-based reasoning. An first version of an experience management tool has been developed and applied for various technical diagnosis applications.

WiMo: Knowledge Engineering for Case-Based Learning

The project WiMo, funded from 11/1995 till 10/1996 by *Stiftung Rheinland-Pfalz für Innovation*[4] from the German state Rhineland-Palatinate, improved the case-based reasoning methods for classification tasks, developed in the IN-RECA project for their practical industrial use (Wilke and Bergmann 1996a). The project contributed to the development of methods and tools for modeling the required experience knowledge (see Sect. 9.8) and provided for the first time an interface for Internet-based experience retrieval.

INRECA-II: Information and Knowledge Reengineering for Reasoning from Cases

The major concern of the ESPRIT IV project INRECA-II[5] (Bergmann et al. 1999a; Bergmann 2001), funded by the European Commission from 6/1996 till 5/1999, was to offer an experience-based development and maintenance methodology and a set of tools to support this methodology (see Chap. 9). Further, the diagnosis of complex technical equipment has been explored extensively (see Chap. 11).

WEBSELL: Intelligent Sales Assistants for the World Wide Web

The ESPRIT IV project WEBSELL[6] (Cunningham et al. 2001; Bergmann et al. 2002), funded by the European Commission from 6/1998 till 1/2000, developed an intelligent sales support framework for electronic commerce applications based on experience management. The requirements that occur in Internet-based applications have been first considered comprehensively, particularly with respect to user communication issues (see chapters 6 and 10).

---

[4] Project 183, Partners: University of Kaiserslautern and tec:inno GmbH

[5] Project 22196, Partners: AcknoSoft (France), DaimlerChrysler AG (Germany), IMS Ltd.(Ireland), tec:inno GmbH (Germany), and University of Kaiserslautern (Germany).

[6] Project 27068, Partners: Adwired Communication AG (Switzerland), IMS Ltd.(Ireland), IWT Verlag (Germany), tec:inno GmbH (Germany), Trinity College (Ireland), and University of Kaiserslautern (Germany).

READEE: Reuse Assistant for Designs in Electrical Engineering

In the course of the project READEE ['redɪ] (Bergmann and Vollrath 1999) funded from 6/1997 till 7/2001 by *Stiftung Rheinland-Pfalz für Innovation*[7] a generic experience management approach for electronic design reuse has been developed (see Chap. 12). The concept of generalized cases for representing design objects has been explored (see Sect. 3.4).

**IPQ: IP Qualification for Efficient Design Reuse *and*
ToolIP: Tools and Methods for IP**

The project IPQ [8] funded from 12/2000 till 11/2003 by the German Federal Ministry for Education and Research (BMBF) and the related European Medea project ToolIP[9] continue the work of the project READEE by aiming at an industrial-strength broker and exchange platform for electronic designs. From an experience management point of view, the focus is on developing representation standards for electronic designs and on handling parameterizable designs as generalized cases.

1.7.3 Structure of the Book

This core of this book is structured in twelve chapters organized in three parts as shown in Fig. 1.3.

Chapter 2 introduces a general model for experience management and defines the basic processes and terms involved. The experience management model provides the top-level framework for the following parts I and II of this book.

Part I covers representation methods for experience and all related knowledge required for experience management. This part consists of the following three chapters:
Chapter 3 describes various approaches for representing experience in a way that is appropriate for experience management.
Chapter 4 deals with the representation of knowledge for assessing the utility of an experience item in a particular problem solving episode. This knowledge is modeled through similarity measures.
Chapter 5 addresses the representation of knowledge about how to adapt an experience item to a new situation.

---

[7] Project 255, Partners: University of Kaiserslautern, Dr. Peter Conradi & Partner, tec:inno GmbH and Zentrum für Mikroelektronik

[8] IPQ Project Partners: AMD, Fraunhofer Institute for Integrated Circuits, FZI Karlsruhe, Infineon Technologies, Siemens, Sciworx, Empolis, Thomson Multi Media, TU Chemnitz, University of Hildesheim, University of Kaiserslautern, and University of Paderborn. See www.ip-qualifikation.de

[9] See toolip.fzi.de for partners and further information.

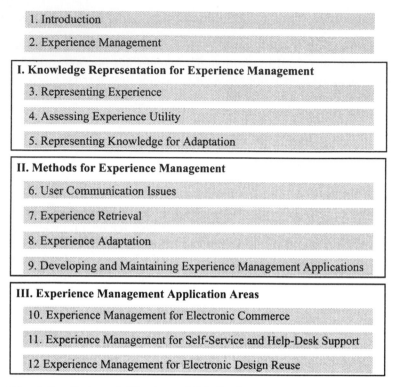

Fig. 1.3. Parts and Chapters of this Book.

Part II includes three chapters that deal with IT methods for implementing Internet-based applications for experience management and a forth chapter that introduces a development methodology for those applications.

Chapter 6 describes basic concepts for the communication between the experience user and the experience management application.

Chapter 7 surveys and compares various algorithms for efficient experience retrieval from large experience bases.

Chapter 8 takes a closer look at the process of experience adaptation and characterizes different approaches relevant for experience management applications.

Chapter 9 presents the basics of an application development and maintenance methodology based on process modeling.

Part III of this book makes the methods discussed previously more concrete by embedding them into concrete application areas. Each of these application areas is discussed in an individual chapter.

Chapter 10 addresses experience management for electronic commerce applications, particularly Web-based product catalogs and shops.

Chapter 11 presents an experience management approach to support the diagnosis of complex technical equipment through an Intranet-based help-desk. *Chapter 12* introduces the new and challenging application area of electronic design reuse.

The first two application areas already led to a number of practical application instances that are in daily use. Hence, we present in detail a generic software architecture for those applications and a specialized development and maintenance methodology. Results of empirical evaluations of those applications in practice is also given. The third application area (electronic design reuse) has not yet reached this state. New companies and business models are just being formed in order to establish the systematic reuse of design objects.

2. Experience Management

> *"Knowledge management is expensive,*
> *but so is stupidity."*
>
> Tom Davenport,
> University of Texas, Austin

Systematic experience reuse supports humans to make better use of their own experience, and more importantly, to make use of experience which is made by a community rather than which is made by an individual. Experience management does not come for free. It involves changing existing or introducing new activities at well as IT technology that efficiently supports these activities. In this chapter we introduce in detail a general model of experience management and define the basic processes and terms involved. Finally, we discuss several related models.

2.1 Knowledge, Experience and Their Characteristics

The experience of the domain that has to be managed for the purpose of reuse is one central issue of consideration now. Experience is a special kind of knowledge. It is specific knowledge that an agent has acquired during past problem solving. However, before clarifying the term *experience* in more detail, we first need to briefly discuss the term *knowledge*.

2.1.1 Data, Information, and Knowledge

Definitions or characterizations for the term knowledge have been given in many scientific disciplines such as philosophy (for example by Plato, Aristotle, Augustine, Descartes, Russel or Popper; see Zalta), economy (Kleinhans 1989; Albrecht 1993; Bellinger et al.; Nonaka 1998), cognitive psychology (Newell 1982; Anderson 1983; Strube and Janetzko 1990), computer science (Aamodt and Nygard 1995; Wolf et al. 1999), and others. We view the term knowledge from the computer science perspective, more precisely, as it is seen in artificial intelligence and knowledge-based systems research. Even in the knowledge-based systems area there are several different attempts to define the term knowledge. An exact or formal definition is not available today and will most likely not be available in the future. For the purpose of this book we try to informally clarify the term knowledge in relation to and distinguished from the terms *data* and *information*. This is because knowledge management and processing by computers is always based on data and information processing. Similar to Aamodt and Nygard (1995) we now describe the terms data, information, and knowledge as follows:

Clarification of Terms 2.1 (Data) Data are syntactic entities, i.e., data are patterns with no meaning. Data can be stored and processed by computers.

Although data has no meaning by itself, it is subject to interpretation by which it is given a meaning. Interpreted data leads to information.

Clarification of Terms 2.2 (Information) Information is interpreted data, i.e., data with meaning. Hence, information is data together with a semantics.

Information is an important entity in problem solving. All complex problem solving is based on a significant amount of information. However, information by itself does not directly describe or imply any activities in problem solving, because information is independent from any pragmatics. This distinguishes it from knowledge.

Clarification of Terms 2.3 (Knowledge) Knowledge is a set of related information with pragmatics. Knowledge puts information into a context given by a certain task or goal.

Knowledge enables an agent to act in a certain way during problem solving and is therefore the primary source of any reasoning process.

The above described relations between data, information, and knowledge are summarized in the knowledge pyramid (Wolf et al. 1999) shown in Fig. 2.1.

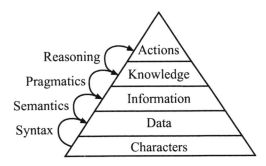

Fig. 2.1. Knowledge Pyramid (adapted from Wolf et al. 1999).

2.1.2 Specific and General Knowledge

Different kinds of knowledge can be characterized among different dimensions, such as: explicit vs. implicit knowledge (Nonaka and Takeuchi 1997; Dienes and Perner 1999), declarative vs. procedural knowledge (McCarthy and Hayes 1969; Winograd 1975), heuristic vs. model knowledge (Lenat 1982). Among those dimensions, the most important distinction when dealing with experience reuse is the distinction between general and specific knowledge. Knowledge can deal with a very specific singular issue in a subject area, giving grounds only for acting in a very narrow situation. On the other hand, knowledge may also have a very broad scope of applicability, such as, for example, a natural law. Knowledge that can be found in textbooks is mostly general knowledge, while case studies, patient records, and lessons learned, are examples of specific knowledge. This distinction is captured in the following clarification of terms.

Clarification of Terms 2.4 (Specific Knowledge) Specific knowledge is knowledge that makes statements about a very narrow subject matter in a domain. Specific knowledge is very much like fact knowledge.

Clarification of Terms 2.5 (General Knowledge) General knowledge is knowledge that makes statements with a broad coverage in the respective domain of problem solving. It may even go beyond the scope of a single domain.

General knowledge is very often the result of some kind of inductive generalization from specific knowledge. Any kind of research in a certain subject area (basic research, but also application-oriented research and research in engineering disciplines) has the goal to discover new general knowledge. Experimental research is a classical example for the inductive creation of general knowledge from specific knowledge, i.e., from experimental observations.

2.1.3 Experience

We now return to what we call *experience*. Experience is specific knowledge that has been acquired by an agent[1] during past problem solving. Experience is therefore always situated in a certain, very specific problem solving context. An additional characteristic is that experience is knowledge that is supposed to be of some value for the agent, i.e., knowledge that is useful for the agent in the future. Therefore experience is stored knowledge. We can summarize this intuition of the term experience as follows.

Clarification of Terms 2.6 (Experience) Experience is valuable, stored, specific knowledge that was acquired by an agent in a previous problem solving situation.

2.1.4 Representation of Experience and Related Knowledge for Reuse

For the management and processing of knowledge with a computer it must be represented as data. Through the processing of this data by algorithms the required semantics and pragmatics are added, thus turning the data into knowledge. For knowledge representation, the computer science and artificial intelligence areas provide a large variety of representation formalisms, most of which are closely related to a preferred way of knowledge processing. Part I of this book comprehensively describes various knowledge representation approaches that are appropriate for representing experience knowledge. Besides all technical differences between the different approaches to represent the knowledge required for experience reuse, we can generally distinguish the knowledge categories: *vocabulary, experience base*, and *reuse-related knowledge*. In the case-based reasoning research this distinction is known as the knowledge container model, first introduced by Richter (1995). Figure 2.2 shows these knowledge containers and their relation to the knowledge pyramid.

---

[1] Here, we don't care whether the agent is a human agent or a fully automatic or a computer supported problem solving process.

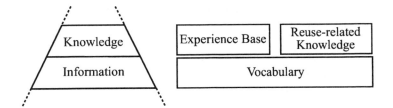

Fig. 2.2. Knowledge Containers.

Vocabulary

The basis of all knowledge and experience representation is the vocabulary of the domain. The vocabulary defines the information entities and structures that can be used to express knowledge. Thereby, the vocabulary defines the "universe" for the representation of experience and reuse-related knowledge. The vocabulary specifies the "language" in which we talk about the domain, but it does not express any knowledge of the domain. It is just the collection of information entities that will become their pragmatics only when they are used to express experience and reuse-related knowledge. Different representations for the vocabulary are discussed in Chap. 3.

Clarification of Terms 2.7 (Vocabulary) The vocabulary defines the information entities and structures that are used to represent experience and reuse-related knowledge.

Experience Base

The experience base is the central knowledge container in the experience-reuse model. It is the collection of the experience that is available for reuse in a domain. We view the experience base as a set of experience items, i.e., a set of closed chunks of experience each of which has a meaning on its own. The experience base can be structured, thereby relating the experience items to each other. Different structures are possible, for example, structures that express a classification of experience items according to certain domain criteria, or structures for the hierarchical organization of experience. The following clarification of terms summarizes this definition of experience base.

Clarification of Terms 2.8 (Experience Base) The experience base is a possibly structured collection of experience items. The experience items are represented using the information entities and structures defined in the vocabulary.

In case-based reasoning an experience item is called a *case* and the experience-base is called *case base* (see also Sect. 2.3.3). In this book we use both pairs of terms synonymously. Different representation formalisms for cases are also discussed in Chap. 3, in relation to the used vocabulary representation.

Reuse-Related Knowledge

To support problem solving efficiently by experience reuse, knowledge in addition to the experience itself is required. This is typically general knowledge about the evaluation of previous experience in a new problem solving context. We call this knowledge *reuse-related knowledge* which is defined as follows.

Clarification of Terms 2.9 (Reuse-Related   Knowledge)   Reuse-related knowledge is general knowledge about the reuse of a certain experience item in a particular problem solving situation. This includes knowledge about the usefulness of reusing a certain experience item for solving a particular problem and also knowledge about how to adapt a certain experience to better suit the current situation. The reuse-related knowledge is represented using the information entities and structures defined in the vocabulary.

This reuse related knowledge can have many different forms, such as

- knowledge about *similarity* between a problem situations,
- domain ontologies,
- transformation knowledge for experience, or
- models of generative problem solving in the domain.

Different forms of reuse-related knowledge and their representation are discussed in detail in the chapters 4 and 5.

2.2 General Model for Experience Management

We now introduce a basic experience management model (EMM), which is shown in Fig. 2.3. This model provides a frame for the whole book in the sense that it relates the different tasks involved in experience management.

The EMM consists of a knowledge kernel and two shells organized around it. The knowledge kernel contains the experience and the reuse-related knowledge, including the vocabulary on which both are based.

The next shell around the kernel consists of the *problem solving cycle* that describes a problem solving that is supported by experience reuse. The processes of the problem solving cycle access the knowledge kernel. IT technology is used to automate these processes (except the problem solving process itself).

The outer shell of the EMM is the *development and maintenance methodology*. The knowledge kernel and the problem solving cycle itself are the subject of the development and maintenance methodology. The various processes

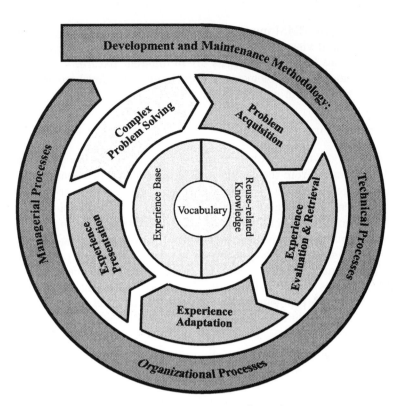

Fig. 2.3. Experience Management Model (EMM).

that occur in this shell (not depicted in the EMM) address the acquisition and maintenance of the knowledge in the kernel as well as the technical, organizational, and also managerial aspects of the problem solving cycle and its implementation. Unlike the processes of the problem solving cycle, the processes that occur in the development and maintenance methodology can usually not be automated by IT technology. However, certain processes can be partially supported by different kinds of support tools.

The development and maintenance activities also form a cycle that must be started each time a kind of maintenance is required. One main difference between these two cycles lies in the frequency in which they are executed. The problem solving cycle is executed continuously, i.e., for every problem or sub-problem instance in which support is required. The maintenance cycle must only be executed if due to the highly dynamic nature of the domain changes have occurred which lead to inefficiencies of the problem solving cycle. Efficient problem solving is established when the problem solving cycle is executed as often as possible and the maintenance cycle is executed as seldom as possible.

Please note that the EMM must not be confused with seemingly similar diagrams of component views of software architectures, such as for operating systems. The relations between the shells are of different nature.

We now introduce the problem solving cycle and the development and maintenance methodology in more detail.

2.2.1 Problem Solving Cycle

The problem solving cycle supports complex problem solving by providing appropriate experience. From the *complex problem solving* process, a problem for which assistance is required is identified. During the *problem acquisition* process this problem is elaborated and described. Then, the available experience in the experience base is *evaluated* and *retrieved* with respect to whether it is appropriate to support solving the particular problem. During the process of *experience adaptation*, the retrieved experience is further tailored to better suit the current problem. Finally, the adapted experience is *presented* to the user who makes use of it during further problem solving. Depending on the complexity of the problem, this cycle must be initiated several times, each times addressing a different sub-problem that occurs during problem solving.

Complex Problem Solving

This process is the core problem solving activity in which the problem owner solves his complex problem. The aim of experience management is to improve this problem solving process. We take the following very general view on problem solving: Problem solving starts with a problem and ends with its solution. During this activity, the problem solver requests relevant experience from the experience provider by either asking for experience about solving the problem as a whole or by asking for experience for solving isolated sub-problems. After the whole problem solving cycle has been completely processed, this experience is available and will (hopefully) help finding a good solution.

Depending on the application domain, problem solving can either be performed without, with partial, or with full support of IT technologies, according to what is the current state-of-the-art in the respective domain. When introducing reuse approaches into an existing problem solving activity, one should not interfere with the ways solutions are further applied; this activity should be mostly left untouched. However, it must be ensured that feedback about the solution quality can be obtained, which might lead to the introduction of some quality measurement activities.

Problem Acquisition

This is the process of eliciting the problem or situation description from the problem owner. The problem acquisition phase is essential to determine the current context for which reusable experience should be provided. Problem acquisition can be supported in many different ways such as filling a questionnaire, following a guided dialog, or browsing through lists of alternatives. The problem acquisition phase results in a problem description, which can be incomplete, vague, or even partially incorrect or inconsistent. Chapter 6 describes in detail different IT methods for problem acquisition.

Experience Evaluation and Retrieval

This is the process of selecting experience items from the experience base that are somehow relevant for the current problem. The retrieved experience items can be useful for solving the whole problem, for solving parts of it, or for helping to find other relevant experience items. The key to experience retrieval is two-fold: first, it requires a good notion of when some kind of experience is relevant for a certain situation. This knowledge is captured in the knowledge container for reuse-related knowledge. Second, it requires methods for efficiently finding such experience in possibly large or distributed experience bases. Different efficient retrieval algorithms are discussed in detail in Chap. 7. The experience retrieval results in a set of relevant experience items that enter the experience adaptation process.

Experience Adaptation

This is the process of adapting or combining the retrieved experience items with respect to the current problem. Experience items might be changed if the current situation differs from the situation in which the experience originally arose. It can be necessary to combine different experience items if each of them only helps to solve some sub-part of the overall problem. Experience adaptation is typically a knowledge intensive task; the required knowledge is also part of the knowledge container for reuse-related knowledge. The experience adaptation results in a single or a set of adapted relevant experience items. Please note that the adaptation sub-process is not always necessary in case there is no need to adapt experience items. Chapter 8 introduces and compares different IT methods for experience adaptation.

Experience Presentation

Experience presentation means communicating the relevant and possibly adapted experience to the experience user in charge of solving the complex problem. The experience must be presented to the user in an appropriate form, i.e., in a way that enables the user to understand the experience and to solve his problem. Chapter 6 describes different experience presentation approaches in relation to the problem acquisition. Both processes together make up the user communication between the experience user and the experience management system.

Feedback from Adaptation to Retrieval

Although it seems that these processes should be performed once and one after the other in sequential order, this must not always be the case. The problem solving cycle shows primarily the flow of data but not the flow of control. A feedback from the experience adaptation process back to the retrieval process can become necessary. If the adaptation fails or leads to inappropriate results, to retrieval must be restarted to find additional, more appropriate experience as a source for the adaptation. This relation between retrieval and adaptation (Smyth and Keane 1993) is also discussed in Chap. 8.

2.2.2 Development and Maintenance Methodology

Experience management applications require development and maintenance processes in order to acquire and update the required experience knowledge and to customize the problem solving cycle. The development and maintenance of the experience kernel requires modeling and maintaining the vocabulary, the reuse-related knowledge, and the cases themselves. Customizing the problem solving cycle includes configuring the IT components that support its processes. The chapters 3 to 8 provide a structured set of building blocks from which appropriate methods can be selected. For certain application areas particularly tailored, so-called *generic vertical platforms* are available. Such a vertical platform combines a certain set of methods into a software tool as a basis for application development. Part III of this book describes three such vertical platforms.

Purpose of a Methodology

The developers of experience management applications must master this development and maintenance process. A methodology makes building an experience management application a systematic engineering activity. A methodology usually combines a number of methods into a philosophy which addresses a number of phases of the software development life-cycle (e.g. Booch 1994, Chap. 1). A methodology should give guidelines about the activities that need to be performed in order to successfully develop a certain kind of product, here an experience management application.

When building an experience management application to be used in the daily practice within an existing complex problem solving scenario, a large variety of different kinds of processes have to be considered. To reach the goals described above, a methodology must cover the following aspects, which naturally occur more or less in every software development project:

- The process of project management (cost and resource assessment, time schedules, project plans, quality control procedures, etc.),

- the specification of the different kinds of products or deliverables (including software deliverables) that must be produced,
- the process of (technical) product development and maintenance, which includes all technical tasks that are involved in the development and maintenance of the software,
- the analysis and (re-)organisation of the environment (e.g. a department) in which the CBR system should be introduced.

All these processes have to be defined and tailored according to the needs and circumstances of the problem solving process.

Technical, Organizational, and Managerial Processes

We distinguish three types of processes that are involved in the development and maintenance methodology.

Technical Processes. Technical processes describe the creation or modification of the experience management software components or the represented knowledge.

Organizational Processes. Organizational processes address those parts of the user organization's business process in which the software system will be embedded. New processes have to be introduced into an existing business process, such as training end-users or the maintenance of the knowledge kernel. Existing processes may need to be changed or re-organized to make the best use of the experience management approach.

Managerial Processes. Managerial processes provide an environment and services for the development of software that meet the product requirements and project goals, i.e., services for enacting the technical and the organizational processes. Examples of managerial processes are project planning, monitoring, and quality assurance.

Development and Maintenance as Cycle

The integration of development and maintenance into a single cycle indicates that there is usually no clear separation between both phases. This holds particularly for the knowledge kernel. Its development is achieved by an incremental extension and modification (Cunningham and Bonzano 1999). This usually involves the monitoring and evaluation of the current problem solving cycle. The evaluation should yield modification needs. Those can be implemented by first modifying the vocabulary (if necessary) and then modifying the reuse-related knowledge and the experience base. All operations performed in the maintenance cycle lead to a changed (hopefully improved) behavior of the problem solving cycle. In the recent literature, different detailed frameworks for the maintenance cycle have been proposed (Nick et al. 2001; Wilson and Leake 2001; Reinartz et al. 2001).

Vocabulary Development and Maintenance. The development of the vocabulary is a very crucial task, since the two other knowledge containers rely on the vocabulary. The vocabulary can be determined by analyzing existing sources of experience knowledge. This process is discussed in Sect. 3.7. Changes to the vocabulary require almost always changes in the reuse-related knowledge and the experience base. Therefore, the knowledge engineer should try to achieve a mostly complete or easily extensible vocabulary from the beginning.

Development and Maintenance of Reuse-Related Knowledge. The development and maintenance of reuse-related knowledge involves modeling knowledge for assessing the relevance of an experience item for the actual problem. This assessment can be made based on the similarity between the current problem and the problem in which a particular experience item was collected. Such an assessment is based on the assumption that problem similarity approximates usefulness of experience. Such issues are discussed comprehensively in Chap. 4. Second, this process also includes modeling adaptation knowledge, which can be a very laborious activity. Adaptation knowledge is usually expressed in the form of rules, operators, or constraints. For this kind of general knowledge a similar knowledge acquisition process is required than for traditional knowledge-based systems. See Chap. 5 for a detailed discussion.

Experience Base Development and Maintenance. The development and maintenance of experience base is initially performed by transforming and integrating existing experience sources like databases, documents, or Web resources. If no such knowledge sources exist, a manual experience acquisition process must be established and integrated into the existing problem solving process. During the life-time of an experience management system, the experience base requires heavy maintenance. Fortunately, this maintenance is much easier to achieve than the maintenance of the other knowledge containers.

The INRECA Approach

A comprehensive description of the development and maintenance methodology that has been created in the INRECA-II Esprit project is given in Chap. 9. Methodology creation is a continuous process that is itself heavily based on experience about application development. Part III of this book illustrates three vertical software platforms, each of which is tailored to a particular application area and connected with a generic development and maintenance model, providing cookbook-like guidance.

2.3 Related Models

The just described EMM has its origins in several related models from different computer science disciplines. Closely related are the already discussed knowledge management models and in particular organizational memory approaches. The quality improvement paradigm and the experience factory approach from software engineering aims at managing software engineering knowledge of various kinds. This model has various relations to the EMM as well. Finally, the case-based reasoning cycle from artificial intelligence research has inspired the problem solving cycle of the EMM. More importantly, it provides the core techniques to support the EMM steps.

2.3.1 Knowledge Management and Organizational Memory

The basic knowledge management activities introduced by Beckman (1997) (see Sect. 1.4.1) are partially related to the EMM. These activities are called: *identify, capture, select, store, share, apply, create*, and *sell.*

Capture and Store

The basic difference is that the EMM deals particularly with knowledge required for experience reuse, i.e., the vocabulary, the experience itself, and the reuse-related knowledge (see Sect. 2.1.4). Unlike general knowledge management models, the EMM is structured according to these knowledge containers. The knowledge management activities *capture* and *store* occur also in the EMM as part of the development and maintenance methodology.

Select, Share, and Apply

In the main EMM model, the knowledge management activities *select, share, apply* occur in the problem solving cycle. During the experience evaluation and retrieval process, the knowledge management activity *select* is performed, i.e., the available experience is assessed for its relevance for the current problem. Knowledge *sharing* is realized in the EMM through the problem acquisition and the experience presentation processes. These processes organize the communication between the experience user and the experience base. From a broader point of view, we can even say that the whole problem solving cycle of the EMM deals with sharing of knowledge in a problem-solving-specific manner. The *application* of knowledge occurs in the EMM mainly during the problem solving process. Here, the experience obtained is used by the problem solver to solve his current problem. The experience adaptation process of the EMM is not explicitly mentioned in knowledge management models. However, it can be regarded as a specific way of knowledge application during which the retrieved experience is transformed into knowledge for problem solving which is more useful for the current problem than the original experience.

Create, Identify, and Sell

The knowledge management process *create* does not occur in its original meaning in the EMM, since experience is not created but captured. However, its effect, i.e., the extension of the previously available knowledge is achieved in the EMM as part of the development and maintenance methodology. On the other hand, maintenance is not explicitly mentioned in the knowledge management model by Beckman. Other models like the corporate knowledge management model by Dieng et al. (1999) explicitly contain a related step named *knowledge evolution*. The knowledge management activities *identify* and *sell* are organizational processes that also occur in the development and maintenance methodology of the EMM.

2.3.2 Quality Improvement Paradigm and Experience Factory

In Software Engineering it has been early recognized that reuse is an important method for improving software development productivity, maintainability, and time to market (Standish 1984; Poulin et al. 1993). Recently, it became obvious that reuse should not only relate to program code, but also to all kinds of software development experience. The experience factory and the related quality improvement paradigm make this idea more precise. They can be considered a knowledge management approach for/from software engineering.

Experience Factory

The experience factory (EF) approach (Basili et al. 1994a) is motivated by the observation that any successful business requires a combination of technical and managerial solutions: a well-defined set of product needs to satisfy the customer, assist the developer in accomplishing those needs, and create competencies for future business; a well-defined set of processes to accomplish what needs to be accomplished, to control development, and to improve overall business; and a closed-loop process that supports learning and feedback. This holds particularly for the software development business.

An experience factory is a logical and/or physical organization that supports project development by analyzing and synthesizing all kinds of experience, acting as a repository for such experience, and supplying that experience to various projects on demand (Basili et al. 1994a). An experience factory packages experience and collects it in an experience base. The experience consists of informal or formal models and measures of various software processes, products, and other forms of knowledge. Figure 2.4 shows a schematized description of the experience factory, its steps, and its relation to the project organization. The project organization is in charge of planning and performing (plan execution) the software development project in an IT company. The experience factory analyzes the lessons learned from executed projects and

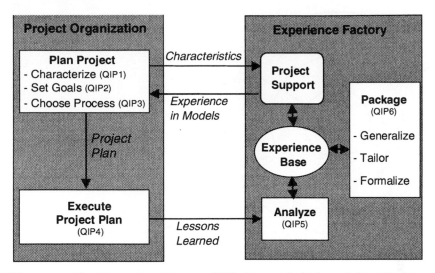

Fig. 2.4. The Experience Factory (EF) Approach (Adapted from Basili et al., 1994).

records them in the experience base. To enable best reuse, these experiences are further packaged, i.e., they are generalized, tailored, and formalized. Further, the experience factory provides access to its experience base and thereby supports the project planning, which goes on in the project organization.

Quality Improvement Paradigm

The steps in the experience factory are organized into a cycle that enables the quality of the software development to be improved continuously. This cycle is called the quality improvement paradigm (QIP, see Fig. 2.5) and orders the six basic steps from the experience factory. In more detail, the six QIP steps are:

- **Characterize (QIP1).** The aim of this step is to characterize the project and its environment based on the available information. Normally, a large variety of project characteristics and environmental factors can be used for this characterization, such as the application domain, susceptibility to changes, problem constraints, techniques, tools, programming language, existing software, available budget, the number of people, the level of their expertise, and so on. This step provides a context for goal definition and for selecting reusable experiences from the experience base.
- **Set Goals (QIP2).** The goals of the project need to be defined. There are a variety of viewpoints for defining goals, like those viewpoints of the user, customer, project manager, corporation, and so on. Goals should be measurable, depending on the business models.

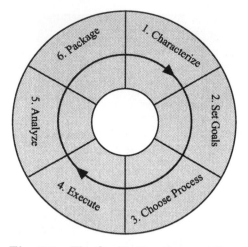

Fig. 2.5. The Quality Improvement Paradigm (QIP).

- **Choose Process (QIP3).** On the basis of the characterization, the goals, and the previous experience from the experience base, appropriate processes for implementing the project must be chosen. This results in the overall project plan.
- **Execute (QIP4).** The project plan is enacted, causing the development project to be carried out. For further analysis, respective records of the development process must be made.
- **Analyze (QIP5).** At the end of each specific project, the data collected must be analyzed to evaluate current practices. Valuable, reusable experience must be identified.
- **Package (QIP6).** The experience in the experience base consists of a variety of models. These models have to be defined and refined. Such models can be, e.g., resource models, process definitions and models, quality models, lessons learned, and so on. On the basis of the new experience, these models might get generalized, tailored to a particular kind of situation, or formalized, so that they can be reused in other projects.

The experience factory/quality improvement paradigm is especially tailored for the software business. It can be compared to approaches used in other fields of businesses, e.g., total quality management. The experience factory and the quality improvement paradigm, provide a mechanism for continuous improvement through the experimentation, packaging, and reuse of experiences based on the needs of a business.

Discussion

Like the experience reuse process model, the experience factory is also a model for improving problem solving through experience reuse. However, its primary focus is on software development, i.e., there is a restriction to a particular kind of problem solving. Also, the EF and QIP target organizational aspects at the first place. IT technology to support the individual EF/QIP steps became only recently a matter of concern. Case-based reasoning (see Sect. 2.3.3) has been proposed as a technology for this purpose (Tautz and Althoff 1997; Althoff et al. 2000).

Besides these general differences, the QIP steps relate as follows to the processes of the EMM: The characterization (QIP1) and goal setting (QIP2) phases are covered by the problem acquisition process of the EMM. The choose process (QIP3) phase covers the remaining parts of the problem solving cycle. It ends up with a proposed solution to the problem, i.e., the project plan in the domain of software development. The execute phase (QIP4) is not explicitly included in the EMM. However, it is assumed implicitly as part of the problem solving process because solution execution is necessary for its evaluation and analysis. The QIP analysis phase (QIP5) and the package phase (QIP6) are primarily maintenance activities that are part of the development and maintenance methodology of the EMM.

Finally, the development and maintenance methodology of the EMM follows an experience based approach and can be considered to be an instance of an experience factory (see Bergmann et al. 1999a and Chap. 9). This comparison is appropriate since both focus on organizational issues rather than on a complete automation of the development process (here the development of an experience management application).

2.3.3 The Case-Based Reasoning Cycle

Case-based reasoning (CBR) (Kolodner 1993; Aamodt and Plaza 1994; Leake 1996; Lenz et al. 1998; Cunningham 1998) is a technique for solving problems by direct reuse of previous experience. Unlike the knowledge management and the experience factory models, case-based reasoning is originally not regarded as an organizational model for experience reuse, but as a cognitive model and a technical architecture. Previous experience comes in the form of a set of *cases*, which are problem solution pairs, that are stored in the *case base*. The terms case and case-base have the same meaning as the previously introduced terms experience base and experience item (see clarification 2.8) and are therefore used interchangeably in this book. Following Aamodt and Plaza (1994), the classical case-based reasoning problem solving cycle (see Fig. 2.6) is as follows: A case that is similar to the current problem is *retrieved* from the case base. Then, the solution contained in this retrieved case is *reused* to solve the new problem, i.e., the solution is adapted in order to come to a solution of the current problem. Thereby, a new solution is obtained and presented to the user who can verify and possibly *revise* the solution. The revised case (or the experience gained during the case-based problem solving process) is then *retained* for future problem solving, e.g., the case can be stored in the case base.

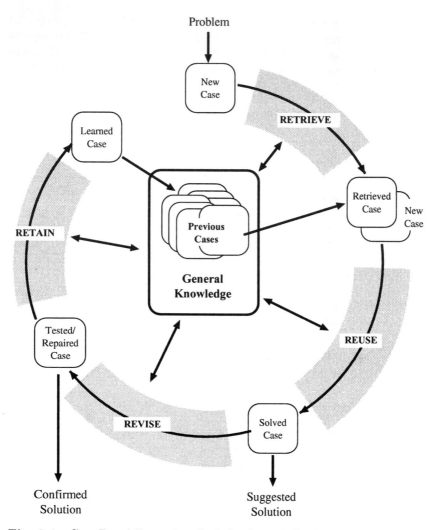

Fig. 2.6. Case-Based Reasoning Cycle by Aamodt & Plaza.

Retrieve

In the CBR cycle, problem solving starts when the users enters a new query to the system (called new case) that consists of a description of a new problem. First, the retrieve phase, selects one or several cases from the case base that are considered useful for solving the new problem. Cases are selected based on the *similarity* of the problem in the new case to the problem that the cases in the case base contain. It is generally assumed that similar problems should also have similar solutions. The accurate formalization of similarity is very crucial to the success of a CBR system. It is important to note that the similarity assessment itself is domain specific knowledge that must be determined for the current domain at hand. In complex case representations, similarity assessment can become a very difficult and computationally expensive task. Moreover, when the case base grows, typically the efficiency of retrieval decreases because an increasing number of cases must be taken into account to find the most similar case from the case base. Most CBR systems apply some kind of indexing in order to find relevant cases more efficiently. However, finding the indexes is often a big problem on its own.

Reuse

Once one or several similar cases have been retrieved, the solution (or other problem solving information) contained in these cases is reused to solve the current problem. This is typically achieved by adapting the retrieved solutions. Several techniques for adaptation in CBR have been proposed so far. A review of adaptation methods is given by Hanney et al. (1995), Voß (1997), and Wilke and Bergmann (1998). The most basic distinction between different adaptation methods is whether transformational adaptation or generative adaptation is applied.

Transformational adaptation relies on a set of adaptation rules or operators that describe how differences in the problem lead to required modifications in the solution. The present differences between the new case and the retrieved case are analyzed, a set of applicable transformations are selected, and the proposed modifications to the solution are performed. This approach has its origin in transformational analogy proposed by Carbonell (1983b).

On the other hand, generative adaptation methods require a complete generative problem solver that is able the solve problems based on general knowledge, i.e., without using any cases at all. Not the solution but the problem solving traces from previous cases are then reused to guide the generative problem solver to find a solution to the new problem. This approach has its origin in derivational analogy proposed by Carbonell (1986).

The reuse phase can become a computationally very expensive activity, especially when case representations are complex and the solution part of the case requires a detailed description. Typically, the effort involved for adaptation depends on the similarity between the retrieved case and the new case. Typically, the more similar the cases are, the less effort must be spent for adaptation.

Revise

The case-based reasoning literature has not much to say about the revise phase. The revision of the solution is typically not the task of the CBR system. The solution determined by the CBR system is verified in the real world and possibly corrected or improved by a human domain expert. The revised case is then entered again into the CBR system for its use in the subsequent retain phase.

Retain

The retain phase is the learning phase of a CBR system. The typical form of learning that occurs in a CBR system is learning by adding the revised case to the case base. Thereby, the new problem solving experience becomes available for reuse in future problem solving episodes. However, this approach has obvious drawbacks, most importantly the continuous growing of the case base which typically results in a decreasing retrieval efficiency (Tambe and Newell 1988; Francis and Ram 1993; Smyth and Cunningham 1996). To avoid this problem, strategies are required for selectively adding cases to the case base (Aha et al. 1991) as well as strategies for forgetting cases that have been already stored in the case base (Smyth and Keane 1995; Smyth and McKenna 1996). Besides this kind of learning, approaches have been developed for improving the similarity assessment (Wess 1993; Wettschereck and Aha 1995; Leake et al. 1996b; Wilke and Bergmann 1996a; Munoz-Avila and Huellen 1996; Branting 2001; Stahl 2001), for learning transformational adaptation knowledge (Hanney and Keane 1996; Wilke et al. 1997), and for combining learned adaptation cases with transformational or generative adaptation (Leake et al. 1996a; Craw et al. 2001).

Discussion

The traditional CBR cycle covers parts of the EMM's problem solving cycle. The CBR cycle does not cover most of the development and maintenance cycle. However, since it has been recently identified that the development and maintenance aspects of experience reuse systems are so important for their long-term success (Bergmann et al. 1999a; Minor et al. 2000; Leake et al. 2001), they have been explicitly included in the EMM.

When comparing the CBR cycle with the EMM it becomes obvious that the retrieve and the reuse phase from the CBR cycle are equivalent to the experience retrieval and experience adaptation processes of the EMM. Further, the revise phase of the CBR cycle relates to the problem solving processes. Finally, the retain phase of the CBR cycle appears in the EMM as part of the maintenance methodology.

Part I

Knowledge Representation for Experience Management

3. Representing Experience

"Experience is that marvelous thing that enables you to recognize a mistake when you make it again."

F. P. Jones

Experience management requires representing experience in appropriate data structures. Experience representation must enable efficient experience retrieval and adaptation. On the other hand, the effort required for experience base development and maintenance must be taken into account.

As shown in the previous chapter, all knowledge related to experience reuse can be subdivided into the three knowledge containers: vocabulary, experience base, and reuse-related knowledge. Since the discussion of the experience representation cannot be separated from the vocabulary, this chapter will address these two issues together. Each of the two following chapters will cover the representation of reuse related knowledge. Chapter 4 deals with the knowledge required for retrieval while Chapt. 5 deals with representing knowledge required for experience adaptation. The representation approaches discussed are primarily based on methods from case-based reasoning and more generally from knowledge-based systems research.

3.1 Cases for Representing Experience

Case-Based Reasoning provides us with appropriate means for representing experience. An experience item is called a *case*. According to Kolodner (1993) "a case is a contextualized piece of knowledge representing an experience that teaches a lesson fundamental to achieving the goals of the reasoner". Kolodner makes the following general observations about cases:

- A case represents specific knowledge tied to a context. It records knowledge at an operational level.
- Cases can come in many different shapes and sizes covering large or small time slices associating solutions with problems, outcomes with situations, or both.
- A case records experience that is different from what is expected. Not all differences are important to record, however. Cases worthy of recording as cases teach a useful lesson.
- Useful lessons are those that have the potential to help a reasoner achieve a goal or set of goals more easily in the future or warn about the possibility of a failure or point out an unforeseen problem.

In the following we explore the principles of case representation in detail.

3.1.1 Basic Case Structure

A case structures an experience item in a certain way. The particular choice of this structure strongly depends on the experience management domain and the task that is to be supported by experience reuse. A case has the following components:

- A *characterization part* describing the experience in a way that allows to assess its reusability in a particular situation.
- A *lesson part* describing the particular lesson the experience item consists of, e.g. the solution to a problem, decisions or problem solving steps that have been taken, justifications for decisions, alternative decisions or failed decisions.

Case Characterization Part

The case characterization part describes all facts about the experience that are relevant for deciding whether the experience can be reused in a certain situation. Thereby this characterization part works as a kind of index for the lesson part. However, compared to a regular index like for example a word in a dictionary, the case characterization part can be rather complex. It must describe the global context in which the experience occurred as well as the specific situation to which it relates. The degree of detail used to characterize the experience determines how accurate its reusability can be assessed, i.e., how accurate the retrieval is. The degree of detail required also depends on the lesson to be reused and on how many similar experience items need to be distinguished.

The characterization part can contain the following information items:

- In a classification or diagnostic situation: type of object, type of problem, observed symptoms, or measured values.
- In an electronic commerce situation: requirements and wishes about a certain product or purpose for which a product was or should be used.
- In a design or planning situation: the goals that should be reached by the design or plan.
- In a general problem solving situation: the goals of the problem solving episode and constraints restricting the searched solution.

Lesson Part

Originally, the term lesson was used for guidelines, tips, or checklists of what went right or wrong in a particular event (Stewart 1997). Today, the term is used in a much broader sense (Weber et al. 2000): "a lesson learned is knowledge or understanding gained by experience" (Secchi 1999). In this thesis we use the term lesson with this general meaning.

The representation of a lesson must include all facts about the experience that are relevant to reuse it. It must be detailed enough to enable the experience user to take the actions in the real world that this experience item suggests. Of course, the degree of detail depends on the particular lesson that is represented as well as on the kind of user. The experience adaptation process may also require representing knowledge about how the particular experience item can be adapted to diverging situations.

The lesson part can contain the following information items:

- In a diagnostic situation: the fault that occurred in a previous situation and the remedy.
- In a classification task: the class that was identified.
- In an electronic commerce situation: a particular product recommendation.
- In a design situation: the design of the object or parts of the design.
- In a planning situation: a solution plan or parts of a solution plan.
- In a general problem solving situation: the particular problem solving decisions taken, the justification for the decision, alternative decisions, failed decisions, etc.

3.1.2 A First General Formalization of Cases

We can now give a first simple formalization for cases based on the structure just discussed. We start by introducing notations for the different components of a case.

Definition 3.1 (Space of Experience Characterization Descriptions)
The *space of experience characterization descriptions* $\mathbb{D}$ is the set of possible
characterizations for experience items.

Definition 3.2 (Space of Lessons) The symbol $\mathbb{L}$ denotes the *space of
possible lessons* recorded in experience items.

In traditional CBR terminology, the experience characterization space is
called *problem space* since the experience characterizations are usually problem descriptions. Here, we explicitly extend this CBR view. The characterization space *can* be the space of problem descriptions, but it can also contain
derived descriptions or properties that were not present in the problem solving situations from which the experience emerges. Also, the lesson space is
usually called *solution space* in CBR. Again, we don't restrict ourselves here
to representing solutions but the lesson space can contain information that
is not the solution itself but useful to find a solution.

Given these notations, we can now give the general straight-forward definition of a case:

Definition 3.3 (Case, General Definition) A *case* is a pair $c = (d, l) \in \mathbb{D} \times \mathbb{L}$.

This definition of a case goes together with the following general definition
of the vocabulary container.

**Definition 3.4 (Vocabulary Container and Case Space, General
Definition)** We call the pair **VOC** $= (\mathbb{D}, \mathbb{L})$ the *vocabulary container*. The
related *case space* is $\mathbb{C} = \mathbb{D} \times \mathbb{L}$.

The above definitions do not specify any internal structure for the components of a case. Therefore it is very general but still useful for specifying general properties and algorithms for the different tasks of experience
management. In Sect. 3.3 we provide several more specific representation
approaches for further structuring case representations.

Finally, we can formally define a case base as follows.

Definition 3.5 (Case Base) A *case base* is a finite set of cases, **CB** $=
\{c_1, \dots, c_n\} \subseteq \mathbb{C}$.

Here, the case base is defined just as a collection of cases. No structure
for navigation or indexing of those cases is implied. Such structures will be
introduced in Chap. 7.

3.1.3 Utility of Experience

Experience is represented for the purpose of being reused. The reuse of a case
in the context of a particular problem must be viewed from the perspective

of the utility. Different cases can be reused with different utility; one lesson can be more useful than another one.

The notion of utility is based on the economics theory of *von Neumann and Morgenstern* (1944) which describes connections between utility, preferences, and human decision making. In the context of experience reuse, the utility makes a connection between a particular problem and a particular lesson captured in a case.

To formalize this important notion of utility we first need to introduce a representation space for problems because all following considerations are related to a particular problem.

Definition 3.6 (Problem/Situation Space) The *problem space* $\mathbb{P}$ is the set of possible problem or situation descriptions.

Given this, we can now formalize utility through *utility functions* as follows:

Definition 3.7 (Utility Function for Experience) A utility function for a problem space $\mathbb{P}$ and a lesson space $\mathbb{L}$ is a function $u : \mathbb{P} \times \mathbb{L} \rightarrow \Re$ that assigns to each problem-lesson pair a utility value from the set of Real numbers, which is the utility of reusing the lesson for solving the problem. If we take the point of view of a particular problem p, we can define a *problem-specific utility function* u_p with a single argument that expresses the utility of the available experience: $u_p(l) := u(p, l)$.

The utility is a property of the problem solving domain when viewed from the perspective of experience reuse. It replaces the traditional truth conditions (e.g. the correctness of a solution of a problem) by a finer graded rating. When investigating a problem solving domain for experience reuse one must explore in depth properties of the underlying utility.

The utility value can have different meanings depending on the current problem solving task. In all cases, an experience with a higher utility value is "better" than an experience with a lower utility value. Utilities for experience can be interpreted in various ways (Bergmann and Wilke 1998), for example, as

- the quality of a solution obtained by reusing the experience,
- the problem solving effort (or cost) saved by reusing experience,
- the monetary cost saved by solving the problem better of faster by reusing the experience,
- the probability that the solution suggested by the experience is correct,
- the satisfaction of the user with the presented experience.

The main problem with utility functions is that they can hardly be determined completely in a complex problem domain. It is unrealistic to assume that it is possible to formalize u completely. We can usually only obtain partial knowledge about u, such as

- whether for some problem the utility of one lesson is higher, equal, or lower than the utility of another lesson, or
- whether the utility of some lesson depends on a certain characteristic of it or of the problem.

Therefore, we now focus on the preference relation induced by a utility function.

Definition 3.8 (Preference Relation for Reusing Experience) In the context of a problem p the action of choosing experience $c_i = (d_i, l_i)$ for reuse is *preferred* over the action of choosing experience $c_j = (d_j, l_j)$ for reuse (we write $c_i \succ_p c_j$) iff $u_p(l_i) > u_p(l_j)$.

The preference relation $\succ_p$ restricts the utility to the decision theoretic information aspect, which is the key aspect during the retrieval phase of the EMM. Also, this preference relation is usually only partially known. What is known are preferences $c_i \succ_p c_j$ for some problems p and some cases c_i and c_j.

3.1.4 Representing Experience with Respect to Utility

When developing a vocabulary for experience representation, the utility function of the problem solving domain must be taken into account. Particularly, the experience characterization space $\mathbb{D}$ must be chosen in a way that it is possible to distinguish different experience items according to their different utilities for a particular problem. If two cases from the case base have the same experience characterization but different lessons, then the lessons must lead to the same utility. This property, which relates to both, the case base and the characterization space, can be formalized as follows:

$$\forall p \in \mathbb{P} \ \forall (d_1, l_1), (d_2, l_2) \in \mathbf{CB} \qquad \text{(Utility Distinguishability of}$$
$$d_1 = d_2 \rightarrow u(p, l_1) = u(p, l_2) \qquad \text{Experience)}$$

This condition, however, causes some problems because it states a relationship between the vocabulary and the experience represented with it. This might cause a need to change the vocabulary when a new case is included into the case base. Although this is a general maintenance problem it can be limited by introducing a general soundness condition for cases in the case base that expresses a relationship between the experience characterization part and the lesson part. This condition states when a case is correctly represented, i.e., when a characterization is appropriate for a lesson. It thereby defines the semantics of the case representation.

Definition 3.9 (Case Base Semantics) A *case base semantics* is given by a relation $\mathbb{B} \subseteq \mathbb{C}$. A case c is called *sound* iff $c \in \mathbb{B}$ holds.

The case base semantics restricts the set of cases we want to deal with to a particular subset of all representable cases. Usually, the case semantics is defined as to include only cases of high utility. It distinguishes cases that are semantically correct from those that express a "wrong" experience. Given this, we can restate the utility distinguishability condition for experience as follows.

$$\forall p \in \mathbb{P} \;\; \forall (d_1, l_1), (d_2, l_2) \in \mathbb{B}$$
$$d_1 = d_2 \rightarrow u(p, l_1) = u(p, l_2)$$

(Utility Distinguishability of Experience, revised)

If the vocabulary (precisely, the experience characterization space $\mathbb{D}$) fulfills this property then we can properly distinguish all sound cases according to their utility.

As we will see, the case semantics just introduced will play an important role with respect to defining the soundness of similarity (see Chap. 4) and experience adaptation (see Chap. 8).

3.2 Overview of Case Representation Approaches

In the following we introduce various approaches for structuring vocabulary and for representing cases according to this structure. There are three main approaches for representing cases that differ in the sources, materials, and knowledge they can make best use of. The approaches are called *textual*, *conversational*, and *structural* case representation. The following analysis of the three approaches has been proposed by Bergmann et al. (1999a).

3.2.1 The Textual Approach

Cases representing experience can be recorded as free text, i.e. strings (Lenz and Ashley 1998; Lenz et al. 1998; Shimazu 1998). For example, this may be product descriptions or service reports. It is very useful in domains where large collections of know-how documents already exist and the intended user is able to immediately make use of the experience contained in the respective documents. Therefore, the textual case representation approach eases case acquisition.

Textual case representation immediately determines the techniques for processing the experience, particularly for retrieving it. An experience management retrieval engine for textual cases usually uses keyword matching techniques to retrieve cases. Keyword search is the most popular technique in current search engines for the Internet. The Web documents that can be accessed by the search engine are indexed by selected keywords or by the whole set of occurring words (e.g. as provided by Altavista). However, textual search approaches are mostly unable to capture the semantics of the text. They are restricted to pure syntactic retrieval criterions, i.e., they select experience based on the occurrence of words rather than on the meaning of the experience.

The textual approach is well suited when there are not too many cases at a time (less than a couple of hundred) and when each case has a short description with quite discriminating words occurring in the text. Due to the mentioned limitations of the retrieval approaches, the cost for controlling the quality of retrieval for textual cases is very high.

Example: Frequently Asked Questions

A company has a collection of documents that represent the current set of frequently asked questions at the company's hotline. Each document contains a single problem and its solution. Navigating and searching in the list of documents is difficult for customers as well as for the people working on the hotline. To avoid this unfriendly search process, customers tend to call the company's hotline instead of solving the well-known problems on their own. The result is that the traffic at the hotline is constantly increasing. The goal of an experience management system is to help customers and employees find solutions to problems whose solutions are already known and documented. Figure 3.1 presents an example of such a textual case.

Frequently Asked Question 241
Title: Order numbers of CPUs with which communications is possible.

Question: Which order numbers must the S7-CPUs have to be able to run basic communications with SFCs?

Answer: In order to participate in communications via SFCs without a configured connection table, the module concerned must have the correct order number. The following table illustrates which order number your CPU must have to be able to participate in these S7 homogeneous communications.

Fig. 3.1. Example of a Textual Case.

3.2.2 The Conversational Approach

A second approach is called conversational case representation (Aha and Breslow 1997; Aha et al. 1998; Aha et al. 2001). The principle is to capture the knowledge contained in customer/agent conversations. A case is represented through a list of questions that varies from one case to the other. There is no domain model and no standardized structure for all the cases as, for example, in the structured approach introduced below.

To index the cases, the case author must also define the order in which the user is asked to answer the questions during the consultation. Problems and questions used to describe the cases are organized into tree-like structures. The developer creates groups of questions that are used to describe a certain subset of the case base. Each case is then positioned by hand in this tree, which must be maintained manually by the developer. This task can be compared to developing an knowledge-based system that relies on decision trees.

The conversational CBR approach is very useful for domains where a high volume of simple problems must be solved again and again. The system guides the agent and the customer with predefined dialogs. However, the case base is organized manually by the case author, which is a complex and costly activity when the cases are described by many attributes (questions). The conversational approach is well suited for applications in which only a few questions are needed for decision making. Maintenance costs are high because the developer must manually position each new case in a decision tree-like structure and update the ordering of the questions.

Example: Call Center for Printer Problems

A company is producing a wide range of different printers for the consumer market. For customer support, it maintains a call center with several agents solving product-related problems by phone. Since the main target market of the company is consumer oriented, most of the problems are simple to solve but the volume of the daily calls is very high. To provide the necessary staff for the call center, the company has hired several part-time agents who should be able to solve most of the simple calls directly. For more advanced problems, the company maintains a highly qualified second-level support team of product specialists. Since the training effort for the first-level agents is constantly increasing and cannot be done just on time anymore, there is a trend that more and more calls are forwarded to the second-level support team. This is not convenient for the customer and causes workload and priority problems at the second level. An experience management system should empower the first-level support agents to solve as many problems as possible on the phone without forwarding the call to the second-level support. The following Fig. 3.2 presents an example of such a conversational case.

3.2.3 The Structural Approach

The idea underlying the structural approach is to represent cases according to a common structured vocabulary (or domain model) (Yokoyama 1990;

```
┌─────────────────────────────────────────────────────────────────┐
│ Case: 241                                                         │
│ Title: Printer does not work in the new release.                  │
│                                                                   │
│ Q1: What kind of problem do you have? Printer Problem             │
│ Q1: Does the printer perform a self-test? Yes                     │
│ Q2: Does the printer work with other software? Yes                │
│ Q3: Did you just install the software? Yes                        │
│ Q4: Did you create a printer definition file? Yes                 │
│ Q5: What release did you install? 4.2                             │
│                                                                   │
│ Problem: Installation procedure overrides printer definition      │
│ Action: Reinstall the printer from disk 2.3                       │
└─────────────────────────────────────────────────────────────────┘
```

Fig. 3.2. Example of a Conversational Case.

Aamodt 1991; Faltings et al. 1991; Manago et al. 1994; Voß 1994; Wess 1995; Althoff et al. 1995; Althoff et al. 1995; Plaza 1995). Once this vocabulary is defined, all cases are restricted to represent experience that can be expressed with this vocabulary. In different structural case representations, the describing features of a case may be organized as flat attribute-value tables, in an object-oriented manner, as graph structures, or by sets of atomic formulas of a predicate logic language. In an object-oriented case base, objects are decomposed into sub-objects. For example, in a PC sales-support application, a PC points to several sub-objects, such as screen and hard disk. Each object has its own set of attributes, such as price and the manufacturer.

To summarize, the domain model defines a standard way to represent all cases. Note that this is different from the textual approach, which may contain a structure using languages such as SGML (for example, the question-and-answer headers in the example in the previous chapter), but where the content associated to each header is not standardized (it contains free text). Even if the content of these headers is stored in a database, this is not sufficient to qualify for the structural approach. In the structural approach, each attribute must be a field in the database and each value must be standardized.

The structural approach is useful in domains where additional knowledge, beside cases, must be used in order to produce good results. The domain model insures that new cases are of high quality and the maintenance effort is low. This approach always gives better results than the two others, but it requires an initial investment to produce the vocabulary.

Example: Sales Support for Electronic Devices

A company has described a catalog of electronic products according to the different sales parameters. Parameters are used to describe technical characteristics of the product, as well as sales characteristics. The application's goal is to find the best matching product based on the characteristics the customer enters for his or her desired product. There are so many characteristics that the chance of retrieving a product that is identical to the user's query is very low (no exact match). Standard database queries almost never retrieve any products from the catalog database. Figure 3.3 presents an example of such a structural case.

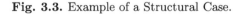

```
Reference : AD8009
Price : 2.25
Input offset voltage : 2 mV
Input bias current : 50 uA
Output voltage : 1.2 V
Output current drive : 175 mA
Single supply : No
PSPS : 70 dB
Number of devices per package : single
Available Package(s) : SOIC
```

Fig. 3.3. Example of a Structural Case.

3.2.4 Comparing the Different Approaches

From a user's point of view, all these approaches may look very similar. A query case is entered and similar cases are retrieved from the case base. From a managerial point of view there are important differences that deal with:

1. the material required to set up the initial case base,
2. the amount of work needed to maintain the case base,
3. the effort required to control the accuracy of the experience management system afterward.

Tables 3.1 and 3.2 show a synthetic overall comparison of the different CBR approaches.

If the material already available in the company corresponds to the material expected by the intended user of the system, choosing the case representation approach is natural and easy. The effort needed to set up an experience management system is always minimized in this case, and if the maintenance process for this material is already in place, the experience management system will often directly fit into it. Unfortunately, this is rarely the case. The material available is rarely the kind of material that is really needed for the case base. For example, in a maintenance management system, historical data about machine faults is usually available, but, unfortunately, it rarely contains the technical information that is needed for decision making.

3.2.5 Effort Required for the Different Approaches

Table 3.3 summarizes the effort caused by the different case representation approaches. Effort to reuse existing material indicates the amount of work

Criteria	Textual CBR	Conversational CBR	Structural CBR
Case Base	A case is represented in free-text format. The cases may be structured according to headers, but the content of the headers is in free-text form. The case base is the collection of free texts that may be, for example, in electronic documents that are accessed on the Internet.	Cases are represented by a list of question and answers. The list of questions and answers may vary from one case to another. There is no common data structure.	The cases in the case base are represented according to the vocabulary, which provides a common structure. A simple approach is to record cases by assigning values to certain attributes that have been predefined. The initial case base may easily be extracted from an existing database.
Query Case	A query is represented by a question in free-text form whose content is similar to the description part of the stored cases.	A list of questions and answers following a dialog with the user.	The query is also expressed according to the vocabulary. It is typically a partially filled case description.
Results	A list of documents that might be useful.	A list of possible actions attached to the cases that have been retrieved.	A list of structured cases, e.g. database records.
Background Knowledge	Dictionaries of similar terms like "install : setup" or "printer : plotter" and information about the relationships between different words.	Ordering of questions, hierarchy of questions in a tree-like structure, possible answers for the questions that have been defined.	Vocabulary that defines the case structure. Rules to deduce values. Information on how to compute the similarity among attributes values.

Table 3.1. Comparison of the Different CBR Approaches (part a).

that typically is necessary to initially create the case base out of existing material and data. Effort for initial modeling refers to the work required to define dictionaries of terms (textual representations), the vocabulary (structural representations), or the lists of questions (conversational representations). With case creation, we state the effort required to enter new cases into an existing case base. Effort to tune the retrieval refers to how the developer or the experience manager controls how the engine retrieves cases. This can be, for instance, achieved by tuning the similarity measures, by defining similarities among attribute values, or by setting weights attached

Criteria	Textual CBR	Conversational CBR	Structural CBR
Initial Effort	Defining terms, synonyms and stop-words. Analyzing and setting up relationships between different words.	Storing dialogs within a case base, structuring the questions to organize the case base manually, ordering the questions manually. This can be done by entering existing decision trees.	Defining vocabulary. Importing an existing database or collecting cases according to the structure of the vocabulary.
Case Creation	Writing new documents.	Adding new dialogs. Depending on the structure of the dialog, new questions must be entered.	Adding a new record to the database. A questionnaire (forms) can be used in order to use the same vocabulary.
Maintenance	Maintaining the dictionary of controlled terms and sentences. Analyzing user queries and results.	Maintaining the list of questions and answers. Eliminating doubles, combining answers and questions. Reordering the questions by hand for the consultation.	Maintaining the case base, the vocabulary, and the reuse-related knowledge.
Multilingual Case Bases	Almost impossible. Must have different documents.	Difficult. Must have different conversations for each language.	Easy to implement with a single case base. Translation based on the vocabulary.
Advantages	Existing documents can be used as cases. No initial investment is required for modeling the cases.	The approach is intuitive and easy to understand. Appropriate for simple applications.	An existing database can be used to produce the initial case base. High accuracy can be achieved. Appropriate for complex applications.
Drawbacks	The user is not guided. The quality of retrieval depends on the syntax and not on the real content of the cases. Difficult to achieve high accuracy. High costs for quality control of the CBR system.	No explicit knowledge represented in the system for computing similarity. The interdependencies among different dialogs cannot be predicted. High maintenance costs.	It can be difficult to create a predefined case structure. This can usually be achieved within most technical domains but becomes harder in softer domains. High investment costs.

Table 3.2. Comparison of the Different CBR Approaches (part b).

to attributes. For example, in a maintenance application, it is preferable to perform two tests that are quick and easy, such as looking at a fault code on a control panel or checking whether a lamp is on, over one that is time consuming and requires, for example, dismantling part of the equipment. With quality control, we look at the effort for verifying that the decision support system works correctly and displays accurate results. Maintenance refers to

Effort per Task	Textual	Conversational	Structural
Reuse existing material	Very Low	High (1)	Medium
Initial Modeling	High (2)	Low	High (3)
Case Creation	Low	High (1)	Medium
Tuning CBR	Very high (4)	High/Impossible (5)	Medium-Low
Quality Control	Very high (4)	High (6)	Low
Maintenance	Low for the case base, High to tune the retrieval (4)	High (6)	Very Low

(1) Cases cannot be loaded directly from a database. For each case, the questions are positioned by the developer manually in a tree-like structure. The ordering of the questions is not done automatically like in the structural approach.

(2) This corresponds to defining the terms, synonyms, stop words.

(3) This corresponds to defining the database structure, the attributes, and their type (domain model).

(4) It is difficult to tune the system so that the right documents are retrieved, and it is also very difficult to maintain this afterward. New documents can drastically alter the retrieval quality (that is, recall and precision).

(5) This technology does not allow the developer to define similarity, and the system functions as a black box. Developer sometimes defines fake attributes/questions in the case in order to work around the problem.

(6) The behavior of the retrieval process can be altered when new cases are entered and new questions are defined to describe cases. The ordering of questions is done by the developer, unlike in the structural approach where this is done automatically.

Table 3.3. Comparison of the Efforts Required for the Different Approaches.

the work required for updating the case base and the experience management system when new cases are added.

In Fig. 3.4, we compare the effort required to build the initial system and the effort required to maintain it. We see that a structural approach requires more effort to create the vocabulary, but less maintenance effort. The conversational approach requires less work initially but the most work for maintenance. The textual approach is half way between the other two.

3.2.6 Focus on the Structural Approach

In the following we focus on the structural approach to case representation since it is best suited to represent experience for complex problem solving. The textual approach does not enable highly accurate retrieval as required for most complex problem solving and the conversational approach does not enable scaling up to large experience bases since maintenance effort increases drastically. Following the structural approach does, however, not mean to formalize all parts of the experience. Formalizing experience, in particularly building a full fledged vocabulary to cover a complete domain also involves

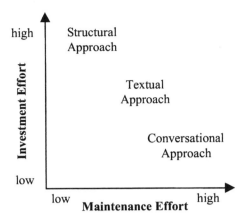

Fig. 3.4. Comparison of Efforts for the Different Representation Approaches.

a large development and maintenance effort. Hence, formalization should be restricted to what is really necessary. A more detailed discussion of this issue is given in Sect. 3.7.

3.3 Formalizing Structural Case Representations

In the following we present formalizations for different structural representation approaches. In particular we will demonstrate the attribute-value representation, the object-oriented representation, the graph-based representation, and representations using predicate logic. These are the basic approaches only. Further, specialized representations and representations that combine several of the basic approaches have been developed as well. Please note that all following formalizations are specializations of the general definition 3.3.

It is important to note that the current section is not meant to be a comprehensive introduction to those representation approaches, since today most of them are common ground in computer science. However, the purpose of this section is to provide a notation that is further used in this thesis and to show the application of the approaches for experience representation.

3.3.1 Attribute-Value Representation

When using attribute-value representation all information contained in the case is represented through sets of attribute values. The set of attributes that are used to represent the case can either be fixed or can vary from case to case. To each attribute a certain type is assigned. The type represents the value range for allowed values.

Attribute-value representations can be formalized as follows, based on the notion of types and attributes.

Definition 3.10 (Type, Type Space) A *type* T is a pair (T_{name}, T_{range}) where T_{name} is a label out of some type name space for referencing the type and T_{range} is a set, which denotes the values that belong to the type. Further, $a \in T$ denotes a value of type T, which is a short notation for $a \in T_{range}$. The *type space* $\mathbf{T}$ is a set of types $\{T_1, ..., T_n\}$ with disjoint $T_{i_{name}}$ labels.

As in standard programming languages where types define allowed value ranges for variables, in case representations they define allowed values for attributes. Examples of types are

- numerical types such as *Integer* or *Real*,
- symbol types that are defined by an enumeration of symbols,
- textual types such as strings,
- special types for multimedia objects, such as a type representing valid URLs,
- set types based on an arbitrary atomic type like those listed before.

Types are used to define allowed value ranges for attributes as shown by the following definition.

Definition 3.11 (Attribute, Attribute Space) An *attribute* A is a pair (A_{name}, A_{range}) where A_{name} is a label out of some attribute name space for referencing the attribute and A_{range} is the label of a type from a type space $\mathbf{T}$. The *attribute space* $\mathbf{A}$ is a finite list of attributes $(A_1, ..., A_n)$ with disjoint attribute names.

Please note that attributes can be either referenced by their attribute name or by their index $1 \ldots n$ in the attribute list.

In attribute value representations, the vocabulary container consists of an attribute space together with the related type space.

Definition 3.12 (Vocabulary Container in Attribute Value Representation) The *vocabulary container* **VOC** *in attribute value representations* is the pair $(\mathbf{A}, \mathbf{T})$ of attribute space and type space.

Given this definition of the vocabulary, we can now define the representation for cases that are constructed using this vocabulary. We distinguish two different ways to represent cases: cases with a fixed set of attributes and cases with a variable set of attributes. The advantage of the first approach is its simplicity while the second gives a little bit more flexibility and efficiency when a large number of attributes must be considered.

Definition 3.13 (Case with fixed set of attributes) A *case with a fixed set of attributes* for a vocabulary $\mathbf{VOC} = (\mathbf{A}, \mathbf{T})$ is a n-dimensional vector $(a_1, \ldots, a_n)$. The vector component a_i specifies the value for the attribute

A_i in this specific case. The value a_i must be an element of the range of the type specified for the attribute A_i.

In situations in which the attributes that are relevant vary from case to case the following representation is appropriate.

Definition 3.14 (Case with variable set of attributes) A *case with a variable set of attributes* for a vocabulary **VOC** $= (\mathbf{A}, \mathbf{T})$ is a set of the following form $\{A_{1_{name}} = a_1, \dots, A_{k_{name}} = a_k\}$, with $A_{i_{name}}$ $(i \in 1 \dots k)$ is the name of an attribute in **A** and a_i is an element from the range of the type specified for this attribute. Further, $A_{i_{name}} \neq A_{j_{name}}$ iff $i \neq j \in 1 \dots k$.

Each equation in this set assigns a value to one attribute. Note that not every available attribute from the attribute space must occur in the case representation. This could save memory when a large number of attributes is present in the vocabulary from which in every case only a small number of attributes occurs.

Example

The example already shown in Fig. 3.3 is represented using the attribute-value representation. The attributes are parameters shown together with their unit, such as "Input offset voltage $[mV]$". Most occurring types in this example are Real values, but we also find a symbol type, for example, to code the temperature range, which is defined as the set $\{COMercial, INDustrial, MILitary, SPAce\}$.

3.3.2 Object-Oriented Representations

Object-oriented case representations can be seen as an extension of the attribute-value representation. They make use of the data modeling approach of the object-oriented paradigm including *is-a* and *part-of* relations as well as the inheritance principle. Several recent CBR systems apply object-oriented techniques for representing cases (Manago et al. 1994; Arcos and Plaza 1995). Such representations are particularly suitable for complex domains in which cases with different structures occur. Cases are represented as collections of objects, each of which is described by a set of attribute-value pairs. The structure of an object is described by an object class that defines the set of attributes together with a type (set of possible values or sub-objects) for each attribute. Object classes are arranged in a class hierarchy, that is usually a n-ary tree in which sub-classes inherit attributes as well as their definition from the parent class. Moreover, we distinguish between simple attributes, which have a simple type like Integer or Symbol, and so-called relational attributes. Relational attributes hold complete objects of some (arbitrary) class from the class hierarchy. They represent a directed binary relation, e.g., a part-of relation, between the object that defines the relational attribute and the object to which it refers. Relational attributes are used to represent complex case structures. The ability to relate an object to another object of an arbitrary class (or an arbitrary sub-class from a specified parent class) enables the representation of cases with different structures in an appropriate way.

We start the following formalization by defining the class hierarchy.

Definition 3.15 (Class Hierarchy) The *class hierarchy* **CL** is a finite set of classes $\{C_1, ..., C_n\}$. A class C is a tuple $(C_{name}, C_{superclass}, (C.A_1, \ldots, C.A_k))$. Here, C_{name} is a label out of some class name space for referencing the class. All class names of a class hierarchy are disjoint. Further, $C_{superclass} \in \mathbf{CL} \cup \{\top\}$ denotes the superclass of class C; the superclass of the root class is $\top$. There is only one root class in a class hierarchy. Finally, $C.A_i$ $(i \in 1 \ldots k)$ are attribute names from some attribute space **A**.

Attributes as they occur in object classes have the following extended definition which allows attributes to have objects as values instead of just simple values defined as types. Additionally, attributes may hold more than a single value or object, i.e., attributes can store sets.

Definition 3.16 (Attribute, Attribute Space (extended definition)) An *attribute* A is a triple $(A_{name}, A_{range}, A_{set-type})$ where A_{name} is a label out of some attribute name space for referencing the attribute. Further, A_{range} is the label of a type from a type space **T** or a label of a class from the class space **CL**. If A_{range} is a type label, we call the attribute *simple attribute*; if A_{range} is a class label we call it *relational attribute*. Further, $A_{set-type} \in \{true, false\}$ is a binary flag which indicates whether the attribute holds a single value or multiple values. In the latter case, the attribute is called *multi-value attribute*. The *attribute space* **A** is a finite list of attributes $(A_1, ..., A_n)$ with disjoint attribute names.

Relational attributes can be used to model arbitrary binary relations between objects. It is typically used for modeling a *part-of* relation. *Is-a* relations are represented in the class hierarchy. We briefly introduce a few notions related to the *is-a* relation (see Fig. 3.5) that will be further used in this thesis. Let C be an inner node of the class hierarchy, then L_C denotes the set of all leaf nodes (classes) from the sub-tree starting at C. Further, $C_i < C_j$ denotes that C_i is a successor node (sub-class) of C_j. Moreover, $\langle C_k, C_l \rangle$ stands for the most specific common object class of C_k and C_l, i.e., $\langle C_k, C_l \rangle \geq C_k$ and $\langle C_k, C_l \rangle \geq C_l$ and it does not exist a node $C' < \langle C_k, C_l \rangle$ such that $C' \geq C_k$ and $C' \geq C_l$ holds. The relation $<$ and the operator $\langle \cdot, \cdot \rangle$ are used with classes as well as with class names.

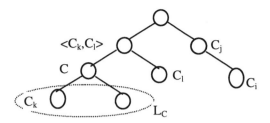

Fig. 3.5. Notations related to the Class Hierarchy.

Definition 3.17 (Vocabulary Container in Object-Oriented Representations) The *vocabulary container* **VOC** *in object-oriented representations* is the tuple $(\mathbf{CL}, \mathbf{A}, \mathbf{T}, C_{\text{case}})$ of class, attribute, and type spaces as well as a specifically marked class $C_{\text{case}} \in \mathbf{CL}$.

The marked class C_{case} determines the class of the objects that constitute cases. This is a kind of main object class for the cases. Please note that this need not to be (and usually is not) the root-class of the class hierarchy.

After the representation of the vocabulary is now defined we need to say in detail how cases are represented. In principle, cases are sets of objects, each of which is an instance of a class defined in the vocabulary.

Definition 3.18 (Object-Oriented Case) An *object-oriented* case c for a vocabulary **VOC** $= (\mathbf{CL}, \mathbf{A}, \mathbf{T}, C_{\text{case}})$ is a set of objects $c = \{o_1, \dots, o_m\}$. An object is a tuple $o = (o_{class}, o_{id}, \{A_{1_{name}} = a_1, \dots, A_{k_{name}} = a_k\})$ with

- o_{class} is a class name from **CL**,
- o_{id} is an object identifier from some object name space; all object identifiers of the objects in a case are disjoint.
- $A_{i_{name}}$ (for all $i \in 1 \dots k$) is an attribute from a class $C \in \mathbf{CL}$ with $C \geq o_{class}$ (this specifies inheritance),
- depending on the attribute definition of the attribute A_i the value a_i is one of the following:
  - If A_i is a single-valued simple attribute then a_i is an element of the range of the type associated with A_i.
  - If A_i is a multi-valued simple attribute then a_i is a finite set that is a subset of the range of the type associated with A_i.
  - If A_i is a single-valued relational attribute then a_i is an object identifier of an object o_j from the case c and $o_{j_{class}} \leq A_{i_{range}}$ (the object is an instance of a class that is equal to or a subclass of the class defined for the attribute).
  - If A_i is a multi-valued relational attribute then a_i is a set of object identifiers $\{o_1, \dots, o_l\}$ such that for each object o_j ($j = 1 \dots l$) holds that o_j is from the case c and $o_{j_{class}} \leq A_{i_{range}}$ (the object is an instance

of a class that is equal to or a subclass of the class defined for the attribute).

Further, the following two conditions must be met:

- c contains exactly one object o^{case} with $o_{class}^{case} \leq C_{case}$.
- for every object $o_i \neq o^{case}$ there exists an object $o_j \in c$ such that o_i occurs as object identifier in a relational attribute of o_j.

This defines a case as a set of connected objects each of which is an instance of a class of the class hierarchy. The case has a clearly marked root object which can be considered the starting node of the object network. This definition allows arbitrarily structured connected object networks to be used as cases as long as they have a marked root node.

However, we further need to introduce an important restriction of object-oriented representations that plays an important role during experience retrieval. We call an object-oriented representation *bounded* if there is an upper limit on the number of objects that can occur in the case representation. This can be ensured through the following property stated for the vocabulary.

Definition 3.19 (Bounded Object-Oriented Representation) An object-oriented representation with a class hierarchy **CL** and an attribute space **A** is called *bounded* if the following two conditions are met:

- the attribute space **A** does not contain a multi-value attribute and
- there does not exist a sequence of classes $C_{i_1}, \ldots, C_{i_k}$ from **CL** with $i_1 = i_k$ such that for each class C_{i_j} there exists a class $C'_{i_j} \geq C_{i_j}$ that has a relational attribute of a class $C''_{i_{j+1}} \geq C_{i_{j+1}}$.

Bounded object-oriented representations restrict the case representation in its size and its structure in the sense that only object-trees with a marked root object o^{case} can occur. Cases represented that way can be easily mapped to a attribute-value representation, although the structural information is lost and not represented explicitly anymore. This is, however, useful to ease the storage of case data (for example in a database) and for efficient retrieval.

Example

A brief example of a class hierarchy for representing experience related to technical objects, here personal computers, is shown in Fig. 3.6. This can be part of an experience representation to support the product search phase in electronic commerce or part of a diagnostic application for representing experience about faulty component behavior. This figure shows 13 classes, some of which have simple and/or relational attributes. The *PC* class, for example, has three relational attributes (printed in *italics*) which hold objects to represent the *Main Board*, the *Hard Disk* and the *Optional Storage*. This is particularly an example of a bounded object-oriented representation.

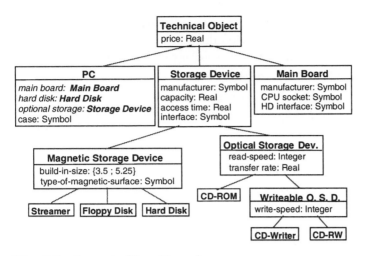

Fig. 3.6. Example Class Hierarchy.

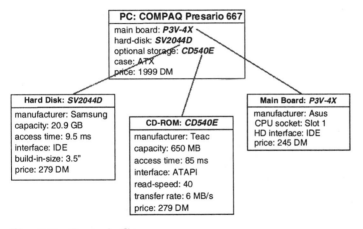

Fig. 3.7. Example Case.

Figure 3.7 shows a fraction of an example case representing a particular PC. It consists of four objects, one representing the whole PC and three for representing components.

3.3.3 Graph Representations

A third approach for formalizing structural case representations is the use of trees and graphs (Börner et al. 1993; Bunke and Messmer 1994; Sanders et al. 1997; Gebhardt et al. 1997; Ricci and Senter 1998). This can be appropriate if the experience to be represented has an inherent natural graph or tree structure. This can, for example, be the case if networks of pipes are part of the experience. Both, nodes and edges of trees or graphs can be labeled or described, for example, in an attribute-value manner.

We start the formalization with the well-known definition of a (directed) graph (Mehlhorn 1984).

Definition 3.20 ((Directed) Graph) A *(directed) graph* is a pair $G = (N, E)$ with N is a finite set called *nodes* and E is a set of (ordered) pairs $(p, q) \in N \times N$ called *edges*. In directed graphs we say that the edge leads from p to q.

We can extend the previous definition to a definition of an attributed directed graph. This representation allows to describe nodes and edges in various ways. Therefore, node and edge descriptors are introduced.

Definition 3.21 (Attributed (Directed) Graph) An *attributed (directed) graph* is a triple (G, α, β) where $G = (N, E)$ is a (directed) graph, α is a mapping $\alpha : N \to V_N$, and β is a mapping $\beta : E \to V_E$. V_N is called *node descriptor domain* and V_E is called *edge descriptor domain*.

When applying graphs for representing cases, the attributed graph itself becomes the case representation and the descriptor domains are the vocabulary, as shown in the following definitions.

Definition 3.22 (Vocabulary Container in Graph Representation) The *vocabulary container* **VOC** *in graph representations* is the pair (V_E, V_N) of the edge and the node descriptor domain.

Both descriptor domains can also be structured as an attribute-value representation. In this case each of the domains V_E and V_N is the set of cases according to definition 3.14. Then, the vocabulary consists of a set of attributes and related types for both, the edge description and the node description.

Definition 3.23 (Vocabulary Container in Graph Representation using Attribute-Value Descriptions) The *vocabulary container* **VOC** *in graph representations using attribute-value descriptions for nodes and edges* is the pair of pairs $((\mathbf{A}_E, \mathbf{T}_E), (\mathbf{A}_N, \mathbf{T}_N))$ of the edge and the node descriptor domain. $\mathbf{A}_E$ and $\mathbf{T}_E$ are attributes and types for representing edge descriptors and $\mathbf{A}_N$ and $\mathbf{T}_N$ are attributes and types for representing node descriptors.

Finally we need to define a case in graph representation as follows.

Definition 3.24 (Case in a Graph Representation) A *case in a graph representation* according to the vocabulary **VOC** $= (V_E, V_N)$ is an attributed graph or an attributed directed graph (G, α, β).

Example

Figure 3.8 shows an example of a fraction of a case in graph representation. It represents a connection structure of a pipe system connecting a supply pipe with several outlets. The nodes, each of which represents a pipe connector, are labeled with attributes describing important properties of the connector. Such a representation can be useful, for example, for representing design experience (Voß et al. 1996).

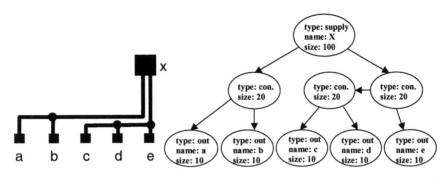

Fig. 3.8. Example Case in Graph Representation.

3.3.4 Predicate Logic Representations

Predicate logic is widely used for knowledge representation. It can also be used in special cases for experience representation (Ashley and Aleven 1993; Börner 1994; Börner et al. 1993; Plaza 1995; Bergmann et al. 1996). However, the typical inference methods connected with predicate logic only play a minor role in experience management, except for areas related to representing planning experience.

We start by some standard definition of first order predicate logic.

Definition 3.25 (Term, Ground Term) Let $\mathbf{F}$ be a set of function symbols, such as $f, g, \ldots, f_1, g_1, \ldots$. Let $\mathbf{V}$ be a set of variable symbols, such as $x, y, \ldots, x_1, y_1, \ldots$. Each function symbol has an arity assigned. *Terms* are defined recursively as follows:

- Each variable symbol and each function symbol with arity 0 is a term.
- When $t_1, \ldots, t_n$ are terms and f is an n-ary function symbol with $n > 0$, then $f(t_1, \ldots, t_n)$ is a term.

A term is called a *ground term* iff it contains no variables.

Definition 3.26 (Formula, Atomic Formula, Ground Fomular) Let $\mathbf{P}$ be a set of predicate symbols, such as $p, q, \ldots, p_1, q_1, \ldots$. Each predicate symbol has an arity assigned. *Formulas* are defined recursively as follows:

- When $t_1, \ldots, t_n$ are terms and p is an n-ary predicate symbol, then $p(t_1, \ldots, t_n)$ is a *formula*. Such formulas are called *atomic formulas*.
- When Φ and Ψ are formulas then $\Phi \wedge \Psi$, $\Phi \vee \Psi$, $\Phi \rightarrow \Psi$, $\neg \Phi$ are also formulas.

A formula is called a *ground formula* iff it contains no variables.

In predicate logic representations, the vocabulary consists of the function and predicate symbols. They must have an interpretation in the real world.

Definition 3.27 (Vocabulary Container in Predicate Logic) The *vocabulary container* **VOC** *in predicate logic representations* is the pair $(\mathbf{F}, \mathbf{P})$ of function and predicate symbols.

Now we can define a case as a set of atomic ground formulas which are coding facts about the situation captured as a case.

Definition 3.28 (Case in a Predicate Logic Representatation) A *case in a predicate logic representation* according to the vocabulary **VOC** $= (\mathbf{F}, \mathbf{P})$ is a set of atomic ground formulas over $\mathbf{F}$ and $\mathbf{P}$.

Instead of representing a case as a single set of ground formulas we can alternatively structure it into subsets each of which represents the characterization part, and the lesson part of the case.

Example

The following Fig. 3.9 gives an example of a diagnostic case represented in predicate logic. It consists of two sets of atomic formulas: the first one represents the characterization part specified by a set of facts and second set represents the lesson which is the particular fault that occurred on the magnetic switch *msw43* that is located in *rack3*.

$$Case = (\{errorcode(i59), errorcode(i59), i/o - state(out7, on),$$
$$relays(rel7, swithed), voltage(vdd, gnd, 23.8)\},$$
$$\{fault(magnetic - switch(rack3, msw43))\})$$

Fig. 3.9. Example of a Case Represented in Predicate Logic.

3.3.5 Relation to the General Definition

All four previously described formalizations for cases are specializations of the general definition 3.3. Although the distinction into characterization and lesson part is not explicit in those definition, it can be easily integrated in two different ways.

Top-Level Structure

Obviously, it is possible to structure the characterization and the lesson part independent from each other by using the four previously mentioned representations. This also enables choosing different representations for both parts, for example, a graph representation for the characterization part and an attribute value representation for the lesson part. If this is done, the vocabulary must also be structured accordingly.

The example from Fig. 3.9 demonstrates this kind of structuring for characterizations and lessons represented in predicate logic.

Annotating Representation Elements

Alternatively, the distinction between characterization and lesson part can also be done within one of the previously introduced representations. We can label attributes, objects, nodes, arcs, or predicates according to the case component to which they belong. A common attribute-value formalization for cases in classification tasks is to represent them as a $(n+1)$-tuple $c = (d_1, d_2, \ldots, d_n, class)$ where the first n attributes describe the situation (characterization) and the last attribute describes the class (lesson).

Representing the Problem Space

Although we have discussed the structural representations primarily in the context of case representation they can also be used to represent the problem space $\mathbb{P}$, which can, but does not necessarily differ from the experience characterization space.

3.3.6 Comparing Different Structural Case Representation Approaches

The advantages and disadvantages of the different approaches for structural case representation are summarized in Table 3.4. Please note also that it is possible to transform representations from each language into one of the others. Therefore one could argue that all representations are equivalent, which is of course true from the formal representational point of view. However, some of the advantages and disadvantages are not primarily caused by the representation itself but by the properties of the related algorithms for experience evaluation and retrieval. Even if this chapter discusses experience representation issues primarily in isolation, the different ways of experience processing depend on the representation. Hence, its choice has many implications besides pure representation issues such as the expressivness of the language.

Criteria	Attribute-Value	Object-Oriented	Graph-Based	Predicate Logic
Advantages	- easy to understand and implement - simple and efficient retrieval - link to databases easy	- flexible representation - arbitrary structures can be represented - more compact storage than for attribute-value representations - structural information available for selecting reusable experience	- enables the representation of simple structures - graph algorithms can be applied for the assessment of the relevance of a case	- very flexible - arbitrary structures can be represented - logical inferences can be used for similarity computation
Disadvantages	- very limited - structural information cannot be represented	- retrieval computationally more complex	- restricted compared to object-oriented representations - applicable graph algorithms typically of high complexity	- numeric values can hardly be handled - inferences are computationally of high complexity
Suited for	- simple analytic problem solving tasks - large case bases with a small number of attributes	- complex analytic problem solving tasks - synthetic problem solving tasks, e.g. design and configuration	- analytic and synthetic tasks if networks need to be represented	- synthetic tasks - tasks in which certain, rule-like knowledge is dominant for assessing the relevance of experience
Inappropriate	- synthetic and complex problem solving	- if no structural information is required	- highly structured domains with different relations	- in domains with many numeric properties - if numeric models for relevance assessment are required.

Table 3.4. Comparison of Different Structural Case Representation Approaches.

3.4 Generalized Cases

In the previous discussion, a case representing experience is regarded as a single point in case space, for example, represented as a pair (see definition 3.3). It assigns a single lesson to a single characterization. This section introduces an extended view on cases which we call *generalized cases*.

A generalized case covers not only a point of the case space but a whole subspace of it. A single generalized case immediately provides lessons to a set of closely related problems rather than to a single problem only. The lessons that a generalized case represents are very close to each other; basically they should be considered as (slight) variations of the same principle lesson. In general, a single generalized case can be viewed as an implicit representation of a (possibly infinite) set of traditional "point cases".

Generalized cases occur naturally in certain experience management application domains, such as the selection of parameterized products within electronic commerce. In such domains, we expect several significant advantages of this approach which can be summarized as follows:

- representation of experience that naturally covers some space rather than a point,
- integration with traditional point-cases in a single case base,
- substitution of several (possibly an infinite number of) point-cases by a single generalized case and thereby reduction of the size of the case base,
- representation of case-specific adaptation knowledge rather than general case-independent adaptation knowledge.

Disadvantages can occur due to the increased representation and acquisition effort for generalized cases. Moreover, depending on the representation approach used, similarity assessment can become more complex for generalized cases (see Chap. 4). Hence, retrieval can become less efficient so that the advantage of reducing the size of the case base is traded against the increased retrieval effort.

The idea of generalizing cases (or examples) was already present since the very beginning of CBR and instance-based learning research (Kolodner 1980; Bareiss 1989; Salzberg 1991; Zito-Wolf and Alterman 1992). For the purpose of adaptation, recent CBR systems in the area of design and planning (Hua et al. 1993; Purvis and Pu 1995; Bergmann 1996) use complex case representations that realize generalized cases.[1] The following considerations are primarily based on work by Bergmann et al. (1999) and Bergmann and Vollrath (1999).

---

[1] The term "generalized cases" was introduced by Bergmann (1996) but was restricted to planning cases. It has its origins in a concept for representing skeletal plans (Bergmann 1992) and for acquiring them by machine learning algorithms.

3.4.1 Extensional Definition of Generalized Cases

We now elaborate the idea of generalized cases in more detail. At first, we basically apply an extensional view on generalized cases by considering them as sets of traditional cases. The definitions we provide in this section should be considered as a specification rather than a means for realizing representation mechanisms or the problem solving process. Representation issues will be addressed in Sect. 3.4.3.

We start from the general definition 3.3 and assume that $\mathbb{D}$ be the characterization space and let $\mathbb{L}$ be the lesson space to be considered. For now we don't make any assumptions about the structure of the elements from $\mathbb{D}$ and $\mathbb{L}$. A traditional case c or *point case* is a point in the $\mathbb{D} \times \mathbb{L}$ space, i. e., $c \in \mathbb{D} \times \mathbb{L}$. A *generalized case*, on the other hand, can now be defined as follows:

Definition 3.29 (Generalized Case) A *generalized case gc* is a relation on the elements of the case space, i.e., $gc \subseteq \mathbb{D} \times \mathbb{L}$.

Hence, a generalized case stands for a set of point cases.[2] However, a generalized case should not represent an arbitrary set. The idea is that a generalized case is an abbreviation for a set of closely related point cases that naturally occur as one entity in the real world. Hence, they represent a uniform relationship between a subspace of the characterization space and a subspace of the lesson space. Unlike point cases, they can be viewed to some extent as general knowledge, which one might also represent using rules. But unlike rules, generalized cases will not be chained for problem solving and need also not be matched exactly.

3.4.2 Different Kinds of Generalized Cases

Given this definition, we can basically distinguish between five types of generalized cases as shown in Fig. 3.10.

- A *point case* (see gc_1 in Fig. 3.10) is a case in the traditional sense, i. e., a point (d, l) in the case space. A point case is a special kind of generalized case which covers one case only: $gc = \{(d, l)\}$.
- A *constant lesson generalized case* (see gc_2) represents a set of characterizations D which all have the same lesson l: $gc = \{(d, l)|d \in D\}$.
- A *functional lesson generalized case* (see gc_3) represents a set of characterizations D, each of which has one particular lesson. Hence, such a generalized case represents a partial function f from the characterization space into the lesson space: $gc = \{(d, f(d))|d \in D\}$.

---

[2] Alternatively, sets of cases could also represent uncertainty as proposed by Bergmann (1998b), but here we don't further discuss this issue.

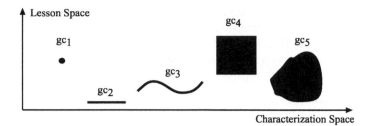

Fig. 3.10. Different Types of Generalized Cases.

- An *independent alternative lesson generalized case* (see gc_4) represents a set of characterizations D together with a set of lessons L. For each of the contained characterizations any of the lessons in the lessons set is appropriate and suited equally well. Hence, $gc = D \times L$.
- A *dependent alternative lessons generalized case* (see gc_5) represents a set of characterizations D and for each characterization $d \in D$ a set of lessons $L(d)$. Unlike the independent alternative lesson generalized case, for each problem there can be a different set of lessons. Hence, $gc = \{(d, l) | d \in D \wedge l \in L(d)\}$.

3.4.3 Representation of Generalized Cases

Obviously, a straight forward approach by applying the definitions from the previous section (e. g. computing the similarity for each point case covered by a generalized case and determining the maximum of the similarity values) can be quite inefficient if the generalized case covers a large subspace. This iterative approach would also not be able to cope with generalized cases that cover an infinite set of traditional cases. Hence, compact implicit representations for generalized cases must be developed.

In the following, we present a representation for generalized cases based on the attribute-value representation (see Sect. 3.3.1). As introduced in Sect. 3.3.5 we can assume that the attribute space **A** is subdivided into a characterization and a lesson space in the following manner: $\mathbf{A} = (A_1, \ldots, A_k, A_{k+1}, \ldots, A_n)$ where $A_1, \ldots, A_k$ represents the k attributes of the characterization space $\mathbb{D}$ and $A_{k+1}, \ldots, A_n$ represents the $n - k$ attributes of the lesson space $\mathbb{L}$. Despite these restrictions these considerations can easily be extended to object-oriented representations.

Representing Generalized Cases as Hyperrectangles

We first discuss representations for generalized cases where the subspace of characterizations and lessons covered by a generalized case can be defined by specifying the possible values of each attribute independent from each other.

For every attribute of the characterization and lesson space, the generalized case specifies an individual set. Thereby, generalized cases are n-dimensional axis-parallel hyperrectangles (Salzberg 1991). We can now define a first representation for generalized cases that builds up on the standard vocabulary definition 3.12 for attribute-value representations.

Definition 3.30 (Hyperrectangle Representation for Generalized Cases) The *hyperrectangle representation* for a generalized case in attribute-value representation, based on the vocabulary **VOC** is of the form $(V_1, \ldots, V_n)$ where V_i is a subset of the range of the type of attribute A_i.

An individual set V_i can be encoded either

- by enumerating its elements (if the set is finite),
- by using intervals in case of ordered types (e.g. real values),
- or by using inner nodes of taxonomic type representations (Bergmann 1998b).

Now it also becomes obvious that the object-oriented representation as introduced in definition 3.18 already covers generalized cases since multi-valued attributes are included. It is only a question whether set-values are treated according to the semantics of generalized cases.

Representing Generalized Cases Using Constraints

The hyperrectangle representation is inadequate for generalized cases which are not axis parallel hyperrectangles, as for example gc_3 of Fig. 3.10. In such situations, more advanced approaches are required. A natural way for representing dependencies is the use of constraints (Freuder 1992). However, such approaches introduce additional computational effort for similarity assessment and therefore must be considered carefully.

First, we need to extend the vocabulary definition by constraints.

Definition 3.31 (Constraint Space) A *constraint space* **CO** $= \{C_1, ..., C_n\}$ is a set of constraint identifiers, each of which has an arity assigned. Further, each k-ary constraint C has assigned a list of k type names $C_{T1}, \ldots, C_{Tk}$, as well as a definition of the relation expressed by the constraint.

The constraint space defines names and definitions for relations that can be used to express particular constraints between certain attributes.

Definition 3.32 (Vocabulary Container for Constraint-based Generalized Cases) The *vocabulary container* **VOC** *for constraint-based generalized cases* in attribute value representation is the triple $(\mathbf{A}, \mathbf{T}, \mathbf{CO})$ of attribute space, types space, and constraint space.

We can now define the syntax for constraints w.r.t. to a given vocabulary.

Definition 3.33 (Constraint) Assume a given vocabulary container **VOC** = $(\mathbf{A}, \mathbf{T}, \mathbf{CO})$ according to definition 3.32. We call $C(x_1, \ldots, x_k)$ a *constraint*, if $C \in \mathbf{CO}$ is a k-ary constraint identifier and if x_i is either an attribute name from **A** such that the attribute type of x_i is C_{Ti} or x_i is a value from C_{Ti}.

According to this definition, a constraint expresses a relationship between certain attributes or between attributes and constants. This definition can be obviously extended to object-oriented representations by introducing object specifiers in addition to the attribute specifiers.

Based on these preceding definitions we can now define a generalized case as follows:

Definition 3.34 (Constraint Representation for Generalized Case) The *constraint representation* for a generalized case has the form $\{C_1, \ldots, C_k\}$, where C_i are constraints based on the vocabulary **VOC** = $(\mathbf{A}, \mathbf{T}, \mathbf{CO})$.

Such a generalized case represents the set of point cases whose attribute values fulfill every constraint in the set C_i. We can also view the definition of a traditional case with a variable set of attributes $\{A_{1_{name}} = a_1, \ldots, A_{k_{name}} = a_k\}$ (see definition 3.14) as a generalized case in the constraint representation, just using the equality relation '=' as constraint.

A Simple Example

As an example, we show how the generalized case shown in Fig. 3.11 can be represented. We have three attributes, the first two for the characterization (values from $[0 \ldots 3]$) and the third for the lesson (values from $[0 \ldots 1]$). The lesson is represented graphically in Fig. 3.11 by the intensity of the shading

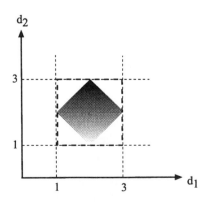

Fig. 3.11. A Simple Example for Generalized Cases.

of the generalized case. The formal representation for this generalized case is shown in Fig. 3.12. Note that the constraints are written in a more readable form than the prefix notation introduced in definition 3.33.

$$gc = \{d_1 + d_2 \geq 3, d_1 + d_2 \leq 5, d_1 - d_2 \leq 1, d_2 - d_1 \leq 1, l_1 = (d_2 - 1)/2\})$$

Fig. 3.12. Example of a Generalized Case Represented using Constraints.

3.5 Hierarchical Representations and Abstract Cases

The previously discussed approaches represented cases at a single level of abstraction. However, in recent CBR literature, the use of multiple representations at different levels of abstraction has been investigated (Smyth and Cunningham 1992; Smyth and Keane 1993; Smyth 1996; Kambhampati and Hendler 1992; Bergmann et al. 1994; Bergmann and Wilke 1995a; Bergmann 1996; Bergmann 1998a; Branting and Aha 1995; Branting 1997; Karchenasse et al. 1997; Cunningham and Bonzano 1998); cf. also (Kolodner 1993, p.576). For this kind of approaches the terms *hierarchical case-based reasoning* (Smyth and Cunningham 1992), *stratified case-based reasoning* (Branting and Aha 1995), and *reasoning with abstract cases* (Bergmann 1996) have been used so far. The basic idea behind these approaches is to supply experience represented at several different levels of abstraction. These cases are stored in a case base for being reused to solve new problems. When a new problem must be solved, one (or several) 'appropriate' concrete or abstract case has to be retrieved from the case base and the lesson that the case contains is reused to derive a lesson for the current problem, e.g., by filling in the details that a retrieved case at some higher level of abstraction does not contain.

3.5.1 Advantages of Abstract Cases

Experience management systems that reason with abstract cases are supposed to have several advantages over traditional approaches, which can be summarized as follows (Bergmann and Wilke 1996):

- Abstraction reduces the complexity of a case, i.e., it can simplify its representation. Cases at higher levels of abstraction are supposed to have a smaller number of features, relations, constraints, operators, etc. Consequently, cases at abstract levels require less storage in the case memory. In certain circumstances, cases at higher levels of abstraction can be used as a substitute for a set of concrete cases. Thereby, the size of the case base may be reduced significantly.

- Due to the above mentioned simplification of the case representation the computational efforts required for experience retrieval and adaptation decrease. Since less features and/or relations are used to describe an abstract case, comparing the new problem to a case is getting easier. Also, since less representational items (e.g. operators) that are used to describe an abstract lesson, adaptation of an abstract lesson to a new abstract problem requires less effort.
- Cases at higher levels of abstraction can be used as a kind of prototypes, which can be used as indexes to a larger set of related, more detailed cases. Such indexes can therefore further help to improve the efficiency of the retrieval.
- Abstraction can increase the flexibility of reuse. Typically, cases at higher levels of abstraction have a larger coverage than concrete level cases. Adapting abstract lessons contained in cases at higher levels of abstraction can lead to abstract lessons useful for a large spectrum of concrete problems.

These advantages seem to be particularly valuable in situations in which a large number of cases is available, the similarity assessment is very expensive, or flexible adaptation is required. Of course, these advantages do not come for free. Abstraction always involves losing information. Cases at abstract levels contain less information about the previous situation than cases at the concrete level. Therefore, the trade-off between the efficiency gains and the loss of information must be considered carefully. Also, building an experience management system that reasons with abstract cases requires a large development effort, first for building the components that realize the retrieval, reuse, and retain phases, and second for performing the knowledge acquisition for each knowledge container.

3.5.2 Levels of Abstraction

Each level of abstraction allows the representation of cases as well as the representation of general knowledge that might be required in addition to the cases. Usually, levels of abstraction are ordered (totally or partially) through an abstraction-relation, i.e., one level is called *more abstract* than another level.

A more abstract level is characterized through a reduced level of detail in the representation, i.e., it usually consists of less features, relations, constraints, operators, etc. Moreover, abstract levels model the world in a less precise way, but they must be designed in a way that they still capture the important properties. For experience management systems, this means that they must capture features that can be easily reused for new problems. At higher levels of abstraction, features must be represented that remain stable even if certain features of the problem (i.e., these are the features considered the details) change. These details should be neglected in the representation of the abstract level.

In traditional hierarchical problem solving (e.g., ABSTRIPS, Sacerdoti 1974), levels of abstraction are constructed by simply dropping certain features (e.g. state predicates in planning) of the more concrete representation levels. However, it has been shown that this view of abstraction is too restrictive and representation dependent (Bergmann and Wilke 1995a; Holte et al. 1995) to make full use of the abstraction idea. In general, different levels of abstraction require different representation languages, one for each level. Abstract properties can then be expressed in terms completely different from the terms used to express concrete properties (Bergmann and Wilke 1995a).

To represent different levels of abstraction, we can structure the vocabulary into several partially ordered sub-vocabularies, one for each level of abstraction.

Definition 3.35 (Hierarchically Structured Vocabulary) A *hierarchically structured vocabulary* $\mathbf{VOC} = (\{\mathbf{VOC}_0, \ldots, \mathbf{VOC}_n\}, \prec)$ is a set of disjoint sub-vocabularies $\mathbf{VOC}_i$ together with a partial order $\prec$ on these sub-vocabularies with a single least element $\mathbf{VOC}_0$. The sub-vocabulary $\mathbf{VOC}_0$ is called the *concrete level*, the other sub-vocabularies are called *abstract levels*.

3.5.3 Kind of Cases

Based on the level of abstraction, we basically can distinguish between two kinds of cases: *concrete cases* and *abstract cases*.

Definition 3.36 (Abstract and Concrete Cases) A *concrete case* is a case located at the lowest available level of abstraction, i.e., it is a case w.r.t the sub-vocabulary $\mathbf{VOC}_0$. An *abstract case* is a case represented at a higher level of abstraction, i.e., it is a case w.r.t. one of the sub-vocabularies $\mathbf{VOC}_i$ with $i > 0$.

If several abstraction levels are given (e.g., a hierarchy of abstraction spaces), one concrete case can be abstracted to several abstract cases, one at each higher level of abstraction. Such an abstract case contains less detailed information than a concrete case. On the other hand several concrete cases usually correspond to a single abstract case (see Fig. 3.13). These concrete cases share the same abstract description; they only differ in the details.

We can define a many-to-one abstraction mapping on cases as follows.

Definition 3.37 (Abstraction Mapping for Cases) An *abstraction mapping* α_{i_k, i_l} abstracts a case from one level of abstraction $\mathbf{VOC}_{i_k}$ to a higher level $\mathbf{VOC}_{i_l}$, i.e., $c_{i_l} = \alpha_{i_k, i_l}(c_{i_k})$ for $\mathbf{VOC}_{i_k} \prec \mathbf{VOC}_{i_l}$. The inverse relation is called *concretization*.

Such an abstraction mapping also encodes domain knowledge. Its definition itself is not considered to be part of the vocabulary or the cases. It can be considered part of the reuse-related knowledge.

Instead of having cases located at a single level of abstraction, a single case can also contain information at several or all levels of abstractions that are available. We call such a case *hierarchical case*.

Definition 3.38 (Hierarchical Cases) A *hierarchical case* is a tuple $(c_{i_1}, \ldots, c_{i_m})$ such that c_{i_k} is case w.r.t. the sub-vocabulary $\mathbf{VOC}_{i_k}$ and if $\mathbf{VOC}_{i_k} \prec \mathbf{VOC}_{i_l}$ then $c_{i_l} = \alpha_{i_k,i_l}(c_{i_k})$.

When constructing an experience base, we can distinguish different approaches with respect to the kind of cases they store in the case-base:

- cases on a single (concrete) level of abstraction,
- abstract cases and concrete cases on several levels of abstraction,
- hierarchical cases on several levels of abstraction.

3.6 Languages for Structural Case Representations

Several languages for vocabularies and cases have been developed. In former days they have been used as modeling languages during the development of an experience management application. Today, graphical modeling tools are available that can be used without knowing the particular syntax of a modeling language (see Sect. 9.8.2). Nevertheless, these languages are still used as a means for storing and exchanging experience.

3.6.1 Common Case Representation Language CASUEL

CASUEL (Manago et al. 1994) is the Common Case Representation language developed in the INRECA project. CASUEL is a flexible, object-oriented

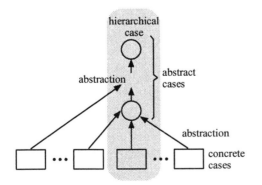

Fig. 3.13. Different Kinds of Cases.

frame-like language for storing and exchanging vocabularies and case libraries in ASCII files. It is designed to model naturally the complexities of real cases. CASUEL represents domain objects in a class hierarchy using inheritance and slots to describe the attributes of these domain objects. Moreover, typing constraints on attribute values, as well as different kinds of relationships between objects can be expressed in the language. In its current version, CASUEL additionally supports a rule formalism for exchanging and storing completion and adaptation rules for cases, as well as a first mechanism for defining similarity measures. Although, CASUEL provides a lot of features, it does not require applications to use all of them. Therefore, CASUEL is a keyword-driven language that allows different system components to easily ignore irrelevant definitions. On the other hand, CASUEL is also open in the sense that new features can be defined if necessary for a particular kind of application or component. In the following we briefly describe the core parts of the language.

```
<CASUEL sources> ::= <domain definition>
                          { <descriptive model> |
                            <case data> |
                            {<descriptive model> <case data>} }
<domain definition> ::= defdomain <symbol>
                  [ declaration_file {<string>}+ ";" ]
                  [ case_file {<string>}+ ";" ]
                  case_structure <class identifier>";"
                  target <class identifier> <slot identifier>";"
                  case_reference <class identifier> <slot identifier>
                  [";" languages { <language identifier>}+ ]
                  {";" {<print name> | <comment>} }* "."
<language identifier> ::= <symbol>
<print name> ::= print_name <language identifier> <string>
<comment> ::= comment <language identifier> <string>
<descriptive model> ::= {<type definition>}*
                          {<value definition>}*
                          {<slot definition>}+
                          {<class definition>}+
                          {<rule definition>}*
                          {<adaptation rule definition>}*
                          {<global object definition>}*
<case data> ::= {<case>}++
```

Fig. 3.14. Syntax Definition for a CASUEL Domain.

Domain Description

The domain description (see Fig. 3.14) specifies the domain of application, including the vocabulary (here called *descriptive model*) and the respective case data. After the *declaration_file* keyword, a list of files containing parts of the descriptive model can be specified. The *case_file* keyword introduces a list of files which contain case data. After the *case_structure* keyword, a name of a class must be stated which specifies the class whose instances represent the cases themselves.

Descriptive Model

The descriptive model consists of a hierarchy of classes (including inheritance) and a set of slots which represent the attributes of each class (see Fig. 3.15). Further the descriptive model specifies a set of types which specify the range of possible values of the slots (see Fig. 3.16).

```
<class definition> ::= defclass <class identifier>
              a_kind_of {<class denoter>}
              [";" slots {<slot identifier>}+]
              [";" discriminant no]
              {";" { <print name>| <comment> } }* "."
<class identifier> ::= <symbol>
<class denoter> ::= class | <class identifier>
<slot identifier> ::= <symbol>
```

```
<slot definition> ::= defslot <slot identifier> [of <class identifier>]
              {{type <type denoter> [";" default <basic value>]} |
               {class <class denoter> [";" properties parts_semantic]}}
              [";" {{cardinal <cardinality restriction>} |
                    interval}]
              [";" discriminant no]
              {";" { <print name> | <comment> | <question> } }* "."
<cardinality restriction> ::=
              "[" <positive integer> ".." {<positive integer> | "*"} "]"
<question> ::= question <language identifier> <string>
```

Fig. 3.15. Syntax Definition for the Classes and Slots of the Descriptive Model.

The *defclass* keyword introduces the definition of a new class with a new class identifier. The class after the *a_kind_of* keyword is defined as the superclass of the new class. The *defslot* definition describes a new global slot identifier, which is further available for all subsequent definitions. The slot

```
<type definition> ::= deftype <type identifier>
        a_kind_of <type denoter>
        [";" range <range restriction>] "."

<type denoter> ::= <type identifier> |
        { integer | real | string | symbol |
          ordered_symbol | taxonomy |
          boolean | date | time }

<type identifier> ::= <symbol>
```

```
<range restriction> ::=
        {<interval range definition> | <enumeration definition> }
<interval range definition> ::=
        "[" {<basic value> | "*"} ".." {<basic value> | "*"} "]"
<enumeration definition> ::=
        { "(" {<basic value>}+ ")" } | { <taxonomy definition> }
<taxonomy definition> ::= "["{ <taxonomy tree>}+ "]"
<taxonomy tree> ::= <basic value> [ "[" {<taxonomy tree>}+ "]" ]
```

Fig. 3.16. Syntax Definition for the Types and Ranges of the Descriptive Model.

definition assigns each slot a unique *type*, which is either a basic type, a type defined with a *deftype* clause or a *class* defined through a *defclass* clause (relational attribute). The *cardinality* definition is used to state or restrict the cardinality of a slot. It can be used to specify a multi-value slot. The first integer number in such a cardinality restriction declares the minimum number of elements required as slots value, while the second integer specifies the maximum number of elements allowed. The *interval* keyword states that the values of the slot are intervals.

The *deftype* definition (see Fig. 3.16) defines a new type with a name. This type is based on a supertype specified after the *a_kind_of* keyword. The supertype is either a type (with type identifier) which was defined by a previous *deftype* clause, or a basic type. Basic types are either ordinal types i.e. *integer, real, time, date*, and *strings* or nominal types i.e., *symbol, ordered_symbol, taxonomy* (hierarchy of values), and *boolean*.

Cases

Figure 3.17 shows the syntax of a case, defined following the *defcase* keyword. A case consists of an unique identifier (a positive integer) and a sequence of objects. Note that each case must contain the slots declared as target and as case reference in the domain definition. An *object* is specified by a class identifier followed by a sequence of slot instantiations. The slot instantiation describes the current values of the slots of the object. For relational slots, the respective objects must be referenced by an object identifier.

```
<class definition> ::= defclass <class identifier>
          a_kind_of {<class denoter>}
          [";" slots {<slot identifier>}+]
          [";" rules { <rule identifier>}+]
          [";" adaptation_rules { <adaptation rule identifier>}+]
          [";" discriminant no]
          {";" { <print name>| <comment> } }* "."

<class identifier> ::= <symbol>

<class denoter> ::= class | <class identifier>

<slot identifier> ::= <symbol>

<rule identifier> ::= <symbol>

<adaptation rule identifier> ::= <symbol>
```

Fig. 3.17. Syntax Definition for a Case.

In addition to the above described language features, CASUEL also contains specific means to represent global objects, rules for specifying functionally dependent features, rules for specifying adaptation possibilities, and similarity measures (see Manago et al. 1994).

3.6.2 The XML-based Orenge Modeling Language OML

A recent follow-up of the CASUEL language is OML, the Orenge (Open Retrieval ENGinE) Modeling Language (Schumacher and Traphöner 2000), developed in part in the WEBSELL project. Orenge follows the idea of using the "internet standard" XML (Bray et al. 2000) as a case representation language (see also related approaches described by Hayes et al. 1998 and Hayes and Cunningham 1999). It consists of several document type definitions (*.dtd* files) that enable the definition of experience and reuse-related knowledge in various forms:

- OMML (Orenge Model Markup Language): modeling of the vocabulary
- OOML (Orenge Object Markup Language): modeling of cases
- OVML (Orenge Valuation Markup Language): modeling of similarity measures
- ORML (Orenge Rule Markup Language): modeling of rules
- OOOML (Orenge Operator Object Markup Language): modeling of adaptation operators.

Additionally, there are several language definitions for the exchange of experience data between different software components. In the following we give a brief overview of the Orenge Model Markup Language and the Orenge Object Markup Language.

Orenge Model Markup Language

The Orenge Model Markup Language is, like CASUEL, an object-oriented language for defining cases. Unlike CASUEL, in which data entities are either modeled as values from types or instances of classes, OMML only knows classes. However, a distinction is made between atomic classes, which correspond to types, and aggregate classes, which correspond to classes as known in CASUEL. Hence, an Orenge model contains the set of classes that define the structure of the data in the application. Each object occurring in a case must be a valid instance of a class in the application model.

Initially, every Orenge model contains a set of system classes. They implement the basic characteristics of the different kinds of classes like numeric or aggregate classes. All user defined classes are constructed by subclassing an existing class. Subclassing a class usually means to restrict the set of possible instances (e.g., atomic values) to a subset of the original class, i.e., the subclass is more specialized than its superclass. This is necessary because a class can inherit features from its superclass, e.g. similarity measures. Thus each instance of a class must also be a possible instance of its superclass. Figure 3.18 shows the hierarchy of system classes. User defined classes will always be subclasses of a leaf in this tree.

Figure 3.19 shows an extract of the document type definition for the OMML. It is restricted to the basic elements required for the specification of user defined classes, i.e., subclasses of *Atomic, Aggregate, Reference, Set, Interval, Compound,* and *Void.*

All class elements have some common attributes (entity *%ClassAttlist*). Each class has two required attributes: *id* gives the name of the class and *super* refers to the superclass this class is derived from.

All atomic classes are defined using the *Atomic* element. The value range can be defined using a *ValueInterval* or a *ValueEnumeration.* If no value range is defined, the new class allows the same values as its superclass.

An enumeration of valid values is defined using the element *ValueEnumeration* together with a set of V-elements each of which defines a valid value. Value enumerations can have orders as properties. Two different orders can be defined: total orders and taxonomies. Taxonomies are used to define hierarchical relations between the values of a class. The element *ValueInterval* can be used to specify the allowed range for numeric and chronologic classes. The *Aggregate*-element (see right side of Fig. 3.19) is used to define aggregate classes. Usually, each OMML-document contains at least one such element, because the class representing cases is usually an aggregate class. A set class

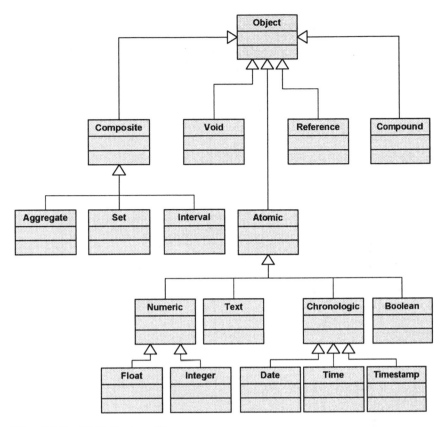

Fig. 3.18. OML System Classes.

is defined using the element *Set*. It is necessary to specify the attribute *elementType*, which must be the name of a class defined in the same document. Optionally, a minimal and maximal size of the instances can be specified. The definition of an interval class is very similar to the definition of set classes: Only the name of the element type, i.e., the class over which the intervals are to be created, has to be specified. The *Compound*-element is used to define compound classes. First of all, it defines that the new class is always abstract. Next, it is possible to define one of the implementing classes of the compound as the default implementor, of which elements are build if nothing else is specified. The element classes of the compound are specified using a list of *ClassReference*-elements. Each such element defines as an attribute the complete name of an element class of the compound.

```
<!ELEMENT Atomic                          <!ELEMENT Aggregate
  ( %ClassProperty; ,                       (%ClassProperty; ,Attribute*)>
  (ValueEnumeration |                     <!ATTLIST Aggregate
  ValueInterval)? )>                        %ClassAttlist; >
<!ATTLIST Atomic                          <!ELEMENT Attribute
  %ClassAttlist;                            (%AttributeProperty;)>
  default  CDATA  #IMPLIED>               <!ATTLIST Attribute
<!ENTITY % ClassAttlist                     name NMTOKEN #REQUIRED
  "                                         type IDREF #REQUIRED>
  id       ID #REQUIRED                   <!ENTITY % AttributeProperty …>
  super    IDREF #REQUIRED
  abstract (true|false) 'false'           <!ELEMENT Reference
  editable (true|false) 'false'             (%ClassProperty;)>
  ">                                      <!ATTLIST Reference
                                            %ClassAttlist;
<!ENTITY % ClassProperty  … >              referenceType IDREF #IMPLIED >

<!ELEMENT ValueEnumeration              <!ELEMENT Set ( %ClassProperty; )>
  ( V*, %EnumerationProperty; ) >       <!ATTLIST Set
                                            %ClassAttlist;
<!ELEMENT V (%ValueProperty;) >            minSize CDATA #IMPLIED
<!ATTLIST V                                 maxSize CDATA #IMPLIED
  v CDATA  #REQUIRED >                      elementType IDREF #REQUIRED >

<!ENTITY % ValueProperty  … >          <!ELEMENT Interval
                                          ( %ClassProperty; )>
<!ENTITY % EnumerationProperty         <!ATTLIST Interval
  "( Taxonomy | TotalOrder )*">           %ClassAttlist;
                                            elementType IDREF #REQUIRED >
<!ELEMENT Taxonomy ( TN ) >
<!ATTLIST Taxonomy                     <!ELEMENT Compound
  id CDATA #REQUIRED >                     (%ClassProperty; ,
                                            ClassReference* ) >
<!ELEMENT TN ( TN* ) >                 <!ATTLIST Compound
<!ATTLIST TN                              abstract CDATA #FIXED 'true'
  v CDATA #REQUIRED >                      %ClassAttlist;
                                            default IDREF #IMPLIED >
<!ELEMENT TotalOrder ( OE* ) >
<!ATTLIST TotalOrder                   <!ELEMENT ClassReference EMPTY >
  id CDATA #REQUIRED>                   <!ATTLIST ClassReference
                                            id IDREF #REQUIRED >
<!ELEMENT OE EMPTY >
<!ATTLIST OE                           <!ELEMENT Void (%ClassProperty;)>
  v CDATA #REQUIRED >                   <!ATTLIST Void
                                            %ClassAttlist; >
<!ELEMENT ValueInterval EMPTY >
<!ATTLIST ValueInterval
  min      CDATA  #IMPLIED
  max      CDATA  #IMPLIED>
```

Fig. 3.19. Extract from the DTD Descriptions for the Modeling Language.

Orenge Object Markup Language

While OMML represents Orenge classes, the Orenge Object Markup Language OOML has been developed for the representation of Orenge objects. In its pure form one can store an object pool, i.e., lists of instances of various Orenge classes, in a single OOML document. So a case base can be loaded from an OOML document and a retrieval engine can use these objects as a case base.

```
<!ELEMENT ObjectPool
   (InstanceList*)>

<!ELEMENT InstanceList
   (%Object;)*>

<!ATTLIST InstanceList
   class CDATA #REQUIRED>

<!ENTITY % Object
"(%Aggregate;|%Set;|%Interval;|
   %Atomic;| %Reference;|%Void;)">

<!ENTITY % ObjectAttlist
   "
   class CDATA #IMPLIED
   id CDATA #IMPLIED
   ">

<!ENTITY % Void "Void">

<!ENTITY % ObjectProperty … >

<!ELEMENT %Void;
   (%ObjectProperty;)*>

<!ATTLIST %Void;
        %ObjectAttlist;>

<!ENTITY % Reference "Ref">

<!ELEMENT %Reference;
      (%ObjectProperty;)*>

<!ATTLIST %Reference;
   %ObjectAttlist;
   v CDATA #REQUIRED>

<!ENTITY % Atomic "Ato">

<!ELEMENT %Atomic;
      (%ObjectProperty;)*>

<!ATTLIST %Atomic;
   %ObjectAttlist;
   v CDATA #REQUIRED>

<!ENTITY % Aggregate "Agg">

<!ELEMENT %Aggregate; (
   (%ObjectProperty;)*,
   (%Attribute;)*)>

<!ATTLIST %Aggregate;
   %ObjectAttlist;>
```

```
<!ENTITY % Attribute
   "%ObjectAttribute; |
    %ValueAttribute; |
    %ReferenceAttribute;" >

<!ENTITY % AttributeAttlist
   "
   n CDATA #REQUIRED
   class CDATA #IMPLIED
   ">

<!ENTITY % ObjectAttribute "A">

<!ELEMENT %ObjectAttribute;
      (%Object;)?>

<!ATTLIST %ObjectAttribute;
   %AttributeAttlist;>

<!ENTITY % ValueAttribute "AV">

<!ELEMENT %ValueAttribute;
      (%ObjectProperty;)*>

<!ATTLIST %ValueAttribute;
   %AttributeAttlist;
   v CDATA #IMPLIED>

<!ENTITY % ReferenceAttribute "AR">

<!ELEMENT %ReferenceAttribute;
      (%ObjectProperty;)*>

<!ATTLIST %ReferenceAttribute;
   %AttributeAttlist;
   v CDATA #REQUIRED>

<!ENTITY % Set "Set">

<!ELEMENT %Set;
   ((%ObjectProperty;)*,(%Object;)*)>

<!ATTLIST %Set;
   %ObjectAttlist;>

<!ENTITY % Interval "Int">

<!ELEMENT %Interval;
   ((%ObjectProperty;)*,
    (%Object;), (%Object;)) >

<!ATTLIST %Interval;
   %ObjectAttlist;>
```

Fig. 3.20. Extract from the DTD Descriptions for the Object Markup Language.

OOML also serves as a common core of the Orenge service languages which can be used for the communication between experience management components. This section gives an overview of the OOML document type definition shown in Fig. 3.20.

ObjectPool is the root element of an OOML file. It contains a set of instance lists, which in turn consists of objects that are all instances of a single class. Therefore, the *InstanceList*-element has to specify the name of a defined class.

The entity *%Object;* shows which types of objects can be used in an OOML file. They correspond to the class elements used in OMML except that there are no compound objects. The *Ref*-element is used to specify a reference object. It has one additional attribute, which specifies the ID of the referenced object. The *Ato*-element is used to specify each kind of atomic objects. The *v*-attribute defines the value of the object, which must be a valid value according to the type definition. The element *Agg* represents an aggregate object. It can contain properties which are defined in a separate property DTD, and a list of attribute values.

There are different ways to specify an attribute: The general way is to use an *ObjectAttribute*-element. The value or reference attribute elements are specified to provide short forms for often used kinds of attributes. They have two attributes in common: *n* specifies the name of the attribute in question and *class* can contain the class of the attribute value. The object attribute element is named simply *A* and can contain exactly one object.

3.7 Choice of the Vocabulary

When choosing the vocabulary for representations, each component of the case is represented by a subset of the used representation entities, e.g. attributes. That is, some attributes are used to characterize the experience while some attributes describe the lessons learned of the experience. Typically we can assign each attribute to one of these three case components. The choice of the attributes is crucial for the success of an experience reuse system. In the following we summarize some brief guidelines that help finding the right attributes and types.

3.7.1 Characterization Part

During the choice of attributes for the characterization part the following criteria should be considered:

- **Independence:** The attributes chosen for the characterization part should be mostly independent. This means that we should avoid, if possible, that an attribute is functionally dependent on other attributes, i.e., that there is a function that computes one attribute value from some others. Independence avoids redundancy, i.e., one piece of information is only stored in one place. However, complete independence can often not be achieved. Sometimes it is necessary to introduce dependent attributes in order to simplify the computation of the relevance assessment.
- **Utility Distinguishability:** The description of the characterization must be complete in the following sense: it must be possible to decide based on the selected attribute values whether it is possible to reuse the experience in a new situation characterized by the same set of attributes. If it is not possible to distinguish two experience items which must be distinguished based on the attributes available in the characterization part of the case,

new attributes must be added to enable the differentiation between the two. This criterion has been formalized in Sect. 3.1.4.

- **Minimality:** The description of the characterization part of the case must be minimal in the sense that there are no attributes that are irrelevant for deciding whether the experience can be reused in a new situation.

3.7.2 Lesson Part

For the lesson part the attributes must be chosen according to the following criteria:

- **Completeness:** The description of the lesson must be complete in the sense that the experience user is able to reproduce the lessons from the experience just by looking at the values of the attributes. This means that all information necessary to reproduce the lesson contained in the experience must be available.
- **Independence:** The lesson information must be split into several independent attributes so that each part of the lesson that needs to be adapted is represented as an individual attribute.
- **Acquirability:** The attribute values can be determined from the experience, e.g. by direct observation, by applying a measurement method, or by derivation from some other attributes.

3.7.3 Choice of Types

Most of the previously introduced case representations make use of types. The types for representing the possible values for attributes must be chosen carefully. The correct choice for the characterization part attribute types depends on the methods used for assessing the utility of an experience in a new situation during the retrieval phase. The correct choice for the lessons part attribute types depends on the methods used for adapting the experience to the new situation. In the following we give some first rough guidelines for choosing appropriate attributes types.

Symbol types are appropriate in case of a small number of possible values for the attribute. Symbols enable simple computation of assessment functions for the utility. Symbols are also suited for most adaptation methods.

Numeric types like Integer and Real are appropriate for representing measured values and other numeric values, which naturally occur in the experience to be represented. The assessment of the utility of the case can be achieved based on the difference of the values in the case and the current situation. Like symbols, numeric values are suited for most adaptation methods.

Text strings are suited for information parts which are unstructured and which require a high degree of flexibility. Representing information in text has many advantages from an experience acquisition point of view. However, handling textual information for assessing the utility of an experience for a new situation is quite difficult and usually results in a low accuracy. Solution adaptation for textual attributes is nearly impossible.

4. Assessing Experience Utility

> *"The problem with similarity is that it has no meaning unless one specifies the kind of similarity."*
>
> Linda B. Smith

The central task for experience management is the retrieval of reusable experience. This retrieval task requires additional knowledge besides the experience itself. It requires knowledge about the utility of an experience item (or case) in a certain problem solving situation. This kind of knowledge is part of the general reuse-related knowledge in the experience management model (see Sect. 2.1). This chapter deals with various approaches for modeling utility through its approximation by similarity measures.

4.1 Approximating Utility with Similarity

In Sect. 3.1.3 we introduced the utility as a function $u : \mathbb{P} \times \mathbb{L} \to \Re$ that assigns each problem-lesson pair a utility value (Def. 3.7). The general problem with those utility functions is that they are usually only partially known. This is because utilities can only be determined a-posteriori, i.e., after the problem is solved and the experience has been applied. Note that all the example interpretations for utility given in Sect. 3.1.3 are a-posteriori measures. A-posteriori measures of utility can, of course, not be used for retrieval since at the time of retrieval the problem in question is not yet solved.

The way out of this problem is to give up the aim of measuring utility directly, but to approximate it. In the following we will introduce an approximation that tries to capture the known preferences $c_i \succ_p c_j$ for some problems p and some cases c_i and c_j instead of the exact utility values.

4.1.1 Traditional View of Case-Based Reasoning

Case-Based Reasoning in its traditional form approximates the utility by similarity while making the following two assumptions:

1. The problem space is identical to the characterization space for experience, i.e, $\mathbb{P} = \mathbb{D}$. This assumption significantly simplifies retrieval and experience base maintenance.
2. *Similar problems have similar solution*, or re-phrased in a more precise wording: *the solution of a problem is also useful for similar problems.*
3. Only cases with a sufficiently high utility are stored in the case base.

Given this, the utility $u(p, l_i)$ of a case $c_i = (d_i, l_i)$ for the problem p is approximated by the *similarity* between the problem p and the problem d_i contained in the cases (see Fig. 4.1). Since the problem space is identical to the characterization space, the similarity measure compares two objects from the same domain.

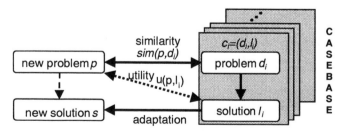

Fig. 4.1. Approximating Utility with Similarity on the Problem Space Level.

4.1.2 Extended View

We can extend this traditional CBR view by generalizing the way in which utility is assessed by means of similarity (Bergmann et al. 2001). In CBR one typically speaks about the similarity on the level of problem descriptions. However, the level on which similarity is assessed is not necessarily the level of problem descriptions, but a level that characterizes the experience appropriately according to its utility. We have already introduced this level, it is the experience characterization space $\mathbb{D}$ which is usually different from the problem space $\mathbb{P}$. It is located between the problem space and the lesson space and mediates between them. As already defined, this level is about properties that are relevant to assess the utility of a solution for a particular problem. This can be properties from the problem space but this doesn't have to be the case.

Figure 4.2 shows this extended view. It requires that the description of the new problem p is transformed into a description d on the level of experience characterization. This is achieved by the following problem transformation.

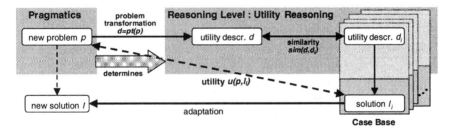

Fig. 4.2. Approximating Utility with Similarity on Experience Characterization Level.

Definition 4.1 (Problem Transformation) A *problem transformation* is a computable function $pt : \mathbb{P} \to \mathbb{D}$.

During retrieval, the description $d = pt(p)$ is compared to the characterizations d_i of the cases from the case base. The purpose of this similarity assessment is to approximate the utility of a given solution for a new problem. In this model, the characterizations d_i of the individual cases are usually part of the case description, but if they depend on the problem itself, they can also be computed during retrieval.

One necessary condition for being able to approximate utility by similarity on the experience characterization space is that also problems can be appropriately distinguished according to their utility on the experience characterization space. If two problems are equal on the characterization space then they have to have the same problem-specific utility function.

$$\forall l \in \mathbb{L} \ \forall p_1, p_2 \in \mathbb{P}$$
$$pt(p_1) = pt(p_2) \to u(p_1, l) = u(p_2, l)$$

(Utility Distinguishability
of Problems)

Like the utility distinguishability condition for experience (see Sect. 3.1.4), this condition also expresses a requirement for the vocabulary, particularly for the experience characterization space, but also for the problem transformation.

Given this property, we can now derive a utility function for an experience characterization and a lesson.

Definition 4.2 (Utility Function on Experience Characterization Space) For a given a utility function $u : \mathbb{P} \times \mathbb{L} \to \Re$ we can define a *utility function for an experience characterization and a lesson* $u : \mathbb{D} \times \mathbb{L} \to \Re$ by $u(d, l) = u(p, l)$ for a $p \in \mathbb{P}$ with $d = pt(p)$.

4.1.3 Similarity Measures

We can now formally introduce a means for measuring similarity through a similarity measure $sim(d, d_i)$, i.e., a function that assesses the similarity and expresses it as a numerical value. The higher the value, the higher is the similarity between the two objects to be compared. The following definition defines similarity measures on the level of experience characterizations and is hence compatible with the previously introduced extended view.

Definition 4.3 (Similarity Measure) A *similarity measure* is a function $sim : \mathbb{D} \times \mathbb{D} \to [0, 1]$.

In the literature one finds various different definitions for similarity measures (Tversky 1977; Richter 1992a; Richter 1994; Wess 1995; Osborne and Bridge 1996; Burkhard 1998; Pal et al. 2000). The one chosen here is specific since it restricts similarity values to the interval $[0, 1]$. This has the advantage that there are values to express the most similar (1) and the least similar (0) situations. Please note also that we do not require any properties for similarity measures. In particular they don't need to be measures in the mathematical sense. Possible properties for similarity measures that *can* be demanded are discussed in Sect. 4.2.2.

4.1.4 Relations between Similarity and Utility

In order to compare similarity measures and utilities directly one has to take into account that they are defined on different domains (Richter and Althoff 1999). Similarity measures sim have pairs of experience characterizations as arguments while utility functions u operate on problem-lesson-pairs. However, both induce preference relations. The preference relation $\succeq_p$ induced by utilities is already introduced in definition 3.8. The preference relation induced by similarities is defined as follows:

Definition 4.4 (Preference Relation Induced by a Similarity Measure) In the context of a problem p or its characterization $d = pt(p)$, a similarity measure sim induces a *preference relation* $\sqsubseteq$ on the case space $\mathbb{C}$ by $(d_i, l_i) \sqsubseteq (d_j, l_j)$ iff $sim(d, d_i) \leq sim(d, d_j)$. We write $\sqsubseteq_p$ to specify the preference relation for a given problem p. We write $\sqsubseteq_d$ to specify the preference relation for a given characterization d. If we want to make clear that the preference relation is induced by a particular similarity measure sim, we write: $\sqsubseteq_p^{sim}$ or $\sqsubseteq_d^{sim}$, respectively.

When we aim at approximating utility functions with similarity measures we do this for the purpose of retrieval. For retrieval the preference relation on cases is more important than the numerical utility values. Therefore, we should try to find a similarity measure operating on an appropriate representation of experience characterizations, such that this similarity measure induces the same preference relation on cases as the utility, or at least a preference relation that does not "contradict" the one induced by the utilities.

Relating Preference Relations

The following requirements express different possibilities for relating the two preference relations of a universe M^1.

$$R_1(\preceq_p, \sqsubseteq_p, M) \text{ iff } \forall a, b \in M \ a \prec_p b \rightarrow a \sqsubseteq_p b$$
$$R_2(\preceq_p, \sqsubseteq_p, M) \text{ iff } \forall a, b \in M \ a \prec_p b \rightarrow a \sqsubset_p b$$
$$R_3(\preceq_p, \sqsubseteq_p, M) \text{ iff } \forall a, b \in M \ a \preceq_p b \rightarrow a \sqsubseteq_p b$$
$$R_4(\preceq_p, \sqsubseteq_p, M) \text{ iff } R_2(\preceq_p, \sqsubseteq_p, M) \wedge R_3(\preceq_p, \sqsubseteq_p, M)$$

These four requirements can be organized in a small lattice in the sense that R_1 is the least restrictive requirement and R_4 is the most restrictive requirement. R_2 and R_3 lie in between but are not comparable. This becomes obvious when looking at the following Table 4.1.

Utility preference	R_1	R_2	R_3	R_4
$a \prec_p b$	$a \sqsubseteq_p b$	$a \sqsubset_p b$	$a \sqsubseteq_p b$	$a \sqsubset_p b$
$a =_p b$	*	*	$a =_p b$	$a =_p b$

Table 4.1. Relating Preference Relations.

---

[1] These considerations are of general nature, but in the following M will be the case space.

This table shows for each of the four requirements what preference the similarity measure can indicate when a certain utility preference is given. In this table $=_p$ means that the cases a and b have the same utility/similarity and $*$ means that any preference can be indicated by the similarity measure. Note also that the requirement R_1 is equivalent to the requirement that the similarity function and the utility function are similarly ordered (Hardy et al. 1967).

The problem with the requirements R_1 and R_3 is that they are usually too weak since even a constant function as a similarity measure, i.e., a similarity measure which does not really distinguish the cases fulfills these requirements. Hence, R_2 or R_4 is usually a good choice. R_2 allows the similarity measure to rank two cases differently although they should be ranked equally.

Scope of Preference Relations

The second question concerning the approximation of utility by similarity is to decide which cases should be ordered appropriately by the similarity measure, i.e., what the set M is in the above introduced relations R_i.

One could think about similarity measures that

- order all possible cases of the case space $\mathbb{C}$ correctly,
- order all sound cases correctly, i.e., all cases from $\mathbb{C}$,
- order all cases of the case base correctly, i.e., all cases from **CB**.

Instead of ordering all cases from the above mentioned sets correctly, one can also require that only the "best" of those cases are ordered correctly since it is usually not necessary to know exactly which of the useless cases is more useless than another one.

Soundness of Similarity Measures

These considerations lead to the following ways of approximating utility by similarity. We call a similarity measure *sound* with respect to one of the following definitions if we consider it a proper approximation of the utility. A necessary condition for the existence of any sound similarity measure is that the characterization space fulfills the utility distinguishability property for problems (Sect. 4.1.2) and cases (Sect. 3.1.4).

Definition 4.5 (Total R_i Soundness of *sim* w.r.t. the Case Base Semantics) A similarity measure *sim* is *totally R_i-sound with respect to the case base semantics* $\mathbb{B}$ iff $\forall p \in \mathbb{P}\ R_i(\preceq_p^{sim}, \sqsubseteq_p, \mathbb{B})$ holds.

Definition 4.6 (Total R_i Soundness of *sim* w.r.t. a Case Base) A similarity measure *sim* is *totally R_i-sound with respect to the case base* **CB** iff $\forall p \in \mathbb{P}\ R_i(\preceq_p^{sim}, \sqsubseteq_p, \mathbf{CB})$ holds.

Definition 4.7 (Partial R_i Soundness of sim w.r.t. a Case Base) A similarity measure sim is *partially R_i-sound with respect to the case base* **CB** iff $\forall p \in \mathbb{P}$ there exists a partition of the case base $\mathbf{CB} = \mathbf{CB}^+ \cup \mathbf{CB}^-$ with $|\mathbf{CB}^+| \geq 1$ and $\forall c^+ \in \mathbf{CB}^+$, $\forall c^- \in \mathbf{CB}^- : c^+ \succeq_p c^-$ and if $R_i(\preceq_p^{sim}, \sqsubseteq_p , \mathbf{CB}^+)$ holds.

These different definitions of soundness of a similarity measure require a different "amount" of knowledge about utility to be captured in the similarity measure. The soundness definition 4.5 requires that the similarity measure encodes the complete knowledge about utility ordering. The advantage of a similarity measure of that kind is that it does not require any maintenance when the case base is changed. The soundness definition 4.6 requires less knowledge of utility to be encoded in the similarity measures. Just enough knowledge is required to handle the cases in the case base. However, this may require to update the similarity measure when new cases enter the case base. Definition 4.7 is even less restrictive and is only able to order the best cases correctly. It may also need an update when new cases enter the case base.

Despite of the different characteristics of those soundness conditions, they all ensure at least the following property.

Proposition 4.1 (Best Case Correctness) If the following is given:

- a problem transformation pt,
- a sound case base **CB**,
- a sound similarity measure sim w.r.t. definition 4.5, 4.6, or 4.7.

Then, for every problem p there is no case in the case base for which it is known that it has a higher utility for the problem p than the case $(d, l) \in \mathbf{CB}$ with the highest similarity $sim(pt(p), d)$.

This property guarantees that always the best case is selected according to the current knowledge of the utility function encoded in the similarity measure.

Pragmatic Criteria for Modeling Similarity

Given the above considerations, the ultimate goal is to model sound similarity measures. However, besides these formal considerations there are several pragmatic issues that must also be taken into account during similarity modeling. They deal with the knowledge acquisition effort required for similarity modeling as well as with the computational effort involved in computing the similarity and computing the best case with respect to a given similarity measure. From those pragmatic considerations it should be taken care that

- the similarity measure can be modeled with reasonable effort,
- the similarity measure is computationally feasible,

- the similarity measure enables an indexing of the case base to handle a large number of cases efficiently.

Defining a similarity measure which approximates an only partially-known utility function results to some degree in performing a kind of sensitivity analysis. This has two aspects:

1. *Choice of the appropriate vocabulary for experience characterization:* Often, the primarily given attributes at the problem or the lessons level are not sufficient for this purpose. This is due to the fact that the utility can depend on a certain relation of values from several attributes rather than on the attribute values alone. This leads to the definition of additional attributes (possibly abstract concepts) and their establishment is an important step towards a successful application. The goal is to achieve mostly independent attributes, each of which expresses a source for a certain preference. This issue has been briefly discussed already in Sect. 3.7.

2. *Decomposing similarity functions:* Modeling similarity means decomposing the similarity function according to the vocabulary defined at the level of characterization. This decomposition should be done such that *local similarity functions* for individual attributes model the influence of certain individual preferences. Local similarities should then be aggregated by taking into account their possibly different importance. This requires comprehensive modeling capabilities for similarities. These will be presented in the remainder of this chapter.

4.2 General Considerations Concerning Similarity and Distance

4.2.1 Distance Measures

A dual formalization for similarity measures are distance measures. They have a long tradition in nearest neighbor classification methods (Dasarathy 1990).

Definition 4.8 (Distance Measure) A *distance measure* is a function $dist : \mathbb{D} \times \mathbb{D} \to [0, 1]$.

As for similarity, the literature gives us different alternative definitions for distance measures (Pal et al. 2000). The one chosen here is specific since it restricts distance values to the interval $[0, 1]$. An alternative definition that is also often used is to express distances as positive Real numbers (including 0). The variant chosen here has the advantage that there are values to express the most distant (0) and the least distant (1) cases. Please note also that we do not require any properties for distance measures. In particular they don't have to be measures in the mathematical sense.

Like similarity measures, distance measures also induce a preference relation on cases as follows.

Definition 4.9 (Preference Relation Induced by a Distance Measure) In the context of a problem p or its characterization $d = pt(p)$, a distance measure $dist$ induces a *preference relation* $\sqsubseteq$ on the case space $\mathbb{C}$ by $(d_i, l_i) \sqsubseteq (d_j, l_j)$ iff $dist(d, d_i) \geq dist(d, d_j)$. We write $\sqsubseteq_p$ to specify the preference relation for a given problem p. We write $\sqsubseteq_d$ to specify the preference relation for a given characterization d. If we want to make clear that the preference relation is induced by a particular distance measure $dist$, we write: $\sqsubseteq_p^{dist}$ or $\sqsubseteq_d^{dist}$, respectively.

We can compare distance measures and similarity measures by comparing the induced preference relations, for example by the requirements introduced in Sect. 4.1.4. In particular we call a similarity measure sim and a distance measure $dist$ *preference equivalent* iff $\sqsubseteq_p^{sim} = \sqsubseteq_p^{dist}$.

A particular way to achieve a preference equivalent counterpart for a similarity measure or a distance measure, respectively, is to transform them via a bijective, strictly monotonously decreasing function f of $[0, 1]$ to $[0, 1]$. For any such function f and any similarity measure sim or distance measure $dist$ holds $\sqsubseteq_p^{sim} = \sqsubseteq_p^{sim \circ f}$ and $\sqsubseteq_p^{dist} = \sqsubseteq_p^{dist \circ f}$.

4.2.2 Possible Properties of Similarity Measures

As mentioned before, we do not state any properties that similarity measures or distance measures must fulfill. However, in certain situations several properties can be stated or must be demanded. In particular, different retrieval approaches as discussed in Chap. 7 have different requirements on the similarity or distance measures on which they can operate. We now define the properties reflexivity, symmetry, triangle inequality for similarity and distance measures (Burkhard and Richter 2000).

Definition 4.10 (Reflexivity) A similarity measure is called *reflexive* if $sim(x, x) = 1$ holds for all x. If additionally $sim(x, y) = 1 \rightarrow x = y$ holds, we call this property *strong reflexivity*. A distance measure is called *reflexive* if $dist(x, x) = 0$ holds for all x. If additionally $dist(x, y) = 0 \rightarrow x = y$ holds, we call this property *strong reflexivity*.

Most similarity measures are reflexive. Interpreted in terms of utility this means that a case achieves the highest possible utility when its lesson is re-applied in the same situation (w.r.t. its representation) in which it was obtained. This condition holds if the case base only contains lessons with the highest utility for a problem with the stored characterization. On the other hand, the strong reflexivity does not always hold since it can often happen

that an experience can be perfectly applied in a situation that differs from
the one in which it was gathered.

Definition 4.11 (Symmetry) A similarity measure is called *symmetric* if
for all x, y it holds $sim(x, y) = sim(y, x)$. A distance measure is called
symmetric if $dist(x, y) = dist(y, x)$ holds for all x, y.

There was a long debate on principles in the literature about whether
similarity measures are symmetric or not (Tversky 1977; Gentner 1980; Martin 1990; Nosofsky 1991; Indurkhya 1992; Jantke 1994). Since in the context
of experience management we use similarity measures to encode knowledge
about utility it becomes obvious that here are many examples for symmetric
similarities as well as many examples for asymmetric similarity measures.
For example, a similarity measure is not symmetric if a lesson gathered in
situation A is also highly useful in situation B, while the lesson gathered in
situation B is not useful in situation A.

Definition 4.12 (Triangle inequality) A similarity measure fulfills the
triangle inequality if $sim(x, y) + sim(y, z) \leq 1 + sim(x, z)$ holds for all x, y, z.
A distance measure fulfills the *triangle inequality* if $dist(x, y) + dist(y, z) \geq dist(x, z)$ holds for all x, y, z.

The triangle inequality can be seen as a kind of extension of the transi-
tivity property for relations. While often demanded for distance functions,
they are not so common for similarity measures. The above stated definition
for similarity measures is derived from the well-known property for distance
functions by applying the transformation $f(x) = 1 - x$ (Burkhard and Richter
2000).

Definition 4.13 (Monotony of a Similarity Measure) If an order re-
lation $<_{\mathbb{D}}$ is defined over $\mathbb{D}$, then a similarity measure $sim : \mathbb{D} \times \mathbb{D} \rightarrow [0, 1]$ is
called *monotonic* if the following holds: $sim(x, y) \geq sim(x, z)$ if $x <_{\mathbb{D}} y <_{\mathbb{D}} z$
or $z <_{\mathbb{D}} y <_{\mathbb{D}} x$. A distance measure is called *monotonic* if the following
holds: $dist(x, y) \leq dist(x, z)$ if $x <_{\mathbb{D}} y <_{\mathbb{D}} z$ or $z <_{\mathbb{D}} y <_{\mathbb{D}} x$.

The monotony property for a similarity measure can be considered if an
ordering on the domain $\mathbb{D}$ is available. This property states that the similarity
or distance measure is somehow "compatible" with this ordering.

4.2.3 Similarity and Fuzzy Sets

We can also interpret similarity and distance measures in the sense of the
Fuzzy theory. We use the notation $A \subseteq_f U$ to express that A is a fuzzy
subset of some set U. Further, $\mu_A : U \rightarrow [0, 1]$ is the membership function of
A.

From a given similarity measure sim we can define a fuzzy subset on
$\mathbb{D} \times \mathbb{D}$ through $\mu_{sim}(x, y) = sim(x, y)$. This fuzzy subset can be seen as a

fuzzy formalization of the relation 'x is useful for y'. Further, we can associate to each characterization of a situation d a fuzzy subset of the case base $F_d \subseteq_f \mathbf{CB}$ through $\mu_{F_d}((d_i, l_i)) = sim(d, d_i)$. This is a fuzzy formalization for the relation "useful for d". It can be regarded as a formalization of how the case base $\mathbf{CB}$ is structured by sim from the viewpoint of d.

Additional remarks about the relation between fuzzy theory and case-based reasoning can be found in papers by (Wang et al. 1994), Richter (1997), Dubois et al. (1997), Liao et al. (1998), and Pal et al. (2000).

4.3 Similarity Measures for Attribute-Value Representations

We now discuss various ways for representing utilities through similarities. These considerations are strongly connected to the representation formalism used for experience.

We start with the simplest representation language, namely attribute-value representations. Hence, we assume that the representation is given by a set of attributes (see 3.3.1) each of which has some predefined type. Here, $\bar{x} = (x_1, \ldots, x_n) \in \mathbb{D}$ and $\bar{y} = (y_1, \ldots, y_n) \in \mathbb{D}$ are the two attribute vectors to be compared.

4.3.1 Simple Measures for Binary Attributes

Several similarity and distance measures have been proposed for binary attribute vectors, i.e., $x_i, y_i \in \{0, 1\}$. The well-known *Hamming distance* is a first and simple example for a distance measure that operates on cases represented through binary attributes. It computes a distance value that is proportional to the number of attributes with different values.

$$dist_H(\bar{x}, \bar{y}) = \frac{1}{n} \cdot |\{i \mid x_i \neq y_i\}| \qquad \text{(Hamming Distance)}$$

The Hamming distance fulfills the properties strong reflexivity, symmetry, and triangle inequality. The corresponding similarity measure is called the *simple matching coefficient*, which is also strong reflexive, symmetric, and fulfills the triangle inequality.

$$sim_H(\bar{x}, \bar{y}) = \frac{1}{n} \cdot |\{i \mid x_i = y_i\}| \qquad \text{(Simple Matching Coefficient, SMC)}$$

A first generalization of the simple matching coefficient is the *weighted simple matching coefficient* that introduces a weight $\omega_i \geq 0$ for each attribute such that $\omega_1 + \cdots + \omega_n = 1$. The weight allows to express the importance of the attribute for the similarity.

$$sim_{H,\overline{\omega}}(\overline{x}, \overline{y}) = \sum_{\substack{i=1\ldots n, \\ x_i=y_i}} \omega_i \qquad \text{(Weighted SMC)}$$

A second generalization of the simple matching coefficient results from weighting the number of equal attribute values different than the number of unequal attribute values. This results in a non-linear strictly monotonic increasing function of the number of equal attributes. A parameter α ($0 < \alpha < 1$) determines the concrete shape of this function.

$$sim_{H,\alpha}(\overline{x}, \overline{y}) = \frac{\alpha \cdot sim_H(\overline{x},\overline{y})}{(\alpha \cdot sim_H(\overline{x},\overline{y}))+(1-\alpha)\cdot(1-sim_H(\overline{x},\overline{y}))} \qquad \text{(Non-linear SMC)}$$

The meaning of α is a follows: $sim_{H,0.5} = sim_H$. If $0 < \alpha < 0.5$ then not matching attributes are weighted higher, if $0.5 < \alpha < 1$ then matching attributes are weighted higher.

The Tversky contrast model (Tversky 1977) is a further generalization of the simple matching coefficient. It allows encoding knowledge about similarity in a function f and three parameters α, β, and γ.

$$\begin{aligned} sim_{T,f,\alpha,\beta,\gamma}(\overline{x}, \overline{y}) = \ &\alpha \cdot f(\{\, i \,|\, x_i = y_i = 1 \,\}) - \\ &\beta \cdot f(\{\, i \,|\, x_i = 1 \wedge y_i = 0 \,\}) - \\ &\gamma \cdot f(\{\, i \,|\, x_i = 0 \wedge y_i = 1 \,\}) \end{aligned} \qquad \begin{array}{l}\text{(Tversky Similarity} \\ \text{Measure)}\end{array}$$

The Tversky similarity measure is not symmetric iff $\beta \neq \gamma$. It has been introduced to compare a prototype described by a set of binary features $\overline{y}$ with a current situation $\overline{x}$. The function f measures the index sets of the matching attributes, e.g. by its size such as with the definition $f(A) = \frac{1}{n} \cdot |A|$, or it can consider different attributes differently, e.g. by using a function such as $f(A) = \sum_{i \in A} \omega_i$. The parameter α determines the importance of features that occur in both, the prototype and the situation. The parameter γ reduces the similarity based on the features that are missing in the current situation while β reduces the similarity based on the features that the current situation has in addition.

4.3.2 Simple Measures for Numerical Attributes

If we assume numerical attribute values, e.g. Real numbers, we can make use of several classical approaches. Most of these have been introduced as distance metrics in the mathematical sense, i.e, they are symmetric, reflexive, and they fulfill the triangle inequality. We now assume an attribute-value range with an upper and lower bound; for reasons of simplicity we assume $x_i, y_i \in [0, 1]$. Given this, the City-Block-Metric (also called Manhattan distance), the Euclidean distance, and the maximum norm are distance measures according to definition 4.8. Unlike the traditional definition of these metrics, we introduce a normalization term to ensure that the distance values are within the interval $[0, 1]$.

$$dist_{|\cdot|}(\overline{x}, \overline{y}) = \tfrac{1}{n} \cdot \sum_{i=1}^{n} |x_i - y_i| \qquad \text{(City Block Metric)}$$

$$dist_{\text{Euklid}}(\overline{x}, \overline{y}) = \sqrt{\tfrac{1}{n} \cdot \sum_{i=1}^{n} (x_i - y_i)^2} \qquad \text{(Euclidean Distance)}$$

$$dist_{\text{Max}}(\overline{x}, \overline{y}) = \max_{i=1}^{n} |x_i - y_i| \qquad \text{(Maximum Norm)}$$

The Minkowski norm is a generalization of these three distance measures. The parameter p determines whether it behaves like the City-Block-Metric ($p=1$), the Euclidean distance ($p=2$) or the Maximum norm ($p \to \infty$).

$$dist_{\text{Minkowski},p}(\overline{x}, \overline{y}) = (\tfrac{1}{n} \cdot \sum_{i=1}^{n} |x_i - y_i|^p)^{1/p} \qquad \text{(Minkowski Norm)}$$

We can also introduce weights into all these measures to express that different attributes have different importance. Attribute weights $\omega_i \geq 0$ are introduced such that $\omega_1 + \cdots + \omega_n = 1$. Very common are the weighted City-Block-Metric and the weighted Euclidean Distance that can be directly derived from the following general form.

$$dist_{\text{Minkowski},p,\overline{\omega}}(\overline{x}, \overline{y}) = (\sum_{i=1}^{n} \omega_i \cdot |x_i - y_i|^p)^{1/p} \qquad \begin{array}{c}\text{(Weighted}\\ \text{Minkowski Norm)}\end{array}$$

Seidl and Kriegel (1997) propose a further extension of the weighted Euclidean distance, called *quadratic form distance* (QFD). It introduces an $n \times n$ weight matrix $\Omega = [\omega_{ij}]$ that enables to consider dependencies between two attributes i and j in the distance measure. In order to ensure that the distance values are in the interval $[0, 1]$ we must demand that Ω is positive definite, i.e., $z \cdot \Omega \cdot z^T > 0$ for all $z \in \Re^n, z \neq 0$ and that $\sum_{i=1}^{n} \sum_{j=1}^{n} \omega_{ij} = 1$. If Ω is a diagonal matrix then this is the standard weighted Euclidean Distance.

$$dist_{\text{Quad-Form},\Omega}(\overline{x}, \overline{y}) = \sqrt{\sum_{i=1}^{n} \sum_{j=1}^{n} \omega_{ij} \cdot (x_i - y_i) \cdot (x_j - y_j)} \qquad \text{(QFD)}$$

Please note that all of the above distance measures can easily be transformed into a preference equivalent similarity measure. However, they are all limited to pure Real valued attributes. Similarity for attribute-value case representation requires, however, to be able to handle various different attribute types within one representation. Therefore we need to extend the above similarity approaches in various ways.

4.3.3 The Local-Global Principle

Similarity modeling can be simplified by decomposing similarity according to a so-called local-global principle. We can describe similarity, first, from a global point of view of the whole case and, second, from a local point of view during which the details of the similarity assessment are taken into account. This leads to the definition of global measures that are defined on the whole case and the definition of local measures defined on the level of the attributes. The general idea is that the global measure reflects the task and has a pragmatic character, while the local measures take care of the details of the technical and domain character and are task independent.

Local Measures

Local measures should represent the main properties. For example, consider an attribute water temperature (in Celsius), which is a Real valued attribute from a range $[-10, +200]$. There are certain domain properties that enable dividing the real axis into certain intervals. So-called *landmarks* can separate these intervals (e.g., 0 degrees and 100 degrees). These landmarks come from physics and are not necessarily related to personal relevances. Each such interval is a qualitative region (where the material behaves in some sense very similar). A local similarity measure reflecting this fact is not uniform: numbers inside the same region have a high degree of similarity but numbers in different regions have a low degree of similarity.

Formally, we can define for each attribute A_i a local similarity measure as follows:

Definition 4.14 (Local Similarity Measure) A *local similarity measure* is a similarity measure for an individual attribute A_i defined through sim_{A_i} : $T_{i_{range}} \times T_{i_{range}} \to [0,1]$, where $T_{i_{range}}$ is the range of the type of A_i.

Global Measures

On the other hand global measures represent task and pragmatics of the user. They reflect importance, relevance, and utility aspects of the similarity. They are modeled by aggregating local similarity by an aggregation function Φ. The aggregation function encodes the knowledge about the importance, relevance and utility.

Definition 4.15 (Global Similarity Measure, Aggregation Function) A similarity measure sim_Φ for cases that is composed from local similarity measures by $sim_\Phi(\overline{x}, \overline{y}) = \Phi(sim_{A_1}(x_1, y_1), \ldots, sim_{A_n}(x_n, y_n))$ is called *global similarity measure*. The function $\Phi : [0,1]^n \to [0,1]$ is called *aggregation function*. An aggregation function must fulfill the following properties:

- $\Phi(0, \ldots, 0) = 0$ and
- Φ is monotonously increasing in every argument.

4.3.4 Local Similarity Measures for Numeric Attributes

We now discuss different variants for modeling local similarity measures for numeric attributes. The advantage of numeric attributes (but also for ordered symbolic attributes) is that there is a predefined order on the domain as well as a notion of difference. Like the similarity measures just discussed in Sect. 4.3.2 we can make use of the difference of the two values to derive a similarity value from it.

Difference Functions

In the following, δ is a function to determine the relevant numerical difference of the two values. Typical difference functions are the following two:

$$\delta(x, y) = x - y \qquad \text{(Standard Linear Difference)}$$

$$\begin{aligned} \delta(x, y) &= ln(x) - ln(y) \quad \text{for} \quad x, y \in \Re^+ \\ \delta(x, y) &= -ln(-x) + ln(-y) \quad \text{for} \quad x, y \in \Re^- \end{aligned} \qquad \text{(Logarithmic Difference)}$$

The logarithmic difference is used when the value range for the attribute spans several orders of magnitude. This is typically the case if the attribute represents a physical measure. For example, we would usually expect that the similarity between $1V$ and $1.2V$ is the same as the similarity between $1mV$ and $1.2mV$.[2] Here, the logarithmic difference yields the same results.

Symmetric and Asymmetric Difference Determined Similarity

Similarity measures can be defined in the following ways:

$$sim_{A_i}(x,y) = f(|\delta(x,y)|) \quad \text{(Symmetric Difference Determined Similarity)}$$

$$sim_{A_i}(x,y) = \begin{cases} f(\delta(x,y)) & : \quad x > y \\ 1 & : \quad x = y \\ g(\delta(y,x)) & : \quad y > x \end{cases} \quad \begin{array}{l} \text{(Asymmetric Difference} \\ \text{Determined Similarity)} \end{array}$$

The functions f and g are monotonic decreasing mappings from $\Re$ to $[0..1]$ such that $f(0) = 1$ and $g(0) = 1$ holds. They describe the decrease of the similarity depending on the increase of the difference. From this follows immediately that the resulting local similarity measure is monotonic for the standard and logarithmic difference function. Figure 4.3 shows several commonly used functions that are described below.

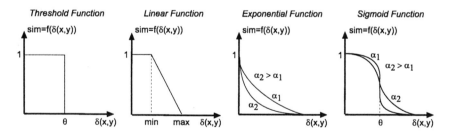

Fig. 4.3. Base Functions for Similarity Measures.

Threshold Function

Threshold functions should be used if there is the possibility that the contribution of an attribute to the utility is binary in the sense that up to a certain difference the case is useful and beyond it is not useful.

---

[2] V stands for the unit Volt.

$$f(d) = \begin{cases} 1 & : \quad d < \theta \\ 0 & : \quad d \geq \theta \end{cases} \qquad \text{(Threshold function with threshold } \theta)$$

Linear Function

In most cases the similarity between two numeric values can be described by a linear function. The idea is that the similarity decreases linearly in an interval $[min, max]$ with the increase of difference between the two values. Below min the similarity is maximal, and above max, the similarity is minimal.

$$f(d) = \begin{cases} 1 & : \quad d < min \\ \frac{max-d}{max-min} & : \quad min \leq d \leq max \\ 0 & : \quad d > max \end{cases} \quad \text{(Linear function on } [min, max])$$

Such linear functions can of course be generalized to piecewise linear functions with different gradients in different intervals for d.

Exponential Functions

Another possibility to describe the similarity between two numeric values is by an exponential function. The semantics of such a similarity function is that little differences between the two values cause a big decrease of similarity. The larger the parameter α the faster is the decrease.

$$f(d) = e^{d \cdot \alpha} \qquad \text{(Exponential function with parameter } \alpha)$$

Sigmoid Functions

We can also use sigmoid functions as a generalization of threshold functions. The parameter $\theta \geq 0$ specifies the difference value at which the similarity has a value of 0.5. The parameter $\alpha > 0$ specifies the steepness of the similarity decrease: the smaller α the steeper is the decrease.

$$f(d) = \frac{1}{e^{\frac{d-\theta}{\alpha}} + 1} \qquad \text{(Sigmoid function with parameters } \alpha \text{ and } \theta)$$

4.3.5 Local Similarity Measures for Unordered and Totally Ordered Symbolic Attributes

We now discuss different variants for modeling local similarity measures for symbolic attributes. We can distinguish different approaches depending on whether there is an order defined on the symbols or not. We first discuss the unordered and totally ordered cases. The case in which the order is of a taxonomic kind requires more explanation and will be introduced afterwards in a section of its own.

Unordered Symbolic Types

If there is no obvious ordering on the set of attribute values $T_{A_i} = \{v_1, \dots, v_k\}$ and no ordering can be defined for the purpose of similarity definition, we can apply the tabular approach. A $k \times k$ matrix $S = [s_{ij}]$ with $0 \le s_{ij} \le 1$ defines the similarity values as follows:

$$sim_{A_i}(x, y) = s_{xy} \qquad \text{(Tabular Similarity Measures)}$$

The similarity measure defined by S is reflexive iff $s_{ii} = 1$ for all $i = 1 \dots k$. The similarity measure defined by S is symmetric iff the upper triangle matrix is equal to the lower triangle matrix, i.e. iff $s_{ij} = s_{ji}$ for all $i, j = 1 \dots k$.

This approach is only feasible if the symbol type only contains a small number of values since the knowledge acquisition effort increases quadratically with the number of attribute values. Otherwise one should first structure the values totally, or partially and apply one of the following approaches.

Totally Ordered Symbolic Types

We assume a total order $<$ on the attribute values $T_{A_i} = \{v_1, \dots, v_k\}$ such that $v_i < v_{i+1}$ holds. If such an order is not naturally available we can try to find such an order for the purpose of similarity measure definition. This can be seen as a sub-task in the knowledge acquisition process for similarity measures. With such an order, we can determine the similarity by using the ordinal numbers of the symbols and applying one of the similarity measures sim_{numeric} just discussed for numeric types (see Sect. 4.3.4). This approach ensures that the resulting local similarity measure is monotonic with respect to the order on the attribute values.

$$sim_{A_i}(v_j, v_l) = sim_{\text{numeric}}(j, l) \quad \text{(Similarity Measures for Ordered Symbols)}$$

4.3.6 Taxonomically Ordered Symbolic Types

A special variant of symbolic types are taxonomies. A taxonomy is an n-ary tree in which the nodes represent symbolic values. The symbols at any node of the tree can be used as attribute values. Unlike a plain symbol type, which only lists possible attribute values, a taxonomy represents an additional relationship between the symbols through their position within the taxonomy-tree. This relationship expresses knowledge about the similarity of the symbols in the taxonomy (Bergmann 1998b). Figure 4.4 shows an example of such a taxonomy in which PC graphics cards are organized.

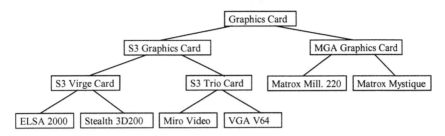

Fig. 4.4. Example of a Taxonomy of Graphics Cards.

Using Taxonomies

We now describe four different example scenarios in which the taxonomy shown in Fig. 4.4 is used with different semantics. We are referring to these examples throughout the remainder of this section.

1a. Consider a sales support application for Personal Computers. A case represents an available PC from the stock. The case representation contains an attribute *graphics card*, and the taxonomy from above represents the set of possible values. Consider a case c_1 with the *ELSA 2000* card and a case c_2 with *Matrox Mystique* card. If we assume that a customer requires a *Miro Video* graphics card, then c_1 is certainly more useful than c_2, because *Miro Video* and *Elsa 2000* have more in common (e.g. the S3 chip) than the *Miro Video* and the *Matrox Mystique*. In general, we could use a similarity measure that assesses similarity based on the distance between case and the query value in the taxonomy tree.

1b. Imagine, the customer states in the query a request for a *S3 Graphics Card*. Then, any of the graphics cards in the *S3* sub-tree are perfectly suited. Hence, we expect the local similarity value between this query and case c_1 (from example 1a) to be 1. From this consideration we can conclude that whenever the query value is located above the case value, the similarity measure should be 1.

2a. Consider a diagnosis experience management system for PCs in which cases encode diagnostic situations and faults that have occurred previously. The domain expert describes a fault that can occur with any *S3* card. Therefore, the respective case contains the attribute value S3 Graphics Card. Assume now, a PC user has a problem and s/he states that there is an *Elsa 2000* card in the PC, than the local similarity for the graphics card attribute should be equal to 1 because the case matches exactly w.r.t. this attribute. From this consideration we can conclude that whenever the case value is located above the query value the similarity measure should be 1.

2b. For the same diagnostics example, imagine now a different query in which the user does not exactly know what kind of graphics card is installed in the PC, but s/he knows that it is a *S3 Trio card*. S/he therefore enters *S3 Trio* as attribute value in the query. Again, the case about *S3* cards mentioned in example 2a matches exactly because, whatever graphics card the user has, we known it is an *S3* card and the situation described in the case applies. However, if we consider a different case that describes a problem with the *Miro Video* card, then this case does not match exactly. Since we don't know what graphics card the user has (it can be a *Miro Video* but it can also be a *VGA V64*) we expect a local similarity value less than 1. Therefore we cannot conclude that whenever the query value is located above the case value the similarity measure should be 1.

Although we have used the same taxonomy in all four examples, it is obvious that they have to be treated differently for the similarity computation. In the query and cases from example 1a, only leaf nodes from the taxonomy are used. The examples 1b to 2b make use of inner nodes of the taxonomy, but in each example the semantics of the inner nodes is different which leads to different similarity measures.

Knowledge Contained in Taxonomies

We now analyze the knowledge that is contained in taxonomies. We will show that a taxonomy contains two different kinds of knowledge:

1. Knowledge about classes of real-world objects[3] (represented by inner nodes).
2. Knowledge about the similarity between leaf nodes.

Basic Notations. We briefly introduce a few notations that will be further used. Let K be an inner node of the taxonomy, then L_K denotes the set of all leaf notes from the sub-tree starting at K. Further, $K_1 < K_2$ denotes that K_1 is a successor node of K_2, i.e., K_2 is on a path from K_1 to the root

---

[3] Here, the word object is not meant in the sense of the object-oriented paradigm.

node. Moreover, $\langle K_3, K_4 \rangle$ stands for the node that is the nearest common predecessor of K_3 and K_4, i.e., $\langle K_3, K_4 \rangle \geq K_3$ and $\langle K_3, K_4 \rangle \geq K_4$ and it does not exist a node $K' \leq \langle K_3, K_4 \rangle$ such that $K' \geq K_3$ and $K' \geq K_4$ holds.

Semantics of Taxonomy Nodes. In a taxonomy, we must distinguish between leaf nodes and inner nodes. Leaf nodes represent *concrete objects* of the real world, e.g., existing graphics cards. Inner nodes, however, describe *classes* of real world objects. An inner node K represents a class with certain properties that all of the concrete objects from the leaf nodes L_K have in common. Unlike classes that occur in the object-oriented paradigm, the classes that are represented by the inner nodes of a taxonomy are not described intentionally by a set of attributes, but extensionally through the set of concrete objects L_K that belong to the class. Therefore, an inner node K stands for the set L_K of real world objects.

In the taxonomy shown in Fig. 4.4, the leaf nodes represent existing graphics cards and the inner nodes represent classes of graphics cards. For instance, *S3 Virge* stands for all graphics cards with the S3 Virge chip on them, i.e, for the set of cards *{Elsa 2000, Stealth 3D 2000}*.

When an application developer builds a taxonomy, s/he should introduce useful sets of real-world objects, i.e., sets that are likely to occur in a case or a query. The taxonomy defines unique names (like *S3 Virge*) for these sets which are then used as abbreviations. Since the sets that are represented by these inner nodes are defined by the taxonomy itself, they are the same in all of the examples shown above, e.g., *S3 Virge* always stands for *{Elsa 2000, Stealth 3D 2000}*. However, the meaning of this set is quite different in the examples.

Similarity between Leaf Nodes

Besides the definition of classes of objects, a taxonomy also encodes some knowledge about the similarity of the real-world objects, i.e., knowledge about the similarity of the leaf nodes of the taxonomy. The inner nodes cluster real-world objects that have some properties in common. The deeper we decent in the taxonomy, the more features do the objects that the inner node represents have in common. For example, all real-world objects (leaf nodes) from the hierarchy in Fig. 4.4 have in common that they are all graphics cards. The objects below the *S3 graphics card* node have in common that the all use some kind of S3 chip, and the objects below the *S3 Trio* node have in common that they all use the specific S3 Trio chip. We can now define local similarity as a measure of how many features the compared objects have in common. The more features are shared, the higher is the similarity. For example, the similarity between *Elsa 2000* and *Stealth 3D200* is higher than the similarity between *Elsa 2000* and *VGA V64*.

This consideration leads to the following general constraint for defining the local similarity measure for the leaf nodes of a taxonomy:

$$sim(K, K_1) \leq sim(K, K_2) \text{ if } \langle K, K_1 \rangle > \langle K, K_2 \rangle \qquad \text{(Similarity Constraint Induced by a Taxonomy)}$$

It states that the similarity between the leaf node K and K_1 is smaller than the similarity between the leaf node K and K_2 if the nearest common predecessor of K and K_1 is located below the nearest common predecessor of K and K_2. It does not state anything about the relationship between $sim(K_1, K_2)$ and $sim(K_3, K_4)$ unless $K_1 = K_3$. Please note that this constraint defines an ordinal similarity measure, i.e., if the value K is given in the query, a partial order of all cases is induced. A similar approach can be also found in a paper by Osborne and Bridge (1996).

Assigning Similarity Values for Leaf Nodes. The taxonomy only represents the constraint shown above, but does not define numeric values for the similarity between two leaf node objects. For this purpose, we have to add additional knowledge to the taxonomy. Basically, there can be different ways of doing this in a way that the resulting cardinal similarity measure is compatible with the constraint. We now present an approach which is quite simple and easy to use, but nevertheless very powerful.

Every inner node K_i of the taxonomy is annotated with a similarity value $S_i \in [0, 1]$, such that the following condition holds: if $K_1 > K_2$ then $S_1 \leq S_2$. The deeper the nodes are located in the hierarchy, the larger the similarity value can become. The semantics of the similarity value is as follows:
The value S_i represents a lower bound for the similarity of two arbitrary objects from the set L_{K_i} or written formally: $\forall x, y \in L_{K_i} \, sim(x, y) \geq S_i$.

Any two objects from L_{K_i} are at least similar to each other with the value S_i, but their similarity can be higher. The similarity value that is assigned to a node should be justified by the properties that all of the objects that belong to this inner node (class) have in common. The fact that the objects belong to this class and have common properties justifies that we can state a lower bound for their similarity. However, objects belonging to one class can of course also belong to a more narrow class further down in the taxonomy, which means that these objects share even more properties and therefore possibly have a higher similarity. We therefore define the similarity between two objects as follows:

$$sim(K_1, K_2) \qquad = \qquad \begin{cases} 1 & : \quad K_1 = K_2 \\ S_{\langle K_1, K_2 \rangle} & : \quad K_1 \neq K_2 \end{cases}$$

(Similarity Measure for
Taxonomy Leaf Nodes)

It can be shown that this similarity definition fulfills the similarity constraint induced by the taxonomy.

As an example, assume that the similarity values from Table 4.2 have been assigned to the taxonomy from Fig. 4.4. Then the similarities that are shown in Table 4.3 arise.

Taxonomy Symbol	Sim. Value
Graphics Card	0.2
S3 Graphics Card	0.5
S3 Virge	0.7
S3 Trio	0.9
MGA	0.8

Table 4.2. Example Similarity Value Assignments.

	Elsa	Stealth	Miro	VGA	M. Mill.	M. Myst.
Elsa	1	0.7	0.5	0.5	0.2	0.2
Stealth	0.7	1	0.5	0.5	0.2	0.2
Miro	0.5	0.5	1	0.9	0.2	0.2
VGA	0.5	0.5	0.9	1	0.2	0.2
M.Mill.	0.2	0.2	0.2	0.2	1	0.8
M.Myst.	0.2	0.2	0.2	0.2	0.8	1

Table 4.3. Example Similarity Values.

Semantics and Similarity of Inner Nodes

If we now recall again the examples, it is obvious that the "graphics card" attribute must be treated differently in the different examples 1a to 2b, although they all use the same taxonomy. From this it becomes clear that some additional knowledge which we have not yet discussed, plays a role during similarity assessment. However, this knowledge is not contained in the taxonomy itself.

The knowledge that we are looking for is the knowledge about the semantics of the inner nodes, i.e., the semantics of the set of concrete objects that they represent. In our example, the question is: what does it mean when the case or query contains the statement: "graphics card: S3 Graphics Card"? In fact, there are different interpretations of this statement that are now discussed.

Any Value in the Query. The user specifies the value K in the query. This means that s/he is looking for a case that contains one of the values from the set L_K. In the example 1b, the user wants an S3 graphics card, but s/he does not care whether it is a *Elsa 2000*, *Stealth 3D 200*, *Miro Video*, or an *VGA V64*. It is clear that the local similarity between this query and any of these four leaf nodes is equal to 1. But what about the similarity to any other leaf node? To answer this question more systematically, we can define the required retrieval result indirectly as follows: Instead of submitting a single query to the system that contains an inner node K, the user could alternatively submit several queries to the system, one for each concrete value from L_K and merge the retrieval results, i.e., select the case with the highest similarity. The result of using the query with the inner node K should yield the same case with the same similarity as the merging of the multiple retrievals. To achieve this, the similarity measure for the inner node must select the maximum similarity that arises from each of the leaf nodes.

Any Value in Case. The case contains an inner node K, which describes a situation in which the case is valid for all attribute values of the set L_K. This is in fact a generalized case as introduced in Sect. 3.4. The generalized case (in which the attribute value K is used) stands for the set of cases that results by replacing K by all of the members of the set L_K. In Example 2a, the case representing a fault for any *S3 graphics cards* stands for a set of four cases, each of which represents a fault for the *Elsa 2000*, *Stealth 3D 200*, *Miro Video*, and the *VGA V64*, respectively. Here, the inner node is used to keep the number of cases in the case base small. However, the retrieval result should of course not be affected. Therefore, the result of having a case in the case-base that contains an inner node K should be the same as having all cases in the case base, one for each concrete value from L_K. Since we are looking for the most similar case, we again have to assess the similarity for the inner node by selecting the maximum similarity that arises from each of the leaf nodes.

Uncertainty. This situation differs significantly from the previous two. Here, the use of an inner node K means that we don't know the exact value for this attribute, but we know that it is one from the set L_K. In Example 2b, we know that the user has a *S3 Trio* card which means it can be one from the set {*Miro Video*, *VGA V64*}. This kind of uncertainty can occur in queries as well as in cases. The user can think of this uncertainty in different ways: treating it optimistically, pessimistically, or as an average case.

Combinations of Different Semantics

We can now define the local similarity SIM(Q,C) between a query value Q and the a case value C each of which can be either a leaf node, an inner node with the "any value" interpretation or an inner node with the "uncertainty" interpretation. This leads to 9 possible combinations shown in Table 4.4. Seven of the 9 combinations in the table are marked with a roman number that is further used to reference the formulas for computing the similarity. These are the ones that occur most frequently. However, the following considerations can easily be extended also to the two missing combinations.

Query / Case	Leaf Node	Any Value	Uncertainty
Leaf Node	I	II	V
Any Value	III	IV	
Uncertainty	VI		VII

Table 4.4. Combinations of Different Semantics for Taxonomy Values in Query and Case.

In the following, $sim(q, c)$ denotes the similarity between two leaf nodes, q from the query and c from the case. It can be computed according to the previously introduced formula.

Case I: Only the similarity between leaf nodes is computed and hence the local similarity sim_{A_i} for the taxonomy attribute A_i is computed as follows:

$$sim_{A_i}(q, c) = sim(q, c) \qquad \text{(Case I)}$$

Case II: The query contains a leaf node and the case contains an inner node representing a set of values each of which is a correct value for the case. Therefore, the use of this set in the attribute is a shortcut for the use of several cases, one for each value in the set. Since we are looking for the most similar case in the cases base, the similarity between the query and our case containing the inner node is equal to the highest similarity between the query and one of the values from the set. Hence,

$$
\begin{aligned}
sim_{A_i}(q, C) &= \max\{sim(q, c) | c \in L_C\} \\
&= \begin{cases} 1 &: q < C \\ S_{\langle q, C \rangle} &: \text{otherwise} \end{cases}
\end{aligned}
\qquad \text{(Case II)}
$$

holds. This definition ensures, that the similarity is the same as the similarity that arises when each of the cases with leaf node values would have been stored in the case base. This measure is appropriate for example 2a.

Case III: Here, the specification of this inner node can be viewed as a shortcut for posing several queries to the system, one for each of the values from the set that the node represents. Since we are again interested in the most similar case, we can again select the most similar attribute value from the set. Hence, it holds:

$$sim_{A_i}(Q,c) = \max\{sim(q,c)|q \in L_Q\}$$
$$= \begin{cases} 1 & : & c < Q \\ S_{\langle Q,c \rangle} & : & \text{otherwise} \end{cases} \qquad \text{(Case III)}$$

This measure is appropriate for example 1b.

Case IV: This is a combination of II and III. We are looking for the highest possible similarity between two objects from the two sets since both, the query and the case, represent alternatives that are suited equally well. Hence, it holds:

$$sim_{A_i}(Q,C) = \max\{sim(q,c)|q \in L_Q, c \in L_C\}$$
$$= \begin{cases} 1 & : & C < Q \text{ or } Q < C \\ S_{\langle Q,C \rangle} & : & \text{otherwise} \end{cases} \qquad \text{(Case IV)}$$

Case V: The case contains an inner node which represents a set of values from which only one value is actually correct for the case, but we don't know which one. Therefore, our similarity measure has to reflect this lack of information. There are three possible approaches: we can assess the similarity in a pessimistic or optimistic fashion, or we can follow an averaging approach:

Pessimistic approach: We assess the similarity between the known object (in the query) and the partially unknown object (in the case) by computing the lower bound for the similarity as follows:

$$sim_{A_i}(q,C) = \min\{sim(q,c)|c \in L_C\} = S_{\langle q,C \rangle} \qquad \text{(Case V: Pessimistic)}$$

Optimistic approach: We assess the similarity between the known object (in the query) and the partially unknown object (in the case) by computing the upper bound for the similarity, which results in the same formula that was already shown in II.

$$sim_{A_i}(q,C) = \max\{sim(q,c)|c \in L_C\}$$
$$= \begin{cases} 1 & : & q < C \\ S_{\langle q,C \rangle} & : & \text{otherwise} \end{cases} \qquad \text{(Case V: Optimistic)}$$

Average approach: We assess the similarity between the known object (in the query) and the partially unknown object (in the case) by computing the expected value of the similarity as follows:

$$sim_{A_i}(q, C) = \sum_{c \in L_C} P(c) \cdot sim(q, c) \qquad \text{(Case V: Average)}$$

Here, $P(c)$ is the probability that the value of the attribute under consideration has the value c given the fact that we know that $c \in L_C$ and given the known information about the current case. Since $P(c)$ is usually hard to determine, we can, for example, estimate $P(c)$ by $1/|L_C|$, assuming that all attribute values are equally distributed and that all attributes are independent.

Case VI: The uncertain information is contained in the query; the information in the case is certain. This case is quite similar to the previous case V, i.e., we can again use a pessimistic, an optimistic, or an average approach. The only change in the formulas for similarity computation is the fact that the minimum, maximum, and sum operations are now performed using the elements from the query L_Q and not the elements form the case.

$$sim_{A_i}(Q, c) = \min\{sim(q, c) | q \in L_Q\} = S_{\langle Q, c \rangle} \qquad \text{(Case VI: Pessimistic)}$$

$$sim_{A_i}(Q, c) = \max\{sim(q, c) | q \in L_Q\}$$
$$= \begin{cases} 1 & : \quad c < Q \\ S_{\langle Q, c \rangle} & : \quad \text{otherwise} \end{cases} \qquad \text{(Case VI: Optimistic)}$$

$$sim_{A_i}(Q, c) = \sum_{q \in L_Q} P(q) \cdot sim(q, c) \qquad \text{(Case VI: Average)}$$

Case VII: The uncertain information is contained in the query and in the case. The similarity is computed as follows:

$$sim_{A_i}(Q, C) = \min\{sim(q, c) | c \in L_c, q \in L_Q\}$$
$$= S_{\langle Q, C \rangle} \qquad \text{(Case VII: Pessimistic)}$$

$$sim_{A_i}(Q, C) = \max\{sim(q, c) | q \in L_Q, c \in L_c\}$$
$$= \begin{cases} 1 & : & C < Q \text{ or } Q < C \\ S_{\langle Q, C \rangle} & : & \text{otherwise} \end{cases} \qquad \text{(Case VII: Optimistic)}$$

$$sim_{A_i}(Q, C) = \sum_{c \in L_C, q \in L_Q} P(c) \cdot P(q) \cdot sim(q, c) \qquad \text{(Case VII: Average)}$$

We see that in all of these cases (except for the average approach to uncertainty), similarity between inner nodes can be computed very easily by determining the position of the query and the case value in the taxonomy and by looking up the similarity value at the appropriate taxonomy node.

4.3.7 Global Similarity Measures

Global similarity measures are defined by applying an aggregation function Φ to the local similarity values. The simple similarity measures for numeric attributes described in Sect. 4.3.2 can be generalized easily to aggregation functions. Such aggregation functions are defined by determining

- a basic aggregation function and
- a weight model that determines weights $\bar{\omega} = (\omega_1, \ldots, \omega_n)$ such that $0 \leq \omega_i \leq 1$ and $\sum_{i=1..n} \omega_i = 1$.

Basic Aggregation Functions

In principle the basic aggregation functions can be arbitrarily complex. However, we restrict ourselves here to the most commonly used functions; more complex functions can also be composed by combining several of these functions.

The weighted average is the most typically used aggregation function. Each attribute contributes to the similarity (and thereby to the utility) in a way that is proportional to its weight.

$$\Phi(s_1, \ldots, s_n) = \sum_{i=1}^{n} \omega_i \cdot s_i \qquad \text{(Weighted Average Aggregation)}$$

The Minkowski aggregation is a generalization of this weighted average. The higher the value of the parameter $p \geq 1$, the higher is the influence of the attribute with the highest local similarity. For $p \to \infty$ this aggregation function becomes the maximum aggregation.

$$\Phi(s_1, \ldots, s_n) = \left(\sum_{i=1}^{n} \omega_i \cdot s_i^p \right)^{1/p} \qquad \text{(Minkowski Aggregation)}$$

When using the maximum aggregation, the overall similarity is determined by the maximum local similarity. This realizes a kind of disjunctive global similarity. If one attribute indicates a high utility the utility for the whole case is high.

$$\Phi(s_1, \ldots, s_n) = \max_{i=1}^{n} \omega_i \cdot s_i \qquad \text{(Maximum Aggregation)}$$

When using the minimum aggregation, the overall similarity is determined by the minimum local similarity. This realizes a kind of conjunctive global similarity. If one attribute indicates a low utility the utility for the whole case is low.

$$\Phi(s_1, \ldots, s_n) = \min_{i=1}^{n} \omega_i \cdot s_i \qquad \text{(Minimum Aggregation)}$$

The k-maximum aggregation is a generalization of the standard maximum aggregation. The k highest local similarity value determines the global similarity. Hence, if k out of n attributes indicate a high utility, the overall utility for the whole case is high.

$$\Phi(s_1, \ldots, s_n) = \omega_{i_k} \cdot s_{i_k}$$
$$\text{with} \, \omega_{i_r} \cdot s_{i_r} \geq \omega_{i_{r+1}} \cdot s_{i_{r+1}} \qquad \text{(k-Maximum Aggregation)}$$

The k-minimum aggregation is a generalization of the standard minimum aggregation. The k lowest local similarity value determines the global similarity. Hence, if k out of n attributes indicate a low utility, the overall utility for the whole case is low.

$$\Phi(s_1, \ldots, s_n) = \omega_{i_k} \cdot s_{i_k}$$
$$\text{with} \, \omega_{i_r} \cdot s_{i_r} \leq \omega_{i_{r+1}} \cdot s_{i_{r+1}} \qquad \text{(k-Minimum Aggregation)}$$

Weight Models

Each of the previously described basic aggregation functions is parameterized by a weight vector $\overline{\omega}$. This weight vector determines the importance of the individual attributes. Different weight models can be distinguished according to the criteria on which these weights depend. This can be domain criteria (in this case the weight vector is denoted by $\overline{\omega_D}$) or user preferences (here the weight vector is denoted by $\overline{\omega_U}$).

Global Weights. The most simple weight model uses one global weight vector for all retrieval tasks. These weights are determined by domain criteria only. Hence, the weight vector $\overline{\omega_D}$ is static and can be considered part of the aggregation function.

Class Specific Weights. Sometimes it is possible to make the assumption that we can achieve an a-priori classification of the current problem p and/or the cases c into one of m classes $K_1, \dots, K_m$. In general we can assume a classifier that assigns each pair (p, c) a class index from $\{1, \dots, m\}$. Such a classification can be achieved, for example, through a rule-based classification or the class can even be part of the case itself, e.g., the class can be part of the lesson stored in the case. The purpose of this classification is to derive a model of importances. For each class we specify a separate weight vector that is justified by the domain. These weight vectors can be combined to an $n \times m$ weight matrix $\Omega_D = \omega_{D_{ij}}$. If a problem p and a case c is classified into the class K_j the similarity between them is computed by using the weight vector $(\omega_{D_{1j}}, \dots, \omega_{D_{nj}})$.

Case Specific Weights. An even more fine-grained weight model consists of defining the weights as part of the case itself. For each case c, we store a weight vector $\overline{\omega_{D_c}}$ as part of the case. This weight vector is then used only during the similarity computations that compare a problem with this particular case c.

User Specified Weights. Weights can also be considered part of the problem description entered by the user. Such user weights $\overline{\omega_U}$ reflect particular user preference. User preferences are usually combined with one of the three previously described domain weight models to the overall weight vector $\overline{\omega}$ through:

$$\overline{\omega} = (\omega_1, \dots, \omega_n) = \frac{(\omega_{D_1} \cdot \omega_{U_1}, \dots, \omega_{D_n} \cdot \omega_{U_n})}{(\overline{\omega_D}) \cdot (\overline{\omega_U}^T)} \qquad \text{(Combining User and Domain Weights)}$$

4.4 Similarity Measures for Object-Oriented Representations

Object-oriented representations differ from attribute value representations discussed above through the introduction of

- a notion of objects that combine certain closely related attributes,
- relational attributes,
- class hierarchies and inheritance of attributes

These extensions must be considered in the similarity modeling. To cope with these extensions, the local-global principle previously described for attribute-value representations must be extended to the object level.

Similarity measures for such object-oriented representations are often defined by the following general scheme (Wess 1995): The goal is to determine the similarity between two objects, i.e., one object representing the case (or a part of it) and one object representing the problem (or a part of it). We call this similarity *object similarity*, which is a kind of global similarity on the object level. The object similarity is determined recursively in a bottom up fashion, i.e., for each simple attribute, a local similarity measure determines the similarity between the two attribute values, and for each relational attribute an object similarity measure recursively compares the two related sub-objects. Then the similarity values from the local similarity measures and the object similarity measures, respectively, are aggregated by an aggregation function to the object similarity between the objects being compared.

However, this approach does not specify how the structure of the object-oriented case model, e.g., the class hierarchy, influences similarity assessment. Intuitively, it is obvious that the class hierarchy contains knowledge about the similarity of the objects. Objects that are closer in the hierarchy should normally be more similar to each other than objects which are more distant in the hierarchy. However, how this knowledge relates to knowledge that could be represented in similarity measures that also consider the local similarity of the attributes is not obvious. In the following we provide a framework for object similarities that allow to compare objects of different classes while considering the knowledge contained in the class hierarchy itself (Bergmann and Stahl 1998). The knowledge about similarity contained in class hierarchies is quite similar to the knowledge contained in taxonomies of symbols as described in Sect. 4.3.6.

4.4.1 Example Use of Class Hierarchies and Object Similarities

We now describe possible uses of class hierarchies in different related application examples in which personal computers are represented as part of the case. In the following we refer to the example class hierarchy introduced in the previous chapter in Fig. 3.6 (and which is included here again for convenience as Fig. 4.5). This class hierarchy contains a class for representing a PC as well as different classes for representing components.

In the example the class *Hard Disk* has no sub-classes and consequently, every object that this attribute refers to has the same structure, i.e., the same set of attributes. In contrast, the relational slot *optional storage* does not have a unique class, because the object-class *Storage Device* has several sub-classes. Hence, the attribute can relate to objects of different structures, but they still have a common super-class (e.g., *Storage Device*) and therefore share at least some common attributes. In our example, one PC can have a second hard-disk as optional storage device, while another PC can have a

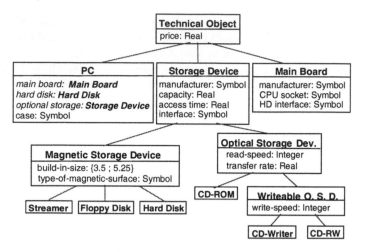

Fig. 4.5. Example Class Hierarchy.

CD-ROM described by a few different attributes (e.g., type of laser) than a hard-disk.

Consider again the *optional storage* attribute. Now we describe four examples in which this attribute is used differently. We first would like to focus on the knowledge contained in the class hierarchy and therefore don't take into account different values for simple attributes.

1a. Consider a sales support application for Personal Computers. A case represents an available PC from the stock. Consider a case c_1 with a second hard-disk as *optional storage device* and a case c_2 with a *CD-Writer*. If we assume that a customer enters a query to such a system in which s/he specifies that s/he wants a *CD-ROM*, then c_2 is certainly closer than c_1, because a *CD-ROM* and a *CD-Writer* have obviously more in common than a *hard disk* and a *CD-ROM*. In general, we could use a similarity measure that assesses similarity based on the distance between the class of the case object (of the respective relational attribute) and the class of the query object in the class hierarchy.

1b. Imagine the customer states in the query a request for an *optional storage device*, i.e., in the query, the relational attribute refers to an instance of the class *Optical Storage Device*. Then any of the devices in the *Optical Storage Device* sub-tree are perfectly suited. Hence, we expect the similarity value for the relational slot between this query and case c_2 (from Example 1a) to be equal to 1. From this consideration we can conclude that whenever the class of the query object is located above the class of the case object, the similarity should be 1.

2a. Consider now a trouble-shooting experience management system for PCs in which cases encode diagnostic situations and faults that have occurred previously. The domain expert describes a fault that can occur with any optical storage device. Therefore, the respective case contains an instance of the class *Optical Storage Device* in the relational attribute *optional storage device*. Now, assuming a PC user has a problem and s/he states that there is a *CD-RW* device in the PC, then the similarity for the respective relational slot should be equal to 1 because the case matches exactly w.r.t. this attribute. From this consideration we can conclude that whenever the class of the case object is located above the class of the query object the similarity should be 1.

2b. For the same trouble-shooting example, imagine now a different query in which the user does not exactly know what kind of storage device is installed in the PC, but s/he knows that it is a writable optical storage device. Therefore, s/he enters an instance of the class *Writable O. S. D.* as attribute value in the query. Again, the case about the *Optic Storage Device* mentioned in Example 2a matches exactly because, whatever storage device the user has, we known it is an *Optical Storage*. Hence, the situation described in the case applies. However, if we consider a different case that describes a problem with a *CD-RW* device, then this case does not match exactly. Since we don't know what *Writable Optical storage device* the user has (it can be a *CD-Writer* but it can also be a *CD-RW*) we expect a similarity value less than 1 to represent this kind of uncertainty. Therefore, we cannot conclude that whenever the class of the query object is located above the class of the case object the similarity should be 1.

Although these four examples are based on the same class hierarchy, it is obvious that they have to be treated differently for the similarity computation. In the query and in the cases from example 1a, only instances of classes without subclasses are used. The examples 1b to 2b make use of abstract classes (classes with subclasses) of the hierarchy, but in each example the semantics of the use these abstract classes is different, which must lead to different similarity measures.

4.4.2 Computing Object Similarities

In general, the similarity computation between two objects can be divided into two steps: the computation of an *intra-class similarity* sim_{intra} and the computation of an *inter-class similarity* sim_{inter}.

Intra-class Similarity between Two Objects

The set of common attributes of the two objects (object o^p from the problem description and object o^c from the case) can be used to determine the intra-class similarity. For this it is necessary to take the most specific common class of these two objects and to compute the similarity based on the attributes of this class only. By considering only the attributes of the most specific common class, the intra-class similarity is defined via a global similarity measure for a particular class.

Definition 4.16 (Intra-Class Similarity) Given a class hierarchy **CL** and for each class $C_i \in \mathbf{CL}$ assume that there is given a global similarity measure $sim_{C_i}(\overline{x}, \overline{y}) = \varPhi_{C_i}(sim_{C_i.A_1}(x_1, y_1), \dots, sim_{C_i.A_k}(x_k, y_k))$ on the attributes of C_i. Further, there are given two objects $o^p = (o^p_{class}, \cdot, \{A^p_{1_{name}} = a^p_1, \dots\})$ and $o^c = (o^c_{class}, \cdot, \{A^c_{1_{name}} = a^c_1, \dots\})$. Let $C_{\langle p,c \rangle} = \langle o^p_{class}, o^c_{class} \rangle$ denote the most specific common object class for the two objects and assume that this class has the attributes $C_{\langle p,c \rangle}.A_1, \dots, C_{\langle p,c \rangle}.A_k$. The *intra-class similarity* between o^p and o^c is defined as follows: $sim_{\mathrm{intra}}(o^p, o^c) = sim_{C_{\langle p,c \rangle}}((a^p_{j_1}, \dots, a^p_{j_k}), (a^c_{l_1}, \dots, a^c_{l_k}))$ with the index sequences defined through $A^p_{j_\nu} = C_{\langle p,c \rangle}.A_\nu$ and $A^c_{l_\nu} = C_{\langle p,c \rangle}.A_\nu$ for $\nu = 1 \dots k$.

Inter-class Similarity

The intra-class similarity alone would not be an adequate object similarity for the two objects. For example, in the domain shown in Fig. 4.5 two instances of *Hard Disk* and *CD-ROM* can have an intra-class similarity of 1, provided that they have the same values in the attributes which they inherit from their common superclass *Storage Device*. But it is obvious that there is a significant difference between a hard disk and a CD-ROM. Hence, the similarity should definitely be less than 1. It is important to note that the difference between two objects is not represented by their shared attributes but by the structure of the class hierarchy. Therefore, it is necessary to use this structure to compute an *inter-class similarity* for the two objects. This inter-class similarity represents the highest possible similarity of two objects, independent of their attribute values, but dependent on the positions of their object classes in the hierarchy. Formally, the inter-class similarity sim_{inter} is defined over the classes of the objects from the problem description and case being compared.

Class Hierarchies and Symbol Taxonomies. Class hierarchies are closely related to taxonomies of symbols and the inter-class similarity can be defined like a taxonomy similarity as introduced in Sect. 4.3.6, too. In a class hierarchy as well as in a taxonomy of symbols, we must distinguish between leaf nodes and inner nodes. In a taxonomy leaf nodes represent *concrete objects* of the real world. Inner nodes, however, describe *classes* of real world objects. An inner node K represents a class with certain properties that all of the concrete objects from the leaf nodes L_K have in common. Unlike classes that occur in the object-oriented paradigm, the classes that are represented by the inner nodes of a taxonomy are not described intentionally by a set of properties, but extensionally through the set of concrete objects L_K that belong to the class. Therefore, an inner node K stands for the set L_K of real world objects.

If we look at the class hierarchy shown in Fig. 4.5, we can notice a difference in the semantics of its nodes compared to the semantics of taxonomy nodes. While a leaf node of a taxonomy represents a concrete object of the real world, a leaf node of a class hierarchy is naturally a class and therefore represents a set of objects. As shown above, inner nodes of a taxonomy describe classes of real world objects, but if we look at the inner nodes of class hierarchies, we can see that these nodes represent abstract classes. Because of this, such a node does not represent a set of real world objects, but a set of *abstract objects*. The instances which belong exclusively to the class *Storage Device* or *Optic Storage Device*, for example, are obviously not objects of the real world. However, abstract objects are sets of real world objects. An instance of *Optic Storage Device*, for example, can be used as abbreviation for the set of all instances of the classes *CD-ROM*, *CD-Writer*, and *CD-RW* that have the same attribute-values in the common attributes as the respective *Optic Storage Device* instance, e.g., the same manufacturer, the same capacity, the same access time, and the same speed.

There is also a difference in the use of the two different structures. A taxonomy tree consists of the symbols that are directly used as values for the attributes. On the other hand, the classes of a class hierarchy are not used as values for the relational slots themselves, but the instances of the classes. If we take this fact into account, we will see that now there is no difference in the semantics of the corresponding values, because the taxonomy symbols must be compared with the instances and not with the classes of the class hierarchy. An instance of a class without subclasses (a leaf node of the hierarchy) represents a concrete object of the real world, and as we have seen before an instance of an abstract class (inner node) can be treated as a set of real world objects. This semantics is equivalent to the semantics of the taxonomy nodes. Therefore, it is possible to apply the similarity measures used to compute similarities between taxonomy symbols for computing the inter-class similarity between objects. As for taxonomies, we need to distinguish between leaf nodes and inner nodes of the class hierarchy.

Inter-class Similarity for Leaf Class Node Instances. To assess the inter-class similarity of two instances of leaf nodes of the class hierarchy we annotate every inner node C_i in the class hierarchy with a similarity value $S_i \in [0,1]$ such that the following condition holds: if $C_i > C_j$ then $S_i \leq S_j$. The value S_i represents a lower bound for the inter-class similarity of two arbitrary instances of the classes from the set L_{C_i}. As illustrated for taxonomies, this defines the inter-class similarity for leaf nodes of the class hierarchy as follows:

$$sim_{\text{inter}}(C_i, C_j) = \begin{cases} 1 & : \quad C_i = C_j \\ S_{\langle C_i, C_j \rangle} & : \quad C_i \neq C_j \end{cases} \qquad \begin{array}{l} \text{(Intra-Class Similarity for} \\ \text{Leaf Node Instances)} \end{array}$$

Inter-class Similarity for Instances of Inner Class Nodes. If we now recall again the examples that we have presented in Sect. 4.4.1, it is obvious that the *optional storage* attribute must be treated differently in the different examples, although they all use the same class hierarchy. The reason for this is that there are different semantics of the instances of inner nodes, as there are different semantics for the use of inner nodes in a taxonomy, as discussed in Sect. 4.3.6.

- *Any value in the query:* The user specifies an abstract object in the query that belongs to the class C_i. This means that s/he is looking for a case that contains a real-world-object that matches with the features of the specified abstract object, i.e., a case that contains an object that belongs to a class of L_{C_i}. This was the situation in example 1b.
- *Any value in case:* The case contains an abstract object that belongs to the class C_i. This describes a situation in which the case is valid for all objects that are instances of a specialization of C_i. This leads to a kind of generalized case and occurs in example 2a.
- *Uncertainty:* This situation differs significantly from the previous ones. Here, the use of an abstract object means that we do not know the concrete object for this relational slot, but we know that it is a specialization of it. This situation occurred in example 2b.

Depending on the appropriate semantics we can now define an inter-class similarity measure $sim_{\text{inter}}(C_i, C_j)$ which computes a value for the inter-class similarity between two objects where each can be either a leaf node (concrete object), an inner node (abstract object) with the "any value" interpretation or an inner node (abstract object) with the "uncertainty" interpretation.

This leads to the nine possible combinations already shown in Tab. 4.4. The taxonomy similarity measures explained for the seven of those nine cases determine exactly the inter-class similarity. We refrain from repeating these formulas here again.

Combining Inter- and Intra-class Similarities

The final object similarity $sim(o^p, o^c)$ between an object $o^p = (o^p_{class}, \cdot, \{\dots\})$ from the problem description p and an object $o^c = (o^c_{class}, \cdot, \{\dots\})$ from the case description c can now be computed by the product of the inter- and the intra-class similarity, as follows:

$$sim(o^p, o^c) = sim_{\text{intra}}(o^p, o^c) \cdot sim_{\text{inter}}(o^p_{class}, o^c_{class}) \quad \text{(Object Similarity)}$$

4.4.3 Handling Multi-value Attributes

Object-oriented representations as introduced in Sect. 3.3.2 allow multi-value attributes, which describe sets of objects or values. Hence we need local similarity measures to compare sets. In the following we assume a multi-value attribute A and a set of attribute values $a^p = \{u_1, \ldots, u_n\}$ for the problem description as well as a set of attribute values $a^c = \{v_1, \ldots, v_m\}$ for the case. We can now define a local similarity measure for $sim_{A*}(a^p, a^c)$ based on an arbitrary similarity measure for the individual set elements $sim_A(u_j, v_j)$. Here, sim_A can be either a local similarity measure if the attribute A is a simple multi-value attribute or it can be an object similarity measure if A is a relational multi-value slot. The definition of the local similarity measure for the multi-value slot A is of the following form.

$$sim_{A*}(a^p, a^c) = \Phi \left(\begin{pmatrix} sim_A(u_1, v_1) & \cdots & sim_A(u_1, v_m) \\ \vdots & \ddots & \vdots \\ sim_A(u_n, v_1) & \cdots & sim_A(u_n, v_m) \end{pmatrix} \right)$$

The concrete function Φ depends on the semantics of the set. The following semantics are the same as those already introduced for inner nodes of class hierarchies or taxonomies.

Any Value in the Query and the Case. The user specifies a set in the query. This means that s/he is looking for a case that matches with any of the specified values. If a case contains a set, this describes a situation in which the case is valid for all elements of the set, i.e. we have the semantics of a generalized case. For this semantics, Φ must be chosen to determine the maximum possible similarity.

$$\Phi((s_{ij})) = \max s_{ij} \hspace{3cm} (\Phi \text{ for Any Value Semantics})$$

Uncertainty. Here, the use of the set means that we do not know the correct value for this attribute, but we know that it is one of the elements in the set. Here we can again distinguish among an optimistic, a pessimistic and an average strategy.

$$\Phi((s_{ij})) = \min s_{ij} \hspace{2cm} (\Phi \text{ for Uncertainty Semantics: Pessimistic})$$

$$\Phi((s_{ij})) = \max s_{ij} \hspace{2cm} (\Phi \text{ for Uncertainty Semantics: Optimistic})$$

$$\Phi((s_{ij})) = \tfrac{1}{n \cdot m} \cdot \sum_{i,j} s_{ij} \hspace{2cm} (\Phi \text{ for Uncertainty Semantics: Average})$$

Multiple Properties Semantics. An alternative semantics that has not been discussed before often occurs with multi-value attributes. The set in the case represents a set of properties that all hold for one single case. This is different from the any value semantics since here the set is used as an abbreviation for several independent cases. We illustrate the difference by the following simple example. Imagine the *hard disk* attribute in Fig. 4.5 is modeled as a multi-value attribute and a case describing a PC contains a set of two hard disk objects. If this attribute has the any value semantics, this means that this PC is available with either of the two hard disks. If the slot has the multiple properties semantics, this means that the PC contains both hard disks. Used in the problem description, a set with the multiple properties semantics states that we are looking for a case that has all the properties stated in the set, rather than a case that has one of the properties.

The multiple properties semantics requires that we need to find a mapping $\gamma : \{1 \ldots n\} \to \{1 \ldots m\}$ from the set elements in the query to the set elements in the case that yields the highest possible overall similarity. The following formula is an example for a function Φ.

$$\Phi((s_{ij})) = \frac{1}{n} \cdot \max\{\textstyle\sum_{i=1}^{n} s_{i\,\gamma(i)} \mid \gamma \text{ with } R(\gamma)\} \qquad \begin{array}{r}(\Phi \text{ for Multiple Properties} \\ \text{Semantics})\end{array}$$

We can distinguish different variants of the multiple properties semantics depending on the requirements $R(\gamma)$ that this mapping must fulfill. The following requirements are quite common.

- *No requirement*: We can assign every element in the problem set an arbitrary element in the case set.
- *Injective:* We require that γ is an injective function and hence only consider mappings in which a case element is only assigned to one problem element.
- *Surjective:* We require that γ is a surjective function and hence only consider mappings in which every element in the case set has a corresponding element in the problem set.
- *Bijective:* We require that γ is bijective and hence only consider mappings in which every element in the problem set has assigned a unique element case set.[4]

Bergmann and Eisenecker (1995) discuss a heuristic algorithm for efficiently computing these kinds of similarity measures.

---

[4] For formal reasons it can be necessary to extend either the problem set or the case set with dummy elements with a similarity value of 0 in order to achieve that both sets have the same size.

4.4.4 Related Approaches

This approach to modeling object-oriented similarity has been applied various times in different application areas some of which are introduced in part III of this thesis.

Currently, there is no other work that proposes similarity measures for object-oriented case representations that make use of the class hierarchy, relational attributes, and flexible local similarity measures for simple attributes. However, similarity measures for different kinds of structured representations are discussed throughout the CBR and instance-based learning literature during recent years. To some extend, object-oriented representations can be compared to representations in first-order logic where a case is a conjunction of atomic formulas. Each atomic formula $P(id, a_1, \ldots, a_n)$ stands for a single object. The argument id of the formula denotes an object identification and the remaining arguments $a_1, \ldots, a_n$ represent the attributes. Relational attributes can be represented by using the object identifications as attribute values.

Emde and Wettschereck (1996) present a relational instance-based learning approach that is based on the computation of similarity between cases represented in first-order logic. However, their approach does not consider class hierarchies or flexible local similarity measures for simple attributes but they can handle multi-value slots. Plaza (Plaza 1995) proposes feature terms for representing structured cases and proposes a similarity computation based on antiunification. This approach allows to consider some kinds of background knowledge during similarity computation but cannot deal with class hierarchies and local similarity measures for simple attributes. The framework by Osborne and Bridge (Osborne and Bridge 1996) is based on lattices of values (somehow similar to a class hierarchy) and applies a logic-oriented approach for defining similarities. However, their work does not cover object-oriented representations, e.g., relational attributes and inheritance of attributes are not considered. Further related work can be found in papers by Maher (1993) and Bisson (1995).

4.5 Similarity Measures for Graph Representations

In the following we discuss a few standard approaches for defining similarity for cases in graph representation. Hence we assume that the two descriptions x and y to be compared by the similarity measure $sim(x, y)$ are graphs. Most of the approaches that will be discussed work in the same way for directed and undirected graphs.

4.5.1 Graph Matching

The first category are the graph matching approaches. They are defined on non-attributed graphs. Here we distinguish among graph isomorphisms, subgraph isomorphisms, and largest common sub-graph measure.

Graph Isomorphism

A binary similarity measure can be defined based on the isomorphism property of two graphs. The standard definition for graph isomorphism is as follows.

Definition 4.17 (Graph Isomorphism) Two graphs $G_1 = (N_1, E_1)$ and $G_2 = (N_2, E_2)$ are called *isomorphic* (we write $G_1 \cong G_2$) if a bijective mapping $f : N_1 \to N_2$ exists such that $(p, q) \in E_1 \Leftrightarrow (f(p), f(q)) \in E_2$ holds.

Two graphs can be said to be similar if they are isomorphic and dissimilar of they are not isomorphic which leads to the following simple similarity measure definition.

$$sim(x, y) = \begin{cases} 1 & : \quad x \cong y \\ 0 & : \quad \text{otherwise} \end{cases} \qquad \text{(Similarity Measure based on Graph Isomorphism)}$$

Graph isomorphism is an equivalence relation and hence this similarity measure is reflexive (but not strongly reflexive), symmetric, and fulfills the triangle inequality.

The graph isomorphism approach has several serious difficulties that restrict its applicability for modeling similarity. First, it does not allow to introduce additional knowledge about different degrees of utility and can therefore only be applied when a binary relation sufficiently approximates the utility. Second, the computation of the graph isomorphism property is very expensive in the general case. The brute-force approach has a factorial worst-case complexity. Various signature approaches (Babai et al. 1980; Babai and Kucera 1979) have been developed that allow to significantly reduce the complexity (down to $O(n)$) but which have a certain rejection probability with which the property cannot be decided. For restricted forms of graphs, algorithms with lower complexity are known. For trees with a marked root node and for plane graphs the isomorphism can be decided in linear time (Aho et al. 1974).

Sub-graph Isomorphism

A different binary but non-symmetric similarity measure can be defined based on the sub-graph isomorphism property of two graphs. The standard definition for sub-graph isomorphism is as follows.

Definition 4.18 (Sub-Graph Isomorphism) A graph G_1 is *sub-graph isomorphic* to a graph G_2 (we write $G_1 \precsim G_2$) if there exists a sub-graph G_2' of G_2 such that $G_1 \cong G_2'$.

The two obvious variants of similarity measures are as follows:

$$sim(x, y) = \begin{cases} 1 & : \quad x \precsim y \\ 0 & : \quad \text{otherwise} \end{cases} \qquad \text{(Similarity Measure (1) based on Sub-Graph Isomorphism)}$$

$$sim(x, y) = \begin{cases} 1 & : \quad y \precsim x \\ 0 & : \quad \text{otherwise} \end{cases} \qquad \text{(Similarity Measure (2) based on Sub-Graph Isomorphism)}$$

Both similarity measures are reflexive (but not strongly reflexive), non-symmetric, and they fulfill the triangle inequality. They have similar shortcomings as the similarity measure based on graph isomorphism. They don't allow to introduce additional knowledge about different degrees of utility and can therefore only be applied when a binary relation sufficiently approximates the utility. The sub-graph isomorphism problem is an NP-complete decision problem (Ullman 1976). For special cases such as for binary trees and biconnected graphs algorithms with polynomial time complexity are known (Mäkinen 1990; Lingas 1986; Lingas and Syslo 1988; Mäkinen 1989).

Largest Common Sub-graph Measure

The largest common sub-graph approach allows defining non-binary similarity measures.

Definition 4.19 (Largest Common Sub-Graph) A graph G is the *largest common sub-graph* of two graphs G_1 and G_2 (we write $G = lcsg(G_1, G_2)$) if $G \precsim G_1$ and $G \precsim G_2$ holds and there does not exist a graph G' such that $G' \precsim G_1$ and $G' \precsim G_2$ and $|G'| > |G|$. Here, $|(N, E)| = |N| + |E|$ is the size of the graph determined by the number of nodes and edges.

The size of the largest common sub-graph can be used as a measure of similarity. A symmetric measure of this kind can be defined as follows and determines the similarity based on the relation between the size of the largest common subgraph and the maximum of the sizes of both graphs to be compared.

$$sim(x,y) = f(1 - \tfrac{|lcsg(x,y)|}{\max\{|x|,|y|\}})$$
(Symmetric Similarity Measure based on the Largest Common Sub-Graph)

Here, the function f is a monotonic decreasing mapping function from $[0,1]$ to $[0,1]$ with $f(0) = 1$, such as the functions introduced in Sect. 4.3.4. Similarly, we can define not-symmetric measures which determine the similarity based on the relation of the size of the largest common sub-graph and the size of one of the graphs to be compared.

$$sim(x,y) = f(1 - \tfrac{|lcsg(x,y)|}{|x|})$$
(Non-Symmetric Similarity Measure (1) based on the Largest Common Sub-Graph)

$$sim(x,y) = f(1 - \tfrac{|lcsg(x,y)|}{|y|})$$
(Non-Symmetric Similarity Measure (2) based on the Largest Common Sub-Graph)

Finding the largest common sub-graph is also an NP-complete problem (Mehlhorn 1984; Brandstädt 1994). Hence this similarity measure should be used quite carefully.

4.5.2 Graph Editing

The weighted *graph edit distance* is a distance measure proposed by Bunke and Messmer (1994) and is a kind of generalization of the string edit distance (Wagner and Fischer 1974). It is defined for attributed directed graphs but can easily be applied in a simplified form to standard graphs as well. Similarity is modeled through a set of edit operations on graphs. Each edit operation e transforms a graph into a successor graph performing a modification of the following kind: insert a new node or a new edge, delete a node or an edge, change a node or an edge label. Each edit operation has assigned a certain cost $c(e) \in [0,1]$. A difference can now be defined based on the total cost of a sequence of edit operations which transform one graph into the other graph. The cheaper and the fewer the operations are that are required to make the two graphs identical the smaller is the difference and hence the higher is the similarity. These considerations lead to the following difference function that can be easily transformed into a similarity measure as introduced in Sect. 4.3.4.

$$\delta(x,y) \qquad = \qquad \min\{\textstyle\sum_{i=1}^{k} c(e_i) \mid (e_1, \dots , e_k) \text{ transforms } x \text{ to } y\}$$

(Graph Editing
    Difference)

The graph edit distance measure is a generalization of the sub-graph isomorphism measure, i.e., we can easily define editing operations such that the sub-graph isomorphism measure is obtained. Its computation is therefore also NP-complete (Bunke and Messmer 1994) and can be performed by a state-space search, e.g. by an A* algorithm. Hence, also this similarity measure should be used quite carefully.

4.6 Similarity Measures for Predicate Logic Representations

Finally, we discuss some similarity measures to be used for cases represented in predicate logic. As introduced in Sect. 3.3.4 a case is a set of atomic formulas. Hence we now define similarity measures that allow comparing two sets of atomic ground formulas.

4.6.1 Treating Atomic Formulas as Binary Attributes

The first obvious approach that we can apply is to view the two sets $x = \{\varphi_1, \dots , \varphi_n\}$ and $y = \{\psi_1, \dots , \psi_m\}$ as two binary vectors of the dimension $|x \cup y|$. The similarity is determined depending on the atomic ground formulas that identically occur in x and y. In the two binary vectors the coordinate i is 1 for both vectors if the i-th formula in $x \cup y$ occurs in x and y (assuming some arbitrary ordering on the atomic formulas). By taking this view, we can apply the simple similarity measures for binary attributes introduced in Sect. 4.3.1 .

This approach is simple, but it does not allow to take into account any semantics of the formulas a case consists of. It is restricted to counting identical occurrences.

4.6.2 Similarity between Atomic Formulas

The disadvantage of the previous approach can be addressed by considering similarity measures between individual atomic formulas. To compare two atomic ground formulas we can use the anti-unification of two formulas in a similar manner as we use the least common sub-graph for comparing two graphs.

Definition 4.20 (Anti-Unification) Given two atomic formulas φ and ψ, we call φ more general than ψ (written as $\varphi \geq \psi$) iff it exists a substitution σ such that $\psi = \sigma(\varphi)$. An *anti-unification* of two formulas φ and ψ is a formula χ (we write $\chi = au(\varphi, \psi)$) such that $\chi \geq \varphi$ and $\chi \geq \psi$ and there does not exist a formula χ' such that $\chi' \geq \varphi$ and $\chi' \geq \psi$ and $\chi' < \chi$. Hence the anti-unification is the most specific generalization of the two formulas.

The size of the anti-unification can be used as a measure of similarity. Here, the size of an atomic formula $|\varphi|$ is defined as the number of function symbols and constants. Variables are not counted. A symmetric measure can now be defined as follows:

$$sim(x, y) = f(1 - \tfrac{|au(x,y)|}{\max\{|x|,|y|\}})$$
(Symmetric Similarity Measure based on the Anti-Unification)

Here, the function f is a monotonic decreasing mapping function from $[0, 1]$ to $[0, 1]$ with $f(0) = 1$, such as the functions introduced in Sect. 4.3.4. Similarly, we can define not-symmetric measures which determine the similarity based on the relation of the size of the anti-unification and the size of one of the graphs to be compared.

$$sim(x, y) = f(1 - \tfrac{|au(x,y)|}{|x|})$$
(Non-Symmetric Similarity Measure (1) based on the Anti-Unification)

$$sim(x, y) = f(1 - \tfrac{|au(x,y)|}{|y|})$$
(Non-Symmetric Similarity Measure (2) based on the Anti-Unification)

If a case consists of several formulas, we can treat this the same way as a multi-value attribute in object-oriented representations (see Sect. 4.4.3), by considering the above defined similarity as element similarity.

Unlike the related similarity measures for graph representations, the similarity measures defined here can be computed in polynomial time. This is due to the fact that the term structures resulting from atomic formulas are trees rather than graphs and hence determining the largest common sub-graph can be done in polynomial time.

4.6.3 Similarity through Logical Inference

A third approach to modeling similarity is though a logical theory Σ. With this approach we can at least model binary similarity measures, i.e. similarity predicates, since classical logic is restricted to the modeling truth. The logical theory must represent the conditions in the domain that ensure that the case is reusable in a certain situation.

$$sim(x,y) = \begin{cases} 1 & : & \Sigma \models x \rightarrow y \\ 0 & : & \text{otherwise} \end{cases} \qquad \text{(Similarity Measure based on a Logic Theory } \Sigma)$$

The applicability of this approach strongly depends on the logic theory (because it impacts the computational effort required to perform the inferences) and on whether a binary similarity measure is appropriate at all.

4.7 Similarity for Generalized Cases

We now extend the notion of similarity to generalized cases. As introduced in Sect. 3.4, a generalized case stands for a set of point cases. However, a generalized case should not represent an arbitrary set. The idea is that a generalized case is an abbreviation for a set of closely related point cases that naturally occur as one entity in the real world.

Modeling similarity for generalized cases can be done implicitly (Bergmann et al. 1999; Bergmann and Vollrath 1999) by modeling similarity for traditional cases (as shown before in this chapter) and extending this definition in a canonical way to generalized cases.

4.7.1 Canonical Extension of a Similarity Measure

For retrieving generalized cases, the similarity between a problem and a generalized case must be determined. We assume that the problem description is a point in the representation space that may be only partially described. We further assume that a traditional similarity measure $sim(q,c)$ is given which assesses the similarity between a problem q and a point case c. Such a similarity measure can be extended in a canonical way to assess the similarity $sim^*(q, gc)$ between a query q and a generalized case gc:

Definition 4.21 (Canonical Extension of Similarity Measures for Generalized Cases) The similarity measure $sim^*(q, gc) := \max\{sim(q,c) \,|\, c \in gc\}$ is called the *canonical extension* of the similarity measure sim to generalized cases.

Applying sim^* ensures that those generalized cases are retrieved that contain the point cases which are most similar to the query.

4.7.2 The General Problem of Similarity Assessment

The similarity assessment between a query $(q_1, \ldots, q_n)$ and a generalized case is as follows. Assume a given traditional similarity measure for point cases $sim(q, c)$ that aggregates individual local similarity measures sim_i for the individual attributes by a function Φ that is monotone increasing in every argument:

$$sim((q_1, \ldots, q_n), (c_1, \ldots, c_n)) = \Phi(sim_1(q_1, c_1), \ldots, sim_n(q_n, c_n))$$

The computation of the canonical extension sim^* given the similarity measure sim and the constraint representation for generalized cases $gc = \{C_1, \ldots, C_k\}$ (according to Def. 3.34) requires searching for values for the variables $v_1, \ldots, v_n$ such that every constraint $C_1, \ldots, C_n$ is satisfied and $sim((q_1, \ldots, q_n), (v_1, \ldots, v_n))$ is maximized.

Nonlinear Programming

For continuous domains, this similarity assessment problem can be formulated as a nonlinear programming (NLP) problem (Buckley and Goffin 1982) or as a problem of nonlinear optimization (Cornet et al. 1987). An NLP problem is of the form:

$$\begin{aligned} \text{minimize} \quad & f(x), \quad x \in \Re^n, \\ \text{subject to} \quad & c_i(x) \geq 0, \quad i \in I, \\ & c_i(x) = 0, \quad i \in E \end{aligned}$$

In our context, the constraints c_i can be identified with the constraints $C_1, \ldots, C_k$ of gc. The *objective function* f corresponds to the similarity function sim. sim (and thus f) is not a linear function (this is true even if Φ is a linear function). Neither are the constraints c_i. So, in general, only numerical algorithms for solving such an NLP problem are applicable. A detailed analysis of the similarity problem for generalized cases with continuous valued attributes has been recently proposed by Mougouie (2001) as well as Mougouie and Bergmann (2002). However, in the general case, efficient algorithms for similarity computation are still an important topic of current research.

Fuzzy Constraint Satisfaction

For discrete and mixed domains, our problem can be formulated as a fuzzy constraint satisfaction problem (FCSP) (Dubois et al. 1993; Ruttkay 1994; Wong et al. 1996). An FCSP is specified by a tuple (V, D, C). $V = \{v_j \,|\, j \in J\}$ is a finite set of variables ("attributes" in our terminology), $D = \{d_i \,|\, i \in I\}$ is a set of domains associated with the variables in V, and C is a set of constraints over these variables. The constraints in C are fuzzy relations with a *satisfaction index* indicating the degree of satisfaction for each variable binding. To model our problem of solution selection one could include in C all constraints from gc as *crisp* constraints. Additionally, the attribute values from the query can be used to derive an appropriate unary fuzzy constraint for each of these variables to be included in C. The satisfaction index si_i of each constraint is defined by the respective local similarity measure: $si_i(v_i) = sim_i(q_i, v_i)$. The overall *solution function* of the FCSP is defined by the function Φ which also defines the overall similarity measure sim. The main difficulty in solving such an FCSP are the mixed (discrete and continuous) domains and the nonlinear continuous constraints occurring in some applications.

5. Representing Knowledge for Adaptation

> *"Adaptation plays a fundamental role in the flexibility of problem solving systems; their ability to solve novel problems depends on their ability to adapt retrieved cases to fit new circumstances [...]."*

> David B. Leake

An important task for experience management is the adaptation of experience in order to improve its reusability. This adaptation task requires additional, general knowledge besides the experience itself. This kind of knowledge is part of the general reuse-related knowledge in the experience management model (see Sect. 2.1). This chapter deals with various approaches for modeling adaptation knowledge.

The modeling approaches for adaptation knowledge have their origin in the projects INRECA, INRECA-II, and WEBSELL. They have been first published by Bergmann et al. (1996), Wilke and Bergmann (1996b), Meyfarth (1997), Schmitt and Bergmann (1999b), Schmitt and Bergmann (1999a), Stahl and Bergmann (2000), and Stahl et al. (2000). Please note also that this chapter is restricted to the knowledge representation issues; the processing of the various kinds of adaptation knowledge is discussed separately in Chap. 8.

5.1 Rule-Based Representations

We first describe an approach to integrate formally represented general knowledge in the form of *rules* with experience knowledge represented in cases. This approach was first published by Bergmann et al. (1996) and Wilke and Bergmann (1996b). We distinguish two different kinds of rules:

- *Completion rules* infer additional features out of known features of a case or the current problem description. Thereby, these rules complete the description of a case.
- *Adaptation rules* describe how the lesson part of a case can be adapted to better fit the current problem.

Both, completion and adaptation rules are rules in the classical sense of knowledge-based systems. As usual, such a rule consists of a precondition and a conclusion that is executed when the precondition holds. What is particular for completion and adaptation rules are the objects to which these rule refer. We will now introduce these particularities and show how the rules can be integrated into an object-oriented case representation.

5.1.1 Different Kinds of Rules

In the following we will explain the two kinds of rules informally before going into the details of their representation.

Completion Rules

Completion rules are used to infer values of attributes of the case description which are directly dependent on some other attributes of the case. We call such attributes *derived attributes*, or *virtual attributes* (Richter 1995). Uncertain, or just probable rules are not considered here.

Definition 5.1 (Derived Attribute) An attribute A_k from some attribute space $\mathbf{A}$ is a *derived attribute* if there is a computable function f and a set of attributes $A_1, \dots, A_m$ from $\mathbf{A}$ (with $k \neq 1 \dots m$) such that $a_k = f(a_1, \dots, a_m)$ holds for all cases $c_i = (a_{i_1}, a_{i_2}, \dots)$ from the case space due to domain principals.

The attributes which are derived using the completion rules can then be used for two main purposes:

1. to compute more informed similarity measures or to determine similarity measures that fulfill certain desired properties, and
2. to derive properties that are used during adaptation.

Definition 5.2 (Completion Rule) A *completion rule* is a rule that represents certain knowledge about how an attribute value of a case can be determined from other attribute values of the same case, under certain conditions.

Informal Example. As a first example for using completion rules we introduce an application in a travel agency domain in which several descriptions of available journeys are collected in a case base. Each journey is described by several attributes such as: *destination, duration, price, kind of transportation, kind of accommodation,* etc.

Assume a case representation for a journey which includes the specification of the number of adults and the number of children which are involved in the journey. Moreover, assume that the representation also specifies the total number of persons because for several journeys only the total number of people is important (e.g. in an apartment). In this situation, the following general rule is useful:

> *The total number of persons is always the sum of the number of children and the number of adults.*

Adaptation Rules

Adaptation rules come into play after a case is retrieved. Most likely, this case does not fully fit the requirements of the user. Some attributes of the retrieved case may exactly match the query while others might differ somehow. According to these differences, the retrieved case can be modified to become better suited to the current query.

Unlike completion rules, adaptation rules combine attributes (including derived attributes) of the retrieved case and attributes of the current problem in the precondition of the rule. In a rule's conclusion, new attribute values for the target (adapted) case are derived (see Fig. 5.1).

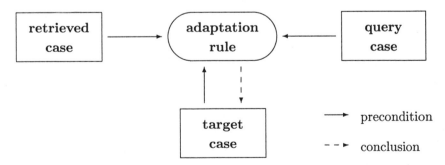

Fig. 5.1. Cases Used for Adaptation.

Definition 5.3 (Adaptation Rule) An *adaptation rule* is a rule that represents certain knowledge about how a retrieved case must be changed if its characterization differs from the current situation.

Informal Example. Suppose, the user's query specifies a journey with a duration of two weeks. Furthermore, assume that the most similar case which satisfies the user best is a journey which takes one week. Since the price for this journey is calculated on a one week basis, it must be adapted to correctly refer to the two week journey:

> *If the duration specified in the query is longer than the duration specified in the retrieved case, then the price specified in the target case is computed by adding the price of the retrieved case and the price for accommodation for the additional period of time.*

5.1.2 Formalization for Rules in an Object-Oriented Framework

Impact of the Object-Oriented Representation

When cases are represented in an object-oriented manner, this has a strong impact on the scope of completion and adaptation rules. For object-oriented representations, we have identified the classes to be the most natural place to attach the rules to. Within the scope of a class, a rule has direct access to the attributes which are defined for that class and to those attributes which are inherited from its superclasses. Additionally, rules must be given access to attributes of those objects which are related to the object the rule belongs to. In the same manner as attributes are inherited from the superclass to a class, the rules can also be inherited. Rules which are defined for a superclass are always valid for all subclasses.

Figure 5.2 shows an example of the simultaneous occurrence of inherited and related objects. Additionally, the figure shows different sets of rules which are attached to the classes and indicates the attributes to which these rules have access to. The figure shows five different classes C1, ..., C5 where C2 is a subclass of C1 and C3 is a subclass of C2. Each class has one simple attribute which are named A1, ..., A5. Moreover, class C2 and class C4 have relational attributes R1 and R2, respectively. To illustrate the scope of the rules associated with the five classes, the attributes that can be accessed by each of the rules are shown. For example, we can see that rules of rule base 2 have access to the attributes of their own class (A2), to the attributes of their superclasses (A1), and to the attributes which are available in related classes (A4, A5). To make a precise reference to attributes of related classes, the relation itself (e.g. R1) must always be noted together with the respective attribute (a possible notation is: R1→A4 or R1→R2→A5). Due to the inheritance of the rules, the rules of rule base 1 are also valid for all objects of the classes C2 and C3, but of course not for objects of the classes C4 and C5 since class C1 is not a superclass of C4 and C5.

Applying the object-oriented representation also to rules enables an efficient way of expressing background knowledge. Due to the rule inheritance, knowledge which applies to many different objects can be expressed in rules

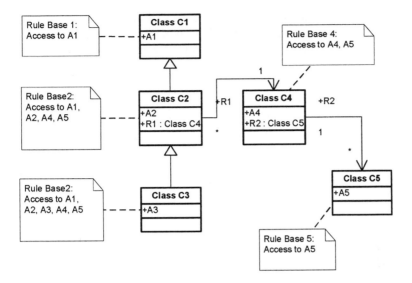

Fig. 5.2. Scope of Rules in the Object-Oriented Case Representation.

which are attached to the respective superclass these objects belong to. Moreover, the restricted set of attributes a rule can access still maintains the principle of information encapsulation of object-oriented representations.

Completion Rules

Like rules in classical knowledge-based systems, each completion rule consists of two parts: a *precondition part* and a *conclusion part*. The precondition part defines a conjunction of conditions. Each condition must be expressed in terms of the accessible attributes with respect to the class to which the rule belongs to. A condition can compare the value of an attribute to values of other attributes, constants, or local variables. Moreover, the precondition can also be used to specify an arbitrary function which calculates a new value using the existing attribute values. The conclusion part of a rule consists of a set of actions which are executed if the precondition is fulfilled, i.e., if all conditions in the precondition are fulfilled. An action in the conclusion of a rule can assign a value to an attribute, create a new object for a relational attribute, or specialize the class of an already existing object in a relational attribute.

Precondition Part of a Completion Rule. The precondition of a rule consists of a set of conditions. The set of these conditions is treated as conjunction, i.e. all conditions of the precondition of the rule must be fulfilled to fire the rule. Additionally, a condition may occur in negated form. Local variables may occur in the precondition of a rule. These variables can become instantiated by a certain condition and can be accessed or tested in conditions evaluated afterwards in the same rule. A condition can be of three different types:

- *Built-in predicates:* A condition can be expressed by using a built-in predicate (e.g., $=$, $\neq$, $<$, $>$, $\in$, etc.) to compare two values. The two values to be compared can be any attributes that lies within the scope of the rule, any constant value, or any local variable (see below). However, one obvious restriction is that the two values to be compared are of compatible types or from compatible object classes.
- *Domain functions and predicates:* Domain functions and predicates can be used to define any kind of domain-specific conditions which cannot be expressed by the built-in predicates.
- *A-kind-of test:* Using the object-oriented features of the case representation, a related object can be from different classes. However, by the definition of a relational attribute, an object's class is already specified, but objects of all respective subclasses are valid objects for such an attribute. Therefore, the a-kind-of test can be used to examine the actual class of a related object.

Variables in Rules. Variables may also occur in the precondition of a rule as a means of sharing values between different conditions contained in the precondition of the same rule. These variables are always local to the current rule. Variables can hold any kind of basic values, objects, or they can hold the class name of an object only. Variables become instantiated by the first (left-most) condition which is either an equal-predicate ($=$), an a-kind-of test, or an external function that calculates and returns a new value. An equality predicate can instantiate the variable with the current value of the attribute (a simple value or a whole object). The a-kind-of test assigns the variable the name of the class of the tested relational object. The external function intantiates the variable with the value which is computed by this function. An instantiated variable can then be used in any further conditions. Moreover, a variable can also be used in an action of the conclusion part of the rule. The value of the variable can then be assigned to a new attribute. Moreover, a new object of a class contained in a variable can be created and assigned to an attribute.

Conclusion Part of a Completion Rule. The conclusion of a rule consists of a set of actions. An action can be either the assignment of a value to an attribute or the creation of a new object which is stored in a relational attribute.

- *Attribute assignment:* An attribute can be assigned a constant value, the value of another attribute, or the value of a variable which was instantiated in the precondition of a rule.

- *Creation of objects:* The second kind of action that may occur in the conclusion of a rule is the creation of new objects for relational attributes. This is necessary to be able to extend the object structure of a case itself. With the creation of a new object, the name of the class of the object must be specified. The name of the class can be stated by specifying the name directly or by selecting a variable which is instantiated by an a-kind-of condition in the precondition of the same rule. If the relational attribute for which the object should be created is still empty, then the new object is created (with unassigned attributes) and directly linked to the attribute. If the relational attribute already contains an object, then this object must be of the same class or it must be a superclass of the object which should be created. If the latter is the case, the existing object is replaced by the more specific (sub-class) object which is to be created, but the filled attributes of the old object are directly copied into the same attributes of the new object.

Adaptation Rules

The basic difference between completion rules and adaptation rules is that completion rules only refer to one case, while adaptation rules always refer to three cases, namely the problem specification (which can be considered a partial query case), the retrieved case, and the target (adapted) case (see Fig. 5.1). These three different cases have to be taken into account when specifying the preconditions and the conclusion of adaptation rules.

The preconditions of an adaptation rule may consist of the same elements as the preconditions of a completion rule, but because an adaptation rule has to take into account three different cases as explained earlier, each reference to an attribute must also state which of the three possible cases is meant to be referenced.

The conclusion of an adaptation rule may consist of the same elements as the actions of a completion rule. Contrary to the precondition part, it is not neccessary to explicitly state the case when an assignment to an attribute is made in the conclusion part because the target case is the only case that may be modified by an adaptation rule.

5.1.3 An Example

We now want to give an example of a completion rule and an adaptation rule. For that purpose we represent the rules from the travel agency domain introduced in the informal examples before. We assume that the descriptive model contains three classes: the classes *vacation*, *transportation* and *accommodation*. In our model, the classes *transportation* and *accommodation* describe objects which are directly related to the *vacation* object as shown in Fig. 5.3. This figure also shows some attributes needed to describe the objects.

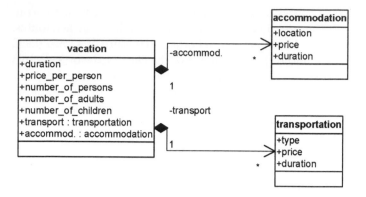

Fig. 5.3. Descriptive OO Example Model of the Travel Agency Domain.

Based on this model, the following completion rule can be formulated to express that *the total number of persons is always the sum of the number of children and the number of adults.*

```
defrule person_calculation of class vacation
    rule
        ?x := number_of_adults + number_of_children
        ⟹
        number_of_persons := ?x.
```

This rule adds the values of the two attributes *number_of_adults* and *number_of_children* and assigns the result to the variable named *?x*. In the conclusion of the rule, the attribute *number_of_persons* is assigned the value stored in *?x*.

The adaptation rule for adapting the price of a journey with respect to its duration can be formulated as follows:

```
defadaptationrule price_adaptation of class vacation
    rule
        query duration > retrieved duration &
        ?additional_days := query duration − retrieved duration &
        ?additional_price := ?additional_days * retrieved accommodation→price &
        ?new_price := retrieved price + ?additional_price
        ⟹
        target price := ?new_price.
```

This adaptation rule first tests whether the *duration* in the query case is longer than the *duration* in the retrieved case. Then the difference between the required and retrieved duration is computed and the *additional_price* is determined. Finally, the last calculation adds the *additional_price* to the price already stated in the retrieved case. In the conclusion of the adaptation rule, the *price* attribute of the target case is assigned the new price.

5.2 Operator-Based Representations

A second approach that is closely related to the rule-based adaptation, is the use of operator-based representations. Operators are introduced that transform a case into an adapted successor cases.

Definition 5.4 (Adaptation Operator) An *adaptation operator* is a partial function that transforms a case into a successor case. An adaptation operator represents valid transformations in the sense that if a valid case is transformed the resulting case after the adaptation is still valid.

Adaptation is achieved by chaining several adaptation operators to a sequence. Unlike in the rule approach, the sequence in which the operators are applied can determine the final results of the adaptation. However, the basic principle for integrating operators into an object-oriented framework is the same as described for the rule approach. The operator-based adaptation was first described by Meyfarth (1997), Bergmann and Wilke (1998), Schmitt and Bergmann (1999b), and Schmitt and Bergmann (1999a).

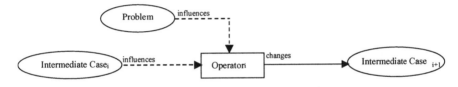

Fig. 5.4. Adaptation Operator.

5.2.1 Basic Approach

First, the adaptation process is divided into atomic units of changes. To model these atomic units, we have developed the concept of adaptation operators (see Fig. 5.4) which hold the whole adaptation knowledge. The first operator applied transforms the retrieved case into an intermediate case. Several operators can be applied sequentially on the intermediate cases until an appropriate target case is reached (see Fig. 5.5). In most cases, an operator is applicable only in certain situations, i.e., for a certain case or intermediate case. The condition when an operator is applicable is part of the operator definition and must be determined during domain modeling.

The operators in this approach can also be compared to the operators used in AI planning (Fikes and Nilsson 1971; Wilkins 1988; McAllester and Rosenblitt 1991). The retrieved case is the initial state and the target case is the goal state. The sequence of operators can be considered the plan. Based on this analogy, we could think about applying generative planning techniques

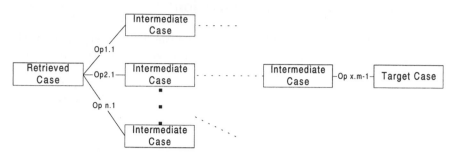

Fig. 5.5. Adaptation Process as Sequence of Operators.

for adaptation, i.e., to automatically find a sequence of adaptation operators which transforms the retrieved product to a target product that fulfills all requirements stated in the query.

5.2.2 Representation

Due to the analogy to state-based planning, we can adopt and extend operator representation approaches from planning (e.g., STRIPS Fikes and Nilsson 1971) to represent adaptation operators. An adaptation operator consists of:

- A *name* which clearly identifies the adaptation step.
- A *precondition* that states for which cases the adaptation is applicable. Basically, the precondition is defined over the attributes of the problem statement, and the current intermediate case. Only when the precondition is fulfilled the operator can be applied. The detailed modeling of preconditions for completion rules as in introduced in Sect. 5.1.2 can be used here as well.
- Additional *parameters* to specify the desired adaptation in more detail.
- For each parameter there can be a *parameter condition* that constraints the set of valid parameter values.
- The *action part* specifies how the current intermediate case is changed. Actions can change slot values of the representation and add or delete new objects. Compared to the representation of the conclusion part in completion rules, operators can additionally delete parts of the case representation.

To integrate this operator representation with an object-oriented case representation, we can attach an operator base to each class description. Operators then only refer to the attributes that are defined in that class to which they are attached and to attributes of related objects. Further, operators can be inherited from a class to its sub-class; additional refinement of inherited operators is possible.

Example for Adaptation Operators. Now, we present an example for an adaptation operator. This is an example for an operator which adapts the duration of the holiday to a customers wish as it can occur in an electronic commerce scenario (see Chap. 10 for details).

- Name: Customize the duration of a vacation.
- Precondition: The duration of the vacation is modifiable.
- Parameters: d: desired duration of the vacation
- Parameter Condition: $d \geq$ minimal duration that can be booked.
- Action part: Set the duration of the vacation to d.

It should be remarked that the example above is rather simplified just for the purpose of presentation. There are dependencies which also have to be considered as well as more actions to be performed.

5.3 Restricting Adaptability with Consistency Constraints

Besides the explicit approaches for representing adaptation knowledge in rules or operators, adaptation knowledge can also be represented implicitly by specifying conditions which guarantee correct cases. Given this knowledge, cases can be adapted according to certain adaptation principles in a way, such that after the modification the resulting case is still correct. This approach is appropriate if cases are composed of different sub-components among which certain dependencies exist which must be considered. In the example introduced in Sect. 5.1.3 a vacation consists of a transportation and an accommodation part. A condition for a valid vacation is that the destination location of the transportation is the same as the location of the accommodation. Adaptation can be achieved by replacing sub-components of a case (for example, the hotel) as long as the conditions for a valid case are not violated (in the example this means that a different hotel at the same place can be chosen) (Wilke et al. 1998; Schumacher 1998; Stahl and Bergmann 2000; Stahl et al. 2000).

Such conditions can be formally represented by a set of constraints. Unlike the constraints that are used to represent a generalized case (see Definition 3.34), these constraints are globally valid and not just in the context of a single case. For this purpose we need to extend the vocabulary by a constraint space **CO** (see Definition 3.31) that provides us with the definition of the constraint relations.

Definition 5.5 (Consistency Constraints) *Consistency constraints* are a set of constraints $\{C_1, \ldots, C_k\}$, where C_i are constraints from the constraint space **CO** that refer to the attributes of the attribute space of the vocabulary.

When cases are represented in an object-oriented manner, the already introduced principle for restricting the access to attributes of rules and operators can also be applied for constraints. Consistency constraints can be added to each class of the case representation. They can refer to attributes of the class to which they belong (including inherited attributes) as well as to attributes that can be reached via relational attributes starting from that class. Further, constraints are inherited by the sub-classes.

Example. The above mentioned consistency constraint can be formally represented as follows. Since it relates to different sub-components it must be attached to the class that combines those sub-components, i.e., the *vacation* class.

> consistency constraint location_compatibility of class vacation
>   transportation → location = accommodation → location

5.4 Generalized Cases

Generalized cases as introduced in Sect.r 3.4 also contain adaptation knowledge, which is the basic motivation in systems like those described by Hua et al. (1993) and Purvis and Pu (1995). By using a generalized case instead of a single point case, the need for traditional adaptation is reduced. Since generalized cases naturally cover a subspace rather than a point, they immediately have a larger coverage (Smyth and Keane 1995) than point cases. To increase the coverage, a traditional system stores a set of point cases and some general adaptation knowledge that is applied to each point case. Thereby, every point case is adapted in the same way. By employing generalized cases, case-specific adaptation knowledge can be encoded into the generalized case. If necessary, case independent adaptation knowledge in the traditional form can be applied additionally.

Part II

Methods for Experience Management

6. User Communication

" The individual communications between the machine and other participants should account for the special characteristics of those participants as the interactions occur. [...] The dialogue machine should track these needs and provide interactions appropriate to the moment."

Alan W. Biermann, Duke University

The ultimate goal of experience management is to achieve a communication of experience between an experience provider and an experience user. Although both, the experience provider and the experience user are usually humans, the communication between them is achieved through an experience management system, which allows bridging time and space frontiers between the two communication partners and to overcome the availability and capacity problems of the experience provider. As a consequence, the computer is inserted into this communication channel, which causes two new communication channels:

- the communication of the experience provider with the experience management system and
- the communication of the experience user with the experience management system.

The first communication channel requires much more effort than the second; the development and maintenance methodology of the experience management model (see Chap. 9) deals with this communication and is not within the scope of this chapter. This chapter addresses the second communication channel. This communication is of bidirectional nature: The user must be able to tell the experience management system about his problem and the experience management system must be able to communicate appropriate experience to the experience user. The difficulties involved here are to organize this communication efficiently and to enable access from several experience users at a time.

6.1 Introduction to User Interaction

We first present a more detailed view of the communication aspects in experience management. Then, we discuss requirements concerning the user interaction and present the main issues to be considered during the design of the communication components.

6.1.1 A Basic Communication Architecture

The communication between the experience user and the experience management system involves two directions.

- *From the experience user to the experience management system:* During the *problem acquisition* phase, the problem must be captured and formalized and transferred to the experience management system.
- *From the experience management system to the experience user:* During the *experience presentation* phase, the experience, or more precisely the lesson contained in the experience, must be presented in an appropriate form to the experience user.

Figure 6.1 shows these two communication phases in relation to the remaining steps of the problem solving cycle of the experience management model. Further, this model also shows the distribution of experience management steps in the problem solving cycle between a client and a server side. A

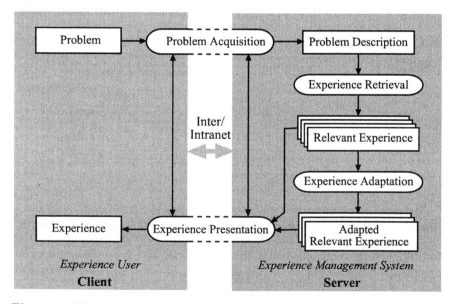

Fig. 6.1. Model for the Communication between Experience User and the Experience Management System.

client-server model is usually necessary due to the common requirement that the experience base is accessed at the same time from many users at different locations. The communication between client and server side requires a data network, which can be a local company Intranet, an Extranet, or the Internet. We do not further discuss these networking issues here, since they are not specific to experience management.

Problem Acquisition

The task of the problem acquisition phase is to acquire sufficient information about the problem from the user in order to present to her/him one or several experience items that are useful to the user for solving the problem. From a formal point of view, problem acquisition deals with specifying a problem $p \in \mathbb{P}$, taking into account the representation language and vocabulary for the problem space.

Definition 6.1 (Problem Acquisition Task) The *problem acquisition task* is the task of acquiring a problem description from the user and formalizing it in terms of the problem space. The outcome of this task is a problem $p \in \mathbb{P}$.

For this purpose, the problem acquisition software component must provide an appropriate user interface that shows input masks or ask specific questions. An important problem is to decide when to ask which question or when to show which input fields to the user (see sections 6.3 and 6.4). All activities involved here can be distributed between the client and the server side. Several options are discussed in Sect. 6.1.3, taking into account the generated network load and the response time.

Experience Presentation

The task of the experience presentation phase is to show the retrieved (and possibly adapted) experience to the user. This requires that the experience is transferred from the server side (if it is stored there) or from an external source (if the cases just maintain links to lessons stored in external sources) to the client. From a formal point of view, the experience presentation simply deals with displaying a lesson $l \in \mathbb{L}$. It requires, however, that the experience is presented to the user in an appropriate way. If different alternative lessons are available, the user must be given the opportunity to browse among them, compare them, and get some explanation of why they are appropriate. Different users may require different kinds of experience presentations, depending on their individual information need.

Definition 6.2 (Experience Presentation Task) The *experience presentation task* is the task of displaying selected lessons $l \in \mathbb{L}$ in a way that is appropriate to the particular user.

For this purpose, the experience presentation software component must provide an appropriate user interface for displaying, browsing, and comparing different lessons. Also this component can be distributed between the client and the server side.

Interactions between Both Components

Problem acquisition and experience presentation can often not be completely separated. The reason for this is that the whole cycle from problem acquisition to experience presentation is usually executed several times until a satisfying lesson has been found. In successive iterations, the problem description is refined, i.e., additional information about the problem is asked that allows to evaluate the utility of the available experience items more properly. Hence, there can be a feedback through the set of retrieved cases to the problem acquisition component. Further questions to be asked can be determined with respect to currently retrieved best experience. On the other hand, explaining a retrieved experience, as done in the experience presentation component, requires also information about the user's problem. From these considerations it becomes clear that both components must communicate with each other. Therefore, and also from a technical implementation point of view, it usually makes sense to combine both components into a single client user interface that provides a single access point to the experience management server.

6.1.2 Requirements

We now discuss some general requirements for user communication, that relate to both, the problem acquisition and the experience presentation component. The ultimate goal of user communication is to achieve an efficient communication. Communication always involves a significant effort from the user for entering information and for understanding the information presented to her/him. This effort should be kept as low as possible. Therefore, the following issues must be taken into account.

Small Number of Questions

During problem acquisition, the number of questions asked should be kept as small as possible. This relates to single questions raised directly, for example in a dialog window, and to questions that are answered implicitly by entering values into an input field of a questionnaire. Therefore it is important to only ask questions that help selecting reusable experience. Asking irrelevant questions increases the communication effort without improving the accuracy of the results. A common problem with this requirement results from the fact that the relevance of a question often depends on many issues, such as the answers given to previous questions, the distribution of the cases, the relevance (weight) of certain attributes, the similarity measure for this attribute, and so forth. Therefore, it is very difficult to find a static sequence of questions that avoids the problem of asking irrelevant questions. Dynamic questioning approaches can help to overcome this problem (see Sect. 6.4).

Comprehensible Questions

The questions asked must be understandable for the user. This means that they must be asked in a language that the user understands and it must be expressed in terms that the user understands. Here the problem can arise that different users may have a different cultural or educational background; there can be domain experts or novices. Depending on the spectrum of users addressed by the experience management approach it might be necessary to provide different questioning styles, multi-lingual access, and different modes for novices and experts.

Low Answering Cost of Questions

Answering a question always causes certain cost. Some questions cause low cost, i.e., they can be answered immediately, while others may cause significant cost and may involve enacting certain examinations or investigations (for example in a medical diagnosis situation). When asking questions, the cost for answering them must be taken into account. Questions that cause low cost should be preferred over questions that cause high cost.

Comprehensible Question Clustering

Usually a series of questions is necessary to capture a problem. These questions are always clustered by some means: Questions can be clustered because they occur together on one page of a questionnaire or they can be clustered by the temporal sequence in which they are asked. Any clustering that occurs should be comprehensible for the user. This means that the cluster should represent a concept known by the user; sequences of questions should represent some "logical" order.

Present Appropriate Amount of Information

When information is presented to the user it must have the appropriate amount. This holds for the information that is contained in a question but more importantly also to the information that is contained in the lesson part of a case. The latter means that experience must be presented in the right amount. The ideal situation is to give exactly the information that the user needs and not to give any information that the user already possesses. Since different users may have different information needs it can be necessary to store and present experience in different forms. Alternatively, experience can be presented in a hyper-text form which gives the user the flexibility to view as much information as s/he wants.

Choose Appropriate Presentation Form

Information (contained both, in questions and in experience) can be presented in different forms, e.g. as plain text, hyper-text, graphics, images, sound, or videos. The presentation form of an information entity should be chosen so that the respective message is communicated with a low effort of the user.

High Interaction Speed

A general requirement that must always be considered is the interaction speed, which should be as high as possible. In a client-server architecture such as the one proposed here, this interaction speed is significantly influenced by the communication time via the data network. Again this is influenced by the amount of data that is transferred (which of course also significantly depends on the presentation form and information amount) and the distribution of the problem acquisition and experience presentation components between the client and the server side.

In general, it should be noted that some of these requirements may contradict each other. For example, the interaction speed requirement usually contradicts requirements concerning the presentation form when sound or videos should be used.

6.1.3 Distribution between Client and Server Side

The problem acquisition and experience presentation component are distributed between the client and server side. Appropriate communication between both sides is necessary. Different distributions are possible.

Thin Client Approach

The thin client approach leaves most of the computation on the server side; client software is reduced to a minimum or standard software such as an HTML compatible Web browser. This approach avoids installing and maintaining specific client software or long client download times such as for example required for a fat client Applet. This is the standard approach used today on the Internet for non security-critical applications. Information is presented to the user as HTML pages, i.e., the information as well as its presentation is determined by the server and transferred to the Web browser, which is only responsible for displaying. Information acquired from the user is entered in input fields of the Web page or through other simple standard dialog GUI components (e.g., check boxes or selection menus). Only little computation is done at the client side and is usually restricted to very simple consistency checks for the entered values. The complete dialog control and presentation generation (e.g. of graphics) must be done at the server side.

This approach is quite appropriate for spontaneous users, i.e., users which do not use the experience management system on a regular basis for their daily work. Therefore, abandoning the client download and installation process turns into an important advantage. A serious disadvantage is the low interaction speed. Each interaction with the problem acquisition and experience presentation component involves the server and therefore also network communication. Since the presentation form of the experience must be determined at the server side (for example as graphics) and transferred to the client, also more data must be transferred via the network compared to a distribution of computation where the presentation form is determined at the client side. Finally, this approach causes a high load at the server side since the computation effort for all users remains at the server.

Fat Client Approach

The fat client approach moves most of the computation required for problem acquisition and experience presentation to the client side. Specific client software is implemented, either as stand-alone software or running as an Applet in a Web browser (which is more common today). The disadvantage of this approach is the higher effort involved in handling the client software, i.e., for downloading, installing, and maintaining. It also requires to transfer some of the knowledge from the server to the client. This particularly includes the vocabulary, but also cases and similarity measures that are required to determine the relevance of a question. Therefore, this approach is mostly appropriate for regular users of an experience management system. Then, the effort must only be invested once (if installed permanently) or once a new version is released. The advantage of this approach is manifold: First, the interaction speed is increased since most interaction can be handled on the client side without involving the possibly highly loaded server and network. Second, the server load is reduced significantly since some computation of the dialog control and the experience presentation is done at the client side. Third, the server can be realized in a state-less manner so that no session management is needed at the server side.

Medium-Sized Client

This third approach is located in between the two extreme positions discussed before. The computational effort for problem acquisition and experience presentation is distributed more equally between the client and server side. This requires downloading a medium-sized client that handles the experience presentation and some of the dialog control and consistency checks for the problem description. However, the knowledge intensive part of the dialog control, which may require access to case data and similarity measures (for example to determine the relevance of a question), is left on the server side. This avoids transferring large amounts of knowledge from the server to the client but still ensures acceptable interaction speed.

6.2 A Formal Dialog Model

We now introduce a general formal model for describing and relating the different dialog components and a dialog strategy (see also Schmitt and Bergmann 2001, Bergmann and Cunningham forthcoming). This model is a framework that allows classifying the detailed approaches presented in the subsequent sections. It is inspired by dialog models that occur in diagnostics (Wetter 1984; Althoff 1992; Richter 1992b; Puppe 1993; Cunningham and Smyth 1994). Diagnostics can be considered as a problem acquisition task plus a classification task. Problem acquisition usually means executing certain examinations that improve the information state of the object to be diagnosed. Examinations are selected according to whether they help to distinguish between several different hypotheses concerning the diagnosis.

6.2.1 Overview

A dialog can be modeled as a state machine. The state (we call it *dialog situation*) characterizes a particular instance in time of a particular dialog enacted between the user and the experience management system. It describes the current information state, i.e., all information gathered from the user up to this point in time, as well as all experience that is considered relevant for the problem as it stands at the moment (e.g., potential hypotheses). In given dialog situation, a certain set of interactions (with the user) can be initiated. We call these interactions *dialog interactions*. A dialog interaction can be to ask a particular question to the user, to present her/him a questionnaire, retrieve some new cases, present retrieved experience to the user, etc. If a dialog interaction is executed, the current dialog situation is changed, which is of course the purpose of the interaction. For example, if a question is asked, the information state is extended by the new information gathered about a certain problem feature.

Usually, there are many different applicable dialog interactions in a particular dialog situation. In order to fulfill the requirements introduced above, a *dialog strategy* is necessary that determines for a given dialog situation one dialog interaction to be executed. Processing a dialog with respect to a given strategy means to start at an initial empty dialog situation and successively execute the dialog interactions proposed by the strategy. Thereby, the dialog state is successively transformed into a successor state until the strategy indicates the termination of the dialog process. We now formalize this view.

6.2.2 Dialog Situation

The following definition formally introduces a dialog situation as a triple.

Definition 6.3 (Dialog Situation Space and Dialog Situation) The *dialog situation space* $\mathbb{S} = \mathbb{P} \times \mathbb{Q} \times \mathbb{H}$ consists of the problem space $\mathbb{P}$, a question state space $\mathbb{Q}$, and a hypothesis space $\mathbb{H}$. A *dialog situation* $s = (p, q, h)$ is an instance of the dialog situation space, i.e., $s \in \mathbb{S}$.

The problem description p contained in the dialog situation is the aggregation of all problem attribute values collected so far. Initially, this problem description is empty. During the dialog more problem attributes are filled and the degree of incompleteness of the problem description is reduced. The question state q usually describes the history of the dialog (for example as a finite state variable) as well as information obtained other than the problem descriptions. For example, it also contains information concerning the user classification such as whether the user is a novice or a domain expert. This can have an influence on the questions asked or the language chosen. The hypothesis h contains current hypotheses concerning the reusability of experience. It is usually some subset of the case base, i.e., $\mathbb{H} = \wp(\mathbb{C})$. It contains, for example, the cases currently rated best (highest similarity) with respect to the current problem description. Additionally, the cases may be annotated with their similarity or some similarity interval.

6.2.3 Dialog Interactions

Dialog interactions are certain actions started by the dialog component to update the dialog situation. The formal definition is as follows:

Definition 6.4 (Dialog Interation Space and Dialog Interation) The *dialog interaction space* $\mathbb{I} = \{i_1, \dots, i_k\}$ consists of a set of *dialog interactions*. A dialog interaction is a function $i_\nu : \mathbb{U} \to (\mathbb{S} \to \mathbb{S})$ that determines from a certain user input (out of the set of possible user inputs) $\mathbb{U}$ a transformation function of the current dialog situation s into a successor situation s', i.e., $i_\nu(u)(s) = s'$.

There are different kinds of dialog interactions.

Gathering Information

The primary reason for dialog interactions is to extend the information about problem. A user interaction can be to ask one particular question that aims at determining the attribute value of a certain problem attribute. Then, the answer given by the user is the user input $u \in \mathbb{U}$ and the transformation function determines the successor situation by assigning u to the respective attribute. Instead of asking a single question, a user interaction can also present a whole questionnaire to the user in which s/he can enter several answer values that are then assigned to the appropriate attributes.

Checking Consistency

Dialog interactions can also be used to model consistency checks for the information entered by the user. If inconsistencies are determined the user can be informed and s/he can be asked to correct mistakes. Such corrections lead to a change in the problem description.

Updating Hypotheses

Another type of dialog interaction is concerned with updating the hypothesis based on the current problem description. This interaction does not usually involve the user but its execution triggers the retrieval and (possibly the adaptation) steps at the server side of the experience management system (see Fig. 6.1). The retrieval result is used to update the current hypotheses.

Presenting Experience

Finally, dialog interactions can also be used to initiate the experience presentation. When such an interaction is executed, the retrieved experience is presented to the user. Additionally, feedback can be obtained about whether the presented experience is reusable or not. The problem description and the hypothesis are not updated by this interaction.

Besides the primary modifications of the dialog situations mentioned above (none for presentation interactions), they usually also update the question state. This is necessary in order to take care of the dialog history, for example, to avoid asking questions twice. The way they are updated depends on the questioning strategy discussed below.

6.2.4 Dialog Strategy and Its Execution

The dialog strategy controls the whole dialog. It determines the interactions to be performed.

Definition 6.5 (Dialog Strategy) A *dialog strategy* is a function *strat* : $\mathbb{S} \rightarrow \mathbb{I}$ that determines for a given current dialog situation the next dialog interaction to be executed.

The dialog strategy is the core of the dialog component. It is responsible for an efficient dialog and for the fulfillment of the requirements discussed in Sect. 6.1.2. The following simple algorithm (Fig. 6.2) describes the top-level loop in which the dialog strategy is executed. It assumes a particular interaction that indicates the termination of the dialog.

In the following we discuss several approaches for user communication in relation to the just described formal framework. These approaches differ significantly in the dialog situation representation, the dialog interaction, and the dialog strategy that is used.

```
procedure DialogControl()
var
    sit: S
    interaction: I
    user_input: U
begin
    sit := (nil,nil,nil)
    repeat
        interaction := strat(sit) (* Determine next interaction *)
        Perform interaction and determine user_input if necessary
        sit := interaction(user_input)(sit) (* Determine successor situation *)
        until interaction=terminate
end
```

Fig. 6.2. Dialog Control Algorithm

6.3 Predefined Static Dialog

The first category of approaches for user interaction is based on a predefined static dialog. The dialog interactions and strategy are manually modeled in advance by the developer of the experience management system. We can distinguish different modeling approaches depending on the degree of flexibility provided by the modeling.

6.3.1 Three-Step Questionnaire-Based Problem Acquisition

The three-step questionnaire-based approach is the most simple and therefore also the most common one in many simple applications. The dialog strategy is a simple sequence of three predefined dialog interactions (see Fig. 6.3):

1. Present a questionnaire to the user and obtain results
2. Retrieve and adapt cases
3. Present the found experience

The questionnaire shows all problem attributes at a time. For each attribute, there is an appropriate way for entering a value of the respective value type of the attribute (Bolender 1999).

- Numeric attribute values are either entered
  - by an input field into which a number must be typed in, or
  - by a slider that must be positioned to the right number

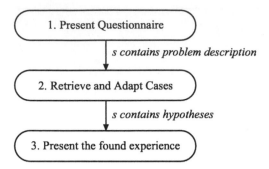

Fig. 6.3. Steps in the Questionnaire Strategy.

- Symbolic attributes' values can either be entered
  - by menus showing all possible values,
  - by a set of radio buttons each of which is associated with a symbolic value, or
  - by an input field into which the symbol value must be typed in.
- Textual attribute values are entered by an input field.

For object-oriented representations, the questionnaire should be structured according to the object structure. However, this is only possible if a fixed object structure can be assumed. If the problem representation requires a flexibility that allows to have arbitrary objects as instances in a relational slot, a dynamic questionnaire is required. Depending on the object class that is selected different input fields for the related attributes must be shown.

Figure 6.4 shows an example of a comprehensive questionnaire for obtaining a PC requirements specification to be used for product experience selection in an e-commerce scenario. This questionnaire is developed particularly for an expert user who is aware of the meaning of the different attributes. For such a user, these attribute descriptions are easily understandable and filling the appropriate fields is an effective way of communication. No further guidance is necessary and a long-lasting dialog would be disturbing for an expert user who knows what s/he wants.

6.3.2 Static Domain Specific Dialogs

The three-step questionnaire-based approach is a fixed dialog model used independent of the application domain. Only the questionnaire itself and the form of the experience presentation is domain specific. *Static domain specific dialogs* discussed now are modeled specifically for the domain at hand. They are static in the sense that they are modeled in advance by the developer of the experience management system and are not changed as a consequence of the available experience or experience with user interactions.

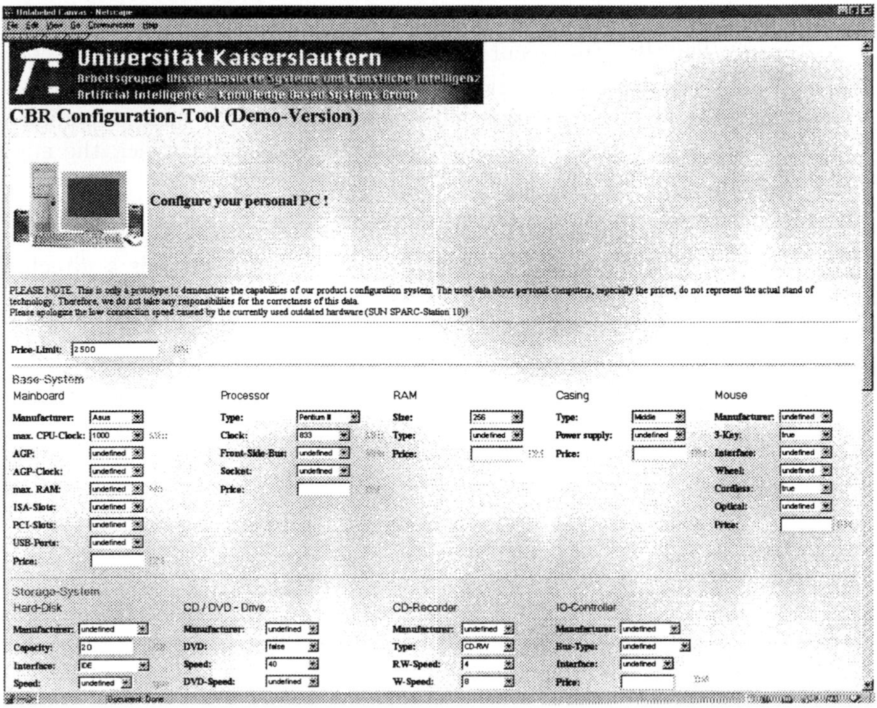

Fig. 6.4. Example Questionnaire.

Dialog Situations

The dialog situation is restricted to only contain the problem description and the question state. The problem description stores the currently acquired information about the problem and the question state is usually one or several state variables.

Dialog Interactions

Dialog interactions that represent user questions, consistency checks, and experience presentations are modeled particularly for the application domain. User questions can involve asking an individual question or presenting a small questionnaire asking for related problem attributes. Typically, such a questionnaire does not ask for all relevant problem attributes such as the example shown in Fig. 6.4 does.

Modeling the Dialog Strategy with a Directed Graph

The modeling of the dialog strategy is most crucial part of this approach. A simple but often appropriate method to model the strategy is to use a directed graph (see Fig. 6.5). The nodes of the graph are labeled with dialog interactions. When they are executed, a successor dialog situation results. The edges in the directed graph describe transitions from one dialog interaction to the next one. They are labeled with conditions on the successor dialog situation that results from the execution of the node from which the edge starts.

Definition 6.6 (Dialog Strategy Graph) For a given dialog interaction space $\mathbb{I}$ and a dialog situation space $\mathbb{S}$, a *dialog strategy graph* is a directed labeled graph (N, E) in which each node $n \in N$ is labeled with a dialog interaction $i_n \in \mathbb{I}$ and each edge $e \in E$ is labeled with a condition $c_e \subseteq \mathbb{S}$. The conditions of outgoing edges from a node are disjoint, i.e., $\forall e_1, e_2 \in E$: $e_1 = (n, n_1) \wedge e_2 = (n, n_2) \wedge n_1 \neq n_2 \rightarrow c_{e_1} \cap c_{e_1} = \emptyset$. The dialog strategy graph contains one distinguished start node n_0.

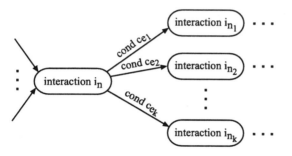

Fig. 6.5. Dialog Strategy Graph.

The dialog strategy graph completely defines the dialog strategy. Its execution starts with the empty dialog situation[1] at the start node n_0. The dialog interaction indicated at a node (initially the start node) is executed and thereby a successor dialog situation is obtained. Then the conditions at the outgoing edges of the node are checked and the dialog proceeds with the node that can be reached from the edge whose condition is fulfilled. If no outgoing edges with fulfilled conditions are available, the question strategy terminates.

Examples of user communication components that are based on this approach are discussed by Rosewitz and Timm (1998), Bolender (1999), Schmitt et al. (2000), Cunningham et al. (2001), and Irish Multimedia Systems (1999). The responsibility for achieving an efficient dialog with respect to the requirements discussed in Sect. 6.1.2 remains with the developer of the experience management system who defines the dialog strategy graph. A simple sequence of interactions is usually not sufficient since in most cases the relevance of

---

[1] The current node can be considered part of the question state.

a question depends on the answers to previous questions. The conditions at the edges of the graph express when a question is relevant.

Modeling the Dialog Strategy with Rules

An alternative way of modeling a dialog strategy is to use rules. Richter and Schmitt (2001) suggest the use of so-called event-condition-action rules. These rules have the following form:

```
IF <Event> AND <Condition> THEN <Action>
```

The event part of the rule relates to an activity issued by the user during a dialog interaction. In the formal dialog model, such activities are encoded in the dialog state. The condition part of the rule is a condition over the current problem description. The action of the rule proposes the dialog interaction to be enacted.

Again, the responsibility for defining a rule base that models an efficient user communication is at the developer's side. Like the conditions in the dialog strategy graph, the preconditions of the rules must not overlap, i.e., for every dialog situation only one rule should fire. If this property is not fulfilled, a conflict resolution mechanism is required, i.e., by adding a priority value to the rules.

An Example

The following Figures 6.6 and 6.7 show a sequence of questions issued by the Carsmart[2] application. The first question asks about the most important attribute. Depending on the answer, the respective attribute is asked in the second question (here the make of the car) together with the problem attribute that contains the model of the car. The third question asks now for more detailed information about the importance of other problem attributes. Finally, the two most important and yet unknown attributes (price and mileage) are asked.

6.4 Dynamic and Adaptable Strategies

The previously discussed dialog strategies must be modeled by hand, which requires a significant knowledge acquisition effort. Changes in the case base will also require updating the dialog strategy. To overcome this problem, several approaches have been developed to realize dialog strategies implicitly.

---

[2] Application developed for demonstration purposes by tec:inno (now empolis).

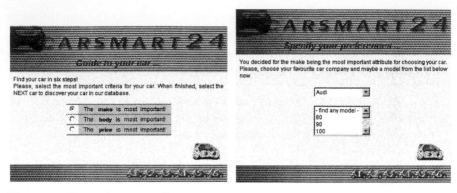

Fig. 6.6. Example Dialog: Questions 1 and 2

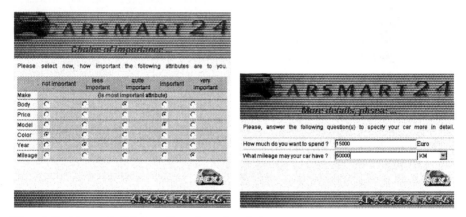

Fig. 6.7. Example Dialog: Questions 3 and 4

The basic idea behind this approaches is to analyze the distribution of cases in the case base to select questions according to their relevance for deciding the reusability of a case. We distinguish different strategies

- according to the selection criterion used and
- according to whether the strategy is compiled into a dialog strategy graph or whether the selection criterion is interpreted dynamically when the dialog is enacted

6.4.1 Criteria for Attribute Selection

Problem attributes to be asked to the user should be selected according to whether they contribute information that is relevant to decide among the reusability of the cases in the case base. The amount of dialog will be reduced to a minimum if irrelevant attributes are not asked. Several attribute selection criteria have been proposed in the machine learning and the case-based reasoning literature. Although, most of the approaches from machine learning do not aim at reducing the amount of dialog but at minimizing the size of generalized concept descriptions, the results can be transferred to a certain degree.

Information Gain Measure for Classified Cases

The information gain measure has its origin in information theory (Hunt et al. 1966) and was used in machine learning for attribute selection during the construction of decision trees (Quinlan 1986; Quinlan 1993). It is based on the concept of *information content* of a message and the *entropy* of a set of items. The information conveyed by a message depends on its probability and can be measured in bits as minus the logarithm to base 2 of that probability. The higher the probability the lower is the information conveyed. If we have a set of k possible messages each of which occurs with the probability pr_i the event has an *expected information content*:

$$H(pr_1, \ldots, pr_k) = -\sum_{i=1}^{k} pr_i \cdot \log_2(pr_i)$$

(Expected Information Content (Entropy))

The information gain measure is traditionally used for classified cases. Classified cases are cases that represent examples of a classification task. The case lesson space is defined as a small set of possible classes. The number of classes is small with respect to the number of cases available, i.e., there are usually several cases that belong to the same class. If we have some set of cases $C = C_1 \cup \cdots \cup C_k$ such that C_i contains only cases of class i, then the expected information content of C is:

$$H(C) = -\sum_{i=1}^{k} \frac{|C_i|}{|C|} \cdot \log_2\left(\frac{|C_i|}{|C|}\right)$$

(Expected Information Content (Entropy) of C)

If C only contains cases of the same class, the expected information content (or the entropy) of C is 0 because we do not need any information to predict the class. If we partition the set of cases C according to an attribute A into m subsets $C = C^1 \cup \cdots \cup C^m$ such that the attribute value[3] of all cases in C^j is v_j we can investigate the expected information content of each subset C^j. The expected conditional information content is

---

[3] This approach usually assumes $\mathbb{D} = \mathbb{P}$, i.e., the problem attributes asked are the same as the experience characterization attributes in the cases.

$$H(C|A) = \sum_{j=1}^{m} \frac{|C^j|}{|C|} \cdot H(C^j) \qquad \text{(Expected Conditional Information Content of } C|A)$$

This value is the expected information content required to determine the class of a case after we know the value of the attribute A. Given a set of cases C, we can now define the *information gain* obtained by knowing the value of the attribute A through:

$$Gain(A) = H(C) - H(C|A) \qquad \text{(Information Gain for Attribute } A)$$

In the traditional ID3 induction algorithm for decision trees (Quinlan 1986) the next attribute used for partitioning the current set of cases is the one with the highest information gain. While this criterion is originally only defined for symbolic attributes extensions to numeric attributes are discussed in connection with the C4.5 algorithm (Quinlan 1993; Quinlan 1996); the continuous value range is partitioned into a finite set of intervals on which the standard definition is applied.

This information gain measure for attributes has also been proposed as a strategy for question selection in case-based reasoning (Cunningham and Smyth 1994; Albin 1997; Göker and Thompson 2000). However, it has several disadvantages. First, it requires classified cases which are not always available; in the next section we discuss how to overcome this limitation. Second, it does not take into account the similarity measure. But the similarity measure also influences the relevance of an attribute. For example, an attribute that does not occur in the similarity measure must not be asked. Third, this approach does not take the answering cost of an attribute into account, which can be different for different attributes. Finally, it is not guaranteed that the clustering of questions, i.e., the sequence in which they, is asked are comprehensible to the user.

Information Gain Measure for Unclassified Cases

In order to overcome the limitation that cases must be classified, Doyle and Cunningham (2000) propose the use of clustering algorithms such as the k-medoid algorithm (Kaufman and Rousseeuw 1990) to derive a classification of originally unclassified cases. This algorithm selects k representative cases, called medoids, and clusters the other cases according to their similarity to the medoids. The medoids are selected such that the average similarity between the medoids and the cases belonging to a cluster is high and the similarity to the cases not belonging to the cluster is low. This clustering yields cases that are classified according to a similarity measure. The information gain measure discussed before is then used for attribute selection on the now classified cases.

Instead of clustering the cases first, one can alternatively use the case identifier as a class label (Albin 1997; Schulz 1999). This means that every case defines its own class. This is the same as turning each case of the case base into a medoid in the clustering algorithm. Given this approach, the entropy of a set of cases C is simplified to

$$H(C) = \log_2(|C|)$$

and the information gain for an attribute A is simplified to

$$Gain(A) = -\sum_{i=1}^{m} \frac{|C^j|}{|C|} \cdot \log_2\left(\frac{|C^j|}{|C|}\right)$$

The clustering approach strongly depends on the number of clusters used, because questions are selected such that the problem can be assigned to a cluster. No questions are generated to differentiate the cases within a cluster. On the other hand, if every case is turned into an individual cluster the relevance of the attributes with respect to the similarity measure is still ignored. Also, the answering costs for attributes are not taken into account and the sequence of questions generated may not be comprehensible to the user.

Similarity Influence Measure

A different attribute selection criterion is the *similarity influence measure* (Kohlmaier et al. 2001, Schmitt et al. 2002, Schmitt forthcomming). The idea is to select an attribute for which a known value has the highest influence on the similarity of a set of cases. The influence on the similarity can be measured by the expected variance of the similarities of a set of selected cases.

For a problem description p and a set of cases C, we can determine the variance of the similarity as follows.

$$simVar(p, C) = \frac{1}{|C|} \cdot \sum_{(d,l)\in C}(sim(pt(p), d) - \mu)^2 \quad \text{(Variance of Similarities)}$$

Here μ denotes the average similarity for the cases in C. When asking a question about the value of an attribute A, we do not know the answer in advance. Therefore we can make the actual attribute selection only on the expected similarity variance as follows.

$$simVar(p, A, C) = \sum_v pr_v \cdot simVar(p_{A \leftarrow v}, C) \qquad \text{(Expected Similarity Influence of an Attribute)}$$

Here, pr_v is the probability that the value v is chosen for the attribute A. This probability can be estimated, from the sample of cases in C, i.e., $pr_v = |C^v|/|C|$.

During the dialog, the attribute A with the highest expected similarity influence $simVar(p, A, C)$ is chosen. It is expected to lead to the highest increase of knowledge about similarity and thereby increases the probability of a correct decision.

Recent results of experimental evaluations indicate a significant advantage of the similarity influence measures compared to the traditional information gain approach (Kohlmaier et al. 2001; Schmitt et al. 2002). Also a very simplified variant of this approach is commonly used in commercial systems (Schulz 1999; tec:inno GmbH 1999). Attributes are selected according to the weight assigned to them in the aggregation function of the similarity measure (see Sect. 4.3.7). The higher the weight of an attribute, the higher its the influence on the similarity. Hence attributes with high weights are asked before attributes with low weights. This approach is an approximation of the expected similarity influence measure. It is only an approximation since it does not take into account the local similarity measures themselves and it also disregards the distribution of cases in the case base. However, the advantage of this approach lies in its simplicity, both in terms of computational complexity and in terms of the required development effort.

Two common disadvantages of all previously discussed question selection criteria also hold for the similarity influence measures. First, they don't consider the answering cost of questions and they may lead to an incomprehensible question ordering. These issues are briefly discussed now.

Integrating Answering Cost

If often occurs that some questions are easier to answer than other questions. Questions may be difficult to answer because they require to make an expensive, time consuming, or disagreeable examination (Tan 1993; Turney 2000). We summarize these issues by introducing the cost of answering a question.

Definition 6.7 (Question Answering Cost) Let A be a problem attribute. The *cost of answering the question* concerning the value of the attribute A in the current situation is denoted by $qc(A) \in [0, 1[$. Cost values are expressed as real values from the interval $[0, 1[$ where a higher values indicates higher cost.

Answering cost are not considered in any of the previously discussed question selection criteria. In the literature, this issue has also been neglected. However, if the answering cost are known they can be easily integrated in any of the previously introduced criteria as follows (the criterion $select\_without\_cost(A)$ can be for example $Gain(A)$ or $simVar(p, A, C)$) :

$$select\_with\_cost(A) = \frac{select\_without\_cost(A)}{1 - qc(A)} \qquad \text{(Cost Sensitive Attribute Selection)}$$

However, the problem of determining the attribute cost remains. They can also vary from user to user or from situation to situation. Hence, adaptive approaches are desirable that automatically determine attribute cost from user behaviour. Kohlmaier et al. (2001) discuss an initial adaptive approach based on Bayes nets.

The Problem of Comprehensible Question Clustering

The second problem ignored by any of the known question selection approaches is that they can cause incomprehensible question orderings. This is due to the fact that relationships between different questions are not considered in any of the criteria. We can express the relatedness of two questions by using a similarity measure as follows:

Definition 6.8 (Question Similarity) Let A_1 and A_2 be two problem attributes. The similarity of the questions asking for the values for A_1 and A_2 is denoted by $sim(A_1, A_2) \in [0, 1]$. The higher the similarity value the more are the two questions related.

Such relationships among attributes are already modeled in an experience management system if an object-oriented modeling is used. The class hierarchy can be regarded also as a hierarchy for questions. Hence, it should be avoided to switch too often from an attribute of one class to an attribute of a class at a distant location in the class hierarchy. By interpreting the class hierarchy as a taxonomy, we can measure the similarity of attributes (or the similarity or relatedness of questions) by using the inter-class similarity measure introduced in Sect. 4.4.2, i.e., $sim(A_i, A_j) = sim_{\text{intra}}(C_i, C_j)$ where C_i is the object class in which the attribute A_i is defined.

The attribute similarity can then be integrated into the attribute selection criterion as a correction term as follows:

$$select\_with\_pref(A) = select\_without\_pref(A) \cdot \qquad \text{(Similar Attribute}$$
$$(1 - \alpha + \alpha \cdot sim(A, A_{prev})) \qquad \text{Preference)}$$

Here, A_{prev} denotes the attribute that has been asked in the previous question. The parameter $\alpha \in [0,1]$ specifies the influence of the attribute similarity on the selection criterion. The higher the parameter α is, the higher is the influence of the attribute similarity. Again, this correction can be used with any of the previously discussed attribute selection criteria.

6.4.2 Compiling Dialog Strategies

The just discussed attribute selection criteria can be used in compiled or interpreted dialog strategies. We now first discuss how strategies can be compiled.

Dialog strategy graphs can compiled during the development of an experience management system from a particular attribute selection approach and a given case base. During problem solving this dialog strategy graph is then used to enact the dialog. The easiest way to construct a dialog strategy graph is to apply a decision tree learning algorithm such as ID3 (Quinlan 1986) or C4.5 (Quinlan 1993). The resulting decision tree can be considered a dialog strategy graph. Alternatively, also learning approaches that construct acyclic directed graphs as an extension of decision trees (Kohavi 1994) can be applied. However, the construction of such decision trees to be used as dialog strategy graphs need some additional considerations.

Fig. 6.8 shows the standard recursive decision tree construction algorithm. In this formulation of the algorithm the four sub-procedures: *SelectAttribute*, *Split?*, *Partition*, and *SelectRangePartition* occur. In decision tree induction algorithms, these are realized in a particular way such that the classification accuracy of the resulting decision tree is optimized. For the purpose of dialog strategy learning these sub-procedures must be reconsidered.

Attribute Selection

Decision tree induction algorithms use the information gain criterion for attribute selection. For learning dialog strategies, different criteria must be considered as already discussed in Sect. 6.4.1.

Partitioning Numeric Attributes

The value range of numeric attributes (continuous value ranges) must be partitioned into a finite set of intervals. This is required to determine a finite set of successor sub-trees (Quinlan 1993). Such a partitioning is also required to compute the attribute selection criterion for numeric attributes. A discussion of this issue for the information gain criterion is given by Quinlan (1996). For decision tree induction this partitioning is done in such a way that the information gain is maximized. For dialog strategy learning it should be done in such a way that the criterion used for attribute selection yields a maximal value.

Input: Case Base **CB**
Output: An Decision Tree

procedure LearnTree(**CB**)
var
  Discriminator: Attribute
  RangePartition: List of Attribute Value Intervals

begin
  if Split?(**CB**) **then return** Leaf Node
  else
    Discriminator := SelectAttribute(**CB**)
    if NumericAttribute(*Discriminator*)
      then *(* Value range of numeric attribute must be partitioned *)*
        RangePartition := SelectRangePartition(**CB**, *Discriminator*)
        return MakeInternalNode(*Discriminator*
        LearnTree(Partition(*Discriminator*,*RangePartition*[1],**CB**))
        , ... ,
        LearnTree(Partition(*Discriminator*,*RangePartition*[m],**CB**)))
      else *(* Attribute is symbolic with the values $v_1, \ldots v_m$ *)*
        return MakeInternalNode(*Discriminator*,
        LearnTree(Partition(*Discriminator*,v_1,**CB**)), ... ,
        LearnTree(Partition(*Discriminator*,v_m,**CB**)))
end

Fig. 6.8. Tree Induction Algorithm

Termination Criterion

The *Split?* predicate is the termination criterion for the tree construction. In decision tree induction it is usually fulfilled when current case base **CB** only contains classified cases of a single class[4]. However, this approach can lead to too many questions and it is also not applicable for unclassified cases. Alternatively, one can set a threshold on the attribute selection criterion. If no attribute extends this threshold, tree construction can be terminated.

---

[4] Alternative tree pruning approaches are also discussed by Quinlan (1993) but are not relevant here.

Case-Base Partitioning

In traditional decision tree induction, a crisp partitioning is made such that a partition only contains cases that match exactly one of the selected attribute value. In the context just discussed this does not make much sense and leads to trees that do not contain enough questions. The reason for this is that with this criterion a tree is constructed that is as small as possible and that completely discriminates all cases. Imagine there is one attribute that already discriminates all cases, e.g., a case identifier attribute. Then, a tree with only one question concerning this identifier would be constructed. However, this is not appropriate although all cases are completely distinguished. In our scenario, questions should be selected such that a problem description is obtained that allows to determine the reusability (measured in terms of similarity) precisely enough. We are basically interested in the similarity of the best cases. Therefore the following partitioning criterion, originally introduced for dynamic strategies (Doyle and Cunningham 2000; Göker and Thompson 2000) should be preferred.

$$Partition(A, v, \mathbf{CB}) = \{(d, l) \in \mathbf{CB} | sim(pt(p_{A \leftarrow v}), d) \geq \theta\} \quad \text{(Similarity Partitioning)}$$

Here p is the problem description that is obtained by traversing the currently constructed tree to the current node to be partitioned and inserting the respective attribute value into p. The threshold θ should be selected in order chose the best cases only. Decreasing the threshold increases the accuracy of the attribute selection criterion, which depends on the current case base, but also increases the computational complexity.

The advantage of the compilation approach is that it requires only little effort during the problem solving phase, since only the dialog strategy graph needs to be traversed. An additional advantage of the explicit representation of the strategy as a tree is that it can be edited manually by the developer of the experience management system. This allows a combination of the automatic approach with the manual approach discussed in Sect. 6.3.

The disadvantages of the compilation approach are the high computational effort required for the tree construction (exponential in the depth of the tree (Martin and Hirschberg 1995)) and the fact that the tree must be reconstructed when the case-base changes significantly. Also, the tree does not immediately provide an alternative question if the current question cannot be answered by the user.

6.4.3 Dynamically Interpreted Strategies

Instead of compiling the attribute selection criterion and the case base into a dialog strategy, a strategy can also be computed at runtime, i.e., during the problem solving phase. Figure 6.9 shows this algorithm. It starts with the empty problem description and chooses a first question according to one of the attribute selection approaches introduced in Sect. 6.4.1. Depending on the answer to the question, the case base is reduced to the set of cases that is closest to the current (partially filled) problem description[5]. This process is iterated until a termination criterion is fulfilled. A useful termination criterion is to stop when the attribute selection criterion does not exceed a certain threshold any more.

Input: Case Base **CB**
Output: Problem Description p

procedure DynamicQuestioning(**CB**)
var
    A: Attribute
    v: Attribute value
    p: Problem description

begin
    p := nil
    while not Terminate?
        A := SelectAttribute(**CB**)
        Ask the question "What is the value of A"
        Let v be the answer given by the user
        CB := Partition(A,v,**CB**)
        $p := p_{A \leftarrow v}$
    end
    return p
end

Fig. 6.9. Dynamic Questioning Algorithm

Figure 6.9 only presents the basic form of a dynamic questioning algorithm. Extensions are required, to handle situations in which the user is not

---

[5] The Partition function refers to the similarity partitioning introduced before.

able to answer a question. Then, for example, the next best question can be chosen. It is also possible to integrate the retrieval step of the problem solving cycle directly into the question loop. Every time a question is answered, a retrieval can be started automatically and a list of the currently best cases can be updated. Dynamic questioning has been described in the literature mostly in combination with some kind of the information gain criterion for attribute selection (Cunningham and Smyth 1994; Albin 1997; Doyle and Cunningham 2000; Göker and Thompson 2000).

The advantage of the dynamic questioning approach is that it is always based on the current set of cases. There is no need to reconstruct a data structure when the case base has changed. Also, the approach can easily provide an alternative question if the originally selected question cannot be answered by the user.

The disadvantage of this approach is the computational effort involved during problem solving. The current set of cases must be analyzed with respect to every attribute for every question to be asked. In order to achieve a fast response time one must restrict the number of cases under consideration.

6.4.4 Learning from User Interaction

The approaches to building dynamic and adaptable dialog strategies investigated in the literature are so far limited to learning from case data. One important source for adaptability has not been taken into account so far: user interaction. Experience management systems that are in daily use easily record large volumes of interaction data. Analyzing this interaction data by means of machine learning algorithms should enable the improvement of a dialog strategy. This requires the identification of "good" and "bad" dialogs, for example by investigating unanswered questions, answers to questions that were revised afterwards, or questions for which additional information was requested (e.g. by pressing a "help" button). Also, the satisfaction of the user with the result can be explicitly asked at the end of the session with the experience management system. This is certainly a topic of interesting future research.

6.5 Experience Presentation

After experience has been retrieved and possibly adapted, it must be presented to the user. First, it is important to present the right amount of information. If the volume of information is too large, the user has to look at more information than s/he needs, which causes a cognitive effort for mental information filtering. On the other hand, if not enough information is presented, the user might not be able to solve the problem. Second, information should be presented in an appropriate way, i.e., such that it can be comprehended as fast as possible by the user.

Both issues also strongly depend on the case representation, or more precisely on the representation of the lesson. Information that is not captured in the lesson cannot be presented. Also different presentation forms cannot be automatically converted into each other. Hence, if necessary, different presentation forms of a lesson must be already contained in the lesson of the case. Hence, the experience presentation task is mainly restricted to *choosing* an appropriate presentation for a particular user. Also, determining the lessons and the appropriate presentation form strongly depends on the application domain. Therefore, we describe here only a few standard approaches.

6.5.1 Simple Lesson Lists

The most simple approach to experience presentation is to show a sorted list of lessons. The top ranked lessons are displayed, ordered according to their similarity. The lower part of the user interface shown in Fig. 6.10 is an example of this approach. Each row shows a possible solution. The similarity, the case identification, and the lesson is shown. Here, the lesson is only presented as a short text that is appropriate for an expert user of this system. A full introduction into this application example is given in Chap. 11.

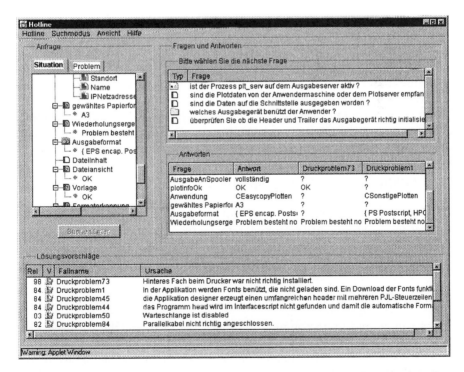

Fig. 6.10. User Communication Interface including Experience Presentation Part.

6.5.2 Experience Lists with External Links

The next, more informative experience presentation approach not only shows the lessons but the whole cases, including the experience characterization part. This helps the user to better understand the reason why a certain experience is proposed. This obviously increases the amount of information that needs to be displayed. In order to preserve the clearness of the presentation the information can be structured into several categories among which the user can switch. The hypertext approach easily supports such a structuring (Auriol et al. 1999). Additional information concerning the meaning of the attribute contained in the experience characterization can be linked to the individual attribute. This is particularly useful since we have to deal with many small and independent pieces of information, each of which relates to one characterization attribute.

Further, the lesson cannot always be restricted to a single line of text. Different users may have a different information need. Hypertext also helps to cope with this problem is a very simple manner. The lesson can be described by a hypertext containing information on different level of detail or different presentations. Then, the user can select what s/he needs to know.

Figure 6.11 shows an example of such a presentation approach for an experience management system for electronic components, here operational amplifiers (Vollrath et al. 1998; Bergmann et al. 1999a). The result page displayed as a static HTML page consists of a table that is structured into different categories of experience characterization attributes, called *Dynamic, Input, Output, Supply, Other*. Each row shows one experience attribute and each column one case. By clicking on the attribute names (left column) an attribute description is presented. By clicking on the cases (here, product identifiers displayed in the first row) a detailed product description including the data sheet of the product is shown (see browser window in the bottom of Fig. 6.11).

6.5.3 Adding Similarity Explanations

To increase the confidence in the reusability of the selected experience, an explanation of the similarity ranking may be required. Since the similarity is based on the experience characterization, this level provides the proper terms for such an explanation.

Coloring Attributes

A very simple and quite common approach is to explain the case selection through the local similarities related to the experience characterization attributes. Depending on the degree of the local similarity, the values of the characterization attributes of the cases are displayed in different color. Typically, the green attribute value indicates a high local similarity (sometimes

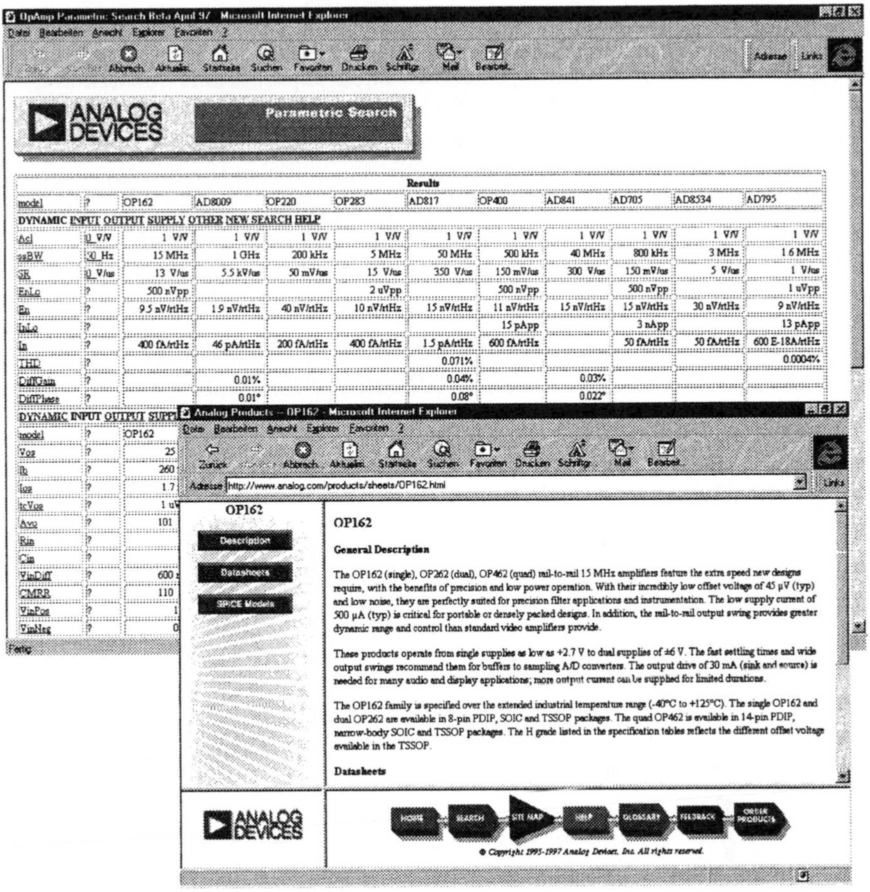

Fig. 6.11. User Communication Interface including Experience Presentation Part.

this color is only used to indicate a perfect match, i.e., the local similarity is 1) while a red attribute value indicates a low local similarity. Sometimes more than two colors are used to indicate local similarity values between 0 and 1. The simple two-color approach is also used in the previously shown example in Fig. 6.11.

Textual Explanations

More elaborated explanations of similarity can be given in the form of structured text. For each attribute a textual explanation is constructed that indicates the causes for a certain local similarity value. This explanation explains the relation between the two attribute values (from the problem description and the case, respectively) in a language that the user understands. Long explanations can also be structured by using hypertext.

Figure 6.12 shows an example of two such explanations constructed by an experience management system for electronic components (here, digital signal processors). The characteristic attributes are listed and for each an explanation is given for the local similarity. The color of the displayed explanations also indicates the local similarity as explained before. Additionally, the weight of each attribute is mentioned and the similarity it contributes to the global similarity is displayed. Such an explanation is particularly tar-

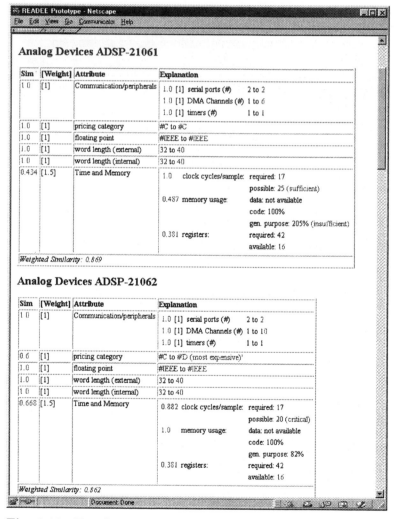

Fig. 6.12. Two Sample Explanations.

geted at expert users, which are the typical users of such a system. From the explanations given in Fig. 6.12 the expert user can see that the first DSP *ADSP-21061* is sufficiently fast for the application the user has in mind, but that it probably does not have enough memory to store the applications code and data. The second possible DSP *ADSP-21062* has sufficient memory, but the processing speed will reach the critical limit for the user's application and the DSP is more expensive than the first one.

6.5.4 Adaptive Experience Presentation

The previously discussed and most common approaches to experience presentation are static in the sense that an experience presentation is created which does not adapt automatically to the users needs. Only hypertext enables the user to get access to the piece of information s/he is interested in. Alternatively, the experience presentation can be made adaptive, i.e., depending on the previous user input (or a user profile) the information need of the user is predicted and compiled to her/his individual needs. Research on adaptive user interfaces (Thomas 1993; Armstrong et al. 1995; Langley 1997; Jameson 1999; Kay 1999) addresses these issues. However little work has been done today in the context of experience management systems. Examples of such work have presented by Brusilovsky and Schwarz (1997), Ardissono and Goy (1999), Waszkiewicz et al. (1999), Hölldobler (2001).

7. Experience Retrieval

> *"To solve a problem, retrieve a similar problem you have solved in the past [...]."*
>
> Alex Goodall

This chapter deals with the process of selecting experience items from the experience base that are relevant for the current problem to be solved. The key to experience retrieval is twofold: first it requires a good notion of when some kind of experience is relevant for a certain situation. This knowledge is captured in the similarity measures which are part of the reuse-related knowledge as discussed in Chap. 4. During retrieval the similarity measures are computed and the experience is evaluated with respect to the similarity results. Second, the retrieval must also be able deal with large case bases in order to ensure the scalability of an experience management system when the amount of available experience increases. Both issues are closely related to each other.

7.1 General Considerations

Retrieval means selecting cases with reusable experience from a case base. We can basically distinguish two kinds of retrieval tasks:

- retrieval tasks that operate on a fixed set of cases stored in a predefined location and
- retrieval tasks that include a search over distributed information sources to identify appropriate case bases.

The discussion here in this chapter is restricted to the first kind of retrieval tasks since for the purpose of experience management, the experience bases need active maintenance to ensure that the contained cases are of high quality. Hence, the location(s) of the case base(s) are known a-priori. Although this restriction is imposed, retrieval from distributed case-bases can be realized by issuing a retrieval job in the sense discussed here on each case base individually and combining the results.

7.1.1 Formal Retrieval Task

The retrieval task can be formally defined as follows:

Definition 7.1 (Retrieval Task) Given are

- a case base $\mathbf{CB} = \{C_1, \ldots, C_n\}$ with $C_i = (d_i, l_i)$,
- a similarity measure $sim : \mathbb{D} \times \mathbb{D} \to [0, 1]$, and
- a problem $d \in \mathbb{D}$ represented in the case description space.

The *retrieval task* is to efficiently determine either (three variants):

1. the set of most similar cases $\{C_1, \ldots, C_k\} \subseteq \mathbf{CB}$ such that $sim(d, d_i) = s$ holds for some s and all $i = 1 \ldots k$ and $sim(d, d_j) < s$ holds for all $C_j \in \mathbf{CB} \setminus \{C_1, \ldots, C_k\}$.
2. for a given k, the set of k most similar cases $\{C_1, \ldots, C_k\} \subseteq \mathbf{CB}$ such that $sim(d, d_j) \leq \min\{sim(d, d_i) | i = 1, \ldots k\}$ holds for all $C_j \in \mathbf{CB} \setminus \{C_1, \ldots, C_k\}$.
3. for a given similarity threshold s the set of cases above s, i.e., $\{C_1, \ldots, C_k\} \subseteq \mathbf{CB}$ such that $sim(d, d_i) \geq s$ holds for all $i = 1 \ldots k$ and that $sim(d, d_j) < s$ holds for all $C_j \in \mathbf{CB} \setminus \{C_1, \ldots, C_k\}$.

This definition includes for all three variants a kind of completeness and correctness condition. *Completeness* means that the retrieved set of cases includes all cases that fulfill the desired retrieval criterion (e.g. being a most similar case for variant (1)). *Correctness* means that all retrieved cases fulfill indeed the retrieval criterion. The difficulty with this retrieval task is that the following two requirements must be fulfilled at the same time:

1. to support arbitrary similarity measures and thereby not to restrict the kind of knowledge about utility that can be considered and
2. to be able to handle large case bases efficiently.

Obviously, a sequential brute-force approach to retrieval is able to handle arbitrary similarity measures (as long as they are computable) and thereby easily fulfills the first requirement, but this approach is not efficient for large case bases and thus fails to fulfill the second requirement. On the other hand, standard databases are able to handle large data sets very efficiently, but they are very restricted to using equality as similarity. Recent database approaches (Seidl and Kriegel 1997; Berchtold et al. 1998; Gionis et al. 1999) try to overcome this restriction and also allow similarity-based queries, but the kind of similarity measures that are supported are still limited and are primarily influenced by spatial relations.

7.1.2 Storing Case Data in Databases

The previous discussion concerning databases gives rise to the more general question of where to store the case data. Small case bases can be easily kept and handled in the main memory, but in practice large case bases require that the case data is stored in a database. To link a database with a similarity-based retrieval function, different architectural variants are possible (Donner and Roth-Berhofer 1999).

Retrieval Inside the Database

From a purely technical point of view, the ideal approach is to integrate the similarity-based retrieval function into the database itself. This enables efficient data access and ensures an up-to-date and consistent view on the data. In such an ideal scenario, the database would be able to automatically process a similarity-based query formulated in a standardized query format enabling flexible representation of similarity measures. The disadvantage of this approach from a commercial point of view is that, if not supported by a database vendor directly, it depends on a proprietary implementation and requires strong linking with the details of the database.

Retrieval on Top of the Database

The second architectural variant is to realize the similarity-based retrieval on top of the database. The retrieval engine becomes a separate module that interfaces with the database to get access to the case data. Such an approach has the advantage of being independent from a proprietary database implementation. Here again, different variants are possible.

- *Bulk-loading all cases into the retrieval engine:* This approach replicates the case base inside the similarity-based retrieval engine. The shortcomings of this approach are that the required storage space is doubled and that it is necessary to update the duplicated case base every time when the database is updated. Hence, major consistency problems arise.

- *Storing only an index structure for the cases in the retrieval engine:* Here, the problem of duplicating the product data is avoided, but the consistency problem of the index structure remains.
- *Approximating similarity-based retrieval with SQL-queries:* The similarity-based retrieval function accesses the data in the database dynamically through SQL queries. This approach avoids the consistency problem and always relies on the up-to-date data.

7.1.3 Overview of Approaches

Several retrieval approaches have been developed so far, some of them are able to handle case data stored in a database. Fig. 7.1 gives an overview.

The brute force retrieval approach evaluates for each issued problem every case with respect to its similarity. It does therefore not imply any restrictions on the similarity measures that can be handled. Index-based approaches compile a kind of index (a tree or a graph) for a give case base and similarity measure. Retrieval is then guided by this index. This allows to reduce the number of similarity computations and thereby increases the retrieval efficiency at the cost of re-constructing the index when the case base or the similarity measure changes. Such an index can also be integrated into a database.

Finally, the SQL approximation approach stores cases in a traditional database and accesses them via standard SQL queries. Similarity-based retrieval is realized by an incremental, dynamic computation of SQL queries that cover successively larger volumes of the representation space. Since no index is constructed, this approach is appropriate for highly dynamic case bases.

All three kinds of approaches support the three variants for retrieval goals (Def. 7.1) and have been intensively investigated. We now discuss these approaches in more detail.

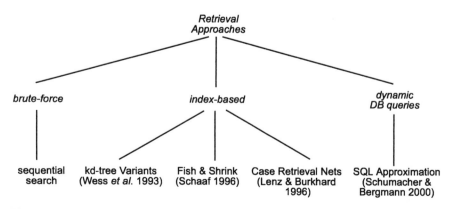

Fig. 7.1. Overview on Retrieval Approaches.

7.2 Sequential Retrieval

Sequential retrieval evaluates the similarity of each case from the case base
with respect to the query and maintains a list that collects the best matching
cases. This simple algorithm is shown in Fig. 7.2.

Input: Case Base **CB**, similarity measure sim, and problem description d.
Output: Sorted list of cases scq

procedure Retrieve(**CB**, sim, d)
   var
   scq: Numerically sorted List of Structure
     object: Case ID
     simval: $[0, 1]$
   s: $[0, 1]$

   begin
     $scq :=$ empty;
     for each $(d_{ID}, l_{ID}) \in$ **CB do**
       $s := sim(d, d_{ID})$ (* Compute similarity *)
       if $Retrieval\_Goal(s, scq)$ **then** $Update\_List(ID, s, scq)$
     return scq
   end

Fig. 7.2. Sequential Retrieval Algorithm

In this algorithm, the predicate *Retrieval_Goal* and the procedure *Up-
date_List* determine the retrieval criterion. They can be defined such that
only the most similar cases are retrieved, such that the k-most similar cases
are retrieved (the similarity queue scq records the best cases seen up to a certain point in time), or such that all cases that extend a similarity threshold
are recorded. This retrieval algorithm has the advantage that it can be implemented very easily and that it can handle arbitrary similarity measures and
case representations. Since it does not pre-compile an index structure prior
to the retrieval, it can also work on highly dynamic case bases. However, it
does not scale-up with growing case bases, which is the major and limiting
disadvantage and the motivation for the subsequent approaches.

7.3 Indexing by kd-Tree Variants

Now, we present a retrieval approach which allows to find the most similar case(s) in an efficient way (Wess et al. 1993; Wess 1995; Althoff et al. 1998). This approach is restricted to cases represented as attribute-value pairs or cases given in a bounded (see Def. 3.19) object-oriented representation. The core idea behind this approach is a new indexing structure we call Inreca-Tree. This indexing structure is based on the concept of the kd-tree (Bentley 1975), which is a multi-dimensional binary search tree. Such a tree – automatically constructed before consultations are performed – structures the space of available cases, based on their observed density. During retrieval, the tree focuses the search for the most similar case(s) and thereby avoids the investigation of all available cases.

Index structures for similarity-based search have also been developed in the database research. Examples are R-trees (Guttman 1984), R^+-trees (Sellis et al. 1987), and X-trees(Berchtold et al. 1996). However, these approaches are limited to similarity measures that are based on geometric distance functions and cannot be easily by extended to arbitrary similarity measures. Recent database research attempts to overcome this limitation. A comprehensive overview of extended approaches that also support quadratic form distance measures (see Sect. 4.3.2) is given by Seidl (1998). However this is still a limitation that is too strong for similarity measures that occur in experience management.

7.3.1 The Standard kd-Tree

The basic idea of a kd-tree (Bentley 1975; Friedman et al. 1977) is to structure the search space for a set of k-dimensional objects by completely partitioning the space into hierarchically structured sub-spaces (see Fig. 7.3). A kd-tree is a binary tree. Each inner node is labelled with an attribute name A_i and the two branches leading to the two child nodes are labelled with a value v for this attribute. More precisely, the left branch is labelled with $<= v$ and the right branch is labelled with $> v$. Every node of a kd-tree represents a subset of the objects. The root node of the tree represents the whole set of objects. Each inner node partitions the represented objects into two disjoint subsets according to whether the objects' value of the attribute A_i is less or equal than v (then it belongs to the left child node) or greater than v (then it belongs to the right child node). Each leaf node of a kd-tree is called *bucked* and is labelled with the subset of objects it represents. In a kd-tree, an attribute can occur more than once.

The basic procedure for building a kd-tree is quite simple and similar to the top-down construction of a decision tree (Quinlan 1983). The whole set of objects is partitioned recursively. For this purpose, a discriminator attribute A_i and a partitioning value v is selected. The two partitions are computed

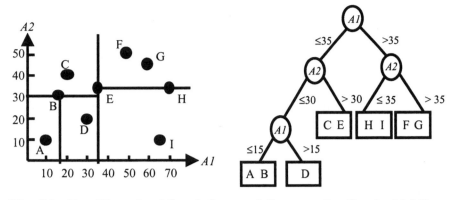

Fig. 7.3. Two-Dimensional Search Space and Corresponding Standard kd-Tree

and the procedure is recursively applied to each of the two partitions, until a certain termination criterion is fulfilled.

The kd-tree supports similarity search with respect to the Euclidean distance. Therefore, it is used as a static index structure. The tree is traversed from the root node to a bucket by following the branches according the query's value of the attribute in the respective branch. The objects in the bucket are first candidates for being most similar to the query. However, more similar objects can be in neighboring buckets and therefore similarity search requires backtracking. This backtracking strategy is guided by a sophisticated criterion. We will explain this in more detail in Sect. 7.3.4 after we have introduced an extension of kd-trees for indexing cases.

7.3.2 The Inreca Tree

The Inreca-Tree is an n-ary tree in which the branches represent constraints for certain attributes of the cases. In contrast to a standard kd-tree, we need to handle ordered and unordered value ranges as well as unknown attribute values. Therefore, we introduce different kinds of branches as shown in Fig. 7.4.

Attributes with an ordered value range partition the set of cases with respect to a certain value v_{ij}. The cases are divided into sets of cases in which the respective attribute has a value which is smaller than v_{ij}, larger than v_{ij}, equal to v_{ij}, or unknown. Attributes with an unordered (finite) value range partition the cases into one set for each value contained in the value range and one additional set for cases in which the attribute value is unknown. The leaves of an Inreca-Tree (we call them buckets as in a kd-tree) contain all cases that fulfill all constraints that occur in the path from the root of the tree to the respective leaf. If cases are given in a bounded object-oriented representation the attribute labels that are used in the tree are in

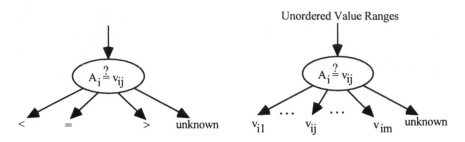

Fig. 7.4. Branches of the Inreca-Tree for Ordered and Unordered Value Ranges.

fact *attribute paths*, i.e., sequences of class name – attribute name pairs that clearly point to a certain value in the case representation.

Fig. 7.5 shows an example of an Inreca-Tree. The top of the tree shows a branch node for the attribute *Voltage*, which holds values from the ordered type *Real*. This node partitions the set of available cases into three subsets in which the voltage attribute has a value which is less than 10, equal to 10, higher than 10, or unknown. The next node partitions the set of cases with a voltage higher than 10 into three subsets, depending on the *switched* attribute. At the leaf nodes of the tree, some buckets are displayed which contain the respective cases. Each case in a bucket fulfills all the constraints recorded from the root of the tree to the bucket. For example, in case 3,

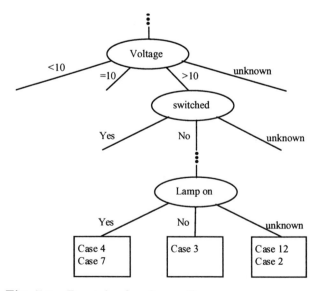

Fig. 7.5. Example of an Inreca-Tree.

the following is known: the *voltage* is higher than 10, the attribute *switched* indicates *no*, and the *lamp* is not on.

7.3.3 Building the Inreca Tree

The Inreca-Tree is built prior to the first consultation of the system. It is assumed that all available cases are already stored in a case base **CB** and are accessible. The basic recursive procedure for building an Inreca-Tree is quite simple and is described in Fig. 7.6. Every node within the tree represents a subset of the case base and the root node represents the whole case base. Every inner node partitions the represented case set into disjoint subsets.

The described algorithm uses the three sub-procedures *SelectAttribute*, *SelectValue*, and *Split?*. The *Split?* procedure determines the depth of the Inreca-Tree. It uses a criterion to determine whether a new sub-tree must be generated or whether the cases in the current partition are collected in a bucket (leaf node). Different termination criteria are possible, e.g., based on the size of the partition, based on the distribution of the cases that occur in the partition, etc. The *SelectAttribute* procedure determines the attribute that is used for partitioning the case base in the current branch. In case of an attribute with an ordered value range, the procedure *SelectValue* determines the exact value used for splitting the case base. Different choice criteria for attributes and values can be used for constructing an Inreca-Tree (Wess et al. 1993):

Inter-quartile Distance/Similarity

To estimate the dispersion, the inter-quartile distance (Koopmans 1987) can be used. While the median splits a given distribution of values into two equally sized areas, quartiles split them into four. The first quartile q_1 (25% quartile) divides the lower half of the distribution into two equally sized areas as the third quartile q_3 (75% quartile) does with the upper half of the distribution. The median is denoted as the second quartile. The greater the distance between these quartiles, the greater is the dispersion of the attribute values. During tree construction the attribute having the maximal dispersion with respect to the used local similarity measure *sim* is selected as the discriminating one. It denotes that we select that attribute for discriminating purposes where the respective quartiles have the lowest local similarity (which corresponds to the greatest distance).

Average Similarity Measure

The idea behind this approach is to build sub-trees and buckets based on cases that are as similar as possible with respect to the global similarity measure. The average similarity measure estimates the dispersion of cases

Input: Case Base **CB**, similarity measure *sim*
Output: An Inreca Tree

procedure CreateTree(**CB**)
var
  Diskriminator: Attribute
  Value: Attribute Value

begin
  if not *Split?*(**CB**) **then return** MakeBucket(**CB**)
  else
    Diskriminator := *SelectAttribute*(**CB**)
    if OrderedValueRange(Diskriminator)
      then
        Value := *SelectValue*(**CB**, Diskriminator)
        return MakeInternalOrderedNode(Diskriminator, Value,
          CreateTree(Partition$_<$(Diskriminator,Value,**CB**)),
          CreateTree(Partition$_>$(Diskriminator,Value,**CB**)),
          CreateTree(Partition$_=$(Diskriminator,Value,**CB**)),
          CreateTree(Partition$_{unknown}$ (Diskriminator, **CB**)))
      else
        return MakeInternalUnorderedNode(Diskriminator,
          CreateTree(Partition$_1$(Diskriminator,**CB**)), ... ,
          CreateTree(Partition$_m$(Diskriminator,**CB**)),
          CreateTree(Partition$_{unknown}$(Diskriminator, **CB**)))
end

Fig. 7.6. Basic Inreca Tree Building Algorithm

with respect to a given partition of the case base. The average similarity between the cases within a partitioning subset is used as choice criterion. The partitioning attribute is the one with the greatest average similarity for a chosen partition.

Information Gain Measure

The information gain measure (see Sect. 6.4.1 and (Shannon 1948)) computes the difference of entropy between a case base and its partition built from a particular attribute. The entropy evaluates the impurity of a set of cases with respect to the target attribute (e.g. a solution class) that must be determined in advance. The procedure selects the attribute that provides the best information gain.

It has been shown that these different criteria have an impact on the structure of the resulting trees (see Fig. 7.7) and on the retrieval efficiency (Wess et al. 1993). For a particular application and case base, an optimal criterion must be selected by systematic experimentation.

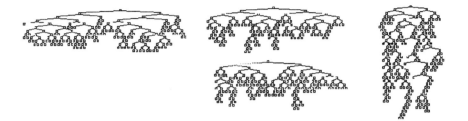

Fig. 7.7. Different Inreca Trees Resulting from Different Partitioning Strategies.

7.3.4 Retrieval with the Inreca-Tree

We now explain how the Inreca-Tree can be used for efficiently retrieving the most similar case(s) for a given new problem case. The search is done via a recursive tree search procedure according to the global similarity measure sim. During the search, the two test procedures called Ball-Overlap-Bounds (BOB) and Ball-Within-Bounds (BWB) are used to focus on the relevant search region. These procedures, to be described in detail, are extensions of equivalent procedures known from kd-trees (Bentley 1975). While the search is performed, a priority list scq is maintained which contains the k most similar cases known so far, together with their similarity to the problem case. This list is updated when new cases are visited. The recursive procedure (beginning with the root node) runs as follows (see Fig. 7.8):

- If the current node is an inner node, the procedure is first iterated on one of the child nodes. The procedure follows the branch whose constraint is fulfilled by the value of the respective attribute contained in the problem description.
- If the current node is a leaf one, the priority list is updated according to the similarity of the cases belonging to the bucket with the problem case. Then the BWB test checks whether it is guaranteed that all k-nearest neighbors have been found. If this is the case, the search terminates. If this is not the case, the search backtracks to a parent node and considers to investigate an additional portion of the tree.

- If the current node is an inner node that is reached through backtracking from a child node, a test is executed to look whether it is necessary to inspect one of the other child nodes. This is done through the BOB test. If this test is false, the partition of the other child nodes cannot contain any k-nearest neighbors with respect to the query. Therefore, they arc not examined further and the search backtracks to the parent of the current node. If this test is true, the procedure is iterated on these nodes, i.e., it continues the search in the respective sub-tree.

Input: Inreca Tree T, similarity measure sim, and problem description d.
Output: Sorted list of cases scq

procedure Retrieve(T, sim, d)
var
   scq: Sorted List of Structure
     object: Case ID
     simval: $[0, 1]$
   s: $[0, 1]$
   T',T^*: Inreca Tree Nodes

begin
  if T is leaf node
    then
    for each case (d_{ID}, l_{ID}) of T **do**
      $s := sim(d, d_{ID})$ (* Compute similarity *)
      if Retrieval_Goal(s, scq) **then** Update_List(ID, s, scq)
    else   (* T is an inner node *)
    Determine the successor node T' of T
      that matches with the attribute in d
    Retrieve(T', sim, d)
    for each successor node T^* of T with $T^* \neq T'$ **do**
      if BOB test is satisfied for T^* **then** Retrieve(T^*, sim, d)
    if BWB test is satisfied **then terminate** Retrieve
end

Fig. 7.8. Basic Inreca Tree Retrieval Algorithm

The BOB (Ball Overlap Bounds) and BWB (Ball Within Bounds) test procedures have relatively simple geometrical interpretations (Fig. 7.9): For these tests, an m-dimensional "ball" is drawn around the current problem description. The radius of this ball is determined by the similarity of the least similar case which is currently in the priority list scq (k most similar case). We only call this shape a "ball" for historical reasons, since it really was a ball in the traditional kd-tree approach, which was defined for a geometrical similarity measure. In the general case in which we are interested here, we can get different kinds of shapes, depending on the similarity measure, particularly depending on the aggregation function. The surface of this shape is defined as the set of points that have the same similarity to the problem description, which is the similarity of the k most similar case in scq. Every case that is outside this ball is less similar than the currently known k most similar cases and need consequently not to be visited. In order to recognize whether a node is "of interest" (it may contain some candidates), the geometrical bounds of the node are used to define a test point that is most similar to the current query but still lies within the geometrical bounds of the current node. If this test point is in the ball it means that the ball overlaps with the node and then there may be a candidate for the similarity list in this node. This search is conducted by the BOB test. Figure 7.9 shows a two-dimensional BOB test, where the test point X_{min1} belonging to the node K1 is in the ball (and therefore it may be of interest to explore this node), but where the test points X_{min2} and X_{min3} for K2 and K3 are not in the ball. Consequently, K1 requires further exploration, while K2 and K3 need not be visited. The other question to answer is, whether the ball around the query Xq lies completely in the geometric bounds of already explored nodes (let us call this set the *bounding box*), or not. To test this, one verifies if the bounding box has no intersection with the ball. Figure 7.9 shows a successful two-dimensional BWB test.

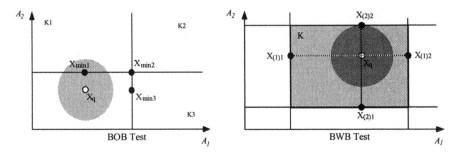

Fig. 7.9. BOB Test (left) and BWB Test (right).

7.3.5 Properties of kd-Tree Based Retrieval

In the best case, when no backtracking is required, retrieval with the Inreca-Tree leads to a computation time that is proportional to the depth of the tree; the retrieval effort is $O(log(n))$, with n being the number of cases in the case base. However, in the worst case in which backtracking is required for every node, the whole tree must be investigated, leading to a retrieval effort of $O(n)$. Experiments conducted in several domains have clearly shown that in the average case important reductions in the retrieval speed compared to a linear retrieval approach can be achieved (Wess et al. 1993; Wess 1995). However, this advantage is getting smaller the more attributes occur in the case representation. This is due to the fact that for higher dimensions, the computational effort for the BOB and BWB test is increasing significantly.

A disadvantage of this approach is that it implies some restrictions on the similarity measures that can be used. Due to the geometrical implications underlying the BOB and BWB test and their extensions, it must be assumed that ordered attributes have a monotonic local similarity measure (see Def. 4.13). An additional problem is that, until now no extensions have been developed so far that enable the use of inter-class similarity measures and class-specific aggregation functions (see Sect. 4.4.2) as well as multi-value attributes as common in object-oriented approaches. A second problem is connected with all index-based approaches. The construction of the Inreca tree is computationally expensive, depending on the criterion for attribute and value selection. Also, some of the suggested criteria for attribute selection depend on the global similarity measure and thereby also on the chosen weights. This leads to problems when weights are at least partially determined by the user preference and hence change from problem to problem. In such situations an "old" Inreca tree still ensures complete and correct retrieval, even if it is not re-constructed for each query (which of course does not make any sense), but the efficiency can decrease. This prevents the application of this approach in highly dynamic domains, since a rapid change of problems and case data requires a rapid re-construction of the Inreca tree.

7.4 Fish and Shrink Retrieval

Fish and Shrink (Schaaf 1995; Schaaf 1996; Schaaf 1998) is the second index-based approach to retrieval which is not limited to simple attribute-value or object-oriented representations. It is particularly suited to applications that require highly complex similarity computations which occur, for example, when cases are represented as graphs. The problem that has to be solved before being able to handle large cases bases is to handle medium size case bases efficiently, which is already a problem due to the inherent complexity of the similarity assessment itself. In such situations, the brute-force approach is not appropriate since it would require computing the similarity to each case during retrieval. In principle, we are now dealing with the same goal as before, which is to reduce the number of similarity computations necessary to perform a complete and correct retrieval.

The Fish and Shrink approach assumes that the case representation can be decomposed into several *complex attributes*. The attributes are complex in the sense that each such attribute has itself a complex data structure, for example, a graph. Hence, the computation of the local similarity with respect to each complex attribute is computationally complex (which justifies calling the attribute complex). In original literature describing this approach, these complex attributes are also called "aspects" (see discussion by Schaaf 1998) which aims at avoiding confusion with standard attribute-value representations. The assumed representation is in fact an attribute-value representation on the top-level, only the types of the attributes are of complex nature, i.e., they can be graphs, object networks, formulas in predicate logic, etc. Therefore, the usual assumption that local similarity measures are computationally inexpensive is not made here. This approach is particularly motivated from experience management applications in the domain of architectural design, where, for example, the topology graph of design objects is one such complex attribute (Coulon 1995).

7.4.1 Basic Idea

The basic idea behind Fish and Shrink is to construct and to continuously refine a network of links between the cases of the case base. One such link connects a complex attribute of one case with the corresponding attribute of a second case. The link has a similarity value assigned which is the local similarity between the two (complex) attribute values of the two cases that are linked. Thereby, the retrieval structure contains pre-compiled knowledge about similarity between the cases in the case base. This pre-compiled knowledge can be used to determine bounds on the similarity between a problem description and certain cases in the case base without the necessity to compute the similarity via the complex similarity measure.

For this purpose, the assumption is made that the triangle inequality holds for the local similarity measures. Expressed in terms of distance measures, Fig. 7.10 illustrates the bounds by considering a geometrical interpretation of the distance. If the similarity (or distance as shown in this figure) between a test case T and some cases C_1, C_2, and C_3, is known and stored as pre-compiled knowledge in a network of links, and the similarity (or distance) between a new problem description P and the test case T is computed, this allows to determine lower and upper bounds on the similarity (or distance) between the new problem P and the cases C_1 to C_3. In Fig. 7.10 the upper and lower bounds for case C_1 are indicated. What is intuitively obvious for the geometrical interpretation of distance, holds in the general case for similarity or distance measures that are symmetric and fulfill the triangle inequality. However, we can waive the symmetry assumption by the cost of pre-computing the similarity between the cases in the case base in both directions.

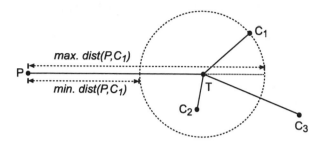

Fig. 7.10. Determination of Upper and Lower Bounds on Distance.

From the triangle inequality immediately follow these two inequations.

$$sim(P,C) \geq sim(P,T) + sim(T,C) - 1 \qquad \text{(Upper Bound)}$$

$$sim(P,C) \leq sim(P,T) - sim(C,T) + 1 \qquad \text{(Lower Bound)}$$

The inequality for the lower bound can be simplified as follows if the symmetry assumption for the similarity measure can be made. This allows to determine the upper and the lower bounds just from knowing the values for $sim(T,C)$; the values for $sim(C,T)$ need not be pre-computed and stored in addition.

$$sim(P,C) \leq sim(P,T) - sim(T,C) + 1 \qquad \begin{array}{l}\text{(Lower Bound in the} \\ \text{Symmetric Case)}\end{array}$$

7.4.2 Retrieval Algorithm

This idea can be turned into the following retrieval algorithm (Schaaf 1996). While the original algorithm makes use of distance measures, we present a variation of this approach based on similarity measures (see Fig. 7.11). This algorithm assumes symmetric similarity measures but it can be easily extended to asymmetrical measures.

The idea of Fish and Shrink is that the similarity between the problem description d and a test case (d_T, l_d) restricts both, the minimum similarity

Input: Case Base **CB**, similarity measure sim, and problem description d.
Output: Sorted list of cases

procedure Retrieve(**CB**, sim, d)
var
   $bounds$: **Array** $[1..|$**CB**$|]$ **of**
     min, max: $[0, 1]$
   p: $[0, 1]$ *(* Precision Line *)*

begin
   for each $(d_{ID}, l_{ID}) \in$ **CB do**   *(* Initialize Intervals *)*
     $bounds[ID].min := 0$
     $bounds[ID].max := 1$
   while not Complete **and not** Interrupted **do**
     Determine precision line p
     Choose (fish) a case $(d_T, l_T) \in$ **CB** with $bounds[T].max{=}p$
     compute $sim(d, d_T)$
     $bounds[T].min := bounds[T].max := sim(d, d_T)$
     for each $(d_{ID}, l_{ID}) \in$ **CB** with
       pre-computed similarity $sim(d_T, d_{ID})$ **and**
       $bounds[ID].min \neq bounds[ID].max$ **do**
         $bounds[ID].min :=$
           $\min\{sim(d, d_T) + sim(d_T, d_{ID}) - 1, bounds[ID].min\}$
         $bounds[ID].max :=$
           $\max\{sim(d, d_T) - sim(d_T, d_{ID}) + 1, bounds[ID].max\}$
   return
      $\{(d_{ID}, l_{ID})$ with $bounds[ID] \,|\, (d_{ID}, l_{ID}) \in$ **CB** $\wedge bounds[ID].min \geq p\}$
end

Fig. 7.11. Fish and Shrink Retrieval Algorithm

as well as a maximum similarity between problem description and some of the "neighbors" of the test case. The algorithm maintains the maximal minimum similarity and the minimal maximum similarity for each case (d_{ID}, l_{ID}). The interval defined by the two values $bounds[ID].min$ and $bounds[ID].max$ describes the range of possible similarities to the problem. Its upper bound only decreases and the lower bound can only rise. Both movements of boundaries are results of one direct comparison between the problem and a test case.

Figure 7.12 describes the behavior of a case which is at first "viewed" from test case T1 and then also "viewed" from test cases T2 and T3. By knowing the similarity between the problem and T1 the interval of possible similarities between the case ID and the problem d can be restricted without having it tested in any way. Direct tests of T2 and T3 further restrict this interval. The test of T2 lowers the upper bound, while test of T3 raises the lower bound such that the interval collapses and a certain similarity value is determined.

By these means, derivable guesses become more and more precise until some definitive statements become possible. The ongoing process leads to the exact similarity between each case and the problem if it runs until its termination. Normally the process is manually or automatically interrupted before termination obtaining the demanded results.

Completion Predicate and Precision Line

The previously described algorithm contains two sub-procedures, one to determine whether the retrieval is complete and a second to determine the so-called precision line. With these two sub-procedures it is possible to realize different retrieval criteria. Fish and Shrink can either supply all cases that are more similar than a given threshold s or deliver the k best cases, optionally including a ranking or giving the exact distance for each of the k best cases. The completeness predicate realizes exactly the retrieval criteria, i.e., it returns *true* if the intervals have been shrunk enough to determine which cases fulfill the retrieval criterion. The precision line p is defined as the highest possible similarity of cases for which it is not yet decided whether they fulfill the retrieval criterion. Fig. 7.13 shows four different scenarios of cases with similarity intervals, each of which shows a different retrieval criterion.

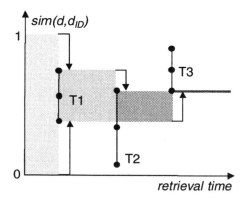

Fig. 7.12. Shrinking of Similarity Intervals during Retrieval.

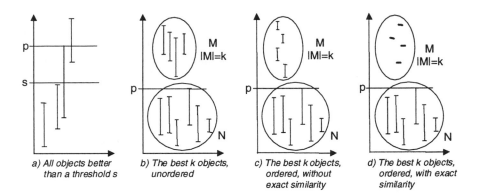

Fig. 7.13. Scenarios for Different Retrieval Criteria.

Suppose the given threshold is s, then it is not necessary to test those cases directly whose minimum similarity is above s (Fig. 7.13a). With the same argument those cases whose maximum similarity is below s need not be tested. It can never exceed the threshold s. Only those cases have to be tested whose intervals overlap s. The number of overlapping intervals decreases permanently because intervals are shrinking continuously.

Figure 7.13b shows how to get the k best cases without a ranking. The case base is partitioned into two subsets of cases M and N such that all similarity intervals of the cases in M are above those of the cases in N and there is no overlapping. The termination criterion is fulfilled if the set M contains k cases, i.e., when k cases have passed the precision line.

If the user asks for k cases with ranking but without exact distances, Fish and Shrink stops if the set M contains k cases whose intervals do not overlap one another (Fig. 7.13c). If the user wants exact similarities of the k best cases, Fish and Shrink stops if the set M contains k cases whose intervals have size 0 (Fig. 7.13d).

7.4.3 Properties of Fish and Shrink

Initial experimental results have demonstrated that the Fish and Shrink retrieval is able to significantly speed-up retrieval compared to a sequential retrieval approach (talk by J. Schaaf at EWCBR'96 in which the paper of Schaaf 1996 was presented). The advantage increases the more costly the similarity computation is and the more similarity values are pre-compiled. A second advantage of this approach is that it can be used as an anytime algorithm. The retrieval can be interrupted at any time and still deliver useful results, although the retrieval criterion has not been completely fulfilled. A third advantage is that this algorithm is incremental in the sense that it can to some degree deal with changing case bases. However, the index, i.e., the network of similarity values between cases, must be maintained when cases become invalid or new cases arise. Inserting and deleting a case and updating the index structure is simple but involves pre-computing certain similarities to existing cases in the case base, which can be computationally complex. Also, invalid cases must not be removed from the network but just marked as invalid. They can still serve as useful test cases to speedup the retrieval.

The disadvantage of the Fish and Shrink approach is the assumption that the triangle inequality holds for the local similarity measures. However, this assumption can be weakened in the sense that it is allowed that the similarity measure makes a certain error with respect to the triangle inequality. If an estimation about the size of this error can be made, this allows to determine an estimation of an upper bound of the error made by the Fish and Shrink retrieval (Schaaf 1998).

7.5 Case Retrieval Nets

The third index-based approach to retrieval are *case retrieval nets* (CRNs) (Lenz 1996; Lenz and Burkhard 1996b; Lenz and Burkhard 1996a; Lenz 1999). A case retrieval net is a directed graph with nodes representing cases as well as the so-called *information entities* (IEs) contained in the cases (e.g. attribute value pairs). These nodes are linked according to the degree to which they influence each other, e.g. through a local similarity or by a contribution to a global similarity. Given a set of cases, such a case retrieval net is constructed prior to retrieval. During retrieval, the IEs that occur in the current problem description are activated and this initial activation is propagated through the case retrieval net by a kind of spreading activation mechanism. Cases that are activated at the end of this process are those selected by the retrieval approach.

7.5.1 The Case Retrieval Net Index Structure

The most fundamental items in the context of CRNs are so-called information entities (IEs). These may represent any basic knowledge item, such as a particular attribute value pair. A case then consists of a set of such IEs, and the case base is a net with nodes for the IEs observed in the domain and additional nodes denoting the particular cases. IE nodes are connected by similarity arcs, and a case node is reachable from its constituting IE nodes via relevance arcs. Different degrees of similarity and relevance may be expressed by varying arc weights.

Information Entity

An information entity (IE) is an atomic knowledge item in the domain, i.e. an IE represents the lowest granularity of knowledge representation, such as a particular attribute value pair. A case is subdivided into sets of information entities. This view of cases does not only cover attribute value representations but also object-oriented representations (Magnus 1999) and particularly well textual case representations (Lenz et al. 1998).

Case Retrieval Net

For a given case base **CB** we define a case retrieval net as a directed labeled graph (see Fig. 7.14). It contains two kinds of nodes:

- *IE nodes* **E:** for each different IE in the cases of the case base an IE node is introduced
- *Case nodes* **C:** for each case in the case base a case node is introduced.

Two IE nodes IE_1 and IE_2 are linked with a directed link from IE_1 to IE_2 if a local similarity between the two IEs can be established that is greater than 0. This is, for example, the case if the two IEs represent two attribute value pairs with the same attribute A and with values v_1 and v_2 such that $sim_A(v_1, v_2) > 0$. The link from IE_1 to IE_2 is labeled with the local similarity value between the two IEs. If the local similarity function is symmetric, this link can be extended to a bidirectional link; if it is asymmetrical, we can get two links, with exchanged source and destination nodes, each of which is labeled with the respective local similarity value. The network among the IEs can be represented as an adjacent matrix $\sigma = [\sigma_{ij}] \in [0,1]^{\mathbf{E} \times \mathbf{E}}$.

Further, a case retrieval net contains a link from an IE node to a case node C if the IE is contained in the case C. The link can be labeled with a relevance value that indicates the weight of the IE for the case. For example, this can be the weight of the corresponding attribute in the global similarity measure, but this also allows case specific weights as introduced in Sect. 4.3.7. The network between the IE and case nodes can also be represented as an adjacent matrix $\rho = [\rho_{ij}] \in [0,1]^{\mathbf{E} \times \mathbf{C}}$.

Finally, each node $n \in \mathbf{E} \cup \mathbf{C}$ in a case retrieval net is labeled with a propagation function $\pi_n : [0,1]^{\mathbf{E}} \to [0,1]$. When dealing with attribute value

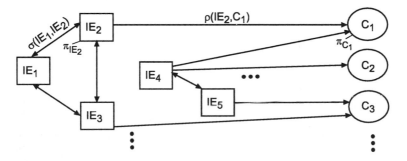

Fig. 7.14. Case Retrieval Net.

representations, this propagation function is the aggregation function Φ from which the global similarity measure is composed (see Def. 4.15).

7.5.2 The Retrieval Algorithm

Retrieval with CRNs is realized by a propagation of activations through the network. An activation can formally be considered a function $\alpha : \mathbf{E} \cup \mathbf{C} \rightarrow [0..1]$ that assigns each node in the network an activation value. The algorithm basically works in three steps. First, the IEs that occur in the query are activated ($\alpha(IE) = 1$). Second, the activation is propagated along the σ links to other IEs. Third, the activation is propagated along the ρ links to the case nodes. Figure 7.15 shows this algorithm in pseudo code.

Input: Case Retrieval Net $(\mathbf{E}, \mathbf{C}, \sigma, \rho, \pi)$ and problem description d.
Output: Sorted list of cases

procedure Retrieve($(\mathbf{E}, \mathbf{C}, \sigma, \rho, \pi)$, d)
var
  α : **array** $[1..|\mathbf{E} \cup \mathbf{C}|]$ of $[0, 1]$

begin
  for each IE$\in \mathbf{E} \cup \mathbf{C}$ **do** α[IE] := 0   (* *Initialize Activations* *)
  for each IE$\in d$ **do** α[IE] := 1
  for each IE$\in \mathbf{E}$ such that it exists IE'$\in \mathbf{E}$ such that σ(IE',IE) > 0 **do**
    α(IE) := $\pi_{\mathrm{IE}}(\sigma(\mathrm{IE}_1,\mathrm{IE}) \cdot \alpha(\mathrm{IE}_1), \ldots, \sigma(\mathrm{IE}_k,\mathrm{IE}) \cdot \alpha(\mathrm{IE}_k))$
  for each C$\in \mathbf{C}$ with it exists IE$\in \mathbf{E}$ such that ρ(IE,C) > 0 **do**
    α(C) := $\pi_{\mathrm{C}}(\rho(\mathrm{IE}_1,\mathrm{C}) \cdot \alpha(\mathrm{IE}_1), \ldots, \sigma(\mathrm{IE}_k,\mathrm{C}) \cdot \alpha(\mathrm{IE}_k))$
  return sort(C with $\alpha(C) \,|\, C \in \mathbf{C} \wedge \alpha(C) > 0$)
end

Fig. 7.15. CRN Retrieval Algorithm

The activations propagated by this algorithm are nothing else than similarity values. The activation of an IE after the propagation is the local similarity between this IE and the respective IE in the problem description. The activations of the case nodes are the global similarities of the case for the current problem description. Through the CRN, the computation of similarities with a value of 0 is avoided and cases for whose it is known that their similarity is 0 are not considered. A problem not taken into account in this basic form of the algorithm occurs when the problem description contains an

IE that is not yet included in the CRN. This can happen if, for example, an IE refers to a numeric attribute and the attribute value in the problem description does not occur in the case. In such situations it is necessary to first extend the retrieval net to include also the new IE and to link it according to the local similarity measure to related IEs.

Some extensions to this basic case retrieval net approach have been proposed. This includes new kinds of nodes that allow to represent concepts as required for object-oriented representations (Lenz and Burkhard 1996a; Magnus 1999). Further, a more efficient, so-called lazy spreading activation algorithm for retrieval has been developed that avoids propagating activations to cases that do not have a change to become a k-best case, since their activation can never exceed those of other cases (Lenz and Burkhard 1996b).

7.5.3 Properties of Case Retrieval Nets

Case retrieval nets speed up retrieval compared to sequential retrieval under certain circumstances. The retrieval effort depends on a number of factors (Lenz 1999). The size of the problem description determines the number of IEs that are activated in the beginning and determines thereby the total number of IEs and case nodes that are activated. The larger the query the higher the retrieval effort. The connectivity of the CRN also influences the retrieval effort significantly. The larger the number of non-zero local similarity values, the higher is the connectivity and the more IEs and case nodes are activated during the propagation. A worst case scenario for a CRN is the following: a CRN is constructed for an attribute-value representation with many numeric attributes and with many non-zero local similarities. If one attribute is present in all cases and the query (e.g. a price attribute in an electronic commerce application), the whole case base must be searched during retrieval, i.e., every case node becomes activated. Hence, we can consider case retrieval nets useful if the similarity measures are simple from a representational point of view. Despite such a worst case, many practical experiments have demonstrated significant performance gains during retrieval (Lenz 1996). A big advantage of the CRN approach is its ability to cope with arbitrary similarity measures, since the similarity is pre-computed and coded into the CRN. However, this leads to the disadvantages that the CRN must be re-computed when the similarity measure changes. Despite of this, user weights can be considered quite simply by coding them into the initial activation of the IEs that occur in the query. Also, a CRN can be easily adapted if the case base changes. If a case is deleted, the respective case node only needs to be removed from the CRN. If a new case arises, a node for this case and nodes for newly included IEs can easily be added to the existing CRN, without a need to change the already constructed part of it.

7.6 SQL Approximation

This section presents an approach to establish the similarity-based case retrieval on top of a relational database (Schumacher and Bergmann 2000). In a nutshell, the core idea is to approximate a similarity-based retrieval with SQL-queries, an idea already proposed by Kitano and Shimazu 1996. The approach avoids duplicating the case data or compiling index structures and is therefore ideal for huge case bases which are often subject to changes. Similar strategies have already been investigated for answering other kinds of complex queries with relational databases that cannot directly be handled by the database.

7.6.1 The Basic Idea

We view a case base as a set of points in an m-dimensional space. Then, the k most similar cases lie within a certain m-dimensional ball around the problem description such that the k most similar case is on the surface of this ball. In Sect. 7.3.4 we have already introduced this consideration in the context of the BOB and BWB test that occurs during kd-tree retrieval. What is called a ball here, is not necessarily really a ball but an n-dimensional volume which shape is determined by the similarity measure, or more precisely by the aggregation function by which the global similarity measure is defined. For the Euclidean distance this is in fact a ball; for a weighted average the shape is a hyperrhombus as shown in Fig. 7.16(a).

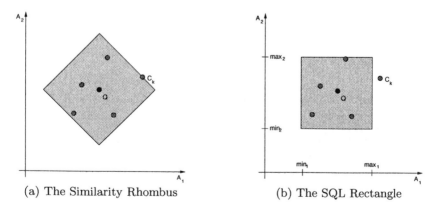

(a) The Similarity Rhombus   (b) The SQL Rectangle

Fig. 7.16. Volumes Covered by Queries.

If we view in the same way an SQL-query of the form

SELECT $a_1, \ldots, a_m$ FROM CaseTable
WHERE $(a_1 \geq min_1$ AND $a_1 \leq max_1)$ $\ldots$
          AND $(a_m \geq min_m$ AND $a_m \leq max_m)$

where $a_1, \ldots, a_m$ are the attributes in the query, we get a hyperrectangle (see Fig. 7.16(b)). The goal is now to use the hyperrectangle SQL-queries to retrieve the cases inside the similarity-rhombus from the database.

The solution is to construct a series of rectangular "rings" around the point that specifies the problem description, as shown in Fig. 7.17(a). In step 0 the retrieval starts with the problem description itself and the cases from the next ring are retrieved as long as more cases are needed to determine the retrieval result. This process is called *query relaxation*. The cases read from the database are ordered according to their similarity to the query, and finally the k most similar cases are returned.

With this approach the real form of the similarity-rhombus is approximated by rectangular rings. The smaller the difference volume between the similarity-rhombus and a rectangular ring that completely covers the rhombus, the more efficient is the retrieval. Further the amount in which the rectangle is increased during each iteration is also crucial to the performance of the retrieval. In the ideal case, the first rectangular has exactly the "right" size such that the k-most similar cases are included and not too many irrelevant cases are retrieved.

This retrieval approach can be seen as a kind of extension of the two stage MAC/FAC retrieval discussed in case-based reasoning research for some time (Forbus et al. 1995). The SQL query is the MAC (Many Are Called) preselection step and the subsequent sorting with respect to the similarity measure is the FAC (Few Are Chosen) step. The main difference here is that

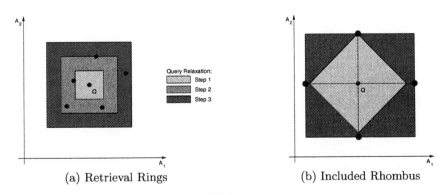

(a) Retrieval Rings   (b) Included Rhombus

Fig. 7.17. Retrieval with Rings of SQL-Rectangles.

the SQL approximation approach iteratively repeats these two steps and can thereby avoid α-errors, i.e., avoid that relevant cases are overlooked.

7.6.2 The Retrieval Algorithm

We now present the retrieval algorithm in detail including details for query relaxation and the termination criterion. The basic retrieval algorithm is described in Fig. 7.18.

Input: Database DB, similarity measure sim, number of cases k,
and problem description d.
Output: Sorted list of cases

procedure Retrieve(DB, sim, d, k)
var
  $result, new$: **Sorted List of** case
  $step$: Integer
  $sqlQuery$: String
  $dbRes$: **Set of** case

begin
  $step := 0$
  $result :=$ empty
  while $NotFinished(d, result, k, sim)$ **do**
    $sqlQuery =$ RelaxQuery(d, $step$, k)
    $dbRes =$ ExecuteSQLQuery(DB, $sqlQuery$)
    $new =$ SortCases(d, sim, $dbRes$)
    insert new into $result$
    step = step + 1
  return $result$
end

Fig. 7.18. SQL Approximation Retrieval Algorithm

Termination Criterion

The function $NotFinished$ implements a suitable criterion to decide if the retrieval can be terminated. One criterion could be that the retrieval should always yield a complete result list, i.e., there are no other cases in the case base which are more similar to the query than those in the result list. The similarity rhombus already covered by the SQL-queries is defined by the most similar object (which is not necessarily a case in the case base) lying exactly on the borders of the rectangle (see Fig. 7.17(b)). If the k most similar case in the *result* list is more similar to the query than this object, we know that we will not find more similar cases by relaxing the query any further.

Query Relaxation

The speed of the relaxation is crucial to the performance of the retrieval: If we relax the query too fast, we risk retrieving too many cases from the database which have to be imported in the search engine and evaluated. This would cost both much main memory and the ordering of the cases would take long. On the other hand if the relaxation is too slow, we would have to do a lot of SQL-queries. While this may be optimal for memory use and evaluation, it would slow down the retrieval due to the overhead involved with each database query. Often the database runs on another machine than the search engine and so this would create a lot of network traffic as well. Therefore, we want to retrieve the necessary cases with only a few database queries.

For the following considerations we view the space of cases as an m-dimensional hyper-cube of volume 1, i.e., all edges of the cube have the length 1. The distance between two values x and y of the same type is defined as $d(x, y) = 1 - sim_i(x, y)$ where sim_i is the local similarity measure for this type. Further we assume that the cases are distributed equally in this space. The goal of the following consideration is to find parameters for the first step of the query relaxation so that in this step already enough cases are retrieved from the database to build an acceptable query result. For this we introduce the parameter N_{max}, which is the maximum number of cases we want to read from the database in a single step. It clearly has to be a function of k because we want the k most similar cases to be included in this number of cases, therefore we write it as a function $N_{max}(k)$.

To generate the bounds of the database query we now have to determine which *volume* the query should cover in order to have a result of $N_{max}(k)$ cases. For an SQL-query this volume can be computed as:

$$V = \prod_{j=1}^{m}(1 - sim_j(min_j, max_j))$$

If the problem description is $d = (d_1, \ldots, d_n)$ and if we select the bounds of the SQL-query so that the speed of the relaxation is equal for all attributes (uniform distribution assumption), we get:

$$\forall_{j=1}^{m} : sim_g = sim_j(d_j, min_j) = sim_j(d_j, max_j)$$
$$\Rightarrow V = (2 \cdot (1 - sim_g))^m$$

We call sim_g the *minimal local similarity threshold* because we retrieve all cases for which the local similarity in every attribute is above this threshold. Because we assume the cases to be distributed equally we can describe the volume of one case as $V_C = 1/N$ where N is the number of cases in the case base, which leads to:

$$V = V_C \cdot N_{max}(k) \Rightarrow sim_g = 1 - \tfrac{1}{2}\left(\tfrac{N_{max}(k)}{N}\right)^{\frac{1}{m}}$$

In this way the minimal local similarity threshold for the first relaxation step $sim_g^1 = sim_g$ depends only on the number of defined attributes, the requested size of the result set and the number of cases in the database.

SQL Query Construction

To construct the SQL-query, the local similarity measures have to be invertible in the sense that it must be possible to determine the following set efficiently:

$$SIM_j(q_j, sim_g) = \{x_j \in T_j \mid sim_j(q_j, x_j) \geq sim_g\}$$

This set contains all attribute values for which the local similarity to the query is greater than the given minimal local similarity threshold. If the attribute type is totally ordered and of the local similarity measure is monotone with respect to this ordering (see Def. 4.13), we can also express this set as an interval $SIM_j(q_j, sim_g) = [min_j, max_j]$. Both forms of the set can be used easily to construct an SQL-query; the WHERE-Clause of the query in step s we denote with C_s.

For further steps s we can compute sim_g^s the same way by either

- using a linear growth of the query volume, or
- using a linear decrease of the minimal local similarity threshold, for example by $sim_g^s = 1 - s \cdot (1 - sim_g)$.

Finally, we have to modify the SQL queries so that in each step not the complete rectangle but only the current ring is read from the database. This can be done by excluding the rectangle of the step before in the query:

SELECT attributes FROM table WHERE C_s AND NOT (C_{s-1})

7.6.3 Properties of SQL Approximation

The SQL approximation retrieval approach has the following advantages:

- *Efficient Retrieval:* It can significantly improve retrieval performance compared to a sequential retrieval and is thereby able to handle large case bases. This has been demonstrated in several experiments (Schumacher and Bergmann 2000).
- *Handle Dynamic Case Bases:* Since no index is constructed prior to the retrieval, cases can be retrieved immediately after they are entered into the case base. This allows to handle highly dynamic case bases.
- *Independence of the Database System:* Any standard SQL database implementation can be used for this technique. No database-specific programming has to be done inside or outside the database.
- *Use of Existing Databases:* If the tables are in the required form they can be used directly for retrieval. Otherwise one can apply a database view to provide the data in a suitable form, but usually nothing has to be changed in the database schema.
- *Appropriate as Any Time Algorithm:* This retrieval approach can also be used as an anytime-algorithm, where the user can examine an intermediate result and trigger another step, until the result is sufficient.

On the other hand, there are some known limitations. First, the efficiency of the approach decreases in high dimensional attribute spaces. The reason for this is that the higher the dimensionality of the space, the larger becomes the difference between the hyperrectangle and the hyperrhombus. Hence, more cases are retrieved from the case base that are potentially irrelevant. However, if it is possible to tolerate a certain amount of α-errors, a less restrictive termination criterion can be used, e.g. to terminate the retrieval after k cases are retrieved from the database. Experiments in practical domains demonstrated a high performance gain and only a small α-error (Schumacher and Bergmann 2000).

Second, the current query relaxation approach is based on the idealistic assumption of a uniform distribution of the cases in the representation space. If this assumption is violated the efficiency of the retrieval will decrease because either too many cases will be retrieved from the database or too many SQL queries are created. We expect that this problem can be avoided by incorporating an introspective learning approach that estimates the density of the case base in different regions.

Third, the retrieval technique presented so far is limited to attribute value representations and bounded object-oriented representations. For bounded object-oriented representations, each attribute path must be turned into a column of a database table. As a first extension towards full object-oriented representations, simple multi-value attributes can be handled (Schumacher and Bergmann 2000).

7.7 Summary

We end this chapter by summarizing and contrasting the central properties of the just discussed retrieval approaches. Table 7.1 compares them from three different perspectives that are now briefly discussed.

	Sequential	kd-Tree Variants	Fish & Shrink	Case Retrieval Nets	SQL Approximation
Similarity Measure Restrictions:					
local measures		monotonic	triangle inequality		
aggregation function		not class specific			not class specific
weights		not class and case specific	not class and case specific		not class and case specific
Applicable for Case Representation:					
attribute-value	+	+	+	+	+
object-oriented	+	bounded only	+1	+	bounded only
graph representations	+	-	+1	-	-
predicate logic	+	-	+1	-	-
generalized cases	+	-	-	hyper-rectangular only	hyper-rectangular only
Efficient if:					
large case base	-	+	o	+	+
many attributes	+	-	+	+	-
dynamic case base	+	-	o	+	+
comput. complex sim.	-	-	+	-	-
represent. complex sim.	+	+	+	-	+
dynamic sim.	+	-	-	-	+

1representation can be used within a single complex attribute

Table 7.1. Overview of the Properties of the Different Retrieval Approaches

Restrictions on Similarity Measures

The approaches differ in the formal restrictions they impose on the similarity measure in order to guarantee retrieval completeness. These restrictions relate to

- properties that the local similarity measures must fulfill.
- restrictions on the aggregation function for object-oriented representations. The kd-tree variants and the SQL approximation only allow one single aggregation function for all object classes.
- the weight model that can be used; some approaches cannot deal with class and case specific weights.

Applicable Case Representations

The five approaches differ in the case representations they can deal with. All approaches can handle attribute value representations and bounded object-oriented approaches. The Fish and Shrink approach is also suited for other representations but they are treated within a single complex attribute.

Domain Characteristics Required for Efficient Retrieval

Finally, the discussed approaches have different strengths and weaknesses concerning domain properties. They relate to the efficiency of retrieval. Obviously, efficiency is a relative criterion that depends on many factors besides the retrieval algorithm. Therefore, the following criteria are no crisp formal conditions but more of a fuzzy nature. The expressed characterization can therefore only be seen as a tendency that is expressed and that helps to choose an appropriate approach. These criteria need a little more explanation.

- *Large case base:* This criterion expresses whether the approach is able to handle "large" case bases. In the experiments reported in the literature to these approaches, a cases base is considered large if it contains some 10000s of cases that are retrieved on a single state-of-the-art workstation computer. However, since the complexity of all retrieval approaches only increases linearly (or less) with the number of cases, this figur ecan easily be extended by increasing the computing performance or by introducing parallel computing.
- *Many attributes:* This criterion expresses whether the approach easily scales up with an increasing number of attributes. Here we distinguish approaches that are influenced by the number of attributes form those that are not.
- *Dynamic case base:* This criterion expresses whether the approach easily scales up with an increasing dynamics of the case base. Here we distinguish approaches according to the effort it takes to insert or delete cases.

- *Computationally complex similarity measures:* This criterion expresses whether the approach is able to deal efficiently with similarity measures that have a high computational complexity. Every similarity measure whose computational complexity is higher than polynomial with the size of the case should be considered complex. The measures discussed for object-oriented representations usually don't fall into this category. The measure connected with graph representations usually do.
- *Complex similarity measure representation:* This criterion expresses whether the approach easily scales up with "amount" of knowledge encoded in the similarity measure. The "amount" of knowledge can be measured by the number of non-zero similarity values that occur.
- *Dynamic similarity measures:* This criterion expresses whether the approach easily scales up with rapidly changing similarity measures. This distinguishes approaches according to the degree to which they make use of pre-computed similarity values that would need to be updated.

8. Experience Adaptation

> *"The reuse of past experience is trivial if it is just the direct application of concrete knowledge or the instantiation of established, abstract knowledge. One of the key insights in CBR and analogy is that prior knowledge that is not directly relevant to the current situation can be made relevant by perturbing or adapting it to fit the current situation."*

Mark T. Keane

In this chapter we will have a closer look at the process of experience adaptation. In situations in which the available experience captured in the lesson part of a case is not suited for solving the current problem at hand, it is necessary to modify it appropriately. This is particularly important if the number of available cases is low with respect to the variety and complexity of the domain and its solutions.

The results presented in this chapter stem primarily from research on adaptation in case-based reasoning, considering also configuration approaches. Initial versions of these results have been published already by Bergmann et al. (1996), Wilke and Bergmann (1998), Bergmann and Wilke (1998), Schmitt and Bergmann (1999b), Schmitt and Bergmann (1999a), Stahl and Bergmann (2000), and Stahl et al. (2000).

8.1 Overview and Characterization of Different Adaptation Approaches

In this section we have a closer look at several adaptation techniques that have their origin in case-based reasoning (related surveys are given by Kolodner 1993, Hanney et al. 1995, Voß 1996). The differences of these techniques are demonstrated using a simple example from the application domain of managing product knowledge for sales support of personal computers.

8.1.1 The Continuum of Adaptation Models

From a case-based reasoning perspective there is a natural relationship between the complexity of the problem solving task and the complexity of the CBR adaptation process. Even adaptation is a special kind of problem solving for the desired task with the helpful input of a problem description, similar problems and belonging similar solutions.

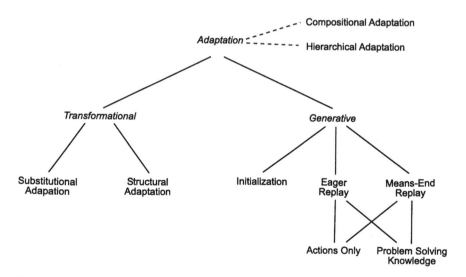

Fig. 8.1. The Continuum of Adaptation Models.

An overview of several basic adaptation approaches which are exploited in recent research is given in Fig. 8.1. We see the main distinction between *transformational* and *generative* approaches. Further, using multiple cases for adaptation is called *compositional adaptation* and performing adaptation on several levels of abstraction is called *hierarchical adaptation*. Compositional and hierarchical adaptation are independent properties that can be combined with any transformational or derivational adaptation approach. We will now describe these different approaches and illustrate them with an example.

Transformational Adaptation

Transformational adaptation means that the old lesson of the similar case is transformed into a new lesson for the new problem. Transformational adaptation (Carbonell 1983a) supports the reorganization of solution elements and permits the modification, addition, and deletion of these elements under certain conditions. Typically, transformational adaptation systems employ a fixed set of adaptation operators and/or rules (see Sections 5.1 and 5.2). Depending on the difference of problem attributes in the problem and the problem attributes in the similar case, the actual solution is modified. Thus, transformational adaptation requires domain knowledge on how certain differences in the problem lead to differences in the solution. Depending on the degree of modification we distinguish between substitutional adaptation and structural adaptation.

Substitutional Adaptation. For simple problem solving tasks simple substitutional adaptation is sufficient. It is promising when the retrieved case will typically be very close to the problem at hand and consequently will require only minor modifications. In this adaptation model it is only possible to change the values of attributes (Bain 1986). The structure of the new solution remains unchanged. Of course, the values of the attributes are reused from the old case, too, but it is possible to change some of them to get a lesson of a better utility. Here, adaptation means a recalculation of several parameters depending on the relation of the attributes of the problem description of the current problem and the similar case.

In the domain of managing product knowledge for sales support of personal computers, a possible substitutional adaptation is the modification of the hard disk space depending on the usage of database systems with the configured PC. If the value for database usage in the problem descriptions differs there is the necessity to add hard disk space.

Structural Adaptation. If we consider changes of the structure of the lesson during adaptation we speak of structural adaptation. Structural adaptation (Goel and Chandrasekaran 1989; Smyth and Keane 1996) supports the reorganization of lesson elements and permits the addition and deletion of such elements under certain conditions. Also structural adaptation systems employ a fixed set of adaptation operators and/or rules which modify the structure of the solution, depending on relations between the problem description and the retrieved similar case. Structural changes can occur when complete components are added or deleted or when another object replaces an existing one.

If in the PC domain the similar case being retrieved was not intended for playing computer games, which is required according to the current problem description then a joystick component must be added. In contrast to the first example, joystick is a new object in the object-oriented model of the solution and not an already existing part of the solution which is modified only.

8.1.2 Generative Adaptation

Generative adaptation is radically different from transformational adaptation. Generative adaptation requires an automatic generative from-scratch problem solver for solving the complex problems that the user deals with. Typically, such a problem solver (e.g., a configuration system in the introduced PC management domain) is in principle able to solve the type of problem that the user deals with alone, i.e., even without the use of experience. However, in practice such a pure generative problem solver is usually insufficient because of the computational complexity of the generative problem solving process or because of the insufficient quality of the solutions it produces. During generative adaptation, the generative problem solver is of course not used to solve the whole new problems from scratch, but only to generate those parts of the solution that are inadequate due to differences between the current problem and the retrieved case. Thus, drawbacks like the lack of efficiency or quality don't have a great impact as long as the retrieved case is sufficiently similar to the current problem.

As a consequence of the use of a generative problem solver, generative adaptation requires a different kind of knowledge than transformational adaptation. Instead of having knowledge that describes how differences in the problem description lead to differences in the solution, knowledge that allow constructing a solution from scratch is required. The particular knowledge needed strictly depends on the generative problem solver that is used. For example, in the introduced PC domain, a configuration system needs knowledge about the components like the function they fulfill and the constraints that exist between different components.

Unlike transformational adaptation which transfers a previous solution to a new problem, generative adaptation transfers the *derivation* of a previous solution (the reasoning trace) to the new problem. Therefore, this kind of adaptation is also called *derivational analogy* (Carbonell 1983a). Reasoning traces record information about the derivational process that led to a particular solution in the past, including decision information, justifications, and reasoning alternatives. During generative adaptation, these traces are essentially *replayed* in the context of the new target problem, i.e., the same or similar decisions are also tried to solve the current problem. If certain decisions from a previous reasoning trace cannot be transferred to the current problem, the generative problem solver will come up with a decisions by itself, without reusing information contained in the cases.

In order to enable the replay of reasoning traces, they must of course be stored in the cases, i.e., the representation of cases must be extended accordingly.

We can basically distinguish two different kinds of replay strategies: *one shot replay* and *interleaved replay* (see Fig. 8.1) which we will discuss now.

One Shot Replay. In one shot replay, one first identifies which portions of the solution trace can be reused in the context of the new situation. These

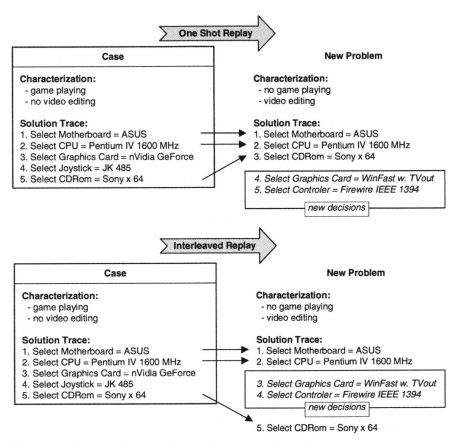

Fig. 8.2. Example for One Shot and Interleaved Replay.

decisions are then replayed by the problem solver. After the replay is finished, the problem solver will make the remaining decisions on its own. The top part of Fig. 8.2 shows an example in the PC domain. The new problem is to configure a PC basically used for video editing and not used for playing games. The retrieved case in the case-base, however, is configured for being used for playing games and not for video editing. The depicted solution trace for the case shows the configuration steps that had been taken to configure this particular PC. In one shot replay, the decisions 1,2, and 5 from the case are replayed first because they are also valid decisions for the new problem too. Then, the remaining decisions concerning a different graphic adapter with TV output and a Firewire card for the digital video connection are taken. CAPLAN/CBC (Muñoz-Avila and Weberskirch 1996) is an example of a case-based planning system that uses one-shot replay.

Interleaved Replay. In interleaved replay, we can switch several times between the replay of a previous solution trace and the generation of certain new decisions by the problem solver. The solution trace is followed up to a certain point where following it further would not be beneficial any more. Then, the generative problem solver takes over until a point is reached where the previous solution trace can be followed again. The bottom part of Fig. 8.2 shows interleaved replay for the same problem used already for demonstrating one shot replay. First, decisions 1 and 2 are replayed. Then, the problem solver takes over and determines a different graphic adapter and the Firewire card. Then, again, step 5 from the case is replayed, i.e., the CD-ROM is selected. PRODIGY/ANALOGY (Veloso 1994) is an example of a case-based planning system that uses interleaved replay.

We see that the basic difference between the two approaches is only the sequence in which replay occurs and not the steps that are replayed. In this examples it might seem easy to decide whether a step can be replayed for a new situation or not. However, in many situations this is not the case, particularly when there is a lot of interaction between the reasoning steps. In interleaved replay, it can also become very difficult to decide when to switch between replay and problem solving. Up to now, there is no general solution to this problem.

Solution Trace Replay Vs. Complete Decision Replay. An other important difference between different techniques is the amount of information about the solution trace that is reused. In *solution trace replay*, only the selection of the solution elements (selection of PC components in Fig. 8.2) is recorded and replayed. In *complete decision replay* all reasoning information in the problem solving process are recorded and possibly taken into account. These reasoning information can be justifications, and reasoning alternatives, or failed attempts.

8.1.3 Compositional Adaptation

In addition to these adaptation models, recent research has demonstrated the power of delivering solutions through the retrieval, adaptation, and subsequent composition of multiple cases. This leads to *compositional adaptation*, (Redmond 1990; Sycara and Navinchandra 1991) in which newly adapted solution components from multiple cases are combined to produce a new composite solution. This is possible if the solution consists of different parts which can be adapted more or less independently and it is effective if there are few conflicts between these components so that a change in one component does not have a lot of side-effects on other components. Examples of compositional adaptation methods are described by Smyth and Cunningham (1992), Maher and Zang (1993), Veloso (1994), Purvis and Pu (1995), Purvis and Pu (1996), Muñoz-Avila and Weberskirch (1996), and Stahl and Bergmann (2000).

Please note that compositional adaptation can be realized with a transformational or derivational approach as main adaptation method. It is independent on this distinction but the details of the realization differ significantly.

8.1.4 Hierarchical Adaptation

Hierarchical adaptation is another recent development that is used in combination with the shown adaptation models (Bergmann and Wilke 1996). Cases are stored at several levels of abstraction and the adaptation is performed in a top-down fashion. At first, the solution is adapted at the highest level of abstraction (omitting less relevant details). Then, the solution is refined in a stepwise manner and the required details are added. Hierarchical adaptation can either reuse a single case or it can reuse different cases for different levels of abstraction or for refining different details of the solution. Examples of systems using hierarchical adaptation are given by Smyth and Cunningham (1992), Bergmann and Wilke (1995b), and Branting and Aha (1995).

8.1.5 Adaptation for Experience Management for Complex Problem Solving

In the context of managing experience for complex problems, the just described basic adaptation approaches drawn from case-based reasoning must be considered carefully. Due to the complexity characteristics of the domain it is usually infeasible to completely model and formalize the knowledge required for a complete generative problem solver. However, this would be the prerequisite for applying a generative adaptation model. Therefore, the generative approaches are usually not applicable here. On the other hand, transformational approaches are easily scalable to the required degree of adaptation. The knowledge engineer can decide how much adaptation knowledge to encode. However, the disadvantage of transformational adaptation is that it can never be guaranteed that useful adapted experience can be provided to the user.

Given this considerations we restrict the remainder of this chapter to transformational adaptation approaches, including compositional extensions.

8.2 Theory of Transformational Adaptation

For pure case retrieval systems, the theory and mathematical formalization focusing on similarity measures, preference relations, and properties of retrieval algorithms have been described in the previous chapters. This solid foundation laid the ground for the success of such systems in practice. For experience management systems involving adaptation such a formalization has been first proposed by Bergmann and Wilke (1998) and is introduced here in a revised form. This is a step into the direction of developing a formal model of transformational adaptation that is based on the notion of utility as introduced in Sect. 3.1.3.

In Sect. 3.1.3 we introduced the utility as a function $u : \mathbb{P} \times \mathbb{L} \to \Re$ that assigns each problem-lesson pair a utility value (Def. 3.7). The general problem with those utility functions is that they are usually only partially known. What is known are preferences $c_i \succ_p c_j$ for some problems p and some cases c_i and c_j. Further, we introduced the case base semantics (Def. 3.9) which is given by a relation $\mathbb{B} \subseteq \mathbb{C}$, where $\mathbb{C} = \mathbb{D} \times \mathbb{L}$ is the case space, $\mathbb{D}$ is the experience characterization space and $\mathbb{L}$ is the lesson space. A case c is called *sound* iff $c \in \mathbb{B}$ holds. The case base semantics restricts the set of cases we want to deal with to a particular subset of all representable cases. Usually, the case semantics is defined as to include only cases of high or at least acceptable utility. It distinguishes cases that are semantically correct from those that express an "undesired" experience.

8.2.1 Experience Transformations

As introduced in Chap. 5 adaptation knowledge is knowledge about how cases can be transformed. Adaptation knowledge can be encoded in different representations, e.g., in the form of adaptation operators or rules that are explicitly defined. We will now take a very general view on adaptation knowledge, which covers different representations as well as adaptation approaches in which the adaptation transformations are only defined implicitly.

Definition 8.1 (Experience Transformation) An *experience transformation* is a partial function $\alpha : C \to C$, i.e., it transforms a case into some successor case.

The knowledge container of experience transformations can now be defined as the set of all experience transformations.

Definition 8.2 (Experience Transformation Container) The *experience transformation container* A is a set of experience transformations, i.e., $\mathbb{A} = \{\alpha_1, \alpha_2, \dots\}$.

As we have introduced the soundness condition for cases we also need to introduce a related soundness condition for experience transformations. This condition must ensure that whenever a sound case is transformed then a sound case is obtained. Besides this requirement the soundness condition must also include a second property that is necessary to ensure that adaptable cases can be retrieved. This property states that the projection of an experience transformation on the experience characterization space $\mathbb{B}$ is still a partial function.

Definition 8.3 (Soundness of an Experience Transformation) An experience transformation α is *sound* iff the following two conditions hold:

1. $\forall c \in \mathbb{B}$ if $\alpha(c)$ is defined then $\alpha(c) \in \mathbb{B}$
2. $\forall d, d', d'' \in \mathbb{D} \; \forall l, l', l'', l^* \in \mathbb{L}$ if $(d', l') = \alpha((d, l))$ and $(d'', l'') = \alpha((d, l^*))$ then $d' = d''$.

Further the experience transformation container is called sound iff all experience transformations it contains are sound.

Because of the second condition stated in this soundness definition, we can define the projection of an experience transformation on the experience characterization space $\alpha : \mathbb{D} \to \mathbb{D}$ by $\alpha(d) = d'$ iff it exists $l, l' \in \mathbb{L}$ such that $\alpha((d, l)) = (d', l')$.

8.2.2 The Experience Transformation Process

The experience adaptation step transforms a retrieved case $c = (d, l) \in \mathbf{CB}$ into an adapted case $c' = (d', l') = \alpha_{i_1} \circ \cdots \circ \alpha_{i_m}(c)$, with $\alpha_{i_j} \in \mathbb{A}$. We write

$$c \overset{*}{\longrightarrow} c' \quad \text{iff} \quad \exists \alpha_{i_1} \ldots \alpha_{i_m} \in \mathbb{A} \; c' = \alpha_{i_1} \circ \cdots \circ \alpha_{i_m}(c) \quad \text{and}$$
$$d \overset{*}{\longrightarrow} d' \quad \text{iff} \quad \exists l, l' \in \mathbb{L} \; (d, l) \overset{*}{\longrightarrow} (d', l')$$

Given an experience transformation container $\mathbb{A}$ and a case base $\mathbf{CB}$ we can define the set of transformed cases by

$$\mathbf{CB}^* = \{c' | c \overset{*}{\longrightarrow} c' \wedge c \in \mathbf{CB}\}$$

Given this definition, $\mathbf{CB}^*$ can be considered the (possibly infinite) set of all sound cases we know due to our knowledge about the case base and the transformation knowledge.

Lemma 8.1 (Soundness of Transformed Cases) If the case base $\mathbf{CB}$ and the experience transformation container $\mathbb{A}$ are sound then the set of transformed cases $\mathbf{CB}^*$ is also sound.

The transformation knowledge extends the scope of the cases. It also gives us some representation flexibility. We can distribute our experience knowledge among the case base and the transformation knowledge. The two extreme situations are

- to represent all experience knowledge through cases in the cases base without including any experience transformations.
- to include only one generic case in the case base and store all knowledge in experience transformations for this generic case.

With given sound transformation knowledge, we can easily extend the best case correctness proposition first stated in Sect. 4.1.4 as follows:

Proposition 8.1 (Best Case Correctness) If the following is given:

- a problem transformation pt
- a sound case base **CB**
- a sound similarity measure sim w.r.t. definition 4.5, 4.6, or 4.7
- a sound transformation knowledge container $\mathbb{A}$

Then for every problem p there is no lesson that can be achieved by adapting a case from the case base for which it is known that it has a higher utility for the problem p than the lesson l in a case $(d, l) \in \mathbf{CB}^*$ with the highest similarity $sim(pt(p), d)$.

If experience transformations are present, it is usually not possible to pre-compute the whole set $\mathbf{CB}^*$ in order to use it for similarity-based retrieval. This is because $\mathbf{CB}^*$ is usually too large to allow efficient storage and retrieval even with the efficient retrieval approaches introduced in Chap. 7 or because the set $\mathbf{CB}^*$ is simply infinite. This is why we need adaptation algorithms that compute an adapted case c' from a retrieved case c by $c \xrightarrow{*} c'$.

8.2.3 Similarity Measures in the Context of Experience Transformations

When experience transformation is involved, we basically aim at selecting the most similar case c' from $\mathbf{CB}^*$ with respect to a similarity measure sim that is modeled as an approximation of a utility function. During retrieval we therefore need to select a case c from the case base **CB** such that after applying a sequence of experience transformations a most similar case with respect to sim is obtained. The similarity measure used during this retrieval step therefore needs to consider the transformation possibilities. To goal is to retrieve adaptable cases (Smyth and Keane 1993). This similarity measure is usually different from the original similarity measure sim. However, we can derive such a similarity measure $sim_{\mathbb{A}} : \mathbb{D} \rightarrow \mathbb{D}$ based on a utility-oriented similarity measure sim and an experience transformation container $\mathbb{A}$ as follows:

$$sim_{\mathbb{A}}(d, d_c) := max\{sim(d, d') | d_c \xrightarrow{*} d'\} \qquad \text{(Adaptation-oriented Similarity Measure)}$$

In the general case, for a given similarity measure sim and given experience transformations $\mathbb{A}$ the adaptation-oriented similarity measure $sim_{\mathbb{A}}$ is not computable[1]. Further, even if it is possible to efficiently determine

---

[1] The undecidablity result for action planning (Bylander 1991) can be used to show this property.

the best case with respect to sim_A finding the best sequence of experience transformations by itself is an undecidable problem since it also includes solving a standard AI planning problem. However, experience adaptation can be considered as a numerical optimization function for which the similarity measure sim determines the objective function. Hence optimization algorithms can be applied in principle for experience transformation. Of course, they cannot guarantee to find the global optimum in the general case but they can at least reach a local optimum.

8.2.4 Relation to Rewrite Systems

The just introduced theory of transformational adaptation also reminds one of the theory of rewrite systems (Dershowitz and Jouannaud 1990; Avenhaus 1995); in fact the notation for experience transformations has been adapted from the notation of rewrite rules. However, there are significant difference between both theories. First, the adaptation process is always performed with respect to a certain target. Unlike in rewrite systems, we are not interested in finding a normal-form, but in a result that is most similar to a defined target problem. Second, a similarity measure as used in transformational adaptation cannot be appropriately considered by a rewrite system. Given these differences, traditional considerations of rewrite systems like confluence or termination property cannot be immediately transferred to the transformational adaptation problem. However, the similarity measure for a given target also induces an ordering on the transformed cases that ensures the termination of the transformation process and certain circumstances.

8.2.5 Relation to Generalized Cases

In Sect. 3.4 we introduced the concept of generalized cases. A generalized case covers not only a point of the case space but a whole subspace of it, i.e., $gc \subseteq \mathbb{C}$. In general, a single generalized case can be viewed as an implicit representation of a (possibly infinite) set of traditional "point cases".

Given the above formalizations, we see that we can immediately define a generalized case from a case $c \in \mathbf{CB}$ in the case base as follows:

$$gc := \{c' | c \xrightarrow{*} c'\}$$

In this view the adaptation knowledge transforms each case into a generalized case. The canonical extension of the similarity measure sim (see Sect. 4.7) is exactly equivalent to the adaptation-oriented similarity measures sim_A. In general, the generalized case gc is of course not computable from a case c and an adaptation container A; for restricted representations it can be computable. If it is possible to find an appropriate representation for the generalized cases gc that are derived from an transformation knowledge container, the approaches for similarity computation for generalized cases can be used to retrieve adaptable cases. For example, if each experience transformation unconditionally adapts a single attribute value within a certain interval, the resulting generalized cases can be represented using the hyperrectangle representation and the canonical extension of the similarity measure is easily computable. Further research is necessary to investigate this relationship in more depth.

8.3 Adaptation with Explicit Transformation Knowledge

The transformation knowledge $\mathbb{A}$ required for a transformational adaptation approach can be represented explicitly. In Chap. 5 we have already introduced two representation forms for transformation knowledge:

- adaptation rules and
- adaptation operators

We have developed an integration of those representation concepts with an object-oriented case representation framework that allows to model complex adaptation knowledge in a convenient way.

8.3.1 Rule-Based Adaptation

When applying the rule-based approach to represent adaptation knowledge we decompose the whole adaptation knowledge into several rules each of which deals with an individual part of the modification. During the adaptation phase, the complete set of rules is applied and a definite outcome, the adapted case, is achieved. Therefore, we can view the set of rules in rule-based adaptation as the representation of a single experience transformation. The requirement stated in definition 5.3 that adaptation rules represent certain knowledge means that the resulting experience transformation is sound.

Efficient processing of adaptation rules can be realized by a forward chaining rule interpreter with an underlying Rete-Network (Forgy 1982). However, the existence of *a-kind-of* and *has-part* relations in an object-oriented representation, requires an extension of the standard "flat" forward chaining rule systems. One first approach towards the integration of object-oriented data structures and a forward chaining rule interpreter is the NéOpus system (Pachet 1991). This system offers a mechanism for structuring large sets of rules in separate rule bases. It is also possible to define sub-bases of rule bases where a sub-base inherits the rules of its super-base. The adaptation rules can be grouped into distinct rule bases belonging to the different classes of the case representation. Every rule base has its own Rete-Network. The nodes of such a network are the single preconditions and conclusions of the rules of the associated rule base. The edges of such a directed network connect the preconditions and conclusion that belong to a single rule in such a way that if one starts at the first precondition of a rule and searches the way along the path, one ends up at the node representing the conclusion of the rule.

8.3.2 Interactive Operator-Based Adaptation

While the standard rule-based approach is limited to represent a single (but arbitrarily complex) adaptation transformation, the operator-based approach discussed now enables representing several experience transformations. In Sect. 5.1 we introduced a representation of adaptation operators, which can be viewed as an extension of the adaptation rules. An adaptation operator specifies one atomic unit of change and represents a single experience transformation. Adaptation is achieved by chaining several adaptation operators into a sequence.

User Interaction

The computational complexity of combining experience transformations to achieve an optimal result leads to the idea to avoid this complexity by introducing an interactive adaptation approach instead of achieving complete automation. This also leads to a more flexible user-controlled process to achieve an adaptation according to the user's wishes. This requires a predefined interface to control the adaptation process, i.e., at certain stages in the process, the user has to be able to tell the system how an experience should be changed. Therefore, two major aspects have to be considered:

- The system has to find out which parts of the retrieved experience have to be adapted. A competent user could determine the components of the case to be modified on her own. However, the adaptation component should be able to guide and control the user in her actions. It should be possible to define situations in which changing a part of a case makes sense.
- If in the course of adaptation new parameters or sub-components have to be included into the case, they will have to be determined in cooperation with the user. This allows the user to specify her wishes more precisely only when required. However, the system should control the customer by validating the desired modifications.

Controlling Adaptation

The first operator applied transforms the retrieved case into an intermediate case. The customer will apply sequentially more operators on the intermediate case until she reaches the target case (see Fig. 8.3). Additionally, one can allow the user to specify these changes in more detail by providing parameters after an operator is selected.

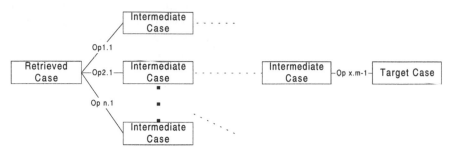

Fig. 8.3. Customization Process as Sequence of Operators.

To enable operator-based adaptation, mechanisms are required to navigate through the space of possible case adaptations. Navigation should include at least mechanisms

- to select one of the applicable operators,
- to undo a previously selected operator, and
- to remove (if possible) an operator from the current sequence.

Hence, for the current intermediate case, the preconditions of all available operators must be checked. Those operators that are applicable must be identified and presented to the user. If the user selects an operator, she must be asked for the values of the operator parameters. If the values entered by the user fulfill the parameter condition, then the action part of the operator is applied. This means that all actions are performed on the current intermediate case. This results in the next intermediate case, which is again presented to the customer. Then, she can either accept this case and terminate the adaptation or new adaptation operators can be offered to further modify the case. To undo previously performed adaptations, the adaptation component must keep track of the computed intermediate cases and operators. If one operator is retracted, all operators that have been applied afterwards must be checked whether they are still applicable. In case they are not, it could be necessary to retract such operators as well. A detailed description of a comprehensive navigation approach is described by Meyfarth (1997) and a Java-based architecture for it is described by Schmitt et al. (2000).

8.4 Incremental Compositional Adaptation

A general problem in particular for the transformation-based approaches to adaptation is that the acquisition of the explicit adaptation knowledge (e.g. in the form of rules or operators) causes a large effort. This turns into a real problem when experience has many different variants or if the domain changes rapidly so that the adaptation knowledge must be updated as well. On the other hand, derivational approaches to adaptation require a complete problem solver and sufficient knowledge for this problem solver. This approach also suffers form intractability, both in terms of computational efficiency and knowledge acquisition effort.

We now present a compositional approach to adaptation in which experience transformations are defined implicitly. Experience is transformed by replacing certain sub-components of the experience with other sub-components. A case base of experience sub-components represents the adaptation knowledge. Additionally, consistency constraints (see Sect. 5.3) must be taken into account. They specify the conditions under which certain sub-components can be combined. This approach avoids huge portions of the knowledge acquisition effort of the previous approaches. It assumes, of course, cases that are structured into sub-components, possibly in a hierarchical manner. The knowledge required is knowledge about available complete cases as well as knowledge about available sub-cases. For example, both kinds of knowledge are easily available in an E-Commerce setting. This approach has been published by Stahl and Bergmann (2000), Stahl et al. (2000), and Stahl (2000).

8.4.1 Highly Structured Problems

Consider the situation that we have a domain in which it is possible to subdivide the arising problems and the related lessons or solutions into more or less independent sub-problems and related sub-solutions. This means, the complete problems, we can also call them *complex problems*, can only be solved if all included sub-problems are solved and combined to an overall solution. When assuming such a problem structure, it is possible to represent the problems and the corresponding solutions in form of part-of hierarchies (see Fig. 8.4). The root-nodes of such part-of hierarchies represent the complex problems or solutions, respectively. Inner nodes represent *complex sub-problems (sub-solutions)* that can be divided again into less complex sub-problems (sub-solutions). Finally, the leaf nodes represent *atomic problems* and the related *atomic solutions*.

Generally, the single sub-problems cannot be considered absolutely isolated because of dependencies between them. The solution of one sub-problem often depends on the solutions of some other sub-problems. Thus, it is unavoidable to handle these dependencies while solving the different sub-problems, or at least when combining them to the final solution.

8.4.2 Compositional Approach

Assuming a highly structured domain as described in the previous section, we can now introduce a special procedure for adaptation. First, a case from the case base is retrieved for the complex problem at hand. Due to the complexity

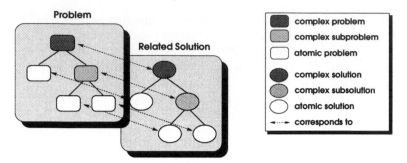

Fig. 8.4. Highly Structured Problems.

of the problem structure, in general, it is unlikely that the complete solution of the retrieved case can be applied to the current problem directly. This means that the retrieved case can include sub-solutions which cannot be reused. Then it is necessary to adapt these unsuitable sub-solutions. Such adaptation can become a very complex task if the unsuitable sub-solutions belong to complex sub-problems.

The idea of compositional CBR is to realize the necessary adaptation by combining solutions from other cases. That is, the adaptation itself is experience-based. This means that we will not try to adapt the retrieved but unsuitable sub-solutions by modifying them with traditional methods. Instead, we use still unsolved sub-problems as new queries for a retrieval in additional case bases. These case bases must contain cases that correspond to the classes of the current sub-problems, i.e., the cases are generally less complex than the cases in the top-level case base (see Fig. 8.5).

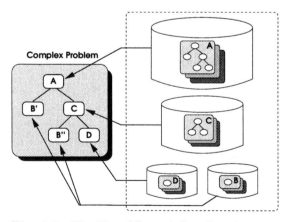
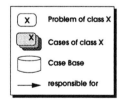

Fig. 8.5. The Use of Several Case Bases.

We now distinguish two situations, depending on the position of an unsolved sub-problem in the hierarchy:

- If the unsolved sub-problem is an atomic problem, the responsible case-base contains atomic solutions only. In this case we suppose that retrieving a case that can be reused directly is possible. Nevertheless, if adaptation is still necessary, it should be quite simple so that it can, for example, be realized by applying few adaptation rules.
- When having an unsolved complex sub-problem and retrieving a suitable case is impossible, we can repeat the described procedure in a recursive manner. This means that we start a retrieval to find a suitable sub-solution. If the retrieved complex sub-solution cannot be reused directly, necessary adaptation can be realized again in the described compositional manner.

To obtain a solution for the overall complex problem which was the starting point of the whole process, it is finally necessary to combine all found sub-solutions. This is why this approach is called compositional adaptation. An illustration of the suggested procedure is shown in Fig. 8.6.

The basic idea of this approach is the principle of "Divide and Conquer", which can often be applied successfully in Computer Science. Generally, it is important to consider one basic limitation of this approach. If it is possible to divide a complex problem into sub-problems that can be solved separately in an easy way, it must also be guaranteed that the final combination of the found sub-solutions will not become too difficult. Otherwise, such a procedure will not be very efficient. Therefore, we assume a limited number of dependencies between the different sub-problems in the application domain to apply our approach.

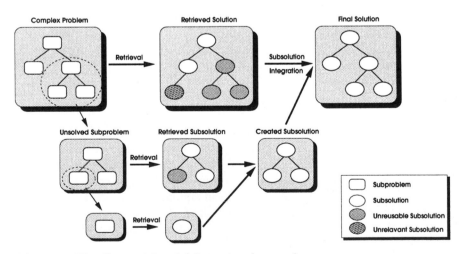

Fig. 8.6. The Compositional Adaptation Approach.

8.4.3 The Adaptation Cycle

We now describe the different steps that occur during adaptation in an adaptation cycle (see Fig. 8.7). For the current complex problem the retrieval yields an initial case from the case base of complete solutions that is then adapted in the adaptation cycle. Please note that this retrieval step must be performed with respect to an adaptation-oriented similarity measure.

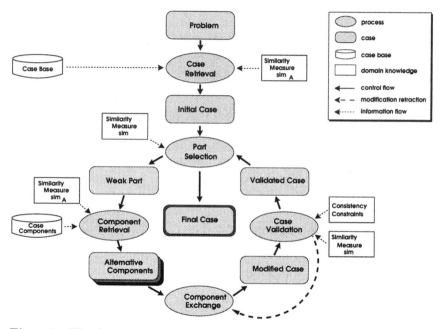

Fig. 8.7. The Adaptation Cycle.

Part Selection

At the beginning of the adaptation cycle, it has to be determined if the current case includes parts that cannot properly be reused for the current problem. This can be done by an examination of the local similarities between the parts of the experience characterization of the case and the respective part of the problem description. Parts with a low local similarity are called *weak parts*. The determination of these parts is the task of the *part selection* process. If the case includes no weak parts at all, the adaptation process is finished and the given case is presented to the user.

Component Retrieval

During the adaptation cycle, a selected weak part leads to a new similarity-based retrieval, called *component retrieval*. In this process, the part-query corresponding to the selected weak part is used to retrieve a collection of alternative components from the component case-base. The elements of this collection are arranged by their similarity to the query in a decreasing order.

Component Exchange

The task of the next process is then the replacement of the weak case component (if existing) by the first (or successive) element of the collection of alternative components. Because of the mentioned order, this alternative component represents the most suitable component that is available within the component case-base. The result of the described *component exchange* is a *modified case*.

Case Validation

To judge the effects of the component exchange, the modified case must finally be inspected during the *case validation* process. The task of this process is the validation of the modified case with respect to two different aspects. On the one hand, it must be guaranteed that the modification leads to a consistent case, i.e., to a case that fulfills the consistency constraints of the application domain. Therefore, a constraint system has to check the modified case. On the other hand, the modified case should naturally represent a better solution as the case before the modification. Therefore, we have to ensure that the global similarity (with respect to the utility-oriented similarity measure sim, not the application-oriented similarity measure) between the problem and the modified case is higher than the similarity between the problem and the previous current case. Either if the modified case is inconsistent or if it has a lower similarity to the query as the case before the modification, retracting the last modification becomes necessary. The latter can happen if the adaptation-oriented similarity measure is not correct, which is quite likely to happen due to the difficulties of finding such adaptation-oriented measures.

Retraction

The *retraction* of the last modification is realized by the repeated application of the component exchange process. This means, the just now installed component that had led to the failure of the case validation is replaced by the next element of the alternative components collection. If no available alternative component is suitable to fulfill the mentioned criteria, it becomes necessary to restore the situation at the beginning of the current iteration of the adaptation cycle. In this case, an adaptation of the respective weak case part is currently impossible.

If the case validation could be passed successfully, one iteration of the adaptation cycle is finished. The result of this adaptation cycle is the next *intermediate case*. In the next step, it is again the task of the part selection process to determine a weak part within this intermediate case which shall be used as the starting point for a new iteration. If it is impossible to determine a weak part whose adaptation could perhaps improve the case, the adaptation cycle terminates.

8.4.4 Controlling the Adaptation Cycle

Generally, we can notice that the adaptation cycle has to solve a combination of a *constraint satisfaction problem (CSP)* and an *optimization problem*. On the one hand, it has to find a combination of different components representing a sound case, i.e., a case that fulfills all consistency constraints of the application domain. On the other hand, it has to find the most useful (optimal) combination with respect to the user's problem.

To solve this special task it is not sufficient to determine weak case parts during the part selection process in any order. It is rather necessary to find adaptation orders which will lead to an optimal configuration result. Generally, we can distinguish between two different approaches to determine adaptation orders:

Preservation of Consistency

Up to now we have assumed that a modification during one iteration of the adaptation cycle must even lead to a consistent case. This means that only adaptation orders that preserve the consistency of the case are allowed.

Temporary Loss of Consistency

In contrast to the previously described approach it is also possible to allow the temporary loss of consistency during the adaptation cycle. That means, if the case validation process determines the violation of constraints after the component exchange process, this must not necessarily lead to an immediately retraction procedure. It is rather possible only to notice the loss of consistency and to continue the whole adaptation process without the retraction of the last modification. However, for the final solution it is of course necessary to re-establish the consistency during the further adaptation.

The advantage of the first approach is the quite simple implementation. Besides that, it represents an *any time algorithm*, i.e., it allows to interrupt the adaptation cycle at any time to obtain the best consistent solution that could be found so far. Nevertheless, with preservation of consistency it is often impossible to get optimal configuration results.

8.4.5 Adaptation as Hill-Climbing Search

The above presented incremental compositional adaptation approach can be interpreted as a hill-climbing search in the space of adapted cases $\mathbf{CB}^*$, starting at the retrieved case. Each iteration of the adaptation cycle corresponds to the application of one experience transformation and is one step in the search procedure. The utility-oriented similarity measure *sim* is the goal function for the search whose value should be maximized. The adaptation steps are selected according to whether they increase the utility-oriented similarity measure; each application of an experience transformation increases the similarity and thereby increases the utility of the current experience. The algorithm terminates if the similarity cannot be improved any further by replacing a single component. Thereby a pareto-optimum[2] is achieved.

Further improvements of this approach can be achieved by allowing the replacement of not just one, but k components at a time. However, this decreases the efficiency since the number of experience transformations increases exponentially with k. Hence, this is an instance of the traditional trade-off between optimal and efficient behavior.

---

[2] This term was introduced by the economist *Vilfredo Pareto* in 1906 and describes an optimum that cannot be improved by just improving an individual allocation.

9. Developing and Maintaining Experience Management Applications

"Experience is a good school, but the fees are high. "

Heinrich Heine

Today, there is already an increasing number of successful companies developing industrial experience management applications. In former days, these companies could develop their early pioneering applications in an ad-hoc manner. The highly-skilled expert of the company was able to manage these projects and to provide the developers with the required expertise. The experts did not have guidelines or methods which helped their developers implementing new projects and there was no way to preserve the experience made in previous projects for future use. This could cause serious problems when members of the staff left, taking their experience with them, and new staff had to be trained. The result was an inefficient and/or ineffective system development. Nowadays, the situation has changed. The market for experience management applications increased significantly. Therefore, these companies have to face the fact that the market demands companies executing more and larger projects than in earlier days. It is required that they develop software fulfilling current quality standards. Consequently, contemporary IT companies can no longer sustain inefficient or ineffectual application development. What is required is a development and maintenance methodology for experience management applications. This methodology is located in the outer shell of the experience management model as introduced in Sect. 2.2.

This chapter presents the INRECA methodology targeted at industrial experience management applications. The methodology has been developed in the INRECA-II European ESPRIT project (1996-1999). Full details are discussed by Bergmann et al. (1997), Bergmann and Althoff (1998), Bergmann et al. (1998), Bergmann and Göker (1999), Bergmann et al. (1999a) and on electronic media (Bergmann et al. 1999b; INRECA Consortium 1999).

9.1 Introduction

The outer shell of the EMM (see Fig. 2.3) is the *development and maintenance methodology*. The knowledge kernel and the problem solving cycle itself are the subject of the development and maintenance methodology. The various processes that occur in this shell address the acquisition and maintenance of the knowledge in the kernel as well as the technical, organizational, and also managerial aspects of the problem solving cycle and its implementation. Unlike the processes of the problem solving cycle, which have been discussed in the previous chapters, the processes that occur in the development and maintenance methodology can usually not be automated by IT technology. However, certain processes can be partially supported by different kinds of support tools.

9.1.1 General Purpose of a Methodology

A methodology usually combines a number of methods into a philosophy which addresses a number of phases of the software development life-cycle (e.g. Booch 1994, Chap. 1). A methodology should give guidelines about the activities that need to be performed in order to successfully develop a certain kind of product, e.g. any kind of software system, a knowledge-based system, or – as in our case – an experience management application. A methodology should make the development an engineering activity rather than an art known by a few experts (Shaw 1990; Gibbs 1994).

Clarification of Terms 9.1 (Methodology) A methodology is a collection of methods and guidelines that enables a person to work effectively and efficiently in the domain for which the methodology has been developed.

The use of an appropriate methodology should provide significant quantifiable benefits in terms of

- productivity, e.g., reduce the risk of wasted efforts,
- quality, e.g., inclusion of quality deliverables,
- communication, a reference for both formal and informal communication between members of the development team, and
- it will provide a solid base for management decision making, e.g., planning, resource allocation, and monitoring.

One of the main driving forces behind the development and the use of a Methodology relates to the need for quality in both the products and processes of the development of computer-based systems. Some methodologies and approaches for software development in general already exist, but software engineering methodology is still a major issue in current software engineering (SE) research. By adapting techniques originating in this area we present a Methodology based on recent SE techniques which are enriched by experience on building and maintaining experience management applications.

9.1.2 Methodology for Experience Management

When building an experience management application to be used in the daily practice within an existing client organization, a large variety of different kinds of processes have to be considered. To reach the goals described above, a methodology must cover the following aspects which naturally occur more or less in every software development project:

- The process of project management (cost and resource assessment, time schedules, project plans, quality control procedures, etc.),
- the specification of the different kinds of products or deliverables (including software deliverables) that must be produced,
- the process of (technical) product development and maintenance which includes all technical tasks that are involved in the development and maintenance of the software.
- the analysis and (re-)organization of the environment (e.g. a department) in which the CBR system should be introduced.

All these processes have to be defined and tailored according to the needs and circumstances of the current client. This is an activity that requires a lot of practical experience. Although this experience is available in the minds of experienced application developers, it is usually not collected and stored systematically. This creates serious problems, e.g., in case of staff departures or when the companies grow and new staff must be trained. But, there is also an additional reason for the relevance of documenting the software development process. It is described in the ensuing section.

9.1.3 Contributions to Methodology Development

Contributions to the goal of developing a methodology for experience management can be found in books on CBR (Kolodner 1993; Wess 1995) and in papers reporting about the experience of people who have successfully developed CBR applications (e.g., Lewis 1995; Bartsch-Spörl 1996; Curet and Jackson 1996). Also, CBR research activities devoted to systematically analyzing CBR systems (Richter 1992a; Aamodt and Plaza 1994; Althoff and Aamodt 1996; Bergmann and Wilke 1996; Voß 1996; Kitano and Shimazu 1996) contribute. Initial experience-based contributions arose from projects where methodology development was explicitly included as one project task, like INRECA[1] (Althoff et al. 1995; Johnston et al. 1996) or APPLICUS (Bartsch-Spörl 1997). Recently, a new branch of CBR research is developing, particularly dealing with methodologies for maintaining CBR applications (Nick et al. 2001; Wilson and Leake 2001; Reinartz et al. 2001).

---

[1] The European Project INRECA (1992-1995) was predecessor of the project INRECA-II, whose results are discussed in this chapter.

Contributions also arose from other areas such as live cycle models from software engineering (e.g., Boehm 1988) or from knowledge engineering (e.g. Van de Velde 1994), requirements engineering (Shaw and Gaines 1996; Jarke and Pohl 1994), object-oriented analysis and design (Booch 1994), schema evolution for databases (Roddick 1995) as well as knowledge acquisition and elicitation (Voß 1994; Strube et al. 1995).

9.2 INRECA Methodology Overview

The basic philosophy behind the INRECA methodology is the experience-based construction of experience management applications. The idea is to support the development of experience management applications by an experience management approach itself. This experience base of the INRECA methodology contains specific experience related to the development task required for the development of an experience management application. Therefore, the INRECA methodology can be seen as a self-application of the principles of experience reuse.

The main focus of the INRECA methodology lies on the modeling of this kind of experience and, of course, on the experience itself. In certain areas, experience management application development is already a routine task with clearly identified processes. This holds, for example, in the area of simple electronic product catalogs or simple help-desk applications. However, in recent years, CBR has been applied to experience management application areas that require large-scale application development. During the course of the INRECA-II project, three major application areas have been explored and large-scale industrial applications have been developed. The experiences of these developments have been captured and are the core of the INRECA experience base. It is expected that the market for many new experience management applications opens up in the future. Therefore, the involved IT companies need to build up their own area-specific experience. To explore such new fields systematically, the experience base must must be extended and maintained. The experience management model (see Sect. 2.2ff.) is perfectly suited for this purpose.

From a technology point of view, the INRECA methodology uses a semi-formal approach. Experience is represented in the form of structured text documents that are hyper-linked in a special way. The structure of these text documents as well as the linking structure is derived from the principle modeling approach that is applied: software process modeling. This semi-formal approach was favored over a more complete formalization because it gives more flexibility for representing experience as it arises, which, in its current state, is not yet very formal. On the other hand, the limited accuracy of text-based retrieval approaches is not a big disadvantage in that currently the set of available documents is limited. In the future, when the experience base grows significantly, more formal experience representation mechanisms might be needed.

9.2.1 Process Modeling

Within the INRECA methodology, software process modeling (Curtis et al. 1992; Rombach and Verlage 1995) is the means for modeling experience management application development experience. It provides a well-defined terminology. Software process models describe the engineering of a product, e.g., the software that has to be produced. Several formalisms and terminologies for process models have already been developed (Osterweil 1987; Curtis et al. 1992; Armitage and Kellner 1994; Dellen et al. 1997). Although the particular names that are used in the different representation languages vary from one representation to another, all representations have a notation of processes, methods, and products. Figure 9.1 shows a graphical representation of these main elements.

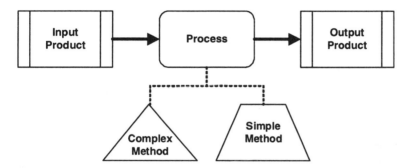

Fig. 9.1. Basic Elements of a Process Model

Processes

A process is a basic step that has to be carried out in a software development project. It is an activity that has the goal of transforming some input product(s) into some output product(s). To enact a process, different alternative methods may be available that allow the required output products to be created in a systematic way, a process is typically defined by the following properties:

- A particular goal of such a basic step. The goal specifies what has to be achieved.
- A set of different alternative methods that can be used to implement the step. Such a method specifies one particular way of carrying out the process, i.e., one way of reaching the process's goal.

- Input, output, and modified products that describe which products are required at the beginning of the step, which products must be delivered at the end, and which products are changed during enactment.
- A set of resources (agents or tools) that are required to perform the step. Here the necessary qualifications or specifications that an agent or a tool must have so that s/he/it can be assigned to the process are defined.

Clarification of Terms 9.2 (Process) A process is an activity that has the goal of transforming some input product(s) into some output product(s). It is a clearly defined step in a development project.

Methods

Methods contain a detailed specification of a particular way of reaching the goal of a process. A method can be either simple or complex. While a simple method provides only a description of what to do to reach the goal of the associated process, a complex method specifies a set of subprocesses, a set of intermediate products (called byproducts), and the flow of products among the sub-processes. This allows the definition of very flexible process models in a hierarchical manner, because very different process refinements can be described by using alternative subprocess models.

Clarification of Terms 9.3 (Method) A method is a particular way of achieving a specific goal in certain processes. A method can be simple or complex. In the latter case, it can embody a number of subprocesses and intermediate products.

Products

The main goal of processes is to create or modify products. Products include the executable software system, as well as the documentation, like design documents or user manuals.

Clarification of Terms 9.4 (Product) A product is an object that is either consumed as input, modified, or created as output of a process.

Resources

Resources are entities necessary to perform the tasks. Resources can be either agents or tools. Agents are models for humans or teams (e.g., managers, domain experts, designers, or programmers) that can be designated to perform a processes. The most relevant properties of agents are their qualifications. Tools (e.g., a modeling tool, a CBR tool, or a GUI builder) are used to support the enactment of a process and can be described by a specification. Therefore, by using the required qualifications and specifications defined in the generic process, it is possible to determine available agents and tools that can be assigned to a certain process.

Clarification of Terms 9.5 (Resources) Resources are objects that might be required to achieve a project goal. They can be financial, temporal, technical or material, as well as human resources.

9.2.2 Experience Captured in Software Process Models

In the INRECA methodology, software process models represent the experience management application development experience that is stored in the experience base. Such software processes can be very abstract, i.e., they can represent some very coarse development steps such as domain model definition, similarity measure definition, and case acquisition. Or they can be very detailed and specific for a particular project, such as analyzing data from Analog Device Inc. operational amplifier (OpAmp) product database, selecting relevant OpAmp specification parameters, and so on. The software process modeling approach allows the construction of such a hierarchically organized set of process models. Abstract processes can be described by complex methods, which are themselves a set of more detailed processes. We make use of this property to structure the experience base.

9.3 The INRECA Experience Base

The INRECA experience base about experience management application development is organized on three levels of abstraction: a *common generic level* at the top, a *cookbook level* in the middle, and a *specific project level* at the bottom (Bergmann et al. 1998). These levels are shown in Fig. 9.2.

Common Generic Level

At this level, processes, products, and methods are collected that are common for a very large spectrum of different experience management applications. The documented processes usually appear during the development of most experience management applications. The documented methods are very general and widely applicable, and give general guidance for how the respective processes can be enacted. At this common level, processes are not necessarily connected to a complete product flow that describes the development of a complete application. They can be isolated entities that can be combined in the context of a particular application or application class. Section 9.5 presents an overview of the experience management development experience on such a common generic level.

Cookbook Level

At this level, processes, products, and methods are tailored for a particular class of applications (e.g., help desk, technical maintenance, product catalogue). For each application class, the cookbook level contains a so-called

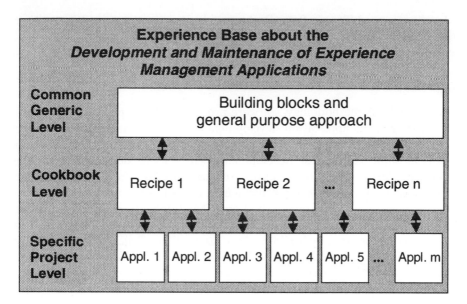

Fig. 9.2. Structure of the Experience Base.

recipe. Such a recipe describes how an application of that kind should be developed and/or maintained. Thus process models contained in such a recipe provide specific guidance for the development of an experience management application of this application class. Usually, these items are more concrete versions of items described at the common generic level. Unlike processes at the common generic level, all processes that are relevant for an application class are connected and build a product flow from which a specific project plan can be developed. The chapters 10 and 11 include two such recipes, one for developing electronic commerce applications and one for developing self-service and help-desk applications.

Specific Project Level

The specific project level describes experience in the context of a single, particular project that has already been carried out. It contains project-specific information, such as the particular processes that were carried out, the effort that was required for these processes, the products that were produced, the methods that were used to perform the processes, and the people who were involved in executing the processes. It is a complete documentation of the project, which is more and more important today to guarantee the quality standards (e.g., ISO 9000, Jackson and Ashton 1994 or SPICE, Software Quality Institute) required by industrial clients.

9.4 Process Modeling in INRECA

Now, the basic concepts and, in particular, the terminology of software process modeling as it is used in the INRECA methodology will be explained more precisely.

9.4.1 Technical, Organizational, and Managerial Processes

We distinguish three types of processes that are involved in a software development project:

- technical processes,
- organizational processes,
- managerial processes.

Technical Processes

First of all, there are the *technical processes,* which describe the development of the system and the required documentation itself. Some of the technical processes that are part of most software development projects are, for instance, requirements analysis, system design, implementation, and testing.

Organizational Processes

The second kind of processes that are part of most standard software development processes are the *organizational processes.* They address those parts of the user organization's business process in which the software system will be embedded. New processes have to be introduced into an existing business process, such as training end-users or the technical maintenance of the system. Existing processes may need to be changed or re-organized to make the best use of the new software system. For example, the introduction of a help-desk system for hot-line support, requires new processes for training the hot-line personnel, for archiving request-records, and for updating and maintaining the help-desk system.

Managerial Processes

The third kind of processes are *managerial processes.* The primary goal of managerial processes is to provide an environment and services for the development of software that meet the product requirements and project goals, i.e., services for enacting the technical and the organizational processes. Examples of managerial processes are project planning, monitoring, and quality assurance.

9.4.2 Interaction among Processes

Typically, a process produces an output product that is used as an input to another process. For example, the process "Perform Feasibility Study" produces as its main output an "Evaluation Document" product. Then, this evaluation document is used as input for the process "Perform First Project Phase." Figure 9.3 shows this kind of interaction between these two processes. This figure also shows the graphical notation the INRECA methodology uses for processes and products. For processes, we use rectangles with rounded edges, while products are displayed as rectangles with a double line on the left and right side. Processes and products are connected by different kinds of arrows. An arrow from a process to a product denotes that the product is contained in the output-products description of the process, i.e., it is produced by the process. An arrow from a product to a process denotes that the product is contained in the input-products description of the process, i.e., it is required by the process. A double-headed arrow between a product and a process denotes that the product is contained in the modified-products description of the process, i.e., it is modified by the process (no double-headed arrows occur in Fig. 9.3).

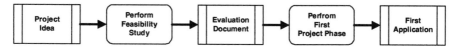

Fig. 9.3. Interaction among Processes.

For each process, there can be several alternative methods that describe alternatives to enacting the process. Simple methods are graphically denoted by a trapezoid, while complex methods are printed as a triangle. Figure 9.4 shows the "Feasibility Study" process together with two alternative complex methods.

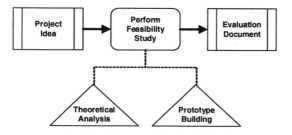

Fig. 9.4. Two Alternative Complex Methods.

Complex methods are called complex because they consist of several subprocesses connected in a particular way. Together, these subprocesses describe the details of how to enact the respective complex method. For example the method "Prototype Building" can be described in further detail by the subprocesses and the product flow shown in Fig 9.5. All these subprocesses have to be enacted in order to implement the complex method "Prototype Building." Please note that as a result of the subprocesses of a method, all required output products of the higher-level process must be produced. In the example shown here, the "Evaluation Document" is created by the product flow shown in Fig. 9.5 and is further used in 9.3 as input to the process "Perform First Project Phase."

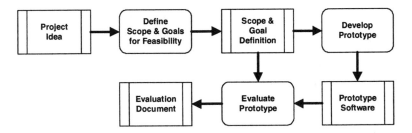

Fig. 9.5. Product Flow for the Complex Method "Prototype Building".

By this approach, the whole software development activity can be divided into several isolated parts that are easy to understand. Also, these parts can be reused individually for new projects or modules.

9.4.3 Combining Processes to Process Models

One of the main ideas behind software process modeling is to make explicit all the processes, products, methods, resources, and interactions of which a software project consists. These are kinds of information that contain very valuable experience about the software development process. They should be captured, stored, and reused for setting up and implementing new projects. The processes, products, and methods must be identified and documented in a clear and understandable way. The diagrams alone are not sufficient for this purpose. Each of the elements that occur in a diagram must be described in sufficient detail. Such a description of processes, products, and methods is called a *process model*. Obviously, making these elements explicit provides a solid basis for project planning. For example, the effort required for the project can be calculated based on the processes involved in the project. Explicitly documented processes and the management of the products that arise also support the execution and monitoring of a project. Documenting processes is also essential for controlling and improving the quality of the product (software) being produced. Documentation is also essential to ensure compliance with current quality standards.

9.4.4 Generic and Specific Descriptions

The INRECA methodology distinguishes between *generic* and *specific* descriptions for processes, products, and methods. The differences will be made clear in the following sections.

Generic Descriptions

The *generic descriptions* describe processes, products, and methods in a way that is independent of a specific development project. They contain generalized information that is likely to be useful in several specific situations.

Again consider, for instance, the process of building a GUI for a experience management application. The process "GUI Development" has one input product, namely the document describing the specification of the GUI, and two output products, one for the software implementing the GUI and one for the documentation describing how to use the GUI. The generic description of the input product (GUI specification document) declares what information in general should be contained in a GUI specification document. It does not say anything about a particular GUI to be developed within a project. Moreover, the generic description of the GUI building process should also specify that one agent is required who has programming capabilities and who is familiar with a GUI-builder, and that a tool is required, namely a GUI-builder, that is flexible enough to produce the kind of GUI that is required. All this is generic information, not restricted to a single project and, therefore widely applicable. The generic description does not contain any information on exactly what the GUI looks like, which person is actually allocated to the task of building the GUI, or which particular GUI-builder is used. The generic information only describes requirements of agents or tools, and general guidelines on how to execute a process.

Generic descriptions are the most important part of the experience base. They are used to document the common generic level and the cookbook level of our experience base.

Specific Descriptions

Specific descriptions elaborate processes, products, and methods for a particular development project. Usually, they are created after the project is finished. Specific descriptions contain information such as the specific agents who were involved in enacting the process and specific tools that were used. For the purpose of documentation, they can also contain information about the effort that was spent for a process, and so forth.

Consider, for instance, a specific GUI development process. The specific description for this process contains information about the input and output products, e.g., the client's GUI specification, the GUI software, and its documentation. It contains references to the specific client's specification document from the project. Moreover, it also contains information about the particular programmer who built the GUI (e.g., James Simon) and about the particular GUI-builder tool that was used (e.g., Visual Basic).

9.5 The Common Generic Level

A large number of processes are involved in an experience management project. As introduced in Sect. 9.4.1, we distinguish between the technical processes (software development and knowledge modeling), the organizational processes (ensuring that the problem solving process itself and the involved problem solvers take advantage of the experience management application), and the management of the associated application development and the introduction of the resulting software into the problem solving process. However, this distinction does not imply that these different kinds of processes can be considered independently.

Fig. 9.6 gives an overview of the top-level processes and products at the common generic level. Only the top-level processes and products are shown in this figure. For most of these top-level processes, refinements have been defined through subprocesses which are combined in the context of complex methods or subproducts. Here, we only give an overview of top-level processes that have been identified. Full details are available on electronic media (Bergmann et al. 1999b; INRECA Consortium 1999).

At this top-level, the processes look very much like processes that might occur in any IT project. While this is in fact true for some of the processes or subprocesses (e.g. some of the managerial processes are standard IT processes) most of them are described at the lower levels in a way that is particularly tailored for CBR application development. In the following we give an overview of all the top-level processes and there interactions, before explaining them in some more detail.

9.5.1 Overview

An experience management project starts with a statement of a client's problem. In the *top-level start-up* process (managerial) a first vision document is created, which preliminary defines the mission of the project. The following *goal definition* process (managerial) is executed in strong interaction with the *preliminary organizational analysis* process (organizational). The organizational problems (that should be addressed by introducing the experience management system) and the respective problem owners are identified. Additionally, a basic goal checklist for the project is created. Based on this goal

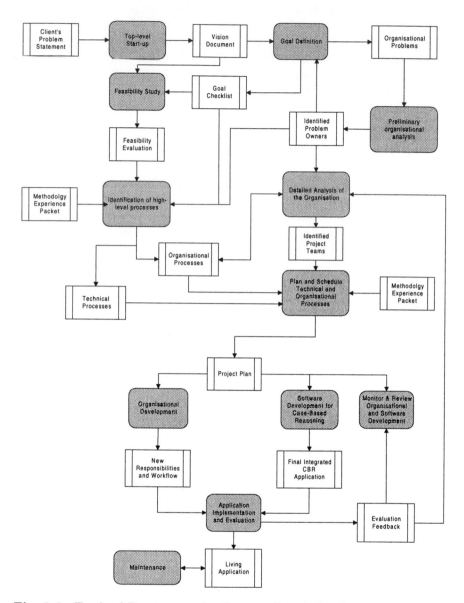

Fig. 9.6. Top-level Processes at the Common Generic Level.

check list and the general project vision, a *feasibility study* (technical) should be carried out. Depending on the results of this study, it must be decided whether

- to continue the project as planned,
- to revise the main project goals,
- to stop the project.

Thereafter, the *identification of the high-level processes* (managerial) leads to a set of technical and organizational processes that should be addressed within the project. The INRECA experience base should be consulted during this process since it gives valuable advice on the processes that are relevant. Additionally, a *detailed analysis of the organization* (organizational process) can be carried out in order to revise and refine the set of organizational processes that should be addressed and to identify possible project teams. Then, the project leader should *plan and schedule the technical and organizational processes* (managerial) and produce an overall project plan. Here, again the experience base should be consulted in order to build on concrete experience from other, similar experience management projects. The resulting project plan is then enacted and monitored during the technical process of *software development for case-based reasoning* and the *organizational development* of the environment into which the experience management system will be introduced. The resulting software implementation and the newly established responsibilities and workflow in the organization will then be *implemented and evaluated.*

Typically, a experience management project requires several development cycles, each of which results in a prototype application that is evaluated by the end-user. The evaluation feedback states whether a new development cycle must be considered or whether a satisfying solution is reached already. At this point, the first living application being in real use has been reached. During the lifetime of this application, some *maintenance* (technical process) will be required during which the application will be modified.

Please note that a separate *monitor & review* process (managerial) is introduced. This process controls the enactment of the software and organizational development. This process does not have a formal output. It also uses the evaluation feedback from the implemented application to allow the project leader to decide whether a new development cycle should be considered to further improve the current system or the organizational structure.

9.5.2 Managerial Processes

This subsection is primarily concerned with the management of the process of development and implementation of the system in its context, but it also touches the other two aspects where necessary given that they are impossible to separate. Managing an experience management project (or any AI project in general) differs from managing other IT projects to the extent that the associated concepts of the technologies are mostly previously unknown to the users. Therefore, there must be more than usual emphasis on early awareness training, and user-participation in the successive iterations of the prototyping process.

Top-Level Start-Up

During the top-level start-up process, client and the top-management of the consulting firm agree on a terms of reference, which specifies the problem or opportunity to be addressed. During this process, the project leader is also identified. This person should have the time and motivation to ensure that the project is a success, and should also have some ownership of the project results. The leader then helps to define the overall project vision stated in the vision document in close interactive consultation with the client and the consultant-firm's management. It is also the duty of the leader to set up a system for monitoring the implementation of the project.

Goal Definition

The first process after start-up is to define the project goal. The vision of what life will be like when the project is completed has to be written down. At this stage, it is appropriate to introduce a high-level abstract concept of a case, and to identify what will be different about the people, their tasks, the technology and organization when the project is finished. This description should also elaborate any associated or dependent goals, in a goal checklist. These goals should be agreed amongst all participants in the project, and by anybody affected by the outcomes of the project. When this has been done, it becomes possible to define the high-level processes which support the performance of scheduled technical and organizational tasks during the whole project.

Identification of High-Level Processes

Even though it is difficult to define precisely each project process in detail, it is possible first to produce a lot of high-level processes that have to be enacted in order to achieve the project goal. As described, the processes can usefully be subdivided into technical and organizational categories. For each process the project planner should check the resource requirements, input- and output products and the dependencies between processes. The determination of the relevant processes should be done based on existing experience management development experience. For this purpose, the project leader should have access to the experience base of INRECA methodology.

Plan and Schedule Processes

During the detailed planning of the technical and organization processes, a couple of important aspects must be considered by the project leader. S/he must

- ensure that the immediate objectives of each project phase are embedded in strategic objectives of the overall project.

- ensure that in the design of the system there is provision for the participative interactive re-design of the work-practices of those using it.
- ensure that when the developed system is implemented, there is timely provision for the necessary level of training in its use by all who interact with it.
- ensure that the implemented system is evaluated critically, with a view to future improvements, identification of possible weaknesses etc., bearing in mind that experience management is an ongoing process.

Monitoring and Review of Organizational and Software Development

There is no difference in monitoring and reviewing the development processes compared to the management of standard IT projects. The implementation of the project plan in the organizational and software development processes must be monitored by the project leader. S/he must ensure that the important project milestones can be reached in time. S/he must control the overall quality of the development process and of the deliverables. Based on the feedback from the evaluation of the application the project leader finally has to decide whether a new organizational or technical development cycle should be considered.

9.5.3 Technical Processes: Software Development

The technical processes described in this subsection are general processes, i.e., such processes that are expected to be part of most experience management application development projects. A number of the technical processes appear in usual software development projects, too. An example is the GUI development process. Such processes can be handled by standard methods. We emphasize on the specific aspects of experience management.

Feasibility Study

The feasibility study consists of a cost/benefit analysis and should deliver an estimation of the commercial success potential of the intended experience management application. A simple mock-up of the intended application should be developed as a means to further clarify the goals and the vision of the project as well as a means to convince the customer to believe in the success of the project. Figure 9.7 gives a brief overview of the subprocesses involved in the feasibility study.

Software Development for Case-Based Reasoning

This is the technical top-level process during which the experience management application itself is developed. An experience management application

Cost/Benefit Analysis
Application Mock-up Development
    GUI Mock-up Development
    Case-Base Mock-up Development
    Retrieval Mock-up Development
    Integration Mock-up Development

Fig. 9.7. Sub-Processes Occurring in the Feasibility Study Process.

Knowledge Modeling
    Domain Analysis
    Identification of Utility Criteria
    Vocabulary Development
        Selection of Case Representation Approach
        Selection of Representation Objects
        Selection of Attributes
        Formalization of Vocabulary
    Similarity Development
        Similarity Characterization
        Similarity Definition
        Similarity Integration and Formalization
    Adaptation Development
        Selection of Representation Approach
        Determination of Adaptation Scope
        Formalization of Adaptation Knowledge
    Case Acquisition
        Develop Case Collection Forms
        Collect Case Data
        Evaluate Selected Good Cases
        Case Entry into the Case Base
GUI Development
    GUI Requirements Analysis
    GUI Design
    GUI Programming
    GUI Manual Writing
    GUI Acceptance Testing
Retrieval Engine Development
    Retrieval Requirements Analysis
    Retrieval Engine Design
    Retrieval Engine Implementation
    Retrieval Engine Test
Adaptation Engine Development
    Adaptation Requirements Analysis
    Adaptation Engine Design
    Adaptation Engine Implementation
    Adaptation Engine Test
System Integration
    Integration Requirements Analysis
    Integration Design
    Integration Implementation
    Integration Test

Fig. 9.8. Sub-Processes occurring in the Software Development Process.

development process in general is a usual software development process with mostly standard ingredients on its top-level. This includes a large number of different subprocesses listed hierarchically in Fig. 9.8. Each of these processes is described in detail by Bergmann et al. (1999b).

Maintenance

Maintenance is the technical top-level process during which the experience management application is maintained during its life-time in the organization (see subprocesses listed in Fig. 9.9). Maintenance usually involves the performance monitoring of the current problem solving cycle. The evaluation should yield modification needs. Those can be implemented by first modifying the vocabulary (if necessary) and then modifying the reuse-related knowledge and the experience base. All operations performed in the maintenance cycle lead to a changed (hopefully improved) behavior of the problem solving cycle. In the recent literature, different detailed frameworks for the maintenance cycle have been proposed (Nick et al. 2001; Wilson and Leake 2001; Reinartz et al. 2001).

```
Maintenance
    Monitoring of the Experience Management Performance
    Change Selection
    Updating the Vocabulary
    Updating the Reuse-related Knowledge
    Updating the Experience Base
        Updating the Similarity Measures
        Updating the Adaptation Knowledge
    Test of Aspired Change
    Apply Update on Living Application
```

Fig. 9.9. Sub-Processes occurring in the Maintenance Process.

9.5.4 Organizational Processes

In analyzing the existing organization's structure and related procedures, there is a preliminary scoping of the environment of the project. This includes a listing of the perceived problems and opportunities at the human and organizational levels.

Preliminary Organizational Analysis

In the preliminary organizational analysis process the first step is to identify the boundaries of the socio-technical problem solving scenario that should be improved by introducing an experience management system. Once this has been identified, it can be regarded as being a 'production' unit embedded in a larger organization. We need to enact this preliminary organizational analysis in strong interaction with the managerial goal definition process. Bearing this in mind, we go on to analyze the processes embedded in the problem solving scenario, and to assess the impact of the technological change. This naturally leads to a synthesis in which the processes are re-organized in the context of experience management.

Detailed Analysis of the Organization

The design of the experience management system will be the result of an iterative process involving all the people in the existing organization who are involved with the cases, the collective of stakeholders who own the material which will end up in the experience base, and who are potential users of the results of the system.

It is useful, having identified the problems and/or opportunities, to set up one or more working groups focused on them, to address the questions

- how is this problem handled elsewhere and
- how does the present situation compare with other experience management applications?

The group should consider the processes, the people, the technologies and the structure within the socio-technical problem solving scenario which deals with the cases. In this way they can begin to tease out the implications for the organization.

Organizational Development

During the organizational development, a new workflow for the organization must be developed that takes care of the processes having to do with the introduction of experience management. The new workflow must cover the continuous acquisition of new experience items as they arise in the organization and should explicitly introduce experience utilization steps. Measures should be included that motivate knowledge owners to give away and formalize their experience (e.g. an incentive or credit point system) and means for ensuring the quality of experience items should also be considered (e.g. an experience certification board). Finally, an overall performance monitoring approach for the experience management system should be considered. This is particularly necessary for maintenance purposes.

Besides the development of the new workflow the new responsibilities that result from the aspired organizational change must identified and the impact for each individual person should be estimated. Training material for the involved personal must be developed.

Application Implementation and Evaluation

During this process, the new organizational workflow and the experience management IT system are integrated and implemented in the organization. This requires

- the installation of the new hard- and software to run the experience management system,
- training the personnel in performing the new workflow and in using the experience management system,
- testing the aspired change of the organizational workflow in a trial run, and
- implementing the new organizational workflow.

9.6 Documenting the INRECA Experience

Generic and specific processes, products, and methods are documented (and stored in the experience base) using different types of sheets. One such sheet is like a structured page containing all relevant information about the respective item in a predefined format. The sheets help to standardize the documentation of the experience. They are created as Web pages, which can be viewed using a standard Internet browser. Hence, accessing the experience base becomes a very easy task that does not require any specialized knowledge. Also the just described common generic level is documented in this form and consists of more than 150 linked sheets. Altogether, the following types of sheets are available:

- generic process description sheet,
- generic product description sheet,
- generic simple method description sheet,
- generic complex method description sheet,
- specific process description sheet,
- specific product description sheet,
- specific simple method description sheet,
- specific complex method description sheet.

Each sheet is a structured form that contains several predefined slots that should be filled in to document the process, product, or method. Before introducing these sheets in detail, we will give a brief overview of the different kinds of sheets and how they are related (see Fig. 9.10). A single sheet is used to describe processes. This sheet will contain references to the respective input, output, and modified products of the process. Every product is documented by using a separate description sheet. The process description also contains references to the applicable methods. A method can be either a *simple method* (which is elementary and does not contain any references to

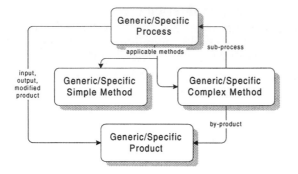

Fig. 9.10. Link Structure of Description Sheets.

other description sheets) or a *complex method*. A complex method connects several subprocesses (each of which is again documented as a separate generic process description), which may exchange some byproducts (documented as separate descriptions).

The sheets for the generic and specific items look very similar. They have the same fields for entering information. The difference is that in the specific sheets, the fields are filled with project-specific information, while in the generic sheets the fields contain project-independent, generalized information.

9.6.1 Process Description Sheets

Generic and specific *process description sheets* contain several fields to hold the information that is necessary for understanding what the process is supposed to do. Figure 9.11 shows an example of a generic process description sheet.

Recipe/Project Name. Every process belongs to a particular level in the experience base and within this level to a particular recipe or project. For generic description sheets, the name of the recipe is noted, for specific description sheets the name of the project is noted.

Process Name. The process name assigns each process description a unique identifier, i.e., a text string. The name should be as short as possible but should clearly identify the process. Names of generic process descriptions are subsequently used as references to the generic process description itself.

Process Goal. The goal describes *what* the process is supposed to do, specified by a textual description. The process goal does not state how the process is performed. This information is recorded in the methods. Obviously, the goal of a process is partially contained in the process name. Since the process name should be as short as possible, a more detailed goal specification is often required.

Input Product, Output Product, Modified Product. Input products are products that are required during the enactment of the process to achieve the desired result. Output products are products that are produced during the enactment of the process. Usually, the production of these output products is one of the goals of the process. Modified products are products that are changed or extended during the enactment of the process. Usually, the modification of these products is also one of the goals of the process. All products are referenced through the product name. The respective product sheets can be reached by following the included HTML links.

Applicable Method. Applicable methods specify a set of alternative methods to implement the process. Typically, a process can be implemented by different methods from which one is selected to perform the process. A method describes *how* the goal of the process can be achieved. Here, we do not specify the contents of the methods, but only the names of the methods. Each method should be described in a separate sheet that includes all required details. The respective method sheets can be reached by following the included HTML links.

Agents. Agents fields specify the type of agents (personnel) who are involved in the process, together with their qualifications and the kinds of the organizations to which they belong. The qualifications that the agent must have in order to execute the respective process is a very important issue. For instance, "experience in GUI development" is a proper qualification for a programmer involved in the GUI development process. One of the agents involved in the process has to be declared "responsible" for the process.

Required Tools. The required tool specification lists all kinds of tools that are required to enact the process. For each tool, the most important requirements should be noted as well. For instance "can import Word documents and export HTML" might be proper requirements for a word processor.

Administrative Information. Additionally, some administrative information about a sheet is required. This is important in order to maintain the sheets and to distinguish among different versions. This information is the name of the sheet author, the version of the sheet, and the date of the last change.

9.6.2 Product Description Sheets

Products may be software, text documents, graphics, sound, and so on. Generic and specific *product description sheets* contain several fields to hold the information that is necessary for understanding what the product consists of or should consist of. Figure 9.12 shows an example of a generic product description sheet.

Module/Project Name. This field mentions the recipe (for generic sheets) or the project (for specific sheets) to which the product belongs. This is the same as for the process description sheets.

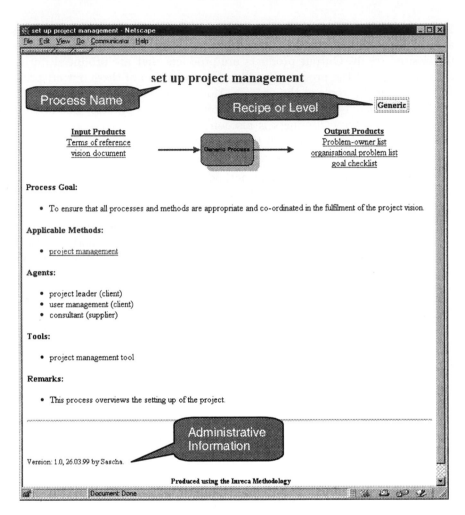

Fig. 9.11. Example Process Description Sheet.

Product Name. The name should be as short as possible but should clearly identify the product. Product names are used in the process description to specify the input, output, or modified product. Examples of appropriate product names are "Requirements Document" or "CBR Prototype Software."

Product Description. This is a detailed textual description of the product or a reference to a detailed "external" specification. From this description, it should become clear what product must be produced. If necessary, quality standards for the product also can be noted.

Administrative Information. The same administrative information is required as for the process description sheets.

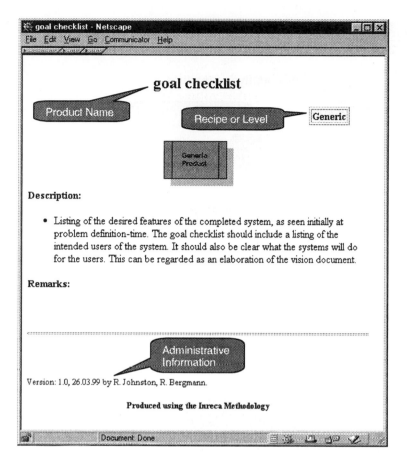

Fig. 9.12. Example Product Description Sheet.

9.6.3 Simple Method Description Sheets

Typically, there are several ways to enact a process. A *method* describes one such way. While the process declares *what* should be done, a method explains *how* to do it. Simple methods describe the "how-to" using a short section of text. If a method needs to be described in more detail, complex method descriptions should be used. Figure 9.13 shows an example of a generic simple-method description sheet. It consists of the following fields:

Module/Project Name. This field mentions the recipe (for generic sheets) or the project (for specific sheets) to which the product belongs. This is the same as for the process description sheets.

Method Name. The method name should be as short as possible but should clearly identify the method. Names of simple method descriptions are used in the applicable methods section of process descriptions.

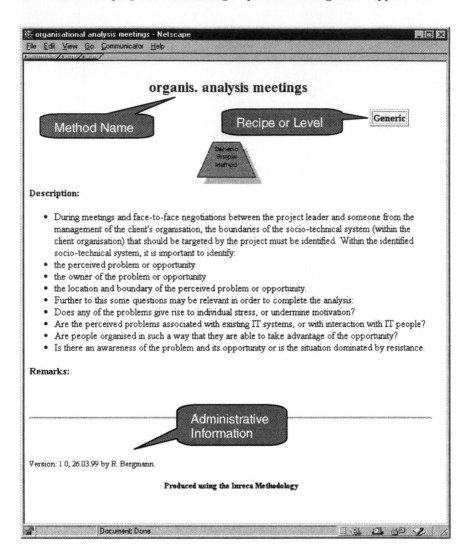

Fig. 9.13. Example Simple Method Description Sheet.

Method Description The method description contains a "how-to" description about the enactment of the actual process. Such a description should contain all information necessary for the assigned agents to produce the specified products. Experiences from earlier projects can be captured in these descriptions by giving descriptions of "good" examples or warnings of steps that were not successful in the past. In general, this description will be informal, i.e., narrative text. However, if formalisms or schemata exist for structuring such descriptions, they should be used. For example, a simple method that describes the design of the similarity measure could give guidelines on how a local similarity measure should be chosen, depending on the kind of attributes.

Administrative Information. The same administrative information is required as for the process description sheets.

9.6.4 Complex Method Description Sheets

Complex methods are necessary when a method needs to be described in more detail. In that case, a method itself can be decomposed into several subprocesses, which interact in a certain way and exchange products. Hence, a complex method consists of several subprocesses and the product flow among them. Figure 9.14 shows an example of a generic complex method description sheet. It consists of the following fields:

Module/Project Name. This field mentions the recipe (for generic sheets) or the project (for specific sheets) to which the product belongs. This is the same as for the process description sheets.

Method Name. Each complex method has a unique name. The method name should be as short as possible but should clearly identify the method. Names of complex method descriptions are used in the applicable methods section of process descriptions.

Method Description. The method description contains a verbal description about the enactment of the actual process, similar to those of the simple methods. It should explain how the subprocesses shown in the "details section" (see below) should be enacted.

Details. The details section links to a product flow description for the complex method, like the one shown in Fig. 9.5. This contains the relevant subprocesses, and the created byproducts. Each of the subprocesses and byproducts has its own description on a separate sheet. Thereby, details can be added at several levels of abstraction, as appropriate, to describe the experience.

Administrative Information. The same administrative information is required as for the process description sheets.

9.7 Reusing and Maintaining INRECA Experience

When a new experience management project is being planned, the relevant experience from the experience base must be selected and reused. This relates to the problem solving cycle of the EMM (see Sect. 2.2.1). The recipes at the cookbook level are particularly useful for building a new application that directly falls into one of the covered application classes. The recipes are the most valuable knowledge captured in the methodology. Therefore, one should

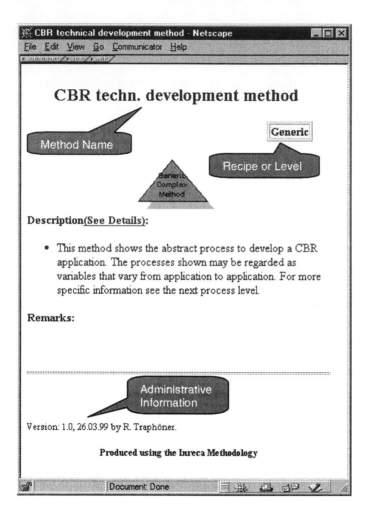

Fig. 9.14. Example Complex Method Description Sheet.

first investigate the cookbook-level to identify whether a cookbook recipe can be reused directly. If this is the case, the new experience management project can be considered a standard application, and the processes from the respective recipe can provide immediate guidance for setting up the new project. On the other hand, if the new project does not fall into one of the application classes covered by the recipe, then the new project enters a new application area. In that case, the new project plan must be constructed from scratch. However, the individual processes described in the common generic level can be used to assemble the new project plan.

9.7.1 The INRECA Reuse Procedure

Figure 9.15 shows the overall procedure for reusing the INRECA experience. It is a special variant of the problem solving cycle of the EMM that takes care of the three-level structure of the experience base.

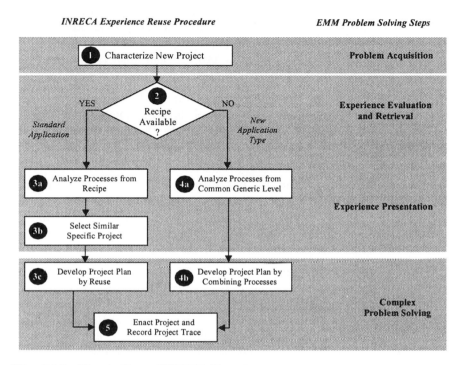

Fig. 9.15. How to Reuse INRECA Experience.

1. Characterize New Project. Identify the application area of the experience management project. The goal is to decide whether an existing recipe from the cookbook level of the methodology covers this application.

2. Recipe Available. Identify whether an appropriate recipe is available. If this is the case then continue with step 3a; otherwise continue with step 4a.

3a. Analyze Processes from Recipe. An appropriate recipe is available. The process model contained in this recipe must now be analyzed to see whether it can be mapped and tailored to the application at hand.

3b. Select Similar Specific Project. Analyze the project descriptions on the specific project level. If a similar project is available then it should be identified as to whether some of the specific experience can be reused within the scope of the current project. This might be a specific way to implement a certain process or software component. It can help to identify existing software components from previous projects that can be reused immediately on the code level.

3c. Develop New Project Plan by Reuse. Develop a project plan for the new project. This project plan is based mainly on a process model from the selected experience recipe. However, application-specific tailoring and pragmatic modifications are typically required. If components from similar projects can be identified for reuse, the project plan must take care of this fact to avoid re-development efforts.

4a. Analyze Processes from Common Generic Level. The set of processes described at the common generic level should be analyzed in the context of the new project. The goal is to identify those processes that are important for the new application. These processes can be considered the building blocks from which the new project plan can be assembled.

4b. Develop Project Plan by Combining Processes. Based on the selected processes, a new project plan must be assembled. For this purpose, the processes must be made more precise and operational. Depending on how innovative the new application area is, it might even be necessary to develop new methods or software component.

5. Enact Project and Record Project Trace. Execute the project by enacting the project plan. Document the experience during the enactment of this project. Particularly, note all deviations from the developed project plan. This is important for two reasons. First, to ensure that the development is performed according to the necessary quality standards and, second, to feedback the new experience into the experience base for reuse.

9.7.2 Relations to the EMM Problem Solving Cycle

The right side of Fig. 9.15 shows to relations between the INRECA reuse procedure and the steps of the problem solving cycle of the EMM. The complex problem to be solved in the context of the INRECA methodology is the development of the experience management application itself or the implementation of certain functions of the applications. This includes the creation of the new project plan. The INRECA experience management approach supports solving this problem.

The characterization of the new project realizes the problem acquisition phase. The characterization must be achieved in terms of

- in terms of the application type, such as "Help Desk" or "Product Catalog",
- in terms of the functions to be realized such as "similarity measure" and/or
- in terms of the experience item that should be reused such as "process", "product", or "method".

The steps 2, 3a-b, and 4a realize the experience evaluation and retrieval step combined with the experience presentation step. The retrieval step which is followed by the presentation of the retrieved experience helps answering the question whether an appropriate recipe is available. The presented experience (whole recipe or items from a process model) can then be analyzed by the application developer whose task is to select from the presented set of retrieval results to most appropriate items. Experience adaptation does not occur in the INRECA methodolgy since the adaptation of process models is not supported. However, manual adaptation occurs during the steps 3c and 4b during which the new project plan is created since retrieved process model elements can usually not by reused unmodified.

During the complex problem solving step of the EMM, the project plan is developed and enacted. This new project plan as well as its modification during its execution is new experience that enters the development and maintenance cycle of the EMM as feedback. This feedback must then be included into INRECA experience base.

9.7.3 Development and Maintenance of the INRECA Experience Base

After a project is finished, it is very important that the experience and the lessons learned are not lost, but are captured for inclusion into thc experience base, which is the core of the INRECA methodology. This is necessary for continuous improvement of the experience management software-development process. This maintenance activity is a kind of maintenance methodology for the INRECA methodology itself.

For the INRECA methodology, a particular extension and update procedure for the experience base has been developed (see Fig. 9.16).

6. Analyze Project Trace. Collect all information that had been captured about the finished project. Analyze this information and identify the processes that were actually performed during the enactment of the project.

7. Add Specific Project. Document the project by creating a specific process description that accurately describes what has been done in the project. Add this process description to the specific project level of the INRECA experience base. If appropriate, create links to the cookbook-level recipes from which this project had been derived.

8. Create or Update Recipe (Optional). Based on the experience collected from the new project, it might become necessary to update an existing recipe or even to create a completely new one. An existing recipe might need to be updated if the following situation was encountered: A recipe was used to setup the project plan for the current project (step 3a in Fig. 9.15) but the experience from enacting the project indicated significant deviations from this plan. In this case, an update of the recipe is required to cover this newly learned lessons.

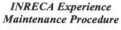

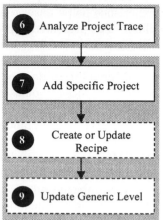

Fig. 9.16. Adding New Experience.

A new recipe might need to be created, if a new type of application was developed that was not covered by any of the existing recipes (steps 4a+b in Fig. 9.15). The process description for the new specific project can then be generalized into a new cookbook-level recipe. For this purpose, all project-specific information must be abstracted so that only those pieces remain that are likely to be reused for new, similar applications. It is very likely that this generalization process can be achieved only after several projects of this new application area have been realized. This avoids generalizing single experiences and is more reliable.

9. Update Generic Level (Optional). If during the previous steps some new generic processes, methods, or products can be identified that are of more general interest, i.e., relevant for more than one application class, then they should be added to the common generic level of the experience base.

9.8 Tool Support for the INRECA Methodology

The IT tool support for the INRECA methodology focuses on the two main problem areas:

1. the modeling and publication of the experience in form of process models and
2. specialized knowledge modeling tools for the vocabulary and the reuse-related knowledge

9.8.1 INRECA Experience Modeling Methodology Tool

We can document a specific experience management project, a recipe for an application class, or common generic experience management development experience using the INRECA experience modeling methodology tool. This tool describes projects in terms of a process diagram where each element of the diagram links to information about the process or product in a database. The tool supports the creation of a web site for a given project, allowing the documentation to be shared among distributed members of a development team. The INRECA experience modeling methodology tool is implemented using the Visio modeling software from Visio Corporation. Visio is a graphical software tool that supports professionals in diagramming systems, structures, and processes in business environments. The basic element of a Visio document is the page. A collection of pages linked together in some sequence is a document. Individual pages generally contain shapes that are linked together on the page to create a drawing. Figures 9.3 to 9.5 give examples of such drawings created with the INRECA experience modeling methodology Tool.

Shapes, in turn, can be linked to other pages in the document. A given shape has a range of properties that can be edited using the Visio Professional software tool or using the developer's environment provided by Visual Basic for Applications. Visio provides a range of shape stencils, each of which contains the symbols for a specific kind of diagram or modeling approach.

Rationale for Selecting Visio

Reasons for selecting Visio to support the INRECA methodology are the following.

- Visio gives a good variety of standard shapes, which can be labeled, linked, and manipulated singly or in groups. Thus, we can have special shapes for products, processes, and methods.
- Shapes can be hot-linked to explanatory material to support the explanations of the meanings of the shapes and their linkages. We used this feature to attach the information contained in description sheets to the shapes.
- A recursive structure of Visio pages can be constructed, with an overview of the total project on page 1 and the shapes being hot-linked to subsequent Visio pages. Those pages develop the underlying detail, still in diagram form, and the shapes on these detail pages themselves can be hot-linked down to the underlying documentation.
- The Visio diagram can be saved in runtime mode as an HTML file with its hotlinks to other HTML files preserved, thus forming an integral part of a robust HTML system.
- Visio supports application development through an implementation of Visual Basic for Applications. This allows us to customize the Visio functionality to meet the needs of the INRECA methodology.

- Access to databases is supported by Visio, allowing us to maintain in a consistent database structure the documentation for a specific project or a recipe.

Standard Recursive Structure

The first page of the Visio diagram consists of a set of high-level process-shapes connecting input product shapes and output product shapes, possibly via one or more intermediate product-shapes. The page header has the project name (if specific), or the recipe name (if cookbook), or just states "Common Generic" for the top-level of the experience base.

In general the processes can be linked to complex-method shapes, which are hot-linked to related Visio documents, each of which constitutes an overview explanation in diagram form of the complex method itself, and so on. The recursion stops when all processes in a diagram can be implemented using simple methods.

Managing Several Recipes and Projects

Typically, the development experience resides in an R&D group or a developmental IT department. Within this unit, the INRECA experience base is likely to exist on one person's system, or on a local server accessible to a named group of experts. The directory structure supporting this experience base might consist of a root directory called "CBR Experience" that contains a set of Visio diagrams and associated explanatory sheets filled in at an abstract, generic level.

Within this directory there is also a set of subdirectories, each representing a domain of experience within which projects may be developed using a common set of cookbook experiences. Within each cookbook directory there is a set of project subdirectories, each containing the experience of a specific project.

The tool supports the creation of a plan for a specific project from a cookbook recipe. The resulting Visio document can then be used to allocate tasks in the project and to record the experience of the project team. This experience then can be used to revise the cookbook recipe, if necessary.

HTML Publication

Each project in the methodology can be easily published in HTML format. The tool will create the diagrams and sheets for the entire project, which can then be published on an Intranet or Internet site. The best practices of performing the development processes are maintained, and they become valuable means of sharing project knowledge and maintaining reference points.

9.8.2 Knowledge Modeling Tools

A set of tools has been developed to support the knowledge modeling processes of the development and maintenance methodology. These tools, which are integrated in the CBR-Works tool (tec:inno GmbH 1999), are now briefly sketched.

Vocabulary Modeling

The CBR-Works Concept Hierarchy Editor (see Fig. 9.17) enables the object-oriented modeling of vocabularies for case representation according to the representation framework described in Sect. 3.3.2. The left side of this editor shows the current hierarchy of object classes in a tree-view. Classes can be added, removed, or moved to a new position in the hierarchy.

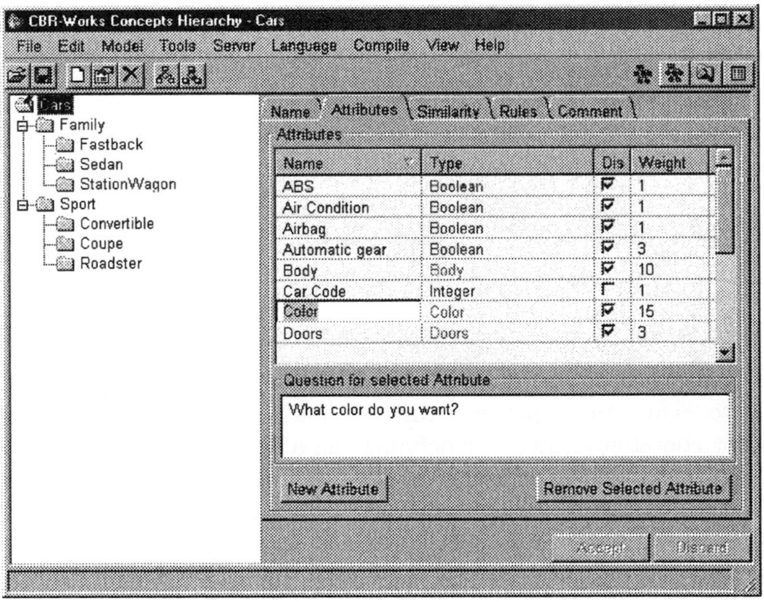

Fig. 9.17. CBR-Works Concept Hierarchy Editor.

The definition of an object class can be edited in the Concept Editor Dialog Region (right side of the window), which is integrated in the Concept Hierarchy Editor. The Name tab is used to add additional information to a class, i.e., naming and annotation for different languages, comments to the concept, and information about its creator.

The Attribute tab (see right side of Fig. 9.17) is used to define the attributes of a concept. An attribute entry has several parts: The name of the attribute, its type, a discriminant check-box that specifies whether the attribute can be used during similarity assessment, as well as a default value for a weight.

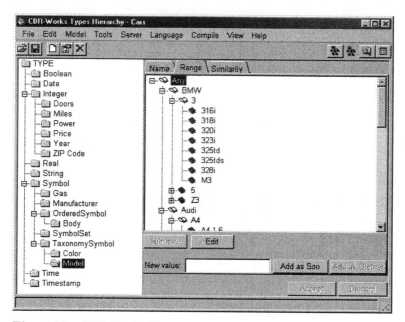

Fig. 9.18. CBR-Works Type Hierarchy Editor.

The CBR-Works Type Hierarchy Editor is shown in Fig. 9.18. It serves as an editor to define the types and their similarity measures being used in the Concept Hierarchy Editor for defining the attributes. Types are also arranged in a hierarchy that is displayed and edited in a tree-view. Different types require different kinds of specifications. The left side of Fig. 9.18 shows the definition editor for a taxonomy type.

Modeling Similarity Measures

The similarity modeling tools are integrated with the concept and the type editor since the modeling strongly refers to the defined vocabulary. For each type a local similarity measure can be defined. The kind of similarity modeling depends on the kind of the type. While for a symbolic type an editable table is shown that holds the local similarity values, numeric types can be graphically edited as shown in Fig. 9.19. First, the characteristic properties of the local similarity measure are selected (e.g. symmetry, monotony, etc., see Sect. 4.2.2) and then the curve representing the similarity value with

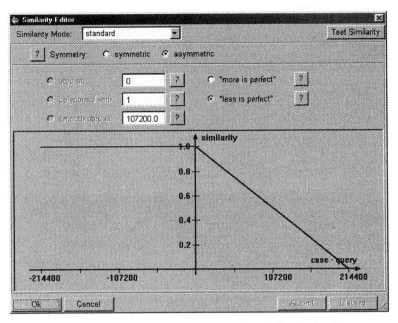

Fig. 9.19. Similarity Editor for Numeric Local Similarity Measures.

respect to the difference of the query and the case value (see Sect. 4.3.4) can be modeled.

For taxonomic attribute types, the similarity modeling approach as described in Sect. 4.3.6 is supported by the editor (see Fig. 9.20). On the left side of the editor the semantic characteristics for using the taxonomy are specified by radio buttons. On the right side of the editor, the taxonomy is shown in a tree-view and similarity values can be assigned to the inner nodes of the taxonomy. The same editor is also used for modeling the intra-class similarity for structured cases (see Sect. 4.4.2). In this case the tree-view shows the class hierarchy instead of the taxonomy of symbols.

Modeling Rules

The CBR-Works modeling tools also include an editor for adaptation and completion rules. This editor allows the modeling of rules, according to the representation introduced in Sect. 5.1. This editor is shown in Fig. 9.21. Rules can be assigned to any class in the class hierarchy. The class, which rules are currently displayed and which can be edited, is shown in the tree-view on the left side of this window. For each rule, preconditions and actions can be specified. For both, specific editors are used that enable the definition of a condition without knowing the particular rule syntax.

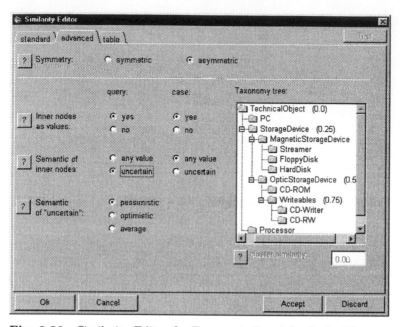

Fig. 9.20. Similarity Editor for Taxonomic Local Similarity Measures.

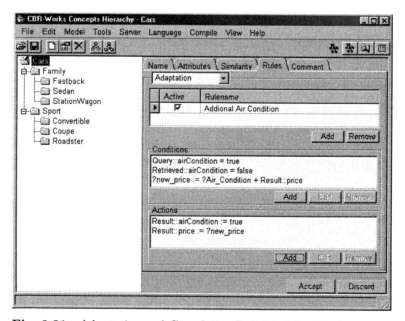

Fig. 9.21. Adaptation and Completion Rule Modeling Tool.

Part III

Experience Management Application Areas

10. Experience Management for Electronic Commerce

> *"On the Internet companies only have computers representing them. They better be intelligent computers"*
>
> Chuck Williams, CEO Brightware

A major requirement of today's online shops is the availability of competent virtual sales agents that guide the customers through the vast space of available products, services, and other opportunities. Today's state-of-the-art online shops provide search functions that should help customers to find relevant product information. While these search functions are considered quite important by the online sellers, the quality of the retrieval results is miserable (Hagen 2000). The key to enhancing search quality, and more generally, to approach the vision of intelligent knowledgeable virtual sales agents, is to incorporate more knowledge about products, customers and the sales process into the sales agent. This is particularly important in the world of today and tomorrow, which is characterized through continuously increasing globalization. The quality of service becomes the dominating factor for achieving customer satisfaction and a good customer relationship. As a consequence customer relationship management (CRM) (Martin 1999; Newell 1999; CRM Forum 1999) and knowledge management (KM) have been recognized as core disciplines with strategic importance for successful future business. In the context of companies which communicate with their customers and partners via electronic online media, this requires making the company knowledge available and visible thorough the virtual agents that are supposed to be the primary access points to the company.

This chapter describes a generic experience management approach for electronic commerce. The results presented in this chapter have been achieved as part of the WEBSELL project and have been previously published in part by Vollrath et al. (1998), Wilke (1999), Schmitt and Bergmann (1999b), Schmitt and Bergmann (1999a), Cunningham et al. (2001), Schmitt et al. (2000), Bergmann, Traphöner, Schmitt, Cunningham, and Smyth (2002), and Bergmann, Schmitt, and Stahl (2002).

10.1 Introduction to the Electronic Commerce Scenario

We will start from a definition and a generally accepted transaction model of electronic commerce to derive opportunities for experience management approaches. Further, we will derive specific requirements for this application area.

10.1.1 Electronic Commerce Definition

The terms "electronic commerce" and "electronic business" have recently achieved a strong recognition. These terms are commonly used to refer to a broad class of activities which we generally understand to be associated with the use of the Internet to trade goods and services. However, due to the rapid technological development, these terms do not really have a precise definition yet.

In the following, we treat the terms electronic commerce and Electronic Business synonymously, according to the following meaning (Klein and Szyperski 1998; Centre for Electronic Commerce 1999):

Clarification of Terms 10.1 (Electronic Commerce) Electronic commerce is the process of electronically conducting arbitrary forms of business between entities in order to achieve the organization's objectives.

Today, electronic commerce typically deals with exchanging information, goods, or services via electronic media. The development moved from private and proprietary networks to open networks with non-proprietary protocols, such as the Internet. Electronic commerce via the Internet is therefore also often called *Internet Commerce* or *Web Commerce* if implemented by agents or HTML pages that that are accessed through Web browsers.

10.1.2 Transaction Model

If we have a closer look at the business process of general commerce, we can identify three consecutive phases (see Fig. 10.1).

Pre-sales

During *pre-sales* a potential customer is concerned with preparing the purchase of a product that fulfills her/his particular wishes and demands. The pre-sales phase can be subdivided into three steps: *supplier search*, *product search*, and *negotiation*.

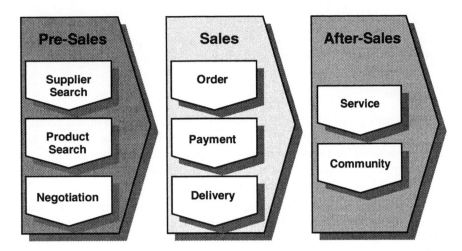

Fig. 10.1. Transaction Processes in Electronic Commerce.

Supplier Search. During supplier search, the client investigates which supplier is basically able to solve her/his problem or to satisfy her/his needs. Usually, there are different suitable suppliers available offering appropriate products, but under different conditions, prices, etc. However, it might also be possible that products from different suppliers must be combined in order to satisfy the customer's need. During supplier search the customer tries to get an overview of suppliers that come into question. Typically, the selection of supplier is primarily based on the type of product that is required rather than on its particular features.

Product Search. After a supplier or a set of suppliers has been chosen, a detailed product selection must be performed. This product selection is based on the detailed identification of wishes, requirements, and preferences of the customer. Product search means mapping of customer criteria to products. Depending on the kind of product, this step can be more or less complex. For fixed, unchangeable products, this is a pure selection process. For more complex products, which can be parameterized or configured, a buyer-directed customization is required in order to achieve a product that best satisfies the user's needs.

Negotiation. After the desired product has been determined, buyer and seller can start negotiations to come to an agreement about

- the price and the way of payment,
- the details of delivery,
- certain regulations about cost and delivery.

After the negotiation step, all details about the transaction related to the product have been determined and agreed between buyer and seller.

Sales

In the *sales* phase, the main business transaction happens. The previously selected product is ordered, paid, and delivered to the customer.

After-sales

The *after-sales* phase starts after a customer has already bought a product. If the customer needs some kind of support related to the product, s/he enters the after-sales phase. After-sales support aims at increasing customer satisfaction and customer relationship. We can distinguish two different after-sales activities: *service* and *community*.

Service. Service aims at increasing the utility of a product for the client. This can be achieved through a troubleshooting service, service related to product maintenance, information related to the usage of the product, or offers for product updates or accessories.

Community. Community support means to to enable different customers to exchange experience about products or vendors. This can help new customers during the buying decision and can therefore be seen as a link to the pre-sales phase. It also provides useful information for the vendor about customer requirements, desired product improvements, and acceptance of the products in the market.

10.1.3 Knowledge Involved in Electronic Commerce

When observing the traditional trade scenario from a knowledge perspective, we can see that many kinds of knowledge play an important role:

- *knowledge about products*: product properties and technical specification, application areas, product structure, compatibility with other products, pricing, experience about faults, etc.
- *knowledge about clients*: requirements, wishes, preferences, shopping type, product experience, product language, cultural affiliation, etc.
- *strategic knowledge*: about recommendation, communication, negotiation, sales, etc.

Typically, the vendor, distributor, or manufacturer is the only one who possesses the full knowledge about products. On the other hand, the client is the only one who possesses the client knowledge. This leads to what we call "knowledge gap" (Bergmann et al. 2001) that must be bridged during the sales process (see Fig. 10.2).

Clarification of Terms 10.2 (Knowledge Gap in Electronic Commerce) The knowledge gap in electronic commerce is the lack of product knowledge at the client side and the lack of customer knowledge at the vendor side.

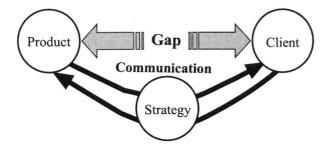

Fig. 10.2. The Knowledge Gap in Electronic Commerce.

In the traditional sales scenario, this knowledge gap is bridged by the human sales agent who makes use of her/his strategic knowledge to mediate between the client and the vendor. This mediation requires communication during which the knowledge is transferred from the vendor to the client and vice versa. In an online sales process, this communication process must be realized by the virtual sales agent which must also bridge the knowledge gap through appropriate communication means. Current search technology enables only a very limited form of communication and hardly bridges the knowledge gap. Hence, it can only work in cases where the knowledge gap is not too big, as for example, for products that are well known by most customers (e.g., CDs or books).

In the future, we expect the knowledge gap to grow significantly. This is due to the fact that products to be sold online will become much more complex. First, products are getting more complex in general and second, after online sales has focused on simple products it will move to the more complicated cases. Additionally, the number of products available for online sale will increase as well. Together, the amount of relevant product knowledge increases. On the other hand, the number of online shoppers is increasing and new classes of shoppers will discover the Internet. This, the increasing diversity of customer wishes and the demand for individual customized products, will increase the uncertainty on the seller's side about the customer and how s/he is individually treated best. The resulting growth of the knowledge gap will become the critical problem for increasing or even maintaining the acceptance of online shopping in the near future.

10.1.4 Opportunities for Experience Management Support

Experience management approaches can help bridging the knowledge gap in electronic commerce, since most of the knowledge related to products can be regarded as experience. This enables to build intelligent virtual sales assistants based using experience management technology. Like a real sales agent, such an virtual sales agent possesses the product knowledge and knowledge about typical customer behavior. Product knowledge is stored as experience in a case base. During the communication between the customer and the virtual sales agent, the sales agent makes recommendations based on the stored experience.

Today, virtual sales agents based on experience management technology have been developed to support the pre-sales and the after-sales phases of electronic commerce. The different processes to be supported require different kinds of experience to be managed.

Experience Management during Pre-sales

From a customer point of view, experience management during pre-sales always has to start from the customer wish. The customer wish provides the overall context for selecting reusable experience.

Supplier Search. During the *supplier search* process, the task is to determine experience about suppliers who can fulfill the customer needs. In this process, experience is needed that maps customer wishes to supplier information. Typically, this experience is not available or maintained by a single supplier, but, for example, by a shopping mall operator or an information service provider[1].

Product Search. During the *product search* process, the task is to determine a product, or a bundle of products that fulfill the customer wish. Sales assistants for product search are typically operated by a vendor or distributor. This gives a special focus on the products that are sold by this organization. Experience in this context needs to map a customer wish to a product or product bundle. In this scenario, there is the additional opportunity for experience adaptation. Experience adaptation then relates to product adaptation or parameterization and is suitable for products that have customization possibilities.

Experience Management during After-sales

Experience management during after-sales is determined by the fact that it typically relates to a particular product. Therefore, the experience can be organized around the products. However, a strict partitioning according to the individual products is very often not appropriate, since experience that originally relates to one product may also be important for a different but somehow similar product. Experience should therefore map descriptions containing products and the particular problem or situation to lessons about fault, remedies, or different forms of advice. Experience management applications for the after-sales phase can replace or support traditional help-desks or call-centers.

---

[1] One example for such a supplier search application is the *European Dealer and Solution Provider* search agent, which supports the selection of an IT service provider based on its specific competence. See www.edsp.de .

Summary

Table 10.1 summarizes the characteristics of the previously described application types. The remainder of this chapter focuses on experience management applications for pre-sales. Service applications are discussed in detail in Chap. 11.

EC Process	Experience	
	Characteristic	Lesson
Supplier Search	Customer Wish	Supplier Information
Product Search	Customer Wish	Product Information
Service and Community	Product and Problem	Fault, Repair, Advice

Table 10.1. Relating EC Processes to Experience.

10.2 Analyzing Pre-sales Scenarios

To bridge the knowledge gap, the virtual sales assistant has to guide the customer during supplier or product search. The customer is searching for a product s/he actually needs and the sales agent tries to support the customer during her/his search. The customer has a set of wishes concerning the product s/he is searching for. These wishes are derived from a particular need in the customer's real life. Roughly spoken, the customer enters an electronic shop to satisfy those needs with a product s/he hopes to find inside. The sales agent operated by the supplier has different kinds product knowledge. The task of the sales agent is to establish a communication with the customer.

10.2.1 Customer Wishes

If a customer enters an electronic shop s/he will be searching for a product that satisfies her/his needs. The customer may not be completely aware of her/his needs or of all details of her/his needs. The customer expresses her/his needs by a set of wishes s/he states during the dialog with the sales agent. The problem of dealing with wishes is that they can be

- vague,
- uncertain,
- expressed incorrectly,
- contradictory to other wishes, or
- unsatisfiable.

Therefore, customer wishes cannot always be regarded has irrevocable. The virtual sales agent should try to elaborate these wishes and determine their nature as well as possible. We now characterize wishes and the possible relations to the available products.

Properties of an Individual Wish

If we analyze an individual statement expressing a single customer wish, independent of the set of available products, we can identify the following important properties.

Wish Importance. Wishes can be of different importance. A wish can be hard, i.e., it expresses a product feature that is mandatory. Products not fulfilling this property are excluded. On the other hand, wishes can also be soft, expressing only a certain preference concerning a particular product feature. In general, there is a continuum of importance for a wish, which endpoints we can call *hard* and *soft*. When recommending products the sales assistant must first fulfill the hard wishes, and as a second step as many of the soft wishes as possible.

Wish Precision. Wishes can be expressed with different precision. Wishes can specify a certain product feature exactly or they can explicitly leave space for variations. In general, there is a continuum of wish precision, which endpoints we can call *precisely determined* and *undetermined*. Precise wishes do not give room for recommending products that do not match exactly (however, it might be necessary to recommend products that do not fulfill certain wish as long as it is not a hard wish). Vague wishes, on the other hand, enable the sales agent to choose from a larger set of products, making recommendation choices based on other wishes as well.

Wish Certainty. The expression of wishes can have different certainty, i.e., the customer can be absolutely certain or uncertain about his wish. During sales the agent should try to increase the certainty of a certain wish. Recommending products based on uncertain wishes bears the risk of suggesting something that does not satisfy the customer's needs, which is only observed after the product has been purchased.

Properties of the Overall Wish

During a sales dialog a customer usually expresses not just one wish but a set of different wishes. In the ideal case, each of these wishes makes statements about an individual product feature. However, this must not be the case. When we look at a set of wishes, we can identify the following properties:

Redundancy. A wish set can be redundant in the sense that also a smaller subset of wishes already expresses the same overall need. When product wishes are acquired interactively through a series of questions by the sales agent, redundancy should be avoided since answering redundant questions requires unnecessary effort by the customer.

Consistency. A wish set can be consistent or inconsistent. It is inconsistent if certain wishes contradict each other. Inconsistency is an indication of the knowledge gap, i.e., the customer does not have the knowledge that is required to specify her/his needs consistently. Inconsistency can either be handled by notifying the customer about the inconsistency and to force her/him to specify consistent wishes only. It can also be handled by accepting the inconsistency and suggesting products which most likely fulfill the anticipated customer needs best, but not exactly.

Relations between Wishes and Product Base

Finally, we can identify certain relations between the customer's wish (or wish set) and the offered products.

Satisfiability with Respect to a Certain Product. The dominant relation to be determined during pre-sales is the satisfiability relation. The question is to determine whether a certain product satisfies the stated customer wishes. The satisfiability relation is typically not a crisp relation, but a fuzzy relation. Of course, a certain product can fully satisfy the customer's needs, or it can be completely inappropriate. However, very often a product satisfies a need only to a certain degree.

Satisfiability with Respect to a Product Set. The satisfiability relation can also be regarded with respect to the whole set of available products. Here, the degree of satisfiability relates to the highest satisfiability that a product from the set of available products can achieve.

10.2.2 Products

After analyzing wishes, we need to take a look at the product side. A classification of different kinds of products is important for determining the technology best suited for developing a sales assistant. The following classification of products is motivated by the *continuum of design tasks* (Brown and Chandrasekaran 1985; Gero 1990), which classifies different products according to the creation process.

Within the set of possible products we identify a *continuum of products* (see Fig. 10.3). It classifies different products according to their ability to be customized.

Fixed Products. At the lower end of this continuum we find fixed products. These products cannot be modified and as a result the sales agent cannot customize them. Examples are music CDs, books, integrated circuits, etc.

Parameterizable Products. Next on the continuum, we find products that are parameterizable by certain values. The values can be either discrete, like the speed of a CPU, or continuous, like the length of a cable. The sales agent needs to determine appropriate values for these parameters.

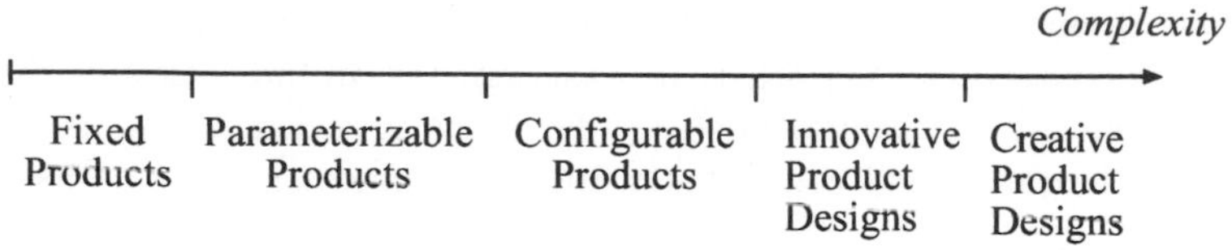

Complexity

| Fixed Products | Parameterizable Products | Configurable Products | Innovative Product Designs | Creative Product Designs |

Fig. 10.3. The Continuum of Products.

Configurable Products. Configurable products are products that are created by combining several components in a certain way. The components themselves can be fixed or parameterizable. There can be different ways of combining components and typically lots of dependencies must be taken into account. Determining an overall product that satisfies customer needs is a configuration task that must be performed by the sales agent. An example for a configurable product is a personal computer.

Individually Designed Products. Individually Designed Products are products that are created as the result of a design process. Such products show a much larger degree of variation than configurable products and typically, the dependencies between different design decisions are much more complex than for configurable products. Examples of individually designed products are architectural objects, or software.

10.2.3 Experience Representation for Product Search

Experience management for product search should support the task of selecting products that best satisfy the customers' wishes. Due to the nature of the wishes it is often not possible to fulfill this task exactly, for example, if the wish set is inconsistent or if the wishes are not satisfiable. Hence, experience should help to identify products that are at least acceptable.

The experience that is required for this purpose and the way it can be represented strongly depends on the kind of products and on the size of the knowledge gap. The size of the knowledge gap determines the content of the experience while the complexity of the products determines this representation. Both issues are now discussed in more detail.

Required Experience for Small Knowledge Gaps

The knowledge gap is small when the customer possesses the relevant product knowledge for deciding whether a product is appropriate or not and of the seller knows her/his clients quite well. This is often the case in B2B scenarios in which the seller offers a limited number of standard products that are either known by the customer through common sense through a common understanding that is based on a clearly defined terminology in the expert domain.

In such situations, the sellers and customers can communicate via a shared language, which is typically the language of the product features. The advantage of choosing this language is that the required vocabulary can be easily provided by the seller. Products can be easily described according to this language. Choosing this language requires that also the customers express their wishes in terms of product features, which is possible since the knowledge gap is supposed to be small. Experience in this situation is therefore mostly product knowledge. The experience base consists of experience items each of which represents a certain product. The characterization part of the experience contains search-relevant product features and the lesson part contains the detailed product description, the product number, or other information that allows to uniquely identify the product.

Example: Analog Devices Product Catalog. Analog Devices is a major manufacturer and seller of electronic devices in the US. Many of their customers are small electronics firms or electronics departments of larger firms. A product search agent for the operational amplifier products of Analog Devices could be easily developed because Analog Devices can communicate with is customers using the well defined language of electronics (Vollrath et al. 1998). Details of this application example are given in Sect. 10.6.

Required Experience for Large Knowledge Gaps

The knowledge gap is large when the customer does not process enough product knowledge to be able to describe her/his wishes in terms of product features. Then, the customer can only describe her/his wishes in terms of the intended application or the required function of the product. Here, we have to deal with two different languages:

- the language of the customer describing product functions and
- the language of the seller describing product features.

Hence, experience is required that describes that a certain product can be used to realize a certain function. The experience characterization part must describe possible product functions and the lessons part must specify a particular product or the features of a product that is suitable.

Example: Personal Computer Sales for Novice End Users. When selling computers in an electronic shop to novice end users who are not familiar with computer technology, the knowledge gap is quite large. Novice end users do not know about the different components a computer consists of and they do not know what requirements concerning the components they have. However, they usually know for what purpose they want to buy the computer. Hence, the user specifies her/his requirements by denoting which applications s/he would like to use his PC for. The wishes consist of a list of application areas like *word processing, database, music & sound, programming* or, *games*, etc. These demands can be modeled by simple attributes each of which represents an importance rating for the application type. Further, the user can give a *price category* for the PC system (see Wilke 1999, Chap. 4).

In this example, an experience item relates an application description to a particular PC or to a particular configuration of PC components. It thereby maps an application profile to a particular product. Of course, one particular PC can be related to many different application profiles, each of which represents a different experience item.

Experience Representation for Simple Fixed Products

Simple fixed products can mostly be represented using flat attribute value representations (see Sect. 3.3.1). Each product or application specific property is coded as an individual attribute. This representation is sufficient if no structural information needs to be represented.

Experience Representation for Parameterizable Products

Parameterizable products can be represented either as a generalized case (see Sect. 3.4) or as a traditional case plus adaptation knowledge (see Sect. 5.4).

Generalized Case. When represented as a generalized case, all parameterization possibilities of the product are represented within this generalized case. Each way to modify the product is represented as an individual parameter. Constraints in the generalized case can be used to represent dependency among those parameters.

Traditional Case Plus Adaptation Knowledge. When a parameterizable product is represented as a traditional case, then this case is prototype product. Adaptation knowledge represented as rules (see Sect. 5.1) or operators (see Sect. 5.2) describes how to change those parts of the product that are variable. This means that product parameters are encoded as adaptation knowledge.

The second approach has advantages over the generalized case representation when many products can be parameterized exactly the same way. In this case, the parameterization knowledge can be represented once for many products. On the other hand, the generalized case approach has advantages when the way products can be parameterized differs significantly from product to product.

Experience Representation for Configurable Products

For configurable products object-oriented representations (see Sect. 3.3.2) are usually more appropriate. Configurable products usually require to represent structural knowledge, for example, knowledge about how the product is constructed. The *is-a* relation can be used to classify products, components, or their application and function according to a product, component, application, or function hierarchy. Inheritance can be employed to parsimoniously represent properties shared by different classes. The *part-of* relation can be used to decompose products into sub-products or components and functions into sub-functions. Constraints between different attribute values are required to represent configuration constraints, e.g., technical constraints concerning the compatibility of certain components.

Experience Representation for Individually Designed Products

Individually designed products are difficult to handle because of the high degree of required flexibility. In principle they can be completely formalized similar as configurable products, but such a representation tends to become quite complex. Depending on the variety of different products one could describe products as well as their application or function on a more abstract level, i.e., as an abstract case (see Sect. 3.5). Thereby one can achieve feasibility of experience management at the cost of reduced retrieval and adaptation accuracy.

10.3 WEBSELL: A Generic Electronic Commerce Architecture

We now introduce the WEBSELL framework shown in Fig. 10.4, which is a generic architecture for realizing electronic commerce applications particularly to support the pre-sales process. This architecture has been developed as part of the WEBSELL project. To manage the requirements that are imposed on such a system in particular by web-based applications, the WEBSELL architecture has been designed as a component-based platform. This offers the highest flexibility in terms of

- being able to deliver tailored solutions,
- integrating with heterogeneous IT environments, and
- reactivity to the fast changing Internet market and its requirements.

The architecture is described in terms of server and client components, data storage and files, as well as XML-based communication protocols to connect these elements.

Building a solution for a specific client then corresponds to configuring a set of components and integrating the resulting system into the environment at the client's side. Whenever additional functionality is needed, new services may be added. Likewise, existing systems can easily be integrated by implementing a specific component organizing the necessary communication between the external system and the affected WEBSELL components.

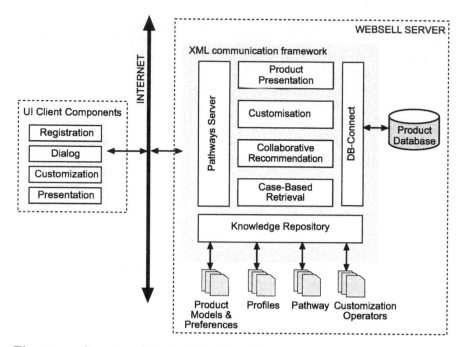

Fig. 10.4. Overview of the WEBSELL Architecture.

10.3.1 Pathways Server and Dialog Components

The objective of Pathways is to allow developers to produce dialogues that will elicit a user's requirements. The dialog component on the client side interviews the customer and reacts to the information provided either to directly recommend a product or service or to perform an intelligent search to find the most suitable product or service. Pathways implements a static domain-specific predefined dialog as introduced in Sect. 6.3. The dialog is modeled as a decision tree that asks questions, does calculations, offers information, and applies rules at each node of the decision tree. When a pathway is processed, the interaction with the prospective customer begins at the top node of the main decision tree and proceeds to the child of that node for which the condition (if any) is satisfied. On reaching a child node the following sequence occurs:

1. Any information on the node is displayed to the user.
2. Any actions on the node are displayed for selection.
3. Any questions on the node are displayed to the user.
4. Any equations on the node are calculated and any sub-pathways run.
5. If there is an unconditional goto, then the interaction jumps to the destination node.

6. If there is a conditional goto, the condition on the destination node is checked, if satisfied, then interaction jumps to the destination node.
7. If there are one or more child nodes, the condition (if any) on each is checked.

If the condition on only one child is satisfied then the interaction proceeds to that node, otherwise the interaction halts. The information that is gathered or calculated at the current node or at any previously visited node may be used in testing conditions. At any node except for the first one it is possible to step back to the previously occupied node, where upon previously entered answers may be changed.

10.3.2 Case-Based Retrieval

Retrieval and adaptation techniques from case-based reasoning have become very important techniques for realizing intelligent agents for product search. The core of such applications is a product database that describes the specific features of each available product. When applying CBR, this product database is treated as a case base, i.e., each product record in the database is interpreted as a case in a case base. During the case retrieval phase, product cases are retrieved based on the similarity between the product features and the requirements elicited by the Pathways component. The similarity encodes the knowledge to assess whether a product is suitable for the customer's requirements. In the WEBSELL retrieval component, similarity is formalized through similarity measures that are modeled by combining several parameterizable local similarity measures for individual product features with a global aggregation function. Thereby global and individual preferences for product selection can be modeled. The main purpose of the retrieval component is then to select from the product database a set of products with the highest similarity as computed by the similarity measure. The challenge is to realize efficient retrieval on a large and highly dynamic product database. The retrieval component provides different similarity-based retrieval algorithms such as complete brute-force search, case-retrieval nets (see Sect. 7.5) similarity-based retrieval by approximation with SQL queries (see Sect. 7.6).

10.3.3 Collaborative Recommendation

In addition to the case-based recommendation approach, WEBSELL also provides a facility for collaborative recommendation based on user profiling (Smyth and Cotter 1999; Smyth and Cotter 2000; Hayes and Cunningham 2000). In the context of WEBSELL, user profiles support the potential personalization of all aspects of the sales process. A user profile stores the past electronic commerce history of an individual user. User profiles are stored and maintained on the server as a profile database. Each user is associated with a single profile, and each profile contains user information that can be separated into three basic category types:

1. Personal Information: This contains various personal details such as name, age, gender, home address, occupation, credit-card details etc.
2. Domain Preferences: This contains user information that is relevant to a particular domain. For example, for an online travel application the domain preferences might include information such as: the type of vacation that the user is interested in (relaxing versus activity, city versus country etc.); their preferred travel arrangements (airline travel with Virgin or British Airways); budget details (the package price should not exceed $2000).
3. Selection Lists: This is the most important type of profile information from the collaborative recommendation viewpoint. Two selection lists are maintained. The positive selection list (+SL) contains a list of products that the user has expressed an interest in or purchased. The negative selection list (-SL) contains a list of products that the user has explicitly ignored in the past.

The collaborative recommendation service in WEBSELL is a recommendation scheme that allows products to be recommended to target users based on their user profile data, and in this sense the recommendations are personalized for the user in question. The key to this form of recommendation is the ability to associate a target user with a group of other users that are similar in the sense that their profiles are similar to the target user profile. Typically, profile similarity is a measure of the correlation between the selection lists of two user profiles; users with a high degree of similarity tend to grade the same products in the same way. A group of users that are similar to the target user form a virtual community for the target, and recommendations are drawn from the profiles of the community members. The result is a list of recommendable products, which can be ranked according to, for example, the frequency of the product in community member profiles. Collaborative recommendation is a three-step procedure:

1. Identify the virtual community associated with a given target user.
2. Produce a ranked list of recommendable products. These are products that are listed in the positive selection lists of community members, but that are not contained within the selection list of the target user. The products are ranked according to their frequency of occurrence in the community.
3. Select the top n recommendable products as recommendations.

The final output of the collaborative recommendation service is a list of products, and ultimately these can be recommended directly to users or combined with the case-based reasoning recommendation. The collaborative recommendation service is responsible for identifying virtual communities (as groups of user ids) within the WEBSELL user population and for associating individual users with the appropriate community.

10.3.4 Customization

One important objective of WEBSELL was to be able to support the sale of complex products requiring configuration or customization. The WEB-SELL customization component allow users to more flexibly and completely configure complex products such as holidays, insurance plans or technical equipment. Two different approaches have been developed:

Operator-Based Customization

The operator-based customization approach (see Sect. 5.2 and 8.3.2) supports interactive modification of products by the customer. After a best-matching product has been retrieved and presented to the customer, a set of customization operators is provided, which may be applied to further customize the product. Each customization operator encodes a particular atomic way of adapting certain products. The description of such an operator contains

- a precondition that specifies under which circumstances the product can be modified,
- a set of parameters to specify the details of the customization
- an action part specifying how the product is affected by the customization.

The customization component enables the customer to navigate through the space of possible customized products and takes care of the applicability of operators, validity of parameter values, and the consistency of the adapted products. In B2C scenarios, the operator-based approach is particularly suited to support products with limited customization capabilities since otherwise the set of applicable operators overstrains the user. However, in B2B scenarios in which clients have expert knowledge about the products, the operator-based approach can be applied to more complex products as well.

Incremental Compositional Adaptation

The incremental compositional adaptation approach (see Sect. 8.4) is particularly suited for complex products that require a sophisticated customization. It is assumed that products are structured into sub-components, possibly in a hierarchical manner. Further, product databases with some pre-configured base products and individual sub-components are required. After retrieving the best pre-configured base product with respect to the customer's requirements, the product is customized by incrementally replacing sub-components by more suitable ones. Components with a low similarity (weak components), i.e., components that do not fulfill the customer's requirements well enough, are candidates for being replaced. By recursively applying CBR to the level of sub-component, alternative components are selected from the product database. Then, the weak component is replaced by an alternative component and the validity of the so created adapted product is checked. During this validation, constraints that exist between the different components are evaluated. Violation leads to backtracking to the component replacement step, giving the next-best component a chance. This adaptation cycle is executed several times. In every run the overall suitability of the product is increased. Generally, we can notice that the adaptation cycle implements a hill-climbing search to solve a combination of a constraint satisfaction problem and an optimization problem for the product suitability (measured by the similarity). On the one hand, it has to find a combination of different components representing a working product, i.e., a product that fulfills all constraints. On the other hand, it has to find an optimal combination that fulfills the demands of the customer as well as possible.

10.4 Methodology Recipe for Retrieval-Based Electronic Commerce Applications

We now describe the development methodology for electronic commerce applications as a recipe at the cookbook level, which is part of the INRECA experience base (see Sect. 9.3). In its current form, the recipe is limited to search in product catalogs of fixed products, i.e., products that cannot be customized. Hence, product adaptation does not play a role here. The reason for this limitation is that currently not enough industrial product catalogs that involve customization have been developed that could provide the necessary experience for a recipe.

The recipe breaks down into five main processes linked as shown in Fig. 10.5. These processes are now described.

10.4.1 Requirements Acquisition

The process of acquiring the user and business requirements for the product search application involves three key activities: analyzing technical and sales materials, eliciting user requirements, and, finally, eliciting business requirements (cf. Fig. 10.6).

Analyze Technical and Sales Materials

An analyst knowledgeable in data modeling and experience management should be assigned to gather and review all available materials used internally or externally to describe the products or services of interest. Material may be available in several forms: product database or catalog, sales literature, technical data-sheets, design specifications, and Web documents. It is possible that the detailed information in these forms will conflict. We have noticed that sales literature often presents a simplified view of the product specifications, making it unsuitable for an experienced or knowledgeable customer.

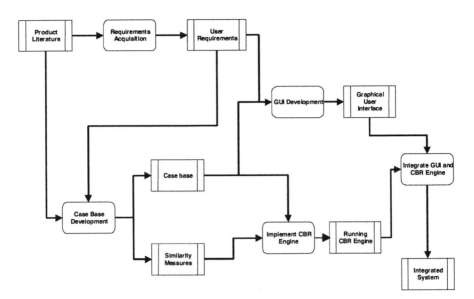

Fig. 10.5. Process Model for Catalog Search Application.

Elicit User Requirements

The intended application user, or stake-holder, should be interviewed and asked to describe the following:

- current work practices in the application area,
- perceived problems or areas that need improvement,
- his or her vision of what the best possible situation would be,
- his or her relationships with other staff members in and out of the area.

From a practical point of view, the team of people involved in this process should include an analyst knowledgeable in data modeling and, ideally, in experience management, a sales person from the company who provides the products or services listed in the catalog, and a technical person who understands the makeup and specifications of the products or services under discussion. The sales person is expected to have an understanding of the customer's needs, the ways in which they currently use company information when selecting a product, and the best way to meet their needs using a experience management catalog search application. The technical person is expected to be in a position to describe how individual products or groupings relate to each other functionally and how values for individual parameters or attributes can be compared to each other. The analyst will interview each of these professionals and use the information to establish the data and interface requirements for the catalog search application.

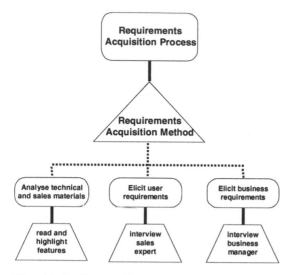

Fig. 10.6. Process Decomposition for Requirements Acquisition.

Elicit Business Requirements

Sales support is a key business function, and the input of an experienced business manager to the creation of an electronic sales support application is essential at this stage in the process. Many possibilities exist to enhance the sales process when a decision is made to create a experience management application. An experienced business manager will be in a position to highlight these opportunities and to make the business case for focusing on them during the course of development.

10.4.2 Knowledge Modeling

Knowledge modeling is a three-stage activity: descriptive model development, similarity development, and case acquisition (see Fig. 10.7).

Vocabulary Development

This will draw on the outputs of the requirements acquisition process to define a list of attributes and organize these into a class hierarchy to construct an object-oriented case representation. This process is supported by the knowledge modeling tools described in Sect. 9.8.2.

Similarity Development

This is not broken down in this diagram, since it is a well-developed, common generic process to almost all experience management projects (see Sect. 9.5.3).

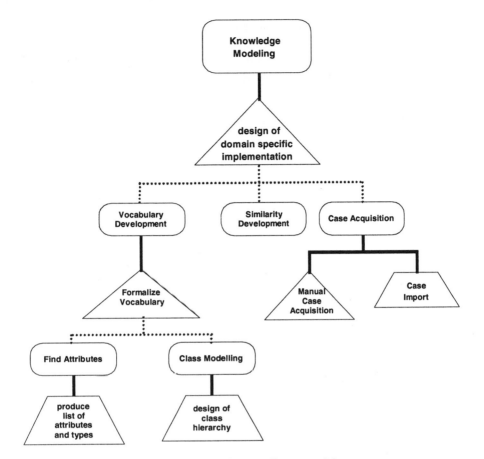

Fig. 10.7. Case Base Development Process Decomposition.

Case Acquisition

This is essentially either a manual input operation or a question of importing existing data. Importing electronic versions of the case base is certainly the most likely scenario in a product catalog application; however, there may be a procedure put in place that allows for manual additions to the case base once the initial import is done.

10.4.3 GUI Development

The development of a graphical user interface for a product search application (see Fig. 10.8) is likely to consume a large part of the development work for the project.

An application without a user interface designed for real users will almost certainly run into problems when it goes live. Where possible, involve users early in the design of the GUI. Get their feedback when creating the graphics for the application and show them screen-shots of the eventual system. These actions will prompt questions regarding the functionality of the system that will be much easier to deal with at the start of a process than at the end. Formal acceptance testing should be conducted at the end of the GUI development to sign off on the interface before integration of the experience management software component begins.

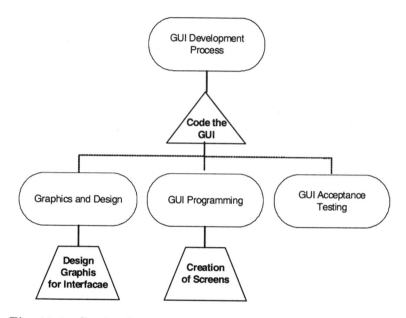

Fig. 10.8. Graphical User Interface Development Process.

10.4.4 Implement CBR Retrieval Engine

The engine that drives the product search application is obviously a key component (see Fig. 10.9). Specific questions should be answered before a final decision is taken concerning the best retrieval approach for the project.

- What is the number of products to be sold now and in the future.
- Is the product spectrum static or is there a high variance in products or the kind of products.
- What is the number of customers expected to access the service at a time.

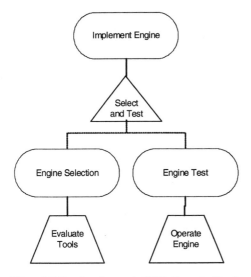

Fig. 10.9. Implement CBR Search Engine Process.

10.4.5 Integrate CBR and GUI

The retrieval engine and GUI components are integrated to form a single application (see Fig. 10.10). The system should, of course, be fully tested in its component and integrated forms. Testing should approximate, as closely as possible, the ways in which actual users will interact with the system. Testing at this stage may raise issues that lead to changes in the model or similarity functions within the system. The final step in deploying the system is to implement the links to the existing product data or literature.

10.5 Application Overview

Within the INRECA-II project, the WEBSELL project, and beyond, a large variety of applications has been implemented. We first provide an overview of applications before going into the details of two selected applications.

Table 10.2 gives an overview of selected applications of the WEBSELL architecture that have been developed by the different project partners. The application type mentioned in the table refers to the main steps of the e-commerce process that is supported by the search application. Current applications involve

- S: the search for an appropriate *Supplier* for the kind of products the client is interested in,
- P: the search for an appropriate *Product* within the product spectrum of one supplier (or broker)

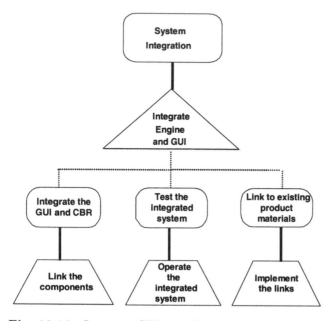

Fig. 10.10. Integrate CBR and GUI Process.

- A: the search for relevant service information as part of an After-sales customer support.

Further, the mentioned applications have a different status. Demo applications have been developed to demonstrate the potential of the technology while applications that are marked as "live" are currently in productive use at the clients' site.

None of these applications exploit all the components that the WEBSELL architecture offers, but a particularly tailored configuration of them. On the right side of the table, the knowledge-based components that are used to implement these applications are marked (X means component in use, P means use of component planned in the future). Besides these components, of course, traditional components that do not involve any knowledge processing (e.g., for product presentation, ordering, payment, etc.) are used as well, but are not mentioned in this table.

10.6 Application: Product Catalog for Operational Amplifiers

Analog Devices, Inc., (ADI) designs, manufactures, and markets a broad line of high-performance linear, mixed-signal, and digital integrated circuits (ICs) that address a wide range of real-world signal processing applications. Analog sells its products worldwide through a direct sales force, third-party industrial distributors, and independent sales representatives.

Application				Components		
Client / Description	Type (Supplier Search Product, Search After Sales)	Status	Pathways	Case-Based Retrieval	Collaborative Rec.	Customization
Check Out Touristik www.reiseboerse.com	P	live		X		
Müritz Online www.mueritz.de/	S	live		X		
Handbook Precision Rhineland-Palatinate	S	live		X		
European Dealer and Solution Provider www.edsp.de	S	live		X		
Hooke & McDonald (residential letting) www.hookemacdonald.com/	P	live		X		
TourIT (City Sightseeing)	S, P	demo	X	X	P	P
Siemens Simatic Knowledge Manager www4d.ad.siemens.de/skm/	A	live		X		
Analog Devices Operational Amplifier	P	live		X		
QUOKA Used Cars Search www.autoaktuell.de	P	live		X		
Shopping24 Search in Warehouse www.shopping24.de	P	live		X		
Digital Signal Processor Search wwwagr.informatik.uni-kl.de/~readee	P	demo		X		
Personal Computer Configuration minsk.informatik.uni-kl.de:8103/launch/WebInterface	P	demo		X		X
Personal Computer Selection www.cykopaths.com/samples.html	P	demo	X	X		
Carsmart (Used Car Search) http://live.tecinno.de/projects/carsmart24com/	P	demo	X	X	X	
Jola Spezialschalter www.jola-info.de	P	live		X		X
Mobile Phone Selection www.cykopaths.com/samples.html	P	demo	X			
Intervox Score Music Sales www.intervox.de	P	live		X		
Bayer AG Plastics Product Advisor www.plastics.bayer.com	P	live		X		
Neckermann White Products Advisor www.neck.nl	P	live		X		
Otto AG Online Retail www.otto.de	P	live		X		
Software AG Knowledge Center www.sag.de	A	live		X		

Table 10.2. Overview of Electronic Commerce Applications

Many of Analog Devices customers are small electronics firms or electronics departments of large firms. Prior to the development of the product search application, a design engineer was the usual contact point with the central applications department. The engineer takes the customers requirements for a product over the phone and tries to find a match in the AD product range. This process can involve weighing dozens of parameters while at the same time interacting with the customer to get an assessment of the customers priorities. Engineers handle about 40 calls per day, 50% of which relate to product selection.

ADI decided to support the customer consultation process on the Internet initially for operational amplifiers. Analog Devices has over 130 operational amplifiers in its catalog, each one specified by up to 40 parameters. Parameters can be real, integer, symbolic, or Boolean.

10.6.1 Vocabulary and User Interface

A requirement for a specific operational amplifier is expressed in terms of the desired parameters for that product (see Fig. 10.11). The parameters are organized into groupings that apply to amplifiers such as are *dynamic, input, output, supply,* and *other.* Much the same groupings would apply to other categories of electronic devices; however, the parameter list would be quite different. For any numerical parameter, the user can enter a desired value. For any non-numerical parameter, the user can either select a value from a list or type a desired value. For any parameter, the user can check "priority", which give this parameter a higher weight during retrieval.

If a parameter has a "=>" symbol to the left of the data-entry field, this means that the value selected or entered by the user is to be interpreted as "greater than or equal to is best". This indicates the kind of local similarity measure that is used for the parameter. Of course, it does not exclude products that have a lower value for this parameter but meet all other requirements. It thus avoids the problem of the near miss in which a product that matches all but one of the requirements is not returned by a normal database search.

The search procedure is almost instantaneous and when it is complete, the application hands the results over to the results page (see Fig. 10.12). The result page displayed as a static HTML page consists of a table that is structured into the different categories of the parameters. Each row shows one parameter and each column one case. By clicking on the parameter names (left column) an attribute description is presented. By clicking on the product identifiers (displayed in the first row) a detailed product description including the data sheet of the product is shown.

10.6.2 Benefit Analysis

An analysis of the project done by one of the partners of the INRECA-II project allowed us to list the following benefits.

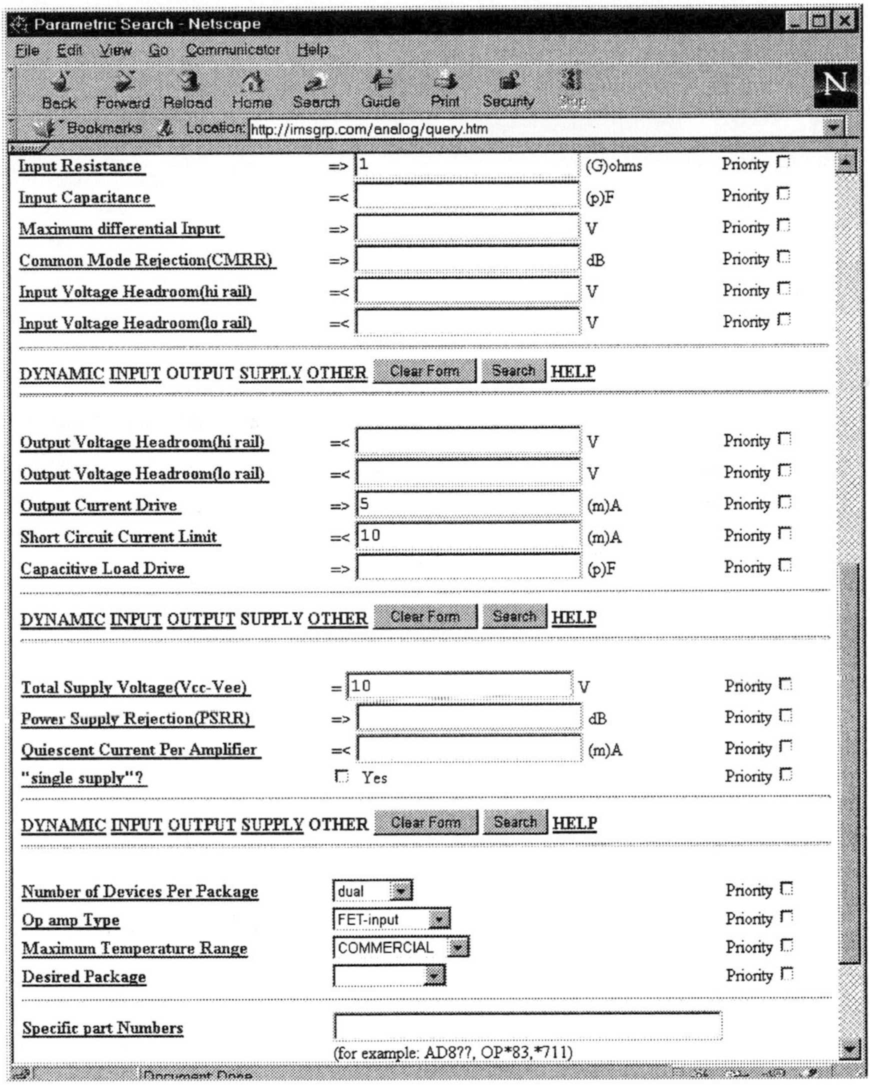

Fig. 10.11. Query Page for Analog Devices Operational Amplifiers.

Benefits for the Customer

The following benefits could be identified for the customer.

- The customer has full flexibility and the opportunity to "negotiate" with the system in order to select a product. The customer can do this using all parameters of the device.

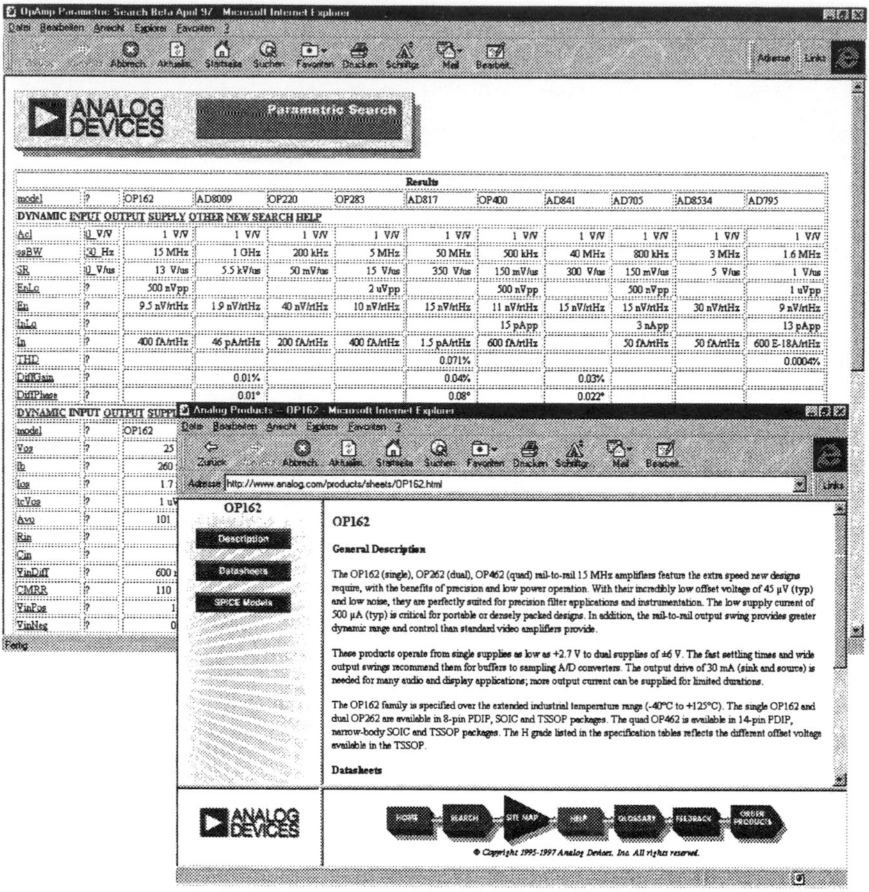

Fig. 10.12. Results Page for Analog Devices Operational Amplifiers.

- The service short cuts the normal research activity and, therefore, reduces testing, design, and direct search costs for the customer.
- The search engine provides an immediate equivalents list, which can save significant time in research and gives greater flexibility at the production stage.
- The search facility always returns a solution, unlike traditional database searches, which only return a value if all conditions are exactly met.
- The facility offers a selection of alternatives, just as an engineer or sales person might.

Benefits for the Manufacturer

The following benefits for Analog Devices could be identified.

- The service frees up the experienced field-applications engineers, allowing them to spend more time addressing complex customer support requirements.
- The service leads to greater product sales at the product design phase (by supporting engineers), and this implies greater sales at the production phase.
- A valuable source of marketing information is generated when the customer specifies his application requirements to the search facility. The information can provide input into the design and production of the products.
- The service is better than anything available and therefore will improve the image of the manufacturer. This progressive image should result in increased product listings by distributors.
- The manufacturer gets to know his customer better and can use the information gathered by the search engine to target promotional materials to specific customers and to tailor other services to customer needs.

Benefits of the Methodology for Product Search Applications

The impact of the methodology on the later applications and its expected impact on future applications can be described as follows:

Development Time Is Shortened. The impact here has, in at least one case, been very large. The first Analog Devices search component took six months to produce, the second (for a different product category) six weeks and the third and fourth only two days (see Fig. 10.13). Some of this is due to automation, but much is due to the systematic reuse of a proven method.

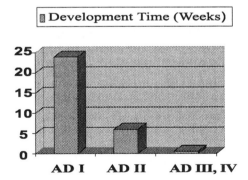

Fig. 10.13. Development Time for Four Different Catalogs for Analog Devices' Products.

New People Can Be Introduced Quickly. Documentation of the development process allows us to quickly bring new people up to speed. We have an independent record of experience and clear documentation on how to apply it.

Steps in the Process Have Been Automated. By formalizing a record of the method we use, we have been able to identify steps in the process that are suited to automation, and we have developed computerized versions of these processes.

Customers Like the Comfort Factor. In any innovative domain, it is important that the customer be comfortable with the concept and the risks involved. A clear method removes the feeling that something is involved that s/he does not understand, and the business decision becomes easier for the customer.

Clear Documentation Is Maintained. Many software quality systems require a systematic documentation regime before approval is granted. The INRECA methodology, when fully applied, generates high-quality and highly usable documentation that meets this need.

10.7 Application: Customization of Electro-mechanical Components

Finally, we now briefly sketch an example application for product search of parameterizable products. The application has been realized for the German company "Jola Spezialschalter K. Mattil & Co" as part of the SMARTSELL project. The company produces thousands of electro-mechanical components and devices like floating and magnetic switches, level controls, liquid level indicators, moisture detectors for cooling ceilings, etc. In general, customers of Jola are neither very knowledgeable about the product variety nor do they know which kind of product is appropriate to their problem. The use of these very special technical parts in industry is underlying specific constraints. Even if a product has been found for the customer's purposes, s/he might have further specifications like length limitations or there is a need for accessories. For some components, the latter are even indispensable.

10.7.1 Vocabulary, Retrieval, Customization, and User Interface

Within the SMARTSELL project an intelligent sales assistant for the products of Jola has been developed. It targets at clients who are not technical experts and who need advice. Hence, for these clients the knowledge gap is particularly large. They need an intelligent sales assistant that asks for their requirements and recommends appropriate products.

Product Retrieval

The behavior of the virtual sales assistant is closer to that of of a human expert. Since communication is performed with an inexperienced user, the focus of the dialog is not on technical details, but on the purpose of the products. Typical questions are:

- What type of substance is in the container (conducting liquid, non-conducting liquid, flammable liquid, water incompatible...)?
- Is the installation area in a explosion hazard area?
- Is the installation area in a water protection area?
- What is the max. temperature of the substance?
- What is the viscosity of the substance (several categories)?
- What is the density of the substance (several categories)?
- What grade of turbulence does the fluid possess?
- Is the container or tank pressurized or not?

In order to be able to search products with respect to the above mentioned purpose oriented characteristics, the product modeling that is used by the retrieval component describes each product in terms of these attributes. They represent knowledge about the purpose for which a particular product is applicable. The similarity measure used for retrieval encodes to what degree a deviation from the ideal application scenario of a product is still acceptable.

Customization

If a product has been found for the customer's purposes, there is very often the need for a customer-specific adaptation. Figure 10.14 shows an example of a customization situation. Suppose the retrieval system has returned a liquid level transmitter. For these types of switches, the customer has several possibilities for modifications. S/he can adapt the length of the shaft, the diameter of the screw-in-nippel, or the type of float of this switch. Furthermore, there are accessory components to choose like a transducer. Only depending on the latter component, further components can be chosen, e.g., a switching unit for signals and/or a display instrument.

Figure 10.15 shows the GUI of the operator-based customization module (see Sects. 5.2 and 8.3.2). With the help of this customization service it is possible to guide the customer, not being familiar with all the modification possibilities and constraints, to his or her target product.

10.7.2 Benefit Analysis

The benefits of the intelligent sales assistant for Jola as reported by Bergmann, Traphöner, Schmitt, Cunningham, and Smyth 2002 are manyfold:

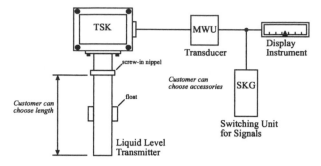

Fig. 10.14. An Example Product from Jola: A Liquid Level Switch.

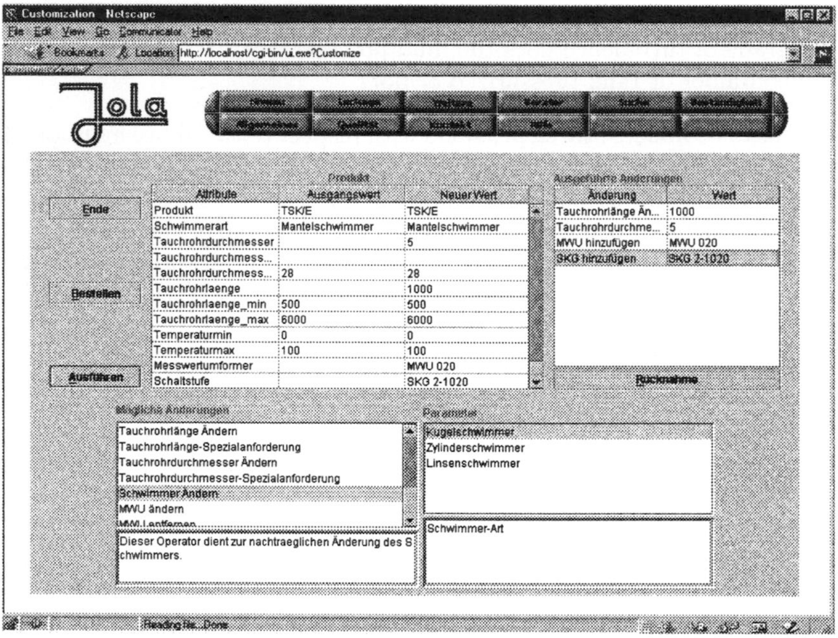

Fig. 10.15. Graphical user Interface to the Customization System of the Jola Domain.

- Building the knowledge model for the sales assistant not only required to re-engineer Jola's product data model but to complete it. Thereby a significant improvement of the product data and its availability was obtained.
- To enable customers to search by product applications rather than the products itself use c ases for all products were collected. This step made a wealth of knowledge of the experienced sales staff explicit that got easily lost in the past. This knowledge enabled Jola to serve their customers better and to optimize their product portfolio.

- Today, customers that use the online system provide the Jola sales department with a detailed description of their application requirements by simply filling the sales assistant questionnaire. If they have not found an appropriate product directly through the internet site then it is at least much easier for the sales engineer to quickly propose alternatives. The questionnaire is also used by the sales force during customer interactions to ensure completeness of information. Both ways, the sales process became much more efficient and more satisfying for the customers.
- The sales assistant is already in use by the external sales force of Jola. It turned out that the lower the experience of the the sales person was, the higher was its usefulness. This finding met our expectations and illustrates the necessity to have the index, the search and the assistant interface according to the seniority level of the user.
- The sales assistant is also an important means to collect very precise market data, i.e. each customer request delivers detailed information on the required application. This will enable Jola to react quickly on new application needs arising and eventually to better predict market needs.
- Monetary effects will stem from increased sales, increased productivity of the sales department and cost reductions. The latter especially when the paper based catalog will be replaced completely by the digital media.

11. Experience Management for Self-Service and Help-Desk Support

"The next wave of economic growth is going to come from knowledge-based business."

S. Davis and J. Botkin,
Harvard Business Review, 1996

The ever-increasing complexity of technical equipment makes it difficult for the users of these systems to operate and maintain them without support. While the probability that technical systems will fail grows exponentially with their complexity, the expertise needed to be able to control every feature of such complex systems usually exceeds the resources available to end-users.

Help-desks support end-users of complex technical equipment. Help-desk operators use their own experiences to solve most of the problems that are relayed to them. However, as systems become more complex, the areas help-desk operators are experts in tend to diverge, i.e., problem solving experience is distributed among experts and the areas of expertise do not necessarily overlap. The goal of developing an experience management system is to create a knowledge repository that contains problem solving experiences for a complex technical domain that changes over time. This knowledge repository will be used in an organization, by a group of people with varying levels of expertise, in a time-critical operation.

The HOMER (in German: "HOtline Mit ERfahrung") system presented in this chapter has been developed as part of the INRECA-II project and has been published by Göker et al. (1998), Göker and Roth-Berghofer (1999a), Bergmann, Breen, Göker, Manago, and Wess (1999a), and Bergmann, Göker, Roth-Berghofer, and Traphoener (1999). Although HOMER has been developed for a specific application in mind, i.e., the CAD/CAM help-desk at DaimlerChrysler in Sindelfingen, it is still a generic vertical platform for realizing help-desk and self-service experience management applications in various domains.

11.1 Introduction

Help-Desks such as the one of DaimlerChrysler in Sindelfingen are usually organized in three levels shown in Fig. 11.1 (Göker et al. 1998). When end-users have a problem with their technical equipment the first person they contact is usually a "key-user". This is a user, working in the same group, that has more experience with the equipment in use. If the key-user is not able to help, the first level support (hotline) is contacted. If the first level help-desk cannot solve the problem, it is escalated to the second level, i.e. to the specialists such as technicians. The personnel at this level is comprised of highly skilled and specialized staff. Problems are transferred to specific people based on their area of expertise. As the overlap in the areas of expertise between the experts can be rather small, problems have to wait if the required expert is not available. Problems that cannot be solved by the second level support are transferred to the vendors of the technical equipment.

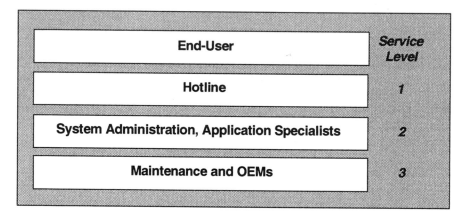

Fig. 11.1. Support Levels at the Help-Desk in the Generalized View.

Traditionally, help-desk operators use a set of tools (e.g. inventory systems, trouble-ticket tools, call-tracking software) that help them in performing their tasks. However, these tools do not give support in diagnosing the problem and cannot serve as a knowledge repository. The growing number of technical equipment as well as the productivity pressure usually heavily increase the responsibility of the help-desk. Although the personnel at the help-desk is very well trained, it is impossible for them to be knowledgeable in all areas.

Since most of the problems recur, the operators end up re-deriving solutions to problems that a colleague of them has already solved in the past. This is not only frustrating to the help-desk operator and the end-user, but also a waste of resources of the company.

11.2 Structure and Representation of the Experience Base

The way the experience base is represented and structured strongly determines the overall experience management approach. The following representation is particularly suited for diagnosis help-desks that deal with complex equipment that can show a large variety of faults that are difficult to diagnose.

11.2.1 Object-Oriented Representation

In HOMER an object-oriented approach to model the experience is used (see Sect. 3.3.2). While the effort necessary to create such a model is obviously higher, it can be used in guiding the help-desk operator while describing and entering cases. The level of abstraction of the domain model must be discussed in detail with the system administrators and a level which they felt comfortable with must be selected. Since the object-oriented domain model forms the basis for case representation an additional effort is necessary in the beginning of knowledge acquisition. However, the better the domain is modeled, the easier it is to maintain and use the system afterwards. The decision to use an object-oriented domain model approach opposed to a shallow approach depends also on the intended users of the system. For inexperienced help-desk operators a tool with which simple problems can be solved by answering a limited number of questions is of great value. However, in our target problem area, the intended users are experienced help-desk operators who would not bother to use a system for (subjectively) trivial problems. In such an environment, a "shallow" system is of limited use. The important advantages of the object-oriented representation in this case are:

- the structure of the technical system to be diagnosed can be represented in the necessary degree of detail,
- symptoms (attributes in the case representation) can be clearly related to the object to which they belong to,
- thereby the semantics of the problem description can be captured and used for selecting appropriate prior experience,
- thereby, a high retrieval accuracy can be achieved.

11.2.2 Case Structure

The cases in the help-desk domain are modeled in accordance with the approach the help-desk operators use in solving problems (see Fig. 11.2). This approach was derived from the DaimlerChrysler application. It is general in the sense that it is feasible for most complex help-desk operations.

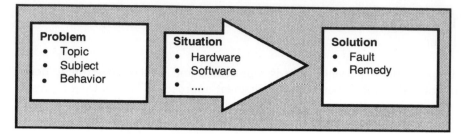

Fig. 11.2. Basic Structure of a Help-Desk Case.

Problem

The first thing a help-desk operator observes, is the *problem* description given by an end user. This description is a subjective description and may or may not have something to do with the actual cause of the problem. The problem in the case model comprises of

- the *topic*: the area in which the problem is located (hardware, software, network, printing or specific service, mailbox system etc.),
- the *subject*: the physical object that the failure is related to (specific software, printer, screen or mobile, router etc.)
- the *behavior*: the way the subject (miss-) behaves (crashes, wrong print size, screeching sound, no dial tone, etc.)

Situation

After the problem has been captured it is necessary to find out about the details of the current *situation*. The situation can be described as a set of attribute-value pairs describing symptoms that are important to diagnose the fault. The symptoms contain the minimum amount of information that is necessary to diagnose the problem. In the object-oriented representation all attributes are related to a certain object.

Solution

The *solution* contains the *fault*, i.e. what the cause of the problem was, and the *remedy*, i.e. how to solve the problem. The solution can be represented as text or hyper-text information, including links to more detailed descriptions describing how to solve the problem.

One has to bear in mind that each solution description can be the result of various situations which in turn can be the result of various problems which can again be solved by applying various remedies. Each complete path from a problem to a solution becomes an individual case.

11.2.3 Partitioning the Experience Base

The complexity and size of the domain as well as the demanded accuracy and consistency of the captured and re-used experience makes it necessary to distinguish among two kinds of cases:

- *Approved cases* represent experience that has been reviewed by top-level experts. The approached cases represent the best practice for problem solving.
- *Open cases* represent experience that was recently captured by the help-desk operators during their daily work. This experience might be worth storing for reuse. However, the open cases have not yet been validated in terms of correctness, completeness and utility.

In order to treat these two kinds of cases separately, the case-base is separated into a *case buffer* and a *main case base*. The main case base contains all approved cases. The case buffer contains all open cases. Since also open cases contain information that might be relevant for the daily operation of the help-desk, they are available to all help-desk operators but marked as being 'not approved'.

11.3 User and Roles

To implement the necessary processes to operate a HOMER experience management application, three user types have been identified:

- the help-desk operator,
- the experience author,
- the experience base administrator.

The help-desk operator has the lowest access rights in the system. S/he is the person that uses the experience management application on a daily basis to solve the problems of the end-users. The main tasks of the help-desk operator are case retrieval and case acquisition.

The experience author is responsible for case maintenance and case approval. S/he checks the cases in the case buffer and transfers relevant cases to the main case-base. The experience author also has the duty to check for redundancy and consistency in the case-base. S/he may modify the value ranges of the attributes in the domain model but is not allowed to modify the domain model itself (i.e. add/remove attributes, move concepts etc.).

The experience base administrator has the highest access rights. S/he has to create and maintain the domain and case model for the system, and administer the users and their access rights.

11.4 Overall Architecture

To ensure that every help-desk operator accesses the same, up-to-date experience base from every point in the network, the system is implemented utilizing a client-server architecture. This enables us to use one central domain model and case-base, and eases the maintenance of the domain model and the case-base.

Figure 11.3 shows the main components of HOMER. The server may be accessed through an intranet or the Internet by the clients. In terms of client-server systems the HOMER client is a fat client. It contains the whole domain model which is loaded on client start-up. It therefore can build up queries and cases based on the domain model and sends requests to the server only when needed. This reduces network traffic. The communications language used is

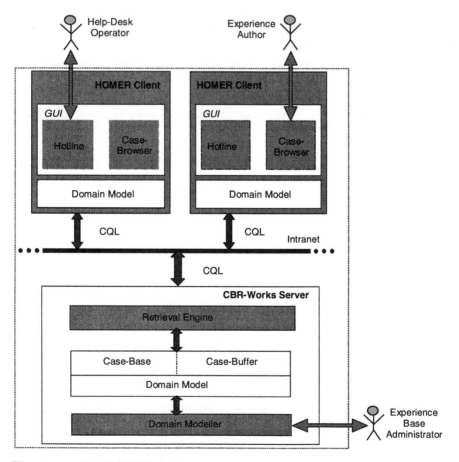

Fig. 11.3. The HOMER Architecture.

CQL (case query language), which was derived from CASUEL (see Sect. 3.6.1), a query language developed in the INRECA project. The HOMER server is based on the standard CBR-Works server (tec:inno GmbH 1999).

11.4.1 The Server

Domain modeling, case and model maintenance, and initial case acquisition is done using the CBR-Works modeling tools (see Sect. 9.8.2). The CBR-Works server stores the model and the case base and provides the tools that the experience base administrator needs to model and maintain the domain.

Figure 11.4 shows a snapshot of a small part of the domain model of HOMER. The tree-view on the left displays the hierarchical structure of the domain concepts. We have selected the *HelpDeskCase* to show the attribute slots.

The slot *Problem* contains an object class *Cproblem*, which describes the failure as mentioned above. *Situation* describes the symptoms. These are structured in sub-concepts to ease the maintenance of the domain model and to speed up the retrieval process. *Loesung* holds the solution to the given problem and *Administrativa* stores organizational and statistical information.

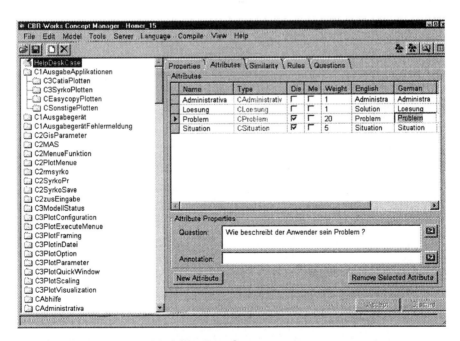

Fig. 11.4. The Domain Modeling Interface.

11.4.2 The HOMER Client

The HOMER client is the interface for case retrieval, case acquisition, and case browsing to the CBR-Works server and was written in Java. Earlier versions were developed as HTML-pages and later with JavaScript, but the dynamics and complexity of the domain model made development with these tools infeasible. Java was chosen because of its networking capabilities and the ease of making it available to the help-desk operator through a web server.

The hotline component of the client is designed for the help-desk operator. It gives the operator all relevant information s/he needs in an easily understandable manner at one glance and assists her/him with two modes of execution: the user-driven mode for the experienced user and the system-driven mode for the novice operator.

The *case browser* component of the client is designed for the experience author. This component

- gives access to the case buffer and the case base,
- enables the revision, extension, and approval of open cases, and
- enables removing outdated cases.

The following section describes the HOMER client in more detail.

11.5 Hotline Component

The Hotline component will be the one used mainly during the hotline operations. Its purpose is to support the help-desk operator during problem solution. Figure 11.5 shows a screen shot of the complete user interface.

11.5.1 Create a New Problem Description

After entering the Hotline Component the first action to be carried out is to describe the new problem to be solved. Entering the problem description is a two stage process:

1. entering a problem part as observed by the user, and
2. entering a situation description by successively adding new symptom values.

Problem Description

The problem description gives the initial information on what the problem is as obtained from the user. Therefore the user has to consecutively answer the following questions:

1. What is the topic of the problem, e.g. "output", "software", "hardware", etc.?

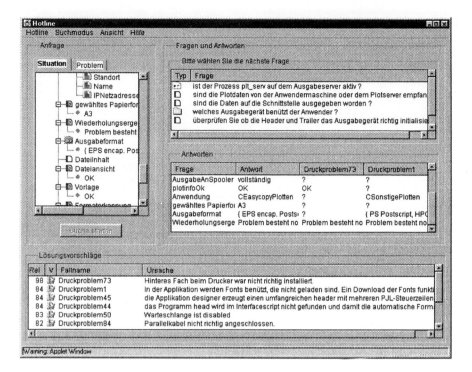

Fig. 11.5. Client Interface.

2. What is this topic's subject, e.g. in case of an output problem: "is the malfunctioning component a plotter or a printer"?
3. After identifying the subject you need to determine the specific behaviour, i.e. what is going wrong, e.g. "no output at all"?

To answer these questions the problem description dialog has been designed (see Fig. 11.6). It opens automatically during the creation of a new problem description. Alternatively, the user can access the problem description in the hotline component shown in Fig. 11.5 by switching its tree view between situation and problem. In the left-hand side tree view the user first selects a topic and then the appropriate subject. Depending on the selection the view on the right offers the choice of possible behaviors that can be specified in an attribute editor.

Situation Description

The previously selected problem description determines which case structure is relevant for the actual problem, i.e. it defines a template for the situation description. It contains a number of possible symptoms related to the problem. Each symptoms is associated with a question and can contain a

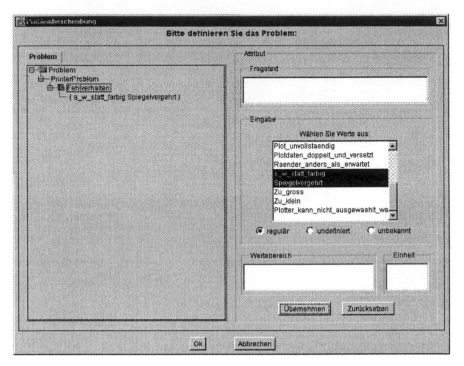

Fig. 11.6. The Problem Description Dialog.

complex or a simple attribute (in the sense of the object-oriented representation), which represents the symptom value.

After the initial problem description has been specified the user must enter a detailed situation description. For this purpose, two different modes of operation are available.

Entering the Situation Description in the User-Driven Mode. In the *user-driven mode* the operator can build a query based on the domain model. This mode is meant for the experienced help-desk operator who does not need guidance on what to ask, knows the case structure, and wants to enter the data directly. The operator enters the symptoms by selecting and specifying the relevant attributes in the situation description shown in the tree view.

Entering the Situation Description in the System-Driven Mode. For the operator with less experience or the operator who wants support in what to ask, s/he can switch to the *system-driven mode*. In this mode the help-desk tool presents the most relevant questions to the operator. The tool generates the questions by selecting the attributes with the highest information gain based on the current case base (see Sect. 6.4.1). These are displayed in the "suggested questions" view. The questions are sorted by their relevance in decreasing order. The help-desk operator can choose which question to ask the end user. Double clicking a question opens the associated attribute editor and allows to answer the question.

11.5.2 Retrieving Problem Solutions

Based on the currently entered problem and situation descriptions, HOMER can retrieve appropriate experience. This retrieval can be carried out in two different modes that can be chosen by the operator:

- Manual: past cases are only retrieved when the user presses the start button. An experienced hotline operator can enter as much information on the problem case s/he wants without delays and interrupts. The retrieval is only invoked if s/he wants new suggestions from the experience management application.
- Automatic: the HOMER application performs a retrieval after any question that has been answered.

Based on the retrieved experience HOMER suggests possible problem solutions, which are displayed in the bottom view of the Hotline Component interface (see Figs. 11.5 and 11.7). Each row shows a possible solution. They are listed in decreasing order of relevance. The relevance displayed shows the degree of similarity between the problem situation and the case to which the suggested solution belongs. Double clicking a solution opens a case entry interface in read-only mode on the past case that is associated with the proposed solution.

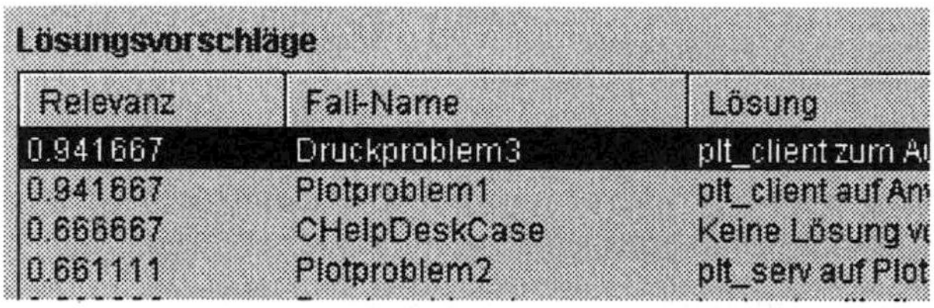

Lösungsvorschläge		
Relevanz	Fall-Name	Lösung
0.941667	Druckproblem3	plt_client zum A
0.941667	Plotproblem1	plt_client auf An
0.666667	CHelpDeskCase	Keine Lösung v
0.661111	Plotproblem2	plt_serv auf Plot

Fig. 11.7. Suggested Solution.

11.5.3 Feedback from Problem Solving

A solved problem can be retained for future use if it contains new reusable experience or if it requires to extend the case model, e.g., to add a new value to a type. To retain a problem the hotline operator selects the "Retain Case" button of the hotline component interface. This will open a case entry interface on the new case. The operator

- can make any final modifications, e.g. complete the case description; and
- can document why s/he thinks that this case should be retained.

The latter is important information for the experience author and the experience base administrator during the maintenance of the case base and the domain model.

The case browser (see Fig. 11.8) is used by the experience author to manage the case base. The browser will be deployed to approved as well as to open cases. The tree view on the left hand side of the screen is used to navigate through the case data. The latter is structured by topics and subjects of the problems. The buttons on the top of the screen allow to perform the following maintenance operations:

- *Case Creation*: The experience author will be asked for the problem, situation, and solution description of the new case.
- *Case Copy*: A complete copy of a case will be created and saved using a new name.
- *Delete Case*: After confirmed by the experience author, a case can be deleted.
- *Approve Case*: An open case is validated and moved from the case buffer to the case base.

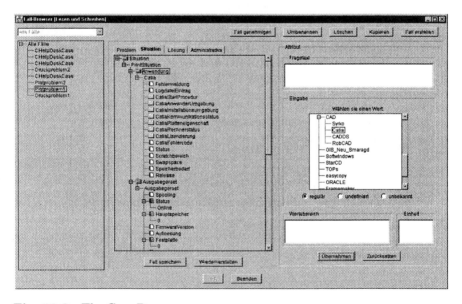

Fig. 11.8. The Case Browser.

11.6 Methodology Recipe for Help-Desk Applications

The following cookbook level recipe (Göker and Roth-Berghofer 1999b; Bergmann and Göker 1999; Bergmann et al. 1999a) describes the processes that must be performed to develop a experience management system to support help-desk operators in diagnosing complex technical equipment. The recipe was created during the development of the DaimlerChrysler application in Sindelfingen and has been applied to the development of several other help-desk systems.

Table 11.1 lists the processes that must be considered and performed during the development and use of an experience management system for help-desk support. As described in Sect. 9.4.1, we distinguish among managerial, organizational, and technical processes.

		System Development	System Use
Managerial Processes		- Goal Definition - Awareness Creation - Tool Selection	- Progress Verification and Controlling
Organizational Processes		- Project Team Selection - Initial Domain Selection - Project Team Training - Knowledge Acquisition Process Development - Utilization Process Development	- End-User Training - Continuous Knowledge Acquisition - Utilization Process
Technical Processes	**General IT-System Related**	- System Specification - System Implementation - System Integration - System Verification	- Continuous System Maintenance
	Knowledge Repository Related	- Initial Knowledge Acquisition - Core Knowledge Acquisition	- Continuous Knowledge Acquisition and Maintenance

Table 11.1. Processes During Help-Desk Support System Development and Use.

11.6.1 Managerial Processes during System Development

The following managerial process must be considered for the development of the system.

Goal Definition

For an experience management project to be successful, precise goals must be determined at the outset. This enables management to fix the direction in which the project should develop and to measure the success of the project upon completion. Hard (quantitative) and soft (qualitative) success criteria should be identified (cf. Stolpmann and Wess 1999). Hard criteria are measurable quantities and cover aspects like:

- *problem solution quality* (first-call resolution rate, solution correctness, and consistency, average cost of proposed solution, and so on),
- *process quality* (average time needed to solve a problem, average number of escalations needed, quality of dynamic priority assignment, and so on),
- *organizational quality* (speedup in help-desk operator training, flexibility of staffing, cost per interaction, and so on).

Soft criteria, on the other hand, measure the subjective quality of the help-desk and cover aspects like:

- *end-user satisfaction* (availability of the help-desk, perceived competence, friendliness, and so on),
- *help-desk operator satisfaction* (workload, work atmosphere, repetitiveness of tasks, intellectual stimulation, and so on), and
- *corporate aspects* (preservation of knowledge, publicity, and so on.).

The goals must be communicated to the project team and the team has to be motivated to achieve them.

When project goals are selected, it is important that these goals be realistic both in terms of their time frame and whether they can be achieved with an acceptable amount of resources. The experience management system for the help-desk must be seen as part of the long-term knowledge management strategy for the company. Since knowledge increases and evolves, the experience in the system must be maintained continuously.

Awareness Creation and Motivation

The experience management project targets the most precious asset of the employees: their experience. The project's goal is to collect the problem solving experience of each relevant employee and make it available to whomever needs it in the organization.

Obviously the help-desk operators will have a motivational barrier to giving away their experience. Every employee knows that "knowledge is power." In help-desk environments or domains where experience is being used to solve problems having experience translates into being superior and indispensable, whereas giving away the knowledge can be perceived as becoming obsolete.

However, as soon as help-desk operators become part of a project team and understand that sharing knowledge means that they will get back much more than they invest, most barriers disappear. It has to be made clear that the user and beneficiary of the developed system is not going to be an anonymous "company," but they themselves. They will be able to access the experience of their colleagues and solve problems they could not solve before, as well as end situations in which colleagues constantly pester them for advice. The resulting experience management system will enable them to work with increased efficiency and effectiveness.

Apart from the help-desk operators, management has to be motivated as well. While to them investing resources into a database project seems to be no problem, investing into experience management technology is investing into a venture with an uncertain outcome. It has to be clarified that experience management is based on an established technology and by no means only an academic playground. It also has to be clarified that the initial installation of the system is only the beginning of a process that will enable the company to capture and reuse experience. Management must be prepared to invest resources on a continuous basis while the system is operational. A experience management approach is only useful if it contains knowledge and is being maintained on a continuous basis.

Without continuous management support and employees who are willing to fill and use the system, any experience management activity is bound to fail.

Tool Selection

Based on the project, domain, and user-group specifications, a suitable tool must be selected. Criteria to be taken into account include:

- the operating environment in which the system is going to be used (hardware and software, network architecture, database type, and so on),
- the complexity of the technical domain (home appliances or networked workstations),
- the level of experience of both the end-users and the help-desk operators,
- the organization of the help-desk (number of levels, physical locations, and so on),
- the project goals that have been defined.

Since the experience management system is going to serve as a (long-term) knowledge repository for the organization, this selection should be based not only on technical criteria, but also should take into account economic and organizational considerations, as well as strategic decisions of the company.

11.6.2 Organizational Processes during System Development

The following organizational process must be considered for the development of the system.

Project Team and Initial Domain Selection

The creation of a project team to serve as the "knowledge engineers" and the selection of a group to serve as initial test users of the system are the first organizational steps that must be taken.

Apart from the person implementing the experience management system, the project team should contain help-desk personnel who are very experienced in the relevant subdomain to be modeled and well respected by the help-desk operators outside the project group. Once selected, the members of the group should be kept constant, i.e., fluctuations should be avoided.

The group of initial users should comprise two types of help-desk personnel: One that is on a comparable level of expertise with the project team with respect to the selected subdomain (i.e., expert users) and help-desk personnel who are less familiar with the specific problem area (i.e., novice users). While the expert test-users can communicate to the project group in their language, the novice users will represent the target group for which the system is being implemented. Feedback from both types of users is required for a successful project. After a first "rapid prototype" has been implemented, the expert users can give hints regarding problems with the knowledge modeled in the system. The members of the novice user group, on the other hand, will serve as models of the help-desk operator who will use the system. The vocabulary in which the cases are being represented and the knowledge contained within them has to be adjusted to the novice user group.

Which domain one selects for the initial knowledge acquisition is of utmost importance. The domain should be representative of the problems that are being handled at the help-desk, both in terms of complexity and frequency. It should also be a problem area that accounts for a considerable amount of the workload and about which the help-desk operators are interested in sharing (obtaining) knowledge.

Training the Project Team

Training the project team is an organizational process that has a major impact on the success of the help-desk project. At the beginning of the project, the project team is (most of the time) inexperienced with respect to knowledge acquisition. Since the project group will be responsible for system maintenance and continuous experience acquisition after the development has finished, it is very important that they are trained in knowledge acquisition and modeling, during the initial knowledge acquisition.

While the project team should also get advanced training to be able to model, fill, and maintain the knowledge in the system, the test users only need to be trained in using the resulting help-desk support system.

Development of the Knowledge Acquisition and Utilization Processes

The introduction and use of an experience management system usually causes a re-evaluation and modification of the existing knowledge and information management processes in a help-desk environment. When the system is used, it must be integrated into the operating environment of the help-desk operators and become part of the standard business process. Existing processes must be altered to facilitate the flow of information to and from the experience management system. When organizational processes are defined, the tasks to be performed, the personnel or roles to perform these tasks, and the communication among the groups/roles have to be fixed.

After the development of the experience management system is complete, it will serve as the central source of information for the help-desk operators. To ensure a smooth flow of information, the knowledge sources and formats, as well as the qualification of the personnel that requires the knowledge, have to be analyzed, and processes that allow efficient and effective acquisition and use of knowledge have to be developed. One should keep in mind that while the group enacting the initial knowledge acquisition process is the project team and rather experienced, the users who use the system in the end (both in terms of knowledge retrieval and continuous acquisition) may be less qualified.

In general, we can define three roles for the organizational processes during the use of the help-desk system:

- the help-desk operator,
- the experience author,
- the experience base administrator.

Help-desk operators are the users from the target group. Their duty is to use the implemented help-desk system in their daily work. If they cannot find an appropriate solution with the system, they will have to solve the problem on their own and generate a new case. Depending on the domain and on managerial decisions, this new case may or may not be made immediately available as an open case to the other help-desk operators. For maintenance purposes, the operators are also encouraged to comment on the quality and applicability of the cases in the case base.

The open cases have to be verified in terms of their correctness and suitability for the case base by the experience author(s). The experience author is a person with experience both in the domain and in using the experience management system. While the experience author can decide on the quality and inclusion of a case in the case base, s/he is not allowed to perform modifications on the vocabulary, the similarity, and the adaptation knowledge. These can only be performed by the experience base administrator.

The personnel enacting the roles of the experience author(s) and the experience base administrator should be included in the project group from the start of the project. It should be noted that both these roles require a considerable amount of resources and should be performed by dedicated personnel. If the organization or the size of the help-desk does not permit dedicating more than one person to these tasks, the duties of the experience author and experience base administrator should be performed by one person.

11.6.3 Technical Processes during System Development

The following technical process occur during the development of the system.

General IT-system Development Related Processes

The development of an experience management system is similar to any other IT project in most aspects. As usual, the system has to be specified, implemented, integrated, and verified. The definition of the requirements, the implementation, and the testing and revision of both the prototype and the actual experience management system are steps that have to be performed in accordance with standard software engineering techniques. However, the user-interface and the connection to supporting programs (integration) are two features that require additional attention.

The essential task in developing a user interface is to present the relevant data, at the right moment, in the right representation, and on a level of abstraction that is suitable for the current users of the system. If the available data is presented to the users in a way that they do not understand, in a representation they are not familiar with, or at a moment when it is irrelevant, it will only cause confusion and be of no use. While the exact specification of the firmware installed on a printer may be necessary information for a second-level help-desk operator, it will be rather useless for a first-level help-desk operator who is just trying to figure out whether the printer is connected to the computer. The user interface of the experience management system has to be developed in accordance with the user group (i.e., second level, first level, or even end-user), the specific domain, and company policies (who is allowed to see what kind of data). It has to present the right data, at the right moment, on the right level of abstraction, and in accordance with company policies.

A experience management system for help-desk support cannot operate in isolation. While the experience management system will store experience, it will not contain data regarding device configurations, maintenance contracts, and users. Maintenance information and device configurations are stored in an inventory system most of the time. Data regarding the end-users is usually stored in another, separate database. Since this information is needed during problem solving, the system has to have interfaces to these databases.

Most help-desks use trouble-ticket tools in their daily operations; they record, manage, trace, escalate, and analyze the calls they receive. While these trouble-ticket tools are very useful in handling calls, they do not provide means to capture and reuse problem-solving experience. Depending on the environment, the experience management system should also either be integrated into the user interface of the trouble-ticket tool or vice-versa. Data from the trouble-ticket system has to be transferred to the experience management system to initialize the attributes that relate to the data that has already been acquired. Except for very complex second-level applications, it is not feasible to have two points of entry to the problem-solving process.

Initial Knowledge Acquisition

An experience management system is useless without experience. When the experience management system is handed over to the help-desk operators, it has to contain enough cases to cover at least part of the relevant problems at the help-desk. Otherwise the system will be considered useless and the project will fail. Initial knowledge acquisition serves three major goals:

- training the project team in knowledge acquisition,
- initializing the knowledge in the system,
- collecting enough help-desk cases to bootstrap the system.

During initial knowledge acquisition, the knowledge in the system can be distributed among the *domain model* (vocabulary), *similarity measure, adaptation knowledge*, and the *case base*. This knowledge has to be captured and formalized. The processes for the acquisition of knowledge for each container run in parallel and cannot be easily separated during the initial knowledge acquisition. Since the vocabulary lays ground for entering the cases and describing the similarity measures and adaptation knowledge, it has to be available first. However, to be able to create a domain model (i.e., the vocabulary), one has to understand how the domain is structured, and this can only be done by looking at the cases, the similarities, and the adaptation rules.

In our experience, the best way to approach this problem is to create and use standardized forms to acquire an initial amount of cases from the project team. The form should be developed in co-operation with the project team. A sample form that was developed for the initial case acquisition for the DaimlerChrysler hotline application is shown in Table 11.2.

The first thing that must be done is to ask the project team to fill out as many case acquisition forms as they can. By looking at the elements of the forms, the vocabulary (i.e., the phrases that have to be used and the domain structure) can be derived and a vocabulary that is capable of describing the cases that have been on the forms can be modeled.

By asking the project team what the range of possible values for each attribute on the forms is and inquiring what would have happened if one of the values on a form were different, a broad range of cases can be created and the vocabulary expanded in a short time. Discussions among the project

Homer Case Acquisition	
Problem Nr : 0816	**Date: 26.04.99**
Author: S. Itani	**Verified by: J. Fleisch**
Problem Description (Failure)	Printer does print pages full of gibberish
Reason (Fault)	File is Postscript, Printer does not understand PS
Solution	Send File to Postscript Printer, delete file from queue
What did you check to find out what the problem was ?	
Printer Model	HP LJ 6L
File Type	Postscript
Other Notes:	The reverse of this problem did also happen, somebody sent a PCL file to a pure PS printer

Table 11.2. Sample Form for Initial Case Acquisition.

team members raise the level of understanding of both the approach and the problems, and should be encouraged in this early phase. One should also keep in mind that the goal is not to model the domain in every detail but on a level that helps the system's user solve a problem (i.e., the system does not have to solve the problem autonomously). Especially during initial knowledge acquisition, it is advisable to have more cases at an "everyday" level rather than having a few extremely specific ones.

While the initial vocabulary is being created and value ranges fixed, questions regarding adaptation rules and similarities should be posed and the results entered into the system.

One of the major challenges one must face when creating a system to capture and represent the experience of domain experts, is determining the level of abstraction with which the domain and the knowledge will be modeled. If the model used is too simplistic, it will cause problems while the experience is being captured and will miss important details. If, however, the domain model is too specific, the user will get lost quickly in useless details, and knowledge acquisition will be very tedious and time consuming. Maintenance is very difficult for both a too-simplistic and a too-complex model.

The decision to use a structured domain model approach as opposed to a textual query-answer-based approach also depends on the system's intended users. For inexperienced help-desk operators, a tool with which simple problems can be solved by answering a limited number of questions is of great value (Thomas et al. 1997). However, for experienced help-desk operators who would not bother to use a system for (subjectively) trivial problems, a structured domain model approach yields better results. The system will be able to present the not-so-obviously similar solutions that the help-desk operators could not find. Since knowledge contained in the domain model is used in similarity calculation, the retrieved solutions will be similar in a semantic and structural manner. The domain model allows the solutions in the case base to be applicable to a broader range of problems. The cases in the help-desk domain should be modeled in accordance with the approach the help-desk operators use in solving problems (see Fig. 11.2).

Once the cases from the initial forms have been entered into the help-desk system, the system should be shown to the project group to verify the results it delivers. Afterwards the initial knowledge acquisition can continue as more cases are entered from additional forms and the knowledge containers are incrementally updated.

Initial knowledge acquisition takes place in two steps. During the first, preliminary knowledge acquisition, the cases for the prototype of the experience management system are collected. While the collected cases will help to initialize the knowledge containers and train the project team, the collection of the "core" cases for the system should be done in a second step, the core knowledge acquisition. Nevertheless, the approach that is used in both processes is similar.

11.6.4 Managerial Processes during System Use

Project progress with respect to the qualitative and quantitative criteria selected as project goals must be monitored constantly during system development and use (cf. Stolpmann and Wess 1999). Regular project reviews should take place. Standard project planning and controlling techniques can and should be applied to experience management projects.

Measuring the impact of the experience management system on the efficiency and effectiveness of the target group (increase in first-call problem resolution, decrease in problem solution time, and so on) and making the results available to both the project and the target groups will motivate the help-desk operators to use the system and help uncover deficiencies.

11.6.5 Organizational Processes during System Use

When the system is in use, the following organizational processes dealing with maintenance and training are important.

Knowledge Utilization and Acquisition Process

The knowledge utilization and acquisition processes that have been defined during system development have to be enacted during system use. The use of the experience management system contains the problem-solving cycle in which the system is used by the help-desk operator and the maintenance cycle in which the system is maintained by the experience author and the experience base administrator (see Sects. 2.2 and 11.6.6).

During the problem-solving cycle, the cases that are stored in the case-based help-desk support system are being used to solve problems. Even if no new cases are being acquired during this cycle, statistical data regarding the quality and usage of the cases (last retrieval time, last application date, success rate and so on) can be collected. This data can be used to determine the quality of the cases and for maintenance purposes.

Whenever a help-desk operator decides that the proposed solution is not appropriate, a new case has to be entered into the case base. However, since the quality of these cases varies according to the user entering them, they cannot be transferred to the case base without being verified by the experience author. This is done in the maintenance cycle. The extension and maintenance of the case base is the duty of the experience author and the experience base administrator.

Training the Help-Desk Operators

Just as the test-users were trained during the project team training, the help-desk operators have to be introduced to the basics of experience management technology and the developed experience management system. Since the operators are going to participate in the continuous acquisition of knowledge, standards on how to store cases have to be introduced and taught. Feedback-channels also should be created and introduced during this training.

11.6.6 Technical Processes during System Use

Maintenance of the experience management system also includes several technical aspects to be considered during system use.

Continuous Knowledge Acquisition and Maintenance

The knowledge contained in an experience management system is an incomplete model of the domain in the real world. Whenever the real world changes, the model in the system has to be updated. The necessity for changes in the model may either arise from real changes in the world or from the learning effect associated with using the experience management system. By learning, the system improves the model's coverage of the real world. Since the model is incomplete by definition (and no such thing as a closed world exists in the real world), with growing knowledge, updates in the knowledge containers will be necessary.

An experience management system comprises two linked process cycles: the problem-solving cycle and the maintenance cycle (see Sect. 2.2). While the problem solving cycle is executed every time a help-desk operator uses the experience management system, the maintenance cycle can be executed less frequently, i.e., only when there is a need for maintaining the system or at regular intervals.

Whenever a new solution is generated during the application cycle, this case is stored in the case buffer, made available to all help-desk operators as an "unconfirmed" case, and sent to the *Maintenance Cycle*. These operations as well as the maintenance cycle are not visible to the standard help-desk operator.

The experience author verifies and approves the representation and content of each case. In terms of representation, the cases should

- contain the information that is necessary and sufficient to solve the problem,
- be described on an abstraction level that is appropriate for the system's end-user.

The content is verified by checking whether the case is

- correct,
- (still) relevant, and
- applicable.

Before a new case is taken into the case base, it must be checked to see

- whether it is a viable alternative that does not yet exist in the case base,
- whether it subsumes or can be subsumed by an existing case,
- whether it can be combined with another case to form a new one,
- whether the new case would cause an inconsistency, and
- whether there is a newer case already available in the case base.

The operations that have to be performed during case base maintenance vary depending on the application domain and the vocabulary that is used to represent the cases.

Both the inclusion of new cases and changes in the domain may have an effect on the validity and quality of the compiled knowledge containers (vocabulary, similarity, adaptation knowledge) as well. Since changes in the vocabulary can cause information in the cases to be no longer available or missing (e.g., attributes can be added and deleted, classes can be moved) maintenance of the vocabulary should be performed with utmost caution (Heister and Wilke 1998).

General IT-system-Related Processes

Once the experience management system has been put into operation, it has to be debugged, monitored, and updated continuously. The necessity for updates does not necessarily have to come from the help-desk system itself, but may also be initiated by changes in the (IT) environment. Since these processes are not specific to experience management but apply to IT systems in general, we refrain from going into their details here.

11.6.7 Process Model for a Help-Desk Project

The overall process for the development and introduction of an experience management system for help-desk support can be divided into six main phases:

1. project planning and initialization,
2. implementation of a rapid prototype,
3. evaluation and revision of the prototype,
4. implementation of the integrated case-based help-desk support system,
5. evaluation and revision of the case-based help-desk support system,
6. utilization of the case-based help-desk support system.

Project Planning and Initialization

During project planning and initialization, the preliminary requirements for the execution of the project are fulfilled. The project goals are defined, the project information is disseminated, the project team is created and trained, and the tool to be used (for example HOMER) is acquired (see Fig. 11.9).

Implementation of the Rapid Prototype

The implementation of the rapid prototype enables the project team to test the validity of the goals and the requirements set forth in the project-planning phase. It also serves to train the project team in knowledge acquisition techniques and in using the tool. The processes that will be used during knowledge acquisition can be defined and refined. The "Rapid Prototype Implementation," "Preliminary Knowledge Acquisition," and "Knowledge Acquisition Process Development" processes are closely interconnected and influence each other. While changes in the prototype will effect the way knowledge is acquired, changes in the domain model will effect changes in the acquisition process as well as the user interface of the system, and so on (see Fig. 11.10). The interaction between processes is shown with dotted lines in the figures.

Evaluation and Revision of the Prototype

During the evaluation and revision of the prototype (see Fig. 11.11), the initial users evaluate the developed a rapid prototype as well as the structure and content of the knowledge containers. The results are collected in a revised-requirements definition document, which serves as a basis for the development of the actual system.

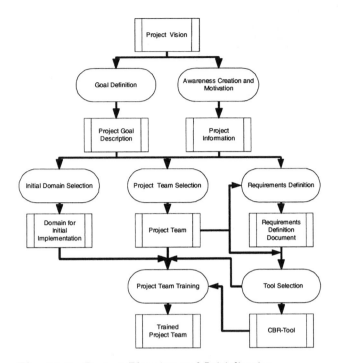

Fig. 11.9. Project Planning and Initialization.

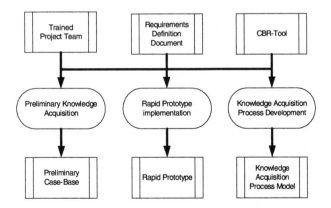

Fig. 11.10. Implementation of the Rapid Prototype.

Implementation of the Integrated Experience Management System

The implementation of the integrated system contains the development of the actual system to be used at the help desk. The implementation is based on the preliminary case base, the revised requirements, the rapid prototype, input from the project team, and the process model for knowledge acquisition.

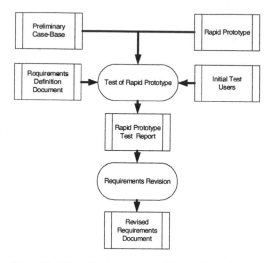

Fig. 11.11. Evaluation and Revision of the Prototype.

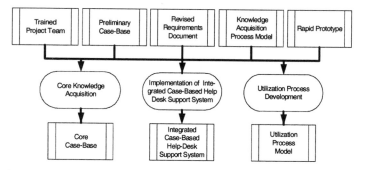

Fig. 11.12. Implementation of the Integrated Experience Management System.

While the system is implemented, the project team acquires the core case base to be deployed with the system after implementation is complete. The processes to be used when the system is used are also developed in close connection with the implementation and the knowledge acquisition in this phase (see Fig. 11.12).

Evaluation and Revision of the Experience Management System

During this phase, the system is evaluated by the initial users and revised according to the results of this evaluation (see Fig. 11.13).

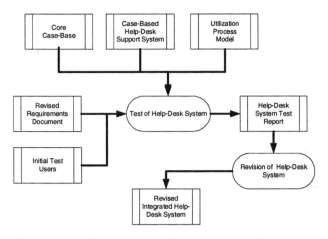

Fig. 11.13. Evaluation and Revision of the Experience Management System.

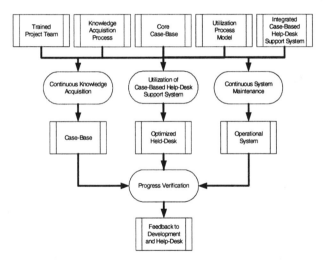

Fig. 11.14. Utilization of the Experience Management System.

Utilization of the Experience Management System

The system is put to use and the impact of the system is continuously monitored and feedback is given to developers and users (see Fig. 11.14).

11.7 Evaluation of HOMER

An application of the HOMER architecture and software components has been realized, using the methodology recipe just described, for the second-level printer/plotter help-desk of DaimlerChrysler in Sindelfingen. An evaluation has been performed by the INRECA-II project partners to identify the benefits of introducing the experience management system for the help-desk operators as well as the benefits for the application developers through the use of the methodology.

11.7.1 Benefits for the Help-Desk Operators

For evaluation purposes, incoming calls were monitored and, depending on their applicability, solved with HOMER. Since this experiment should not interfere with the normal operation of the help-desk and the end-users, the help-desk operator first solves the problem in a conventional manner. After the call had been resolved, the operator solved the same problem using HOMER. If no solution was found, the case was entered as a new case into the case base. During the two month test period, 102 calls were handled by the second-level help-desk operator who performed the test. Forty-five of these calls were either trivial, directed to the wrong help-desk, or could not be reproduced (see Fig. 11.15).

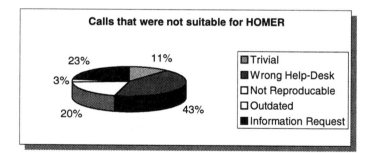

Fig. 11.15. Reasons why Calls were Unsuitable for HOMER.

Of the remaining 57 problems, HOMER solved 18 (i.e., 32%). While the average problem resolution time for these problems was 141 minutes without HOMER, the help-desk operator needed only 9 minutes on average to solve problems with HOMER (see Fig. 11.16). Of course, knowing the correct result might bias the operator while solving the same problem again with HOMER. However, this bias is limited since the dialog with the help-desk operator is controlled to a large extend by the HOMER dialog component.

This result was much better than what was expected when the project was initiated. As a next step, HOMER and the printer-plotter case base are being transferred to another production site of DaimlerChrysler. This site is currently implementing the same process chain for their printer-plotter environment as was done in Sindelfingen. Since the help-desk operators as

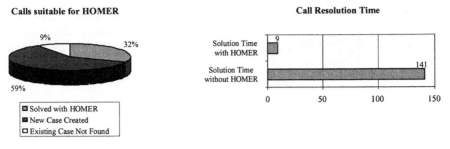

Fig. 11.16. HOMER Performance.

yet have no experience with the process chain, the printer-plotter cases in HOMER are of great value to them. An interesting side-effect is that in the course of initial knowledge acquisition, the help-desk operators gained a much deeper insight into the processes involved in the domain that was being modeled. This resulted in several enhancements and has reduced the number of calls that arrive at the help-desk as well.

11.7.2 Evaluation of the Methodology Recipe

The methodology recipe described in Sect. 11.6 was created during the development of this printer/plotter application. After the process models were complete, the methodology and the developed tools were used during the *project definition, application development,* and *system utilization* phases of new projects. As described in Capt. 9, the methodology should have an impact on *productivity, quality, communication,* and *management decision making.* The advantages of using the methodology could been observed in each of these areas and in all three project phases, both to the customer (management and user) and to the developer.

Impact of the Methodology during Project Definition

During the definition of a project, the processes to be executed have to be detailed. For each process, this involves defining the methods to be used, the project's duration, the resources needed, the results to be produced, the interaction with other processes within the project, and the sequence in which the processes must be executed.

By means of the methodology the developers were able to create project definitions with structured process models, task definitions, roles and responsibilities, duration, and resource allocations. The methodology enabled them to make the experience management system development process traceable both to the customers and to themselves.

While the creation of the project definition for the printer/plotter application from scratch took about three months, a new development team from

DaimlerChrysler was able to reuse the help-desk recipe to define three new projects in less than a week each (see Fig. 11.17). The overall duration of these projects varied between six months and three years. Since a recipe was reused that had been executed before, it could be sure that all aspects that needed be taken into account were covered. Since the basic recipe was available, the developers could concentrate on the peculiarities of each domain. The quality and level of detail that could be achieved in these project descriptions were far beyond the level that can be achieved when a description is created from scratch.

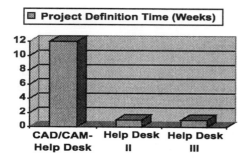

Fig. 11.17. Impact of Methodology During Project Definition.

Apart from these advantages in increased productivity and quality, the methodology was also very useful for communicating with the customer and conveying the message that the development of an experience management system is not an art, but, rather, solid technology. Being able to describe each process in the development of a case based system in detail enabled developers to convince managers of the validity of the approach, clarified the need for continuous maintenance and resource allocation, and let them raise realistic expectations. They were able to give customers figures on how much effort had to be spent by whom and when. Project progress became measurable. This gave them a basis for making decisions, enabled them to plan their resource allocation in advance, and prevented the loss of critical resources in the course of the project.

Impact of the Methodology during System Development

The detailed project plan that was created during project definition served as a guideline during the development of the system. The ability to trace a structured path and the use of the software tools that was developed to support the methodology allowed to speed up the development process by a factor of 12. While the development and testing of the first prototype took up to six months from the initiation of the projects, the developers were able to create a prototype and test it at another site of DaimlerChrysler within two weeks (see Fig. 11.18).

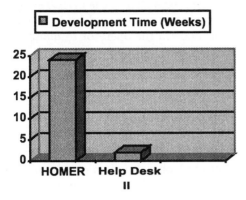

Fig. 11.18. Impact of Methodology During Project Definition.

Since the tasks that have to be performed and the results that have to be achieved during the implementation of the system were described in detail in the recipe and the project definition, some tasks could be transferred from one developer to the other without additional effort, and the progress that was achieved during the project could be measured. A clear-cut definition of the tasks to be performed and the availability of tools for creating and maintaining a domain model allowed DaimlerChrysler to use less-qualified personnel during the development of the system without compromising the quality of the resulting product. This allowed both the developer and the customer to optimize the allocation of personnel resources.

Impact of the Methodology during System Use

During the development and initial use of HOMER, the tasks and qualifications of the personnel needed to operate the system had to be changed several times. Since the processes for the acquisition, use, and maintenance of the knowledge in the experience management system are defined in the methodology, it was possible to introduce new help-desk systems in a much more efficient manner. While the domain modeling and maintenance task could only be performed by a highly qualified help-desk operator in the HOMER project, the domain modeling and model-maintenance tools, as well as the similarity editor that was developed to support the INRECA methodology, enabled to use much-less-qualified personnel in the ensuing projects.

The detailed definition of the duties that have to be performed and the qualification that is needed for the project group also enabled the customers to allocate the necessary resources in advance and monitor the status of the project according to the goals that had been set when the project was initiated.

The methodology was also used to train users in the administration of a case-based help-desk support system. Using process charts, the overall structure of the project was explained to the operator who would be in charge of the project after it was completed. This allowed the operator to maintain and use the system without getting lost in details and neglecting important aspects, like maintaining the case base.

11.8 Summary

HOMER is a generic experience management architecture and a set of related tools that stores the experience of the help-desk operators in a case base and enable them to access, reuse, and extend the knowledge in a natural and straightforward manner. It allows the experience of the help-desk operators to be gathered and preserved, ensuring that solutions to previous problems are available. Since the time needed to solve problems decreased drastically, the productivity of the supported departments increased.

To develop experience management systems for help-desk support to be used in dynamic, corporate environments by a large group of users, one must take into account the managerial, organizational, and technical processes. It has to be kept in mind that once an experience management system is in place, continuous knowledge acquisition and maintenance is necessary. Processes for knowledge acquisition and maintenance have to be developed and put in place, and personnel have to be dedicated to performing these tasks.

12. Experience Management for Electronic Design Reuse

> *"Knowledge management may turn out to be the greatest form of IP to leverage. In this emerging information age, it will become very significant for designers to share know-how, decisions and information characterizing design."*

J. Scott Runner,
Director, Conexant Systems Inc.

The design of electronic circuits is a discipline in which two contrasting tendencies can be observed: On the one hand, modern circuit designs get ever more complex and difficult to handle by electronic engineers. On the other hand, global competition requires a continuous reduction of development times. At the same time, the correctness and reliability of the designs should, of course, not suffer from shorter development cycles.

These requirements have become so dominant that they cannot be met anymore without extensive utilization of design reuse. It is getting vitally important for an electronic engineer to reuse old designs (or parts of them) and not to re-design a new application entirely from scratch.

This chapter describes a generic experience management approach for electronic design reuse. The results presented in this chapter have been achieved as part of the project READEE (Reuse Assistant for Designs in Electronic Engineering), the project IPQ[1] (IP Qualification for efficient system design) and the European MEDEA+ project TOOLIP[2] (Methods and TOOLs for IP) and have been previously published in part (Vollrath 1998; Oehler et al. 1998; Oehler et al. 1998; Bergmann et al. 1999; Bergmann and Vollrath 1999; Koegst et al. 1999; Vollrath 2000).

---

[1] IPQ is funded by the German Ministry for Education and Research (BMBF) from 12/2000 till 11/2003. See www.ip-qualification.de.

[2] MEDEA+ is part of the EUREKA initiative. The TOOLIP consortium includes 30 European partners. See toolip.fzi.de for details.

12.1 Electronic Design Reuse

Reusing designs from the past requires that the engineer has enough experience and knowledge about existing designs, in order to be able to find candidates that are suitable for reuse in his specific new situation. Manually searching databases of existing designs can be an extremely time consuming task because it is difficult to decide whether a given design from a database can be easily adapted to meet the specification of the new application.

The idea of design reuse is not new, but until recently, reusable components in electronic designs were of limited complexity and understandable by application designers. There was no need for experience management approaches. Nowadays, reusable designs are growing ever more complex and are difficult to understand by designers reusing them. To reflect this growing complexity, the term *intellectual property (IP)* has been assigned to those designs and the term *reuse* today means more than just plugging a component into a new environment.

12.1.1 Intellectual Properties

More and more electronic companies do not hesitate to use *intellectual properties* (IPs) from third parties inside their complex electronic systems. An IP is a design object whose major value comes from the skill of its producer (Lewis 1997), and a redesign of it would consume significant time. IP is just a new name for what formerly were called macro/mega cells, cores, or building blocks. What's different is the growing complexity of such cells (10k to 100k gates). Applying such functional blocks to a system-on-chip (SoC) design in a block-oriented way is often called *design by reuse*. For doing so, such complex blocks have to be *designed for reuse*. That means

- standardized pinout for pin compatibility,
- compatibility with industry standards,
- standardized on-chip interfaces (Virtual Socket Interface),
- proper verification of such blocks,
- meaningful documentation and well-documented source code.

This additional effort only makes sense for blocks which will be used very often. An IP with fixed parameters offers just a *design point*. That means, it can only be used for one specific application. On the other hand, an IP which is parameterizable, e.g. a variable wordlength, spans a *design space*. Therefore, parameterizable IPs are more flexible to use and the chances that they will be reused are much better.

IPs can be classified into three main groups.

Hard IP. Hard IPs are not parameterizable, technology dependent, usually optimized for maximum performance, minimum size or low power. Register transfer level (RTL) simulation models available. Measures, which are particular IP characteristics (see Sect. 12.2.2), such as gate count, performance, and power consumption are known.

Soft IP. Soft IPs are parameterizable, technology independent, VHDL (Perry 1991) or Verilog (Thomas and Moorby 1991) descriptions. Measures are unknown or only roughly estimated for a specific target technology.

Firm IP. Firm IPs are intermediate between soft and hard cores: they are characterized by a limited portability but estimations of gate count, performance and power are available.

More and more IP vendors arise, offering their IPs especially in the Internet. Searching in such IP databases can be an extremely time consuming task because, first, the public domain documentation of IPs is very poor and second there are currently no intelligent tools to support the designer in deciding whether a given IP from a database can be easily adapted to meet the specification of her/his new application.

12.1.2 IP Reuse

A simple but typical reuse scenario from the designer's point of view consists of a few main steps:

1. Make a *specification* for a new application.
2. *Find a catalog* of reusable designs that contains IPs of the specific application domain.
3. In the catalog, *search* for the IP that is best reusable for the new application.
4. *Buy* this IP from the IP provider.
5. Try to *reuse* the IP. This usually requires the use of a design and synthesis tool. Often, an IP can be used without modification but the design parameters of soft IPs need further specification.
6. The *profit* gained by reusing the IP depends on the amount of time and effort that could be saved compared to the time and effort that it would have taken to develop the application from scratch. If a bad IP selection has been made in step 3, reusing an IP can be so difficult that the expected profit turns into a loss.

12.1.3 Existing IP Reuse Support

Larger electronic companies try to develop their own reuse tools. The primary focus of most of these systems yet is on design representation issues and related database management problems.

The Internet, of course, provides some information on electronic components and IPs. For hardware components, the information sometimes is provided as data sheets. They contain all the information (and even more) that is needed to evaluate a product regarding a special purpose. Browsing through the data sheets of certain product families and evaluating the information contained therein can take many days.

On the other hand, information on IPs often is so sparse that a designer can only guess whether the IP would be suitable for his purpose. IP providers have to be very careful to protect their intellectual property.

In July 1997 *Design & Reuse*[3] (Behnam et al. 1998) launched an online catalog for IPs. This catalog was a great success right from the start which indicates that there is a big demand for reusable designs. The *Design & Reuse* IP Catalog basically provides two different search facilities: First, there is a hierarchical IP taxonomy which serves as a selection tree for IPs and families of IPs, and second there is a keyword search that enables a user to search across the boundaries of the taxonomy.

There are general points of criticism that apply to these search techniques. The biggest problem is their lack of abstraction capabilities: abstract information like "good for high fidelity audio applications" can not be deduced from low-level attributes like "signal-to-noise ratio" and "dynamic range".

Keyword search is only a syntactical search. A search for a "short cycle time", for example, would fail to find components with a "high clock rate", which is a more or less equivalent quality. In addition to that, more abstract information like "good for high fidelity audio applications" can not be deduced from low-level attributes like "signal-to-noise ratio" and "dynamic range" by a syntactical search.

A taxonomy, on the other hand, holds some more information about categories of designs. A drawback of a purely taxonomic search is that there is no information about the relations (exchangeability or equivalence, for example) between two categories on the same hierarchical level. However, such information would be very beneficial for a reuse tool. Another problem with selection trees is that the user is forced to make decisions in a predefined order. If, for some reason, s/he cannot (or does not want to) make a decision at some point, s/he is forced to make several inquiries in sequence.

Figure 12.1 illustrates this problem with an example taken from the *Design & Reuse* IP Catalog. A user looking for an 8 bit microcontroller is forced to make a decision (RISC or CISC) s/he rather would not care about. It is not possible to generally solve this problem because there might be another user looking for a RISC microcontroller, so the order of decisions cannot be globally optimized.

---

[3] www.design-reuse.com

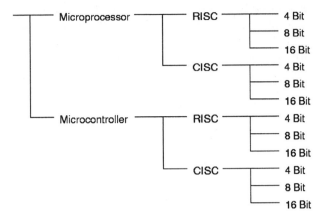

Fig. 12.1. Part of an IP Selection Tree.

12.1.4 Challenges of Experience Management for IP Reuse

There are a number of reasons why experience management approaches are needed to support the designer during IP reuse.

- IP databases can be very large. Standard search approaches, like keyword search or decision trees, tend to fail to keep the number of matching IPs small. The IPs retrieved have to be individually examined by the designer, and this can be very time consuming.
- Evaluating the usability of an IP for a specific problem often requires that the user makes herself/himself familiar with many details of the design. Even if the user is an expert in the application domain of the IP, extracting certain information out of a data sheet can be very difficult because the technical data is partly described on a very low technical level.
- Design information on intellectual property must be protected against pla-giarism. Because of this, a designer does not get much information on a soft IP before s/he actually buys it. It is therefore often impossible to tell in advance the difference between a number of IPs with similar purposes but different implementations .

All these arguments make clear that experience management systems capable of providing real selection support are highly recommended.

For typical soft IPs a complete analysis with respect to a given target application can be extremely complex and calculation intensive. Moreover, it is even more difficult to build a system that can automatically adapt such a complex design to the specification of a new application. On the other hand, a designer who decides to reuse existing hardware components often does not expect to find an IP that *exactly* meets the new requirements – it is usually sufficient to find a design that is *easily adaptable* or to which the implementation of the new application can be easily adapted. Because of this, the READEE approach concentrates on the employment of similarity-based retrieval. It relies on suitable heuristics and makes decisions in a way very similar to the decision making process of a human designer – but hopefully faster and with unlimited access to relevant information. The approach taken avoids the complex analysis of existing hardware descriptions, but relies on more abstract knowledge about the important qualities of a design and about the relations between possible values of design parameters. This knowledge, typically, must be specified by the IP designer or by someone with similar expertise.

12.2 Representation of Intellectual Properties

A hard IP, i.e., an IP with fixed parameters offers just a *design point*. That means, it can only be used for one specific application. On the other hand, a soft IP is parameterizable and spans a *design space*. Therefore, parameterizable IPs are more flexible to use and the chances that they will be reused are much better. Soft IPs are usually written in VHDL or Verilog. The automated analysis of VHDL or Verilog code for the extraction of relevant parameters does not seem to be successful (Lehmann et al. 1996). The reason is that it is not trivial to decide what an algorithm or an RTL description is made for or which function it performs, respectively, just by looking at its code. We take another approach which offers an internal representation structure where an IP provider can characterize the IP. The characterization is done by attributes within an underlying object-oriented representation. The distinction between different IPs results from a functional description. The underlying VHDL or Verilog description is, therefore, not necessary.

12.2.1 IP Taxonomy

IPs can be classified by a taxonomy very similar to that proposed by Behnam et al. (1998), see Fig. 12.2. This figure shows only part of an IP taxonomy, extensions are indicated by ellipses. An edge represents an Is-A relation between a class and its parent class. This classification is reasonable as each class of IPs requires very different kinds of attributes for their characterization. These attributes are organized in an object-oriented way. As new classes or IPs always may arise, both taxonomy and kinds of attributes have to be expandable and must evolve over time. This is the task of the development and maintenance cycle of an experience management approach.

To gain satisfying retrieval results it is important to limit the depth of the taxonomy and use intelligent retrieval methods as early as possible. This eliminates the deficits of simple selection trees as the one shown in Fig. 12.1. The IP taxonomy must only be developed down to a level on which the

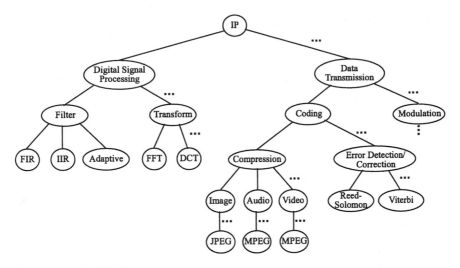

Fig. 12.2. An IP Taxonomy.

occurrence of different attributes must be distinguished. It must not be grown to a level that allows to distinguish IPs by different attribute *values*.

12.2.2 IP Attributes

Attributes of IPs can be divided into the three main groups: *measures, application specific parameters*, and *design specific parameters*.

Measures

Measures are attributes that depend on the structure a design is mapped to. Examples are *area* (gate count), *power dissipation, computational latency* and the *delay* on the critical path ($t_{pd\text{-}max}$) or the *maximum clock frequency* ($f_{clk\text{-}max}$), respectively. These measures differ tremendously for different design styles: synthesis from RTL descriptions, high-level synthesis from algorithmic descriptions or a software implementation on a DSP. Today, soft IPs are mostly described at RT level, but this is not necessarily so. Measures are also influenced by the reference or target technology, like: $0.5\mu m$ CMOS process, Xilinx XC4000 etc. Estimations of measures are only valid for the specified target or reference technology. Approximation models are desirable to convert measures from one technology into another one during reuse.

Application Specific Parameters

Application specific parameters are those that only occur in a certain application or application class. They are important for the user to characterize her/his application for which s/he needs a reusable IP. Every node in the IP taxonomy shown in Fig. 12.2 has its own set of application specific parameters.

Examples for a Discrete Cosine Transform (DCT) or its inverse (IDCT) are attributes such as *internal and external wordlengths, number of rows, number of columns, type of output* and *type of rounding*. For IPs which are (partially) not parameterizable these application specific parameters are fixed. For example, most IP providers offer only 8 by 8 matrix DCT or IDCT, which means that the number of rows and columns are both fixed to a value of 8.

Typical application specific parameters that are important for reuse are relations to existing standards and I/O port specifications. They reflect the quality and the applicability of an IP. Examples from different domains are: ISO/IEC 11172 (MPEG-1), ISO/IEC 13818 (MPEG-2), CCIR 601 NTSC or PAL, PCI Rev. 2.0/2.1, software compatible with TMS320C5x etc. Industry standards sometimes need more parameters than one keyword only. For example:

- MPEG-2 Video (not all combinations are supported by the standard): which profile {Simple, Main, SNR scalable, Spatial scalable, High, Multiview, 4:2:2} which level {Low, Main, High-1440, High}.
- MPEG-1 or MPEG-2 Audio: Layer 1, 2, 3.

Furthermore, industry standards may have different semantics for different IPs (compare to Fig. 12.2):

- MPEG-2 for a video encoder/decoder means: "fullfills the standard" (dependent on the additional parameters)
- MPEG-2 for a DCT/IDCT means: "can be used for MPEG-2 video encoder/decoder".

Design Specific Parameters

Design specific parameters describe the particular design that is realized in the IP. For soft IPs, some of them can span a design space in different ways. Typical examples for such attributes are:

- *Parallel versus sequential:* If one operation, like a MAC (Multiply and Accumulate) operation for a filter, has to be processed m times in parallel, the hardware realization can use one operator in a sequential order (the slowest solution) or m operators in parallel for the fastest solution, or a number of operators between 1 and m.
- *Pipelining at the word-level:* A chain of operations can be processed completely in one clock cycle, or registers can be put between the different operations and the computation needs several clock cycles, where the clock speed can be increased. The length of a pipeline varies from IP to IP.

- *Parallel versus serial (pipelining at the bit-level)*: An operation can be processed in parallel or bit-serial, which means bit by bit. Intermediate solutions may process subwords.

The values of design specific parameters are not necessarily important to know for a user. The main differences between application specific and design specific parameters are the following. Application specific parameters are important for the functionality of a class of IPs whereas design specific parameters are provider/architecture specific. However, application specific parameters, which increase the programmability/flexibility of an IP are provider and architecture specific, too. Both, design specific and application specific parameters have a great impact on the measures, but only the design specific parameters will exchange measures like gate count versus maximum clock frequency.

12.2.3 IP Representation as Generalized Cases

Soft IPs have a number of variable design parameters which can be used to customize the design in some way. A simple example for such a parameterized IP is a description of a multiplier where the word length is a parameter that can be varied between 4 and 32. Concrete values for such parameters must be determined before the design can be synthesized and manufactured.

Representing such parameterized IPs as cases in an experience management system immediately leads to the concept of generalized cases as introduced in Sect. 3.4. A generalized case describes a design space in contrast to a single design point. A soft IP has usually more than one variable parameter and the permissible values of these parameters depend on each other. In a generalized case dependencies between parameters and measures can be expressed by a constraint net which orthogonally overlays the IP taxonomy (Fig. 12.2). They can express the usable design space offered by an IP design. This can be seen as an abstract model of an IP. Such a model is just an estimation, as the measures also strongly depend on the chosen optimization parameters of the synthesis tool, the floorplanning, etc.

Figure 12.3 shows an example of an IP design space where the IP measures *gate count* and *delay* depend on the single design specific parameter *wordlength*. This figure also shows certain limitations (timing and area constraints) that come from the problem description of the user looking for an IP that matches her/his application requirements. When the IP parameters are instantiated as shown in the design point C all requirements are fulfilled.

12.2.4 An Example IP

Because detailed design information on existing IPs is usually confidential and therefore hard to acquire, we developed a representative IP (Wahlmann 1999) to study issues of representation, retrieval, and parameterization. This

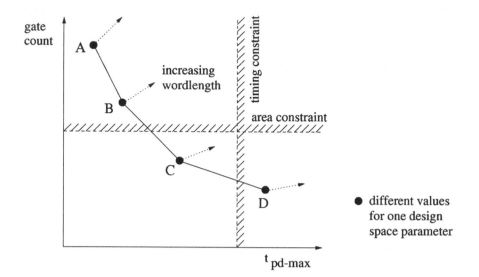

Fig. 12.3. Example of a Design Space

IP implements an algorithm for the *discrete cosine transform (DCT)* and its inverse operation *(IDCT)* which is needed as an important part of decoders and encoders of the widely known MPEG-2 video compression algorithm.

Table 12.1 lists the variable parameters of this IP that are relevant for our example. The parameters f and a are *measures* that are of general importance for most IPs. f, a, and w may be part of a new problem specification. In contrast to that, s is a *design specific parameter*, i.e., it is specific to this individual IP. s will never be part of a problem specification.

parameter		description
frequency	f	The clock frequency that can be applied to the IP.
area	a	The chip area the synthesized IP will fit on.
width	w	Number of bits per input/output word. Determines the accuracy of the DCT. Allowed values are 6, 7, ... , 16.
subword	s	Number of bits calculated per clock tick. Changing this design space parameter may have a positive influence on one quality of the design while having a negative impact on another. Allowed values are 1, 2, 4, 8, and no_pipe.

Table 12.1. Selected Parameters of an Example IP.

Synthesizing an IP is a very complex task and can take up to several hours for a single design point, depending on the complexity of the IP. We synthesized the IP for only a limited number of design points and used fitting algorithms to interpolate the data for the other parameter combinations. These steps lead to approximating functions for f and a, depending on w and s. The fitting error of these functions is below 3% for the synthesized design points.

$$
f \leq \begin{cases}
-0.66w + 115 & \text{if } s = 1 \\
-1.94w + 118 & \text{if } s = 2 \\
-1.74w + 88 & \text{if } s = 4 \\
-0.96w + 54 & \text{if } s = 8 \\
-2.76w + 57 & \text{if } s = \mathsf{no}
\end{cases}
$$

$$
a \geq \begin{cases}
1081w^2 + 2885w + 10064 & \text{if } s = 1 \\
692w^2 + 2436w + 4367 & \text{if } s = 2 \\
532w^2 + 1676w + 2794 & \text{if } s = 4 \\
416w^2 + 1594w + 2413 & \text{if } s = 8 \\
194w^2 + 2076w + 278 & \text{if } s = \mathsf{no}
\end{cases}
$$

Figure 12.4 graphically shows the estimation of the chip area a (in units of gate count) as a function of the frequency f and word width w .

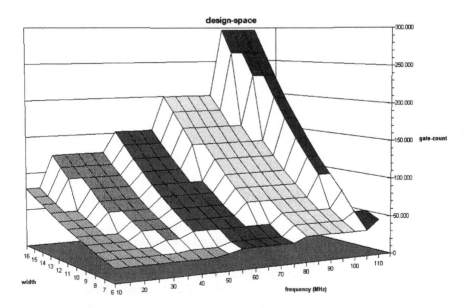

Fig. 12.4. Chip Area of the Example IP Dependent on the Clock Frequency and the Word Width.

12.3 Descriptions of Design Problems and Reuse-Related Knowledge

We now discuss the particularities related to the problem descriptions provided by electronics designers and give some remarks related to similarity measures.

12.3.1 Problem Descriptions

A specification of a design problem usually uses a vocabulary at a much higher level of abstraction than the information contained in data sheets of electronic circuits or IP descriptions as introduced in the previous section. This is because the specification states *what* has to be achieved by the implementation whereas a design description explains *how* something is achieved, where this "something" often is not explicitly mentioned. For example, the specification could say

> *The sum of two vectors of length 1024 must be calculated within 1 ms.*

Whereas a design description could contain the information that

> *The design consists of 8 parallel arithmetic units with a response time of 5 ms.*

The concept "vector sum" might not occur in the IP case description at all, but nonetheless it is important to know this intended application of the design to decide whether it can perform the requested number of calculations fast enough, i. e., whether the task to be performed can benefit from parallelism. This discrepancy between different levels of abstraction of the query and the cases must be bridged by suitable mechanisms that transform the problem description to the experience characterization level. We have introduced this problem transformation in definition 4.1 of Sect. 4.1. Transformation rules can be used to represent such a problem transformation.

12.3.2 Similarity Measures

There is a major difference between experience management systems for design reuse and systems for classification and diagnosis tasks. Experience management systems for diagnosis (see Chap. 11) perform an *abstraction* from known details (symptoms) to the unknown nature of the fault (the diagnosis). The problem is *analyzed*. On the other hand, retrieval for reuse puts a general description of a problem into concrete terms (a complex design) which should be able to solve the problem. The design is *synthesized*. This fact significantly influences the similarity modeling.

Problem Specific Similarity Measures

Some diagnosis applications handle case-specific or diagnosis-specific weights for their similarity measures (see Sect. 4.3.7). This accounts for the observation that different kinds of faults require different interpretations of similarity. The particular fault is "known" to the cases only and hence the similarity measure must be defined for each case (or at least for each kind of fault) individually.

This is different for reuse applications where the problem determines whether a design is reusable. Therefore, the concept of similarity may vary from problem to problem, but not from case to case. Thus, a CBR system for design reuse may need ways to adjust the weights of the similarity measure to the problem. Hence, we need user specific weights. These weights can be automatically derived from the problem description entered by the user. Again, this requires the acquisition of additional expert knowledge.

Similarity Evaluation Models

A similarity measure for electronic design reuse requires a sophisticated *evaluation model*, which is more complicated than the similarity measures used for diagnosis applications. What is required is a kind of abstract simulation of the application problem with the use of the IP under consideration. The similarity can then be assessed based on the degree to which the application requirements stated in the problem description can be fulfilled.

For this purpose, the evaluation model must determine problem dependent characteristic parameters from the case description. Examples of such parameters are:

- effective usable clock frequency depending on the given maximum power consumption
- execution time depending on a given abstract description of a program code fragment to be run on a processor, and
- memory size needed to represent the given program code on the processor

These characteristics enter the calculation of the overall similarity of a case to the query.

Usually, a number of low-level attributes need to be taken into account to compute such characteristics. We call these characteristics that depend on both the problem and the case *virtual attributes* (see Fig. 12.5). The low-level attributes that are used to calculate the values of the virtual attributes we call *supportive attributes*.

Figure 12.6 illustrates the calculation of two virtual attributes in a reuse scenario for DSPs. The virtual case attribute *available clock cycles per sample* depends on the supportive attributes *application sample frequency, max. allowed power consumption* taken from the problem description (left side), and

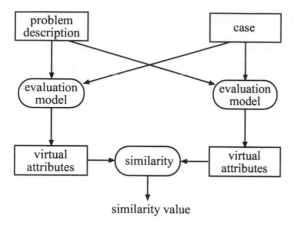

Fig. 12.5. Computation of Virtual Attributes

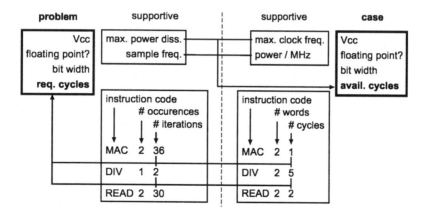

Fig. 12.6. Example for the Determination of Virtual Attributes

the attributes *max. DSP clock frequency*, and *power consumption per MHz* that are taken from the case (right side).

The virtual query attribute *required cycles per sample* depends on the instruction set available on the DSP, and on the number of op-codes and iterations that occur in the abstract machine code for the application to be implemented.

These virtual case and problem attributes can be directly compared by a simple similarity measure. The similarities of the virtual attributes are assumed to be independent of each other and of other basic attributes.

It is difficult to foresee the possible complexity of such evaluation models for IP reuse applications in general. With larger case bases, care must be taken to ensure efficient retrieval. The problem is that none of the currently available retrieval techniques (including those discussed in Chap. 7) except the sequential retrieval does yet support evaluation models and virtual attributes as introduced above. This is not a problem unless the size of the case base exceeds an amount of several thousand IPs and unless a large number of users are accessing the experience management system at the same time. However, this problem can become dominant in the future.

12.4 The READEE Prototype for DSP Selection

The READEE prototype[4] (introduced at DATE98[5], Vollrath and Oehler 1998) is an example of an experience management system for selecting digital signal processors (DSPs). A user can specify her/his requirements of a DSP both on higher and lower levels of abstraction. A typical low-level requirement would be: *supply voltage = 5V.* More abstract specifications could state characteristics of the intended application, for example: *Fast Fourier Transformation (FFT) with up to 512 samples per frame.* Part of the consultation interface of READEE is shown in Fig. 12.7.

This prototype employs the concept of evaluation models, which include knowledge about the key features of the components in the case base. A complex design typically has certain qualities that are difficult to extract – even for experts – from the component's data sheets or from a complex design description. However, an intelligent retrieval assistant must know about these qualities if they are important for the selection decision of a human designer.

The evaluation models compute to which extent a certain DSP has a certain abstract quality, with respect to the user's specification of his application. For DSPs, for example, one of the most abstract qualities of this type is "The processor must run a specific algorithm as fast as possible". To judge how good this quality is fulfilled by a specific DSP regarding the user's specification, the experience management system needs suitable models of

- algorithms that are likely to be implemented on a DSP, and of
- execution times of abstract operations that might be used within those algorithms.

It is not necessary, however, to feed the experience management system with a complete model of possible realizations of the execution units of a DSP. A reusing designer neither needs to care about the number of pipeline stages of the floating point unit, for example, nor is s/he interested in details about the data paths between functional parts of the DSP – if only s/he knows how much time the processor takes to perform his application specific algorithm, or perhaps a certain set of instructions.

---

[4] online at http://wwwagr.informatik.uni-kl.de/~readee/
[5] DATE98: Design, Automation and Test in Europe, Conference in Paris 1998

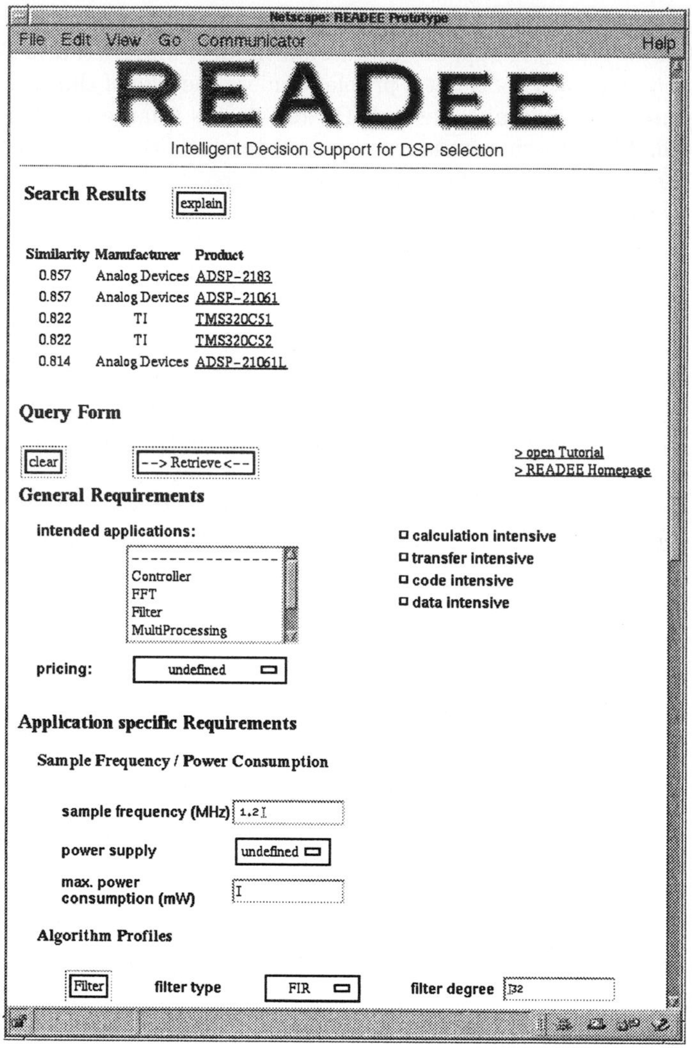

Fig. 12.7. Part of the User Interface of the READEE Prototype for DSP Selection.

The READEE prototype accounts for these decision criteria of human designers and internally represents just the kind of information that is relevant for the selection of reusable designs. Some of this information may not be explicitly found in data sheets and has to be provided by a human expert when the case base is put together. This human expert ideally is the designer of the IP.

After the individual ratings of these high level qualities have been assessed by the evaluation models they are combined to an overall similarity value which is a measure for the expected reusability of the DSP with respect to the user's application. Additional low-level requirements, such as "low cost" or "low power consumption" are also taken into account by the overall similarity value.

The result of a READEE consultation is a list of DSPs sorted by their similarity to the user's specification (see top part of Fig. 12.7). The user has the option to further refine his specification in case his initial specification was not precise enough to produce a satisfying result. The system also has the ability to explain what makes the proposed DSP similar to the specification. It also points out certain problematic attribute values that lead to a significant reduction of similarity.

The READEE prototype shows the suitability of knowledge- and similarity-based retrieval methods for catalogs of reusable design components. However, it should be pointed out that the intelligence of such a system comes at the cost of reduced generality. The READEE-prototype specialized on DSPs, for example, is not suitable for completely different types of designs (e. g. memory blocks). Retrieving IPs for other application areas requires the assessment of evaluation models for the abstract key-features of the respective application. A more general catalog of IPs would therefore consist of a collection of application specific evaluation models.

12.5 Issues of Future Research

With a growing IP market sophisticated experience management systems for IPs will become a must. This is also demonstrated by the increasing interest of the electronics industry, both at the side of IP providers and potential IP users. The just started German project IPQ (**IP Q**ualification for efficient system design) and the European MEDEA+ project TOOLIP (Methods and **TOOL**s for **IP**) with significant participation from industry are a clear indication of this situation.

With the concepts presented in this chapter it is possible to accurately describe IP's and to evaluate them with respect to their utility for a new application. Due to the ability of an experience management system to automatically evaluate IPs it can hide confidential information from the user while still offering high quality retrieval results.

However, there are several open issues that need further research. Most of them are related to the scalability of the presented approach. When the IP market will grow as expected, a large number of IPs is getting available, which imposes the requirement on an experience management system to handle large case bases and high numbers of users. Currently available approaches for assessing the similarity of generalized cases are either limited to specific kinds of constraints (e.g. linear constraints as discussed by Bergmann & Vollrath (1999)) or have a high computational complexity. An important challenge is to integrate expressive representations for generalized cases with efficient retrieval mechanisms.

Also the similarity modeling through evaluation models including virtual attributes are currently not compatible with efficient retrieval approaches since the requirements imposed by those retrieval algorithms are usually not fulfilled.

Finally, a comprehensive experience management system for IP reuse should also support the adaptation of selected IPs for the particular application of the user. Hence approaches for modeling and managing IP adaptation knowledge are desirable.

List of Symbols

$\mathbb{A}$	Experience transformation container
$\mathbb{B}$	Case base semantics
$\mathbb{C}$	Cases space
$\mathbb{D}$	Case characterization space
$\mathbb{H}$	Hypothesis space
$\mathbb{I}$	Dialog interactions
$\mathbb{L}$	Case lesson space,
$\mathbb{P}$	Problem description
$\mathbb{Q}$	Question state space
$\mathbb{S}$	Dialog space

$\mathbf{A}$	Set of attributes
$\mathbf{CB}$	Case case
$\mathbf{CL}$	Set of classes
$\mathbf{CO}$	Set of constraints
$\mathbf{F}$	Set of function symbols
$\mathbf{P}$	Set of predicate symbols
$\mathbf{T}$	Set of types
$\mathbf{V}$	Set of variables symbols
$\mathbf{VOC}$	Vocabulary

$\alpha : C \to C$	Experience transformation
$pt : \mathbb{P} \to \mathbb{D}$	Problem transformation
$sim : \mathbb{D} \times \mathbb{D} \to [0,1]$	Similarity measure
$u : \mathbb{P} \times \mathbb{L} \to \Re$	Utility function
$\sqsubseteq_p \subseteq \mathbb{C} \times \mathbb{C}:$	Preference relation induced by similarity measure
$\succ_p \subseteq \mathbb{C} \times \mathbb{C}:$	Preference relation induced by utility function

References

Aamodt, A. (1991). *A Knowledge-Intensive, Integrated Approach to Problem Solving and Sustained Learning*. Ph. D. thesis, University of Trondheim.

Aamodt, A. and M. Nygard (1995). Different roles and mutual dependencies of data, information and knowledge. *Data and Knoweldge Engineering 16*, 191–222.

Aamodt, A. and E. Plaza (1994). Case-based reasoning: foundational issues, methodological variations, and system approaches. *AI Communications 7*(1), 39–59.

Aamodt, A. and M. Veloso (Eds.) (1995). *Case-Based Reasoning Research and Development, Proc. ICCBR-95*, Lecture Notes in Artificial Intelligence, 1010. Springer Verlag.

Abecker, A., A. Bernardi, K. Hinkelmann, O. Kühn, and M. Sintek (1998, May/June). Toward a technology for organizational memories. *IEEE Intelligent Solutions*, 40–48.

Aha, D. and L. Breslow (1997). Refining conversational case libraries. See Leake and Plaza (1997).

Aha, D., L. A. Breslow, and H. Munoz-Avila (2001). Conversational case-based reasoning. *Applied Intelligence*.

Aha, D., T. Maney, and L. Breslow (1998). Supporting dialogue inferencing in conversational case-based reasoning. Technical Report AIC-98-008, Naval Research Laboratory, Navy Center for Applied Research in Artificial Intelligence, Washington, DC.

Aha, D. W., D. Kibler, and M. K. Albert (1991). Instance-Based Learning Algorithms. *Machine Learning 6*, 37–66.

Aho, A. V., J. E. Hopcroft, and J. D. Ullman (1974). *The Design and Analysis of Computer Algorithms*. Addison-Wesley.

Albin, M. (1997). Konzept und Implementierung eines fallbasierten Systems zur Verkaufsunterstützung im Internet. Master's thesis, Universität Kaiserslautern.

Albrecht, F. (1993). *Strategisches Management der Unternehmensressource Wissen*. Verlag Peter Lang, Frankfurt am Main.

Althoff, K.-D. (1992). *Eine fallbasierte Lernkomponente als integrierter Bestandteil der MOLTKE-Werkbank zur Diagnose technischer Systeme*. Ph.

D. thesis, Dept. of Computer Science, University of Kaiserslautern, Germany.

Althoff, K.-D. and A. Aamodt (1996). Relating case-based problem solving and learning methods to task and domain characteristics: towards an analytic framework. *AI Communications 9*(3), 109–116.

Althoff, K.-D., E. Auriol, R. Barletta, and M. Manago (1995). *A Review of Industrial Case-Based Reasoning Tools*. Oxford: AI Intelligence.

Althoff, K.-D., E. Auriol, R. Bergmann, S. Breen, S. Dittrich, R. Johnston, M. Manago, R. Traphoener, and S. Wess (1995). Case-based reasoning for decision support and diagnostic problem solving: The INRECA approach. See Bartsch-Spörl et al. (1995), pp. 63–72.

Althoff, K.-D., E. Auriol, R. Bergmann, S. Breen, S. Dittrich, R. Johnston, M. Manago, R. Traphöner, and S. Wess (1995). Case-based reasoning for decision support and diagnostic problem solving: The INRECA approach. See Bartsch-Spörl et al. (1995), pp. 63–72.

Althoff, K.-D., R. Bergmann, and L.-K. Branting (Eds.) (1999). *Case-Based Reasoning Research and Development, Proceedings of the Third International Conference on Case-Based Reasoning (ICCBR'99)*, Lecture Notes in Artificial Intelligence, 1266. Springer Verlag.

Althoff, K.-D., R. Bergmann, S. Wess, M. Manago, E. Auriol, O. Larichev, Y. Bolotov-Zhuravlev, and A. Gurov (1998). Case-based reasoning for medical decision support tasks: The INRECA approach. *Artificial Intelligence in Medicine* (12), 25 – 41.

Althoff, K.-D., F. Bomarius, and C. Tautz (2000). Using a case-based reasoning strategy to build learning software organizations. *IEEE Journal on Intelligent Systems. Special issue on Knowledge Management and Knowledge Distribution over the Internet*.

Althoff, K.-D. and M. Nick. *How To Support Experience Management with Evaluation: Foundations, Evaluation Methods, and Examples for Case-Based Reasoning and Experience Factory*. forthcomming.

Anderson, J. R. (1983). *The architecture of cognition*. Cambridge, MA: Harvard University Press.

Arcos, J. and E. Plaza (1995). Reflection in NOOS : An object-centered representation language for knowledge modelling. In *IJCAI'95 Workshop: On Reflection and Meta-Level Architecture and their Applications in AI*.

Ardissono, L. and A. Goy (1999). Tailoring the interaction with users in electronic shops. See Kay (1999), pp. 35–44.

Armitage, J. and M. Kellner (1994). A conceptual schema for process definitions and models. In *Proceedings of the Third International Conferene on Software Process*. IEEE Computer Society Press.

Armstrong, R., D. Freitag, T. Joachims, and T. Mitchell (1995). Webwatcher: A learning apprentice for the world wide web. In *AAAI Spring Symposium on Information Gathering from Heterogeneous Distributed Environments*.

Ashley, K. D. and V. Aleven (1993). Using logic to reason with cases. In M. M. Richter, S. Wess, K.-D. Althoff, and F. Maurer (Eds.), *Preprints First European Workshop on Case-Based Reasoning (EWCBR-93)*, pp. 373 – 378. Fachbereich Informatik, Universität Kaiserslautern. SEKI Report SR-93-12.

Auriol, E., R. Crowder, R. MacKendrick, R. Rowe, and T. Knudsen (1999). Integrating case-based reasoning and hypermedia documentation: An application for the diagnosis of a welding robot at odense steel shipyard. *Engineering Applications of Artificial Intelligence.* *12*(6).

Avenhaus, J. (1995). *Reduktionssysteme: Rechnen und Schließen in gleichungsdefinierten Strukturen.* Springer.

Babai, L., P. Erdös, and S. M. Selkow (1980). Random graph isomorphism. *SIAM Journal of Computation 9*, 628–635.

Babai, L. and L. Kucera (1979). Canonical labelling of graphs in linear average time. In *Proceedings of the 20th Annual IEEE Symposium on Foundations of Computer Science*, pp. 39 – 46.

Bain, W. M. (1986). A Case-Based Reasoning System for Subjective Assessment. In *Proceedings of the 5th Annual National Conference on Artificial Intelligence AAAI-86*, Philadelphia, Pennsylvania, USA, pp. 523–527. AAAI86: Morgan Kaufmann Publishers.

Bareiss, R. (1989). *Exemplar-Based Knowledge Acquisition: A unified Approach to Concept Representation, Classification and Learning.* Academic Press.

Bareiss, R. (Ed.) (1991). *Proceedings: Case-Based Reasoning Workshop.* Morgan Kaufmann Publishers.

Bartsch-Spörl, B. (1996). How to make CBR systems work in practice. See Burkhard and Lenz (1996), pp. 36–42.

Bartsch-Spörl, B. (1997). How to introduce cbr applications in customer support. See Bergmann and Wilke (1997).

Bartsch-Spörl, B., D. Janetzko, and S. Wess (Eds.) (1995). *3rd German Workshop on CBR: Fallbasiertes Schließen - Grundlagen und Anwendungen —*, Kaiserslautern. University of Kaiserslautern.

Basili, V. R., G. Caldiera, and H. D. Rombach (1994a). Experience factory. In J. J. Marciniak (Ed.), *Encyclopedia of Software Engineering, volume 1*, pp. 469–476. John Wiley & Sons.

Basili, V. R., G. Caldiera, and H. D. Rombach (1994b). Goal question metric paradigm. In J. J. Marciniak (Ed.), *Encyclopedia of Software Engineering, volume 1*, pp. 528–532. John Wiley & Sons.

Beckman, T. (1997). A methodology for knowledge management. In *Artificial Intelligence and Soft Computing*, Banff, Canada. International Association of Science and Technology.

Behnam, B., K. Babba, and G. Saucier (1998). IP taxonomy, IP searching in a catalog. In *Design, Automation and Test in Europe Conference (DATE98)*, pp. 147–151.

Bellinger, G., D. Castro, and A. Mills. Data, information, knowledge, and wisdom. http://www.outsights.com/systems/dikw/dikw.htm.

Bentley, J. L. (1975). Multidimensional binary search trees used for associative searching. *Communications of the ACM 18*(9), 509–517.

Berchtold, S., B. Ertl, D. A. Keim, H.-P. Kriegel, and S. T. (1998). Fast nearest neighbor search in high-dimensional space. In *Proc. 14th Int. Conf. On Data Engineering (ICDE'98)*, pp. 209 – 218.

Berchtold, S., D. Keim, and H.-P. Kriegel (1996). The x-tree: An index structure for high dimensional data. In *Proceedings of the 22nd Conference on Very Large Databases*, pp. 28–39.

Bergmann, R. (1992). Knowledge acquisition by generating skeletal plans. In F. Schmalhofer, G. Strube, and T. Wetter (Eds.), *Contemporary Knowledge Engineering and Cognition*, Heidelberg, pp. 125–133. Springer.

Bergmann, R. (1996). *Effizientes Problemlösen durch flexible Wiederverwendung von Fällen auf verschiedenen Abstraktionsebenen*. DISKI 138. infix.

Bergmann, R. (1998a). Efficient retrieval of abstract cases for case-based planning. In T. Ellman (Ed.), *SARA98: Symposium on Abstraction, Reformulation and Approximation*. Rutgers University.

Bergmann, R. (1998b). On the use of taxonomies for representing case features and local similarity measures. In L. Gierl and M. Lenz (Eds.), *6th German Workshop on Case-Based Reasoning*. Institut für Medizinische Informatik und Biometrie der Universität Rostock.

Bergmann, R. (2001). Highlights of the european INRECA projects. In D. Aha and I. Watson (Eds.), *Proceedings of the 4th International Conference on Case-Based Reasoning*.

Bergmann, R. and K.-D. Althoff (1998). *Methodology for Building CBR Applications*, Chapter 12, pp. 299–326. LNAI 1400. Springer.

Bergmann, R., S. Breen, E. Fayol, M. Göker, M. Manago, J. Schumacher, S. Schmitt, A. Stahl, S. Wess, and W. Wilke (1998). Collecting experience on the systematic development of CBR applications using the INRECA-II methodology. See Smyth and Cunningham (1998), pp. 460–470.

Bergmann, R., S. Breen, M. Göker, M. Manago, and S. Wess (1999b). CD-ROM: Developing industrial case-based reasoning applications: The INRECA methodology. Lecture Notes in Artificial Intelligence, Springer Electronic Media.

Bergmann, R., S. Breen, M. Göker, M. Manago, and S. Wess (1999a). *Developing Industrial Case-Based Reasoning Applications: The INRECA Methodology*. LNAI 1612. Springer.

Bergmann, R. and P. Cunningham. Acquiring customers requirements in electronic commerce. *Artificial Intelligence Review*. Forthcoming.

Bergmann, R. and U. Eisenecker (1995). Case-based reasoning for supporting reuse of object-oriented software: A case study (in German). In M. M. Richter and F. Maurer (Eds.), *3rd German Conference on Expert Sys-*

tems, Sankt Augustin, Germany, pp. 152–169. infix Verlag. Proceedings in Artificial Intelligence 2.

Bergmann, R. and M. Göker (1999). Developing industrial case-based reasoning applications using the INRECA methodology. In S. Anand, A. Aamodt, and D. Aha (Eds.), *IJCAI-99 Workshop ML-5 on the Automatic Construction of Case-Based Reasoners.*

Bergmann, R., M. Göker, T. Roth-Berghofer, and R. Traphoener (1999). Specification of the vertical platform. INRECA-II Deliverable D20.

Bergmann, R., H. Muñoz-Avila, and M. Veloso (1996). Fallbasiertes Planen: Ausgewählte Methoden und Systeme. *Künstliche Intelligenz, Themenheft Fallbasiertes Schließen 10*(1), 22–28.

Bergmann, R., G. Pews, and W. Wilke (1994). Explanation-based similarity: A unifying approach for integrating domain knowledge into case-based reasoning. In S. Wess, K.-D. Althoff, and M. Richter (Eds.), *Topics in Case-Based Reasoning*, Volume 837 of *Lecture Notes on Artificial Intelligence*, pp. 182–196. Springer.

Bergmann, R., M. M. Richter, S. Schmitt, A. Stahl, and I. Vollrath (2001). Utility-oriented matching: A new research direction for case-based reasoning. In S. Schmitt, I. Vollrath, and U. Reimer (Eds.), *9th German Workshop on Case-Based Reasoning.*

Bergmann, R., S. Schmitt, and A. Stahl (2002). Intelligent customer support for product selection with case-based reasoning. In J. Segovia, P. Szczcpaniak, and M. Niedzwiedzinski (Eds.), *E-Commerce and Intelligent Methods*, Studies in Fuzziness and Soft Computing. Springer.

Bergmann, R. and A. Stahl (1998). Similarity measures for object-oriented case representations. See Smyth and Cunningham (1998).

Bergmann, R., R. Traphöner, S. Schmitt, P. Cunningham, and B. Smyth (2002). Knowledge-intensive product search and customization in electronic commerce. In J. Gasós and K.-D. Thoben (Eds.), *E-Business Applications: Results of Applied Research on e-Commerce, Supply Chain Management and Extended Enterprises.* Springer.

Bergmann, R. and I. Vollrath (1999). Generalized cases: Representation and steps towards efficient similarity assessment. In W. Burgard, T. Christaller, and A. B. Cremers (Eds.), *KI-99: Advances in Artificial Intelligence.*, LNAI 1701. Springer.

Bergmann, R., I. Vollrath, and T. Wahlmann (1999). Generalized cases and their application to electronic designs. See Melis (1999).

Bergmann, R. and W. Wilke (1995a). Building and refining abstract planning cases by change of representation language. *Journal of Artificial Intelligence Research 3*, 53–118.

Bergmann, R. and W. Wilke (1995b). Learning abstract planning cases. In N. Lavrač and S. Wrobel (Eds.), *Machine Learning: ECML-95, 8th European Conference on Machine Learning, Heraclion, Greece, April 1995,*

Number 912 in Lecture Notes in Artificial Intelligence, pp. 55–76. Berlin: Springer.

Bergmann, R. and W. Wilke (1996). On the role of abstraction in case-based reasoning. See Smith and Faltings (1996), pp. 28–43.

Bergmann, R. and W. Wilke (Eds.) (1997). *5th German Workshop on CBR — Foundations, Systems, and Applications —*, Report LSA-97-01E, Kaiserslautern. University of Kaiserslautern.

Bergmann, R. and W. Wilke (1998). Towards a new formal model of transformational adaptation in case-based reasoning. In *European Conference on Artificial Intelligence (ECAI'98)*.

Bergmann, R., W. Wilke, and J. Schumacher (1997). Using software process modeling for building a case-based reasoning methodology: Basic approach and case study. See Leake and Plaza (1997), pp. 509–518.

Bergmann, R., W. Wilke, I. Vollrath, and S. Wess (1996). Integrating general knowledge with object-oriented case representation and reasoning. See Burkhard and Lenz (1996), pp. 120–127.

Bisson, G. (1995). Why and how to define a similarity measure for object based representation systems. In *Towards Very Large Knowledge Bases*, pp. 236 – 246. IOS Press.

Blanzieri, E. and L. Portinale (Eds.) (2000). *Advances in Case-Based Reasoning (EWCBR'2000)*, Lecture Notes in Artificial Intelligence, 1898. Springer.

Boehm, B. W. (1988). A spiral model of software development and enhancement. *IEEE Communications 21*(5), 61–72.

Bolender, D. (1999). Entwurf und Realisierung von Komponenten zur Akquisition in Electronic-Commerce Verkaufsshops auf der Grundlage von fallbasiertem Schließen. Master's thesis, University of Kaiserslautern.

Booch, G. (1994). *Object Oriented Desing with Applications.* Benjamin/Cummings.

Borghoff, U. M. and R. Pareschi (1997). Information technology for knowledge management. *Journal of Universal Computer Science 3*, 835–842.

Börner, K. (1994). Term-based approach to structural similarity as guidance for adaptation. In A. Voß (Ed.), *Similarity concepts and retrieval methods*, Volume 13 of *Fabel-Reports*, pp. 59–72. Sankt Augustin: GMD.

Börner, K., R. Faßauer, and S. Seewald (1993). Term- und Baumrepräsentationen räumlichen Wissens in der Bauarchitektur. In V. Kamp, M. Kopitsch, M. M. Richter, M. Schick, and A. Schöller (Eds.), *Workshop Räumliche ProblemStellungEn in Technischen Domänen Auf der KI-93*, LKI-M-93/2. Universität Hamburg.

Brandstädt, A. (1994). *Graphen und Algorithmen.* Stuttgart: Teubner.

Branting, K. (1997). Stratified Case-Based Reasoning in Non-Refinable Abstraction Hierarchies. In D. Leake and E. Plaza (Eds.), *Proceedings of the 2rd International Conference on Case-Based Reasoning*, pp. 519 – 530. Wiley.

Branting, K. (2001). Acquiring user preferences from return set selections. In D. Aha and I. Watson (Eds.), *Proceedings of the 4th International Conference on Case-Based Reasoning.*

Branting, K. L. and D. W. Aha (1995). Stratified case based reasoning: Reusing hierarchical; problem solving eposides. Technical Report AIC-95-001, Naval Research Lab.

Bray, T., J. Paoli, C. M. Sperberg-McQueen, and E. Maler (2000). Extensible markup language (XML) 1.0 (second edition). Technical report, W3C.

Brown, D. and B. Chandrasekaran (1985). Expert systems for a class of mechanical design activity. In J. Gero (Ed.), *Knowledge Engineering in Computer-Aided Design*, Amsterdam: North Holland.

Brusilovsky, P. and E. Schwarz (1997). User as student: Towards an adaptive interface for advanced Web-based applications. See Jameson (1999), pp. 177–188.

Buckley, A. G. and J.-L. Goffin (Eds.) (1982, April). *Algorithms for Constrained Minimization of Smooth Nonlinear Functions.* Number 3016 in Mathematical Programming Study. North-Holland – Amsterdam: The Mathematical Programming Society, Inc.

Bunke, H. and B. T. Messmer (1994). Similarity measures for structured representations. In S. Wess, K.-D. Althoff, and M. M. Richter (Eds.), *Topics in Case-Based Reasoning: First European Workshop, EWCBR-93, selected papers*, Volume 837 of *Lecture Notes in Artificial Intelligence*, pp. 106–118. Berlin: Springer.

Burkhard, H.-D. (1998). Extending some concepts of CBR - foundations of case retrieval nets. In M. Lenz, B. Bartsch-Spörl, H.-D. Burkhard, and S. Wess (Eds.), *Case-Based Reasoning Technology: From Foundations to Applications.* Springer.

Burkhard, H.-D. and M. Lenz (Eds.) (1996). *4th German Workshop on CBR — System Development and Evaluation —*, Informatik-Berichte, Berlin. Humboldt University.

Burkhard, H.-D. and M. Richter (2000). Similarity in case-based reasoning and fuzzy theory. In S. Pal, T. Dillon, and D. Yeung (Eds.), *Soft Computing in Case-Based Reasoning*, Chapter 2. Springer.

Bylander, T. (1991). Complexity results for planning. In J. Mylopoulos and R. Reiter (Eds.), *Proceedings of the 12th International Conference on Artificial Intelligence IJCAI-91*, pp. 274–279.

Carbonell, J. G. (1983a). Derivational Analogy and Its Role in Problem Solving. In *Proceedings of the 3rd Annual National Conference on Artificial Intelligence AAAI-83*, Washington, D.C., USA, August 1983. AAAI: Morgan Kaufmann Publishers.

Carbonell, J. G. (1983b). Learning by Analogy: Formulating and Generalizing Plans from Past Experience. In R. Michalski, J. G. Carbonell, and T. Mitchell (Eds.), *Machine Learning: An Artificial Intelligence Approach*, Volume 1. Palo Alto, California: Tioga.

Carbonell, J. G. (1986). Derivational analogy: a theory of reconstructive problem solving and expertise acquisition. In R. Michalski, J. Carbonnel, and T. Mitchell (Eds.), *Machine Learning: an Artificial Intelligence Approach*, Volume 2, pp. 371–392. Los Altos, CA: Morgan Kaufmann.

Centre for Electronic Commerce (1999). Electronic commerce - a definition. `http://www-cec.buseco.monash.edu.au/links/ec_def.htm` .

Cornet, B., V. H. Nguyen, and J. P. Vial (Eds.) (1987). *Nonlinear Analysis and Optimization*. Number 30 in Mathematical Programming Study. North-Holland – Amsterdam: The Mathematical Programming Society, Inc.

Coulon, C.-H. (1995). Automatic indexing, retrieval and reuse of topologies in complex designs. In P. J. Pahl and H. Werner (Eds.), *Proceeding of the Sixth International Conference on Computing in Civil and Building Engineering*, Berlin, pp. 749–754. Balkema, Rotterdam.

Craw, S., J. Jarmulak, and R. Rowe (2001). Learning and applying case-based adaptation knowledge. In D. Aha and I. Watson (Eds.), *Proceedings of the 4th International Conference on Case-Based Reasoning.*

CRM Forum (1999). http://www.crmforum.de.

Cunningham, P. (1998). CBR: Strengths and weaknesses. In A. P. D. Pobil, J. Mira, and M. Ali (Eds.), *Proceedings of 11th International Conference on Industrial and Engineering Applications of Artificial Intelligence and Expert Systems*. Springer.

Cunningham, P., R. Bergmann, S. Schmitt, R. Traphoener, B. Smyth, and P. Mac AnUltaigh (2001). WEBSELL: Intelligent sales assistants for the world wide web. *KI – Künstliche Intelligenz 1.*

Cunningham, P. and A. Bonzano (1998). Hierarchical CBR for multiple aircraft conflict resolution. In H. Prade (Ed.), *Proceedings of the 13th European Conference on Artificial Intelligence*. Wiley.

Cunningham, P. and A. Bonzano (1999). Knowledge engineering issues in developing a case-based reasoning application. *Knowledge Based Systems.*

Cunningham, P. and B. Smyth (1994). A comparison of model-based and incremental case-based approaches to electronic fault diagnosis. In *Proceedings of the AAAI-90 Case-Based Reasoning Workshop*. AAAI.

Curet, O. and M. Jackson (1996). Towards a methodology for case-based systems. In *Expert Systems 96: Proc. of the 16th annual workshop of the British Computer Science Society.*

Curtis, B., M. I. Kellner, and J. Over (1992). Process modeling. *Communications of the ACM 35*(9), 75 – 90.

Dasarathy, B. (1990). *Nearest Neighbor Norms: NN Pattern Classification Techniques*. IEEE Computer Society Press.

Davenport, T., S. Jarvenpaa, and M. Beers (1996). Improving knowledge work process. *Sloan Management Review*, 53–65.

Davenport, T. and L. Prusak (1997). *Working Knowledge: How Organizations Manage What They Know*. Harvard Press.

Dellen, B., G. Pews, and F. Maurer (1997). Knowledge based techniques to increase the flexibility of workflow management. *Data & Knowledge Engineering Journal*.

Dershowitz, N. and J.-P. Jouannaud (1990). Rewrite systems. In *Handbook of Theoretical Computer Science*, Volume B, Chapter 6, pp. 243–320. North-Holland.

Dienes, Z. and J. Perner (1999). A theory of implicit and explicit knowledge. *Behavioral and Brain Sciences 22*(5).

Dieng, R., O. Corby, A. Giboin, and M. Ribiere (1999). Methods and tools for corporate knowledge management. *International Journal of Human-Computer Studies* (51), 567 – 598.

Donner, M. and T. Roth-Berhofer (1999). Architectures for integration CBR-systems with databases for e-commerce. In *7th German Workshop on Case Based Reasoning (GWCBR'99)*.

Doyle, M. and P. Cunningham (2000). A dynamic approach to reducing dialog in on-line decision guides. See Blanzieri and Portinale (2000).

Dubois, D., F. Esteva, L. Garcia, L. Godo, R. Lopez de Mantaras, and H. Prade (1997). Fuzzy modelling of case-based reasoning and decision. See Leake and Plaza (1997).

Dubois, D., H. Fargier, and H. Prade (1993). The calculus of fuzzy restrictions as a basis for flexible constraint satisfaction. In *IEEE International Conference on Fuzzy Systems*, Volume 2, San Francisco, pp. 1131–1136.

Emde, W. and D. Wettschereck (1996). Relational instance based learning. In L. Saitta (Ed.), *Machine Learning - Proceedings 13th International Conference on Machine Learning*, pp. 122 – 130. Morgan Kaufmann Publishers.

Ernst, G. and A. Newell (1969). *GPS: A case study in generality and problem solving*. Academic Press.

Faltings, B., K. Hua, G. Schmitt, and S.-G. Shih (1991). Case-based representation of architectural design knowledge. See Bareiss (1991), pp. 307 – 316.

Fensel, D., M. Erdmann, and R. Studer (1997). Ontology-groups: Semantically enriched subnets of the WWW. In *Proceedings of the International Workshop Intelligent Information Integration at the 21st German Annual Conference on Artificial Intelligence*.

Fikes, R. E. and N. J. Nilsson (1971). Strips: A new approach to the application of theorem proving to problem solving. *Artificial Intelligence 2*, 189–208.

Forbus, K. D., D. Gentner, and K. Law (1995). MAC/FAC: A model of similarity-based retrieval. *Cognitive Science 19*, 144–205.

Forgy, C. (1982). A fast algorithm for many pattern/many object pattern match problem. *Artificial Inteligence 19*, 17–37.

Francis, A. G. and A. Ram (1993, July). The utility problem in case-based reasoning. In D. B. Leake (Ed.), *Case-Based Reasoning: Papers from the*

1993 Workshop, Technical Report WS-93-01, Menlo Park, CA, pp. 168. AAAI.

Freuder, E. (1992). The logic of constraint satisfaction. *Artificial Intelligence 58*, 21 70.

Friedman, J. H., J. L. Bentley, and R. A. Finkel (1977). An algorithm for finding best matches in logarithmic expected time. *ACM Transactions Math. Software 3*, 209–226.

Gebhardt, F., A. Voß, W. Grather, and B. Schmidt-Belz (1997). *Reasoning with Complex Cases*. Kluwer.

Gentner, D. (1980). Metaphor as Structure Mapping. In A. P. Association (Ed.), *Proceedings of the Conference of the American Psychological Association*, Montreal, Canada.

Gero, J. S. (1990). Design prototypes: A knowledge representation schema for design. *The AI Magazine 11*, 26–36.

Gibbs, W. W. (1994). Software's chronic crisis. *Scientific American*, 86–95.

Gionis, A., P. Indyk, and R. Motwani (1999). Similarity search in high dimensions via hashing. In *Proceedings of the 25h VLDB Conference*.

Goel, A. K. and B. Chandrasekaran (1989). Use of Device Models in Adaption of Design Cases. In K. J. Hammond (Ed.), *Proceedings CBR89*, pp. 100–109. Morgan Kaufmann Publishers.

Göker, M. (Ed.) (2000). *8. German Workshop on Case-Based Reasoning (GWCBR'2000)*. DaimerChrysler Research Ulm.

Göker, M. and T. Roth-Berghofer (1999a). The development and utilization of the case-based help-desk support system HOMER. *Engineering Applications of Artificial Intelligence 12*(6), 665 – 680.

Göker, M. and T. Roth-Berghofer (1999b). Development und utilization of a case-based help-desk support system in a corporate environment. See Althoff et al. (1999), pp. 132 – 146.

Göker, M., T. Roth-Berghofer, R. Bergmann, T. Pantleon, R. Traphöner, S. Wess, and W. Wilke (1998). The development of HOMER: A case-based CAD/CAM help-desk support tool. See Smyth and Cunningham (1998), pp. 346 – 357.

Göker, M. and C. Thompson (2000). The adaptive place advisor: A conversational recommendation system. See Göker (2000).

Guttman, A. (1984). R-trees: A dynamic index structure for spatial searching. In *Proceedings of the ACM SIGMOD International Conference on Management of Data*, pp. 47–57.

Hagen, P. R. (2000). Must search stink. The Forrester Report, June 2000.

Hanney, K. and M. Keane (1996). Learning adaptation rules from a case base. In I. Smith and B. Faltings (Eds.), *Proceedings of the 3th European Workshop on Case-Based Reasoning*, pp. 179–192. Springer.

Hanney, K., M. T. Keane, B. Smyth, and P. Cunningham (1995). Systems, tasks and adaptation knowledge: revealing some revealing dependencies. See Aamodt and Veloso (1995), pp. 461–470.

Hardy, G., J. Littlewood, and G. Polya (1967). *Inequalities*. Cambridge University Press.

Hayes, C. and P. Cunningham (1999). Shaping a cbr view with xml. See Althoff et al. (1999).

Hayes, C. and P. Cunningham (2000). Smart radio: Building music radio on the fly. In *Expert Systems*.

Hayes, C., P. Cunningham, and M. Doyle (1998). Distributed CBR using XML. In W. Wilke and J. Schumacher (Eds.), *KI-98 Workshop on Intelligent Systems and Electronic Commerce*, Number LSA-98-03E. Centre for Learning Systems and Applications, University of Kaiserslautern.

Heister, F. and W. Wilke (1998). An architecture for maintaining case-based reasoning systems. See Smyth and Cunningham (1998), pp. 221–232.

Hölldobler, T. (2001). Temoräre Benutzermodellierung für Multimediale Produktpräsentationen im World Wide Web. *KI - Künstliche Intelligenz* (1).

Holte, R. C., T. Mkadmi, R. M. Zimmer, and A. J. MacDonald (1995). Speeding up problem solving by abstraction: A graph-oriented approach. Technical report, University of Ottawa, Ontario, Canada.

Hua, K., I. Smith, and B. Faltings (1993). Integrated case-based building design. See Wess et al. (1993), pp. 436–445.

Hunt, E., J. Martin, and P. Stone (1966). *Experiments in Induction*. Academic Press.

Indurkhya, B. (1992). *Metaphor and Cognition: an Interactionist Approach*. Dordrecht: Kluwer Academic Publishers.

INRECA Consortium (1999). The INRECA Center for Case-Based Solutions. www.inreca.org.

Irish Multimedia Systems (1999). Pathways. http://www.cykopaths.com.

Jackson, P. and D. Ashton (1994). *ISO 9000 - Der Weg Zur Zertifizierung*. Landsberg/Lech: Verlag Moderne Industrie.

Jameson, A. (Ed.) (1999). *User Modeling: Proceedings of the Sixth International Conference, UM97*. Springer.

Jantke, K. P. (1994). Nonstandard concepts of similarity in case-based reasoning. In H.-H. Bock, W. Lenski, and M. M. Richter (Eds.), *Information Systems and Data Analysis: Prospects – Foundations – Applications, Proceedings of the 17th Annual Conference of the GfKl, Univ. of Kaiserslautern, 1993*, Kaiserslautern, pp. 28–43. Springer, Berlin.

Jarke, M. and K. Pohl (1994). Requirements engineering in the year 2001: On (virtually) managing a changing reality. *Software Engineering Journal*.

Johnston, R., S. Breen, and M. Manago (1996). Methodology for developing cbr applications. Technical report, Esprit Project INRECA Deliverable D30.

Kambhampati, S. and J. Hendler (1992). A validation-structure-based theory of plan modification and reuse. *Artificial Intelligence 55*, 193–258.

Karchenasse, N., J.-M. Roger, and F. Sevila (1997). The hierarchical case-based diagnosis. In R. Bergmann and W. Wilke (Eds.), *Proceedings of the*

5th German Workshop ion Case-Based Reasoning, LSA 97-01E, University of Kaiserslautern, Germany.

Kaufman, L. and P. Rousseeuw (1990). *Finding Groups in Data: An Introduction to Cluster Analysis*. Wiley, New York.

Kay, J. (Ed.) (1999). *User Modeling: Proceedings of the Seventh International Conference, UM99*. Springer.

Kitano, H. and H. Shimazu (1996). The Experience-Sharing Architecture: A Case Study in Corporate-Wide Case-Based Software Quality Control. See Leake (1996), Chapter 13, pp. 420.

Klein, S. (1997). Kommerzielle Elektronische Transaktionen: Sektorale Struktur, Umfang und Strategisches Potential. In R. Werle and C. Lang (Eds.), *Modell Internet?*, pp. 23–42. Campus.

Klein, S. and N. Szyperski (1998). Referenzmodell zum Electronic Commerce. http://www.wi.uni-muenster.de/wi/literatur/.

Kleinhans, A. (1989). *Wissensverarbeitung im Management. Möglichkeiten und Grenzen Wissensbasierter Managementunterstützungs-, Planungs- und Simulationsansätze*. Verlag Peter Lang, Frankfurt am Main.

Koegst, M., J. Schneider, R. Bergmann, and I. Vollrath (1999). IP retrieval by solving constraint satisfaction problems. In *FDL '99, Second International Forum on Design Languages*. École Normale Supérieure de Lyon, Lyon, France.

Kohavi, R. (1994). Bottom-up induction of oblivious readonce decision graphs: Strengths and limitations. In F. Bergadano and L. De Raedt (Eds.), *European Conference on Machine Learning*. Springer.

Kohlmaier, A., S. Schmitt, and R. Bergmann (2001). A similarity-based approach to attribute selection in user-adaptive sales dialogs. In D. Aha and I. Watson (Eds.), *Forth International Conference in Case-Based Reasoning (ICCBR 2001)*. Springer.

Kolodner, J. L. (1980). *Retrieval and Organizational Strategies in Conceptual Memory*. Ph. D. thesis, Yale University.

Kolodner, J. L. (1993). *Case-Based Reasoning*. San Mateo: Morgan Kaufmann.

Koopmans, L. (1987). *Introduction to Contemporary Statistical Methods*. Duxbury, Boston.

Langley, P. (1997). Machine learning for adaptive user interfaces. In G. Brewka, C. Habel, and B. Nebel (Eds.), *Proceedings of the 21st German Annual Conference on Artificial Intelligence*, pp. 53–62. Springer.

Leake, D., A. Kinley, and D. Wilson (1996a). Acquiring case adaptation knowledge: A hybrid approach. In *Proceedings of the Thirteenth National Conference on Artificial Intelligence*. AAAI Press, Menlo Park.

Leake, D., A. Kinley, and D. Wilson (1996b). Linking adaptation and similarity learning. In *Proceedings of the Eighteenth Annual Conference of the Cognitive Science Society*. Lawrence Erlbaum.

Leake, D., B. Smyth, D. Wilson, and Q. Yang (Eds.) (2001). *Maintaining Case-Based Reasoning Systems*. Special Issue of the Computational Intelligence Journal.

Leake, D. B. (1996). *Case-Based Reasoning: Experiences, Lessons, and Future Directions*. Menlo Park, CA: AAAI Press.

Leake, D. B. and E. Plaza (Eds.) (1997). *Case-Based Reasoning Research and Development, Proc. ICCBR-97*, Lecture Notes in Artificial Intelligence, 1266. Springer Verlag.

Lehmann, G., B. Wunder, and K. D. Müller-Glaser (1996). VYPER: Eine Analyseumgebung zur rechnerunterstützten Wiederverwendung von VHDL-Entwürfen. In *GI/ITG/GME-Workshop "Hardwarebeschreibungssprachen und Modellierungsparadigmen"*.

Lenat, D. B. (1982). The nature of heuristics. *Artificial Intelligence 19*(2), 189–249.

Lenz, M. (1996). Case Retrieval Nets applied to large case bases. See Burkhard and Lenz (1996), pp. 111–118.

Lenz, M. (1999). *Case Retrieval Nets as a Model for Building Flexible Information Systems*. Ph. D. thesis, Humboldt University Berlin.

Lenz, M. and K. Ashley (Eds.) (1998). *Proceedings of the AAAI98 Workshop on Textual Case-Based Reasoning*. AAAI Press.

Lenz, M., B. Bartsch-Spoerl, H.-D. Burkhard, and S. Wess (1998). *Case-Based Reasoning Technology from Foundations to Applications*. Springer.

Lenz, M. and H.-D. Burkhard (1996a). Case Retrieval Nets: Basic ideas and extensions. In G. Görz and S. Hölldobler (Eds.), *KI-96: Advances in Artificial Intelligence*, Lecture Notes in Artificial Intelligence, 1137, pp. 227–239. Springer Verlag.

Lenz, M. and H.-D. Burkhard (1996b). Lazy propagation in Case Retrieval Nets. In W. Wahlster (Ed.), *Proc. 12th European Conference on Artificial Intelligence ECAI-96*, pp. 127–131. John Wiley and Sons.

Lenz, M., A. Hübner, and M. Kunze (1998). Textual CBR. In M. Lenz, B. Bartsch-Spörl, H.-D. Burkhard, and S. Wess (Eds.), *Case-Based Reasoning Technology – From Foundations to Applications*. Springer.

Lewis, J. (1997). Intellectual property (IP) components. http://www.artisan.com/ip.html.

Lewis, L. (1995). *Managing computer networks: A case-based reasoning approach*. Artech House Publishers, London.

Liao, T., Z. Zhang, and C. R. Mount (1998). Similarity measures for retrieval in case-based reasoning systems. *Applied Artificial Intelligence 12*, 267 – 288.

Liebowitz, J. (Ed.) (1999). *Knowledge Management Handbook*. CRC Press.

Lingas, A. (1986). Subgraph isomorphism for biconnected outplanar graphs in cubic time. In G. Goos and J. Hartmanis (Eds.), *STACS 86: Third Annual Symposium on Theoretical Aspects of Computer Science*, pp. 98 – 103. Springer.

Lingas, A. and M. M. Syslo (1988). A polynomial-time algorithm for subgraph isomorphism of two-connected series-parallel graphs. In G. Goos and J. Hartmanis (Eds.), *Automata, Languages, and Programming, 15th International Colloquium*, pp. 394 – 409. Springer.

Magnus, N. (1999). Design and implementation of case-based reasoning retrieval by case retrieval networks for Structured/Complex domains. Master's thesis, University of Kaiserslautern.

Maher, M. L. and D. M. Zang (1993). CADSYN: A case-based design process model. *Artificial Intelligence for Engineering Design, Analysis, and Manufacturing* 7(2), 97–110.

Maher, P. (1993). A similarity measure for conceptual graphs. *International Journal of Intelligent Systems.* 8(8), 819 – 837.

Mäkinen, E. (1989). On the subtree isomorphism problem for ordered trees. Technical report, Department of Computer Science, University of Tampere, Finland.

Mäkinen, E. (1990). A linear time and space algorithm for finding isomorphic subtrees of a binary tree. Technical report, Department of Computer Science, University of Tampere, Finland.

Manago, M., R. Bergmann, S. Wess, and R. Traphöner (1994). CASUEL: A common case representation language. ESPRIT Project 6322 Deliverable D1, University of Kaiserslautern, Kaiserslautern.

Martin, J. and D. Hirschberg (1995). The time complexity of decision tree induction. Technical report, Technical Report 95-27, Dept. of Information and Computer Science, University of California, Irvine.

Martin, J. H. (1990). *A Computational Model of Metaphor Interpretation.* Academic Press.

Martin, W. (1999). Customer relationship management: Eine geschäftsphilosophie zur optimierung von kundenidentifizierung, -ansprache und -bestandssicherung. Customer Relationship Management Kongress und Messe, http://www.crm-expo.com/.

McAllester, D. and D. Rosenblitt (1991). Systematic nonlinear planning. In *Proceedings of the Annual National Conference on Artificial Intelligence AAAI-91*, Annaheim, California, USA, pp. 634–639. AAAI: Morgan Kaufmann Publishers.

McCarthy, J. and P. J. Hayes (1969). Some philosophical problems from the standpoint of artificial intelligence. In B. Mehler and D. Michie (Eds.), *Machine Intelligence.* Edinburgh University Press.

Mehlhorn, K. (1984). *Data Structures and Algorithms 2: Graph Algorithms and NP-Completeness.* Berlin: Springer.

Melis, E. (Ed.) (1999). *7. German Workshop on Case-Based Reasoning (GWCBR'99).*

Meyfarth, S. (1997). Entwicklung eines transformationsorientierten Adaptions-konzeptes zum fallbasierten Schließen in INRECA. Master's thesis, University of Kaiserslautern, Germany.

Minor, M., P. Funk, T. Roth-Berghofer, and D. Wilson (Eds.) (2000). *ECAI 2000 Workshop on Flexible Strategies for Maintaining Knowledge Containers.*

Mougouie, B. (2001). Optimization of distance/similarity functions under linear and nonlinear constraints with application in case-based reasoning. Master's thesis, University of Kaiserslautern.

Mougouie, B. and R. Bergmann (2002). Similarity assessment for generalizied cases by optimization methods. In *Proceedings of the European Conference on Case-Based Reasoning (ECCBR-02)*. Springer.

Munoz-Avila, H. and J. Huellen (1996). Feature weighting by explaining case-based planning episodes. In I. Smith and B. Faltings (Eds.), *Proceedings of the 3th European Workshop on Case-Based Reasoning*. Springer.

Muñoz-Avila, H. and F. Weberskirch (1996). Planning for manufacturing workpieces by storing, indexing and replaying planning decisions. In B. Drabble (Ed.), *Proceedings of the 3rd Int. Conference on AI Planning Systems (AIPS-96)*. AAAI-Press.

Newell, A. (1982). The knowledge level. *Artificial Intelligence 18*, 87–127.

Newell, F. (1999). *Loyalty.Com: Customer Relationship Management in the New Era of Internet Marketing*. McGraw-Hill Professional Publishing.

Nick, M., K.-D. Althoff, T. Avieny, and B. Decker (2002). How experience management can benefit from relationships among different types of knowledge. In M. Minor and S. Staab (Eds.), *Proceedings of the First German Workshop on Experience Management*. GI-Editon – Lecture Notes in Informatics.

Nick, M., K.-D. Althoff, and C. Tautz (2001). Systematic maintenance of corporate experience repositories. *Computational Intelligence – Special Issue on Maintaining CBR Systems 17*(2), 364–386.

Nonaka, I. (1998). The knowledge-creating company. In *Harward Business Review on Knowledge Management*, pp. 21–46. Harvard Business School Press.

Nonaka, I. and H. Takeuchi (1997). *Die Organisation des Wissens*. Campus.

Nonaka, I., H. Takeuchi, and H. Takeuchi (1995). *Knowledge-Creating Company - How Japanese Companies Create the Dynamics of Innovation*. Oxford University Press.

Nosofsky, R. M. (1991). Stimulus bias, asymmetric similarity, and classification. *Cognitive Psychology 23 b*, 94–140.

Oehler, P., I. Vollrath, P. Conradi, and R. Bergmann (1998). Are you READEE for IPs? In A. Kunzmann and R. Seepold (Eds.), *Proceedings of the 2nd GI/ITG/GMM-Workshop "Reuse Techniques for VLSI Design"*. FZI-Report 3-13-9/98, Karlsruhe.

Oehler, P., I. Vollrath, P. Conradi, R. Bergmann, and T. Wahlmann (1998). READEE - decision support for IP selection using a knowledge-based approach. In *Proceedings of IP98 Europe*. Miller Freeman.

O'Leary, D. (1998). Enterprise knowledge management. *IEEE Computer 31*(3), 54–61.

Osborne, H. and D. Bridge (1996). A case base similarity framework. See Smith and Faltings (1996).

Osterweil, L. (1987). Software processes are software too. In *Proceedings of the Ninth International Conference on Software Engineering*, pp. 2 – 13.

Pachet, F. (1991). Reasoning with objects: The neopus environment. Technical Report 13/91, University of Paris VI.

Pal, S., T. Dillon, and D. Yeung (2000). *Soft Computing in Case-Based Reasoning.* Springer.

Perry, D. (1991). *VHDL.* McGraw Hill.

Plattner, H. (1999). Customer relationship management. In A.-W. Scheer and M. Nüttgens (Eds.), *Electronic Business Engineering / 4. Internationale Tagung Wirtschaftsinformatik*, pp. 2–12. Physica-Verlag.

Plaza, E. (1995). Cases as terms: A feature term approach to the structured representation of cases. See Aamodt and Veloso (1995), pp. 265–276.

Poulin, J., J. Caruso, and D. Hancock (1993). The business case for software reuse. *IBM Systems Journal 32*(4), 567–594.

Puppe, F. (1993). *Systematic Introduction to Expert Systems.* Springer Verlag.

Purvis, L. and P. Pu (1995). Adaptation using constraint satisfaction techniques. See Aamodt and Veloso (1995), pp. 289–300.

Purvis, L. and P. Pu (1996). An approach to case combination. In *Proceedings of the Adaptation in Case Based Reasoning Workshop of the European Conference on Artificial Intelligence (ECAI96)*, Budapest, Hungary.

Quinlan, J. (1996). Improved Use of Continuous Attributes in C4.5. *Journal of Artificial Intelligence Research 4*, 77–90.

Quinlan, J. R. (1983). Learning efficient classification procedures and their application to chess end games. In R. S. Michalski, J. G. Carbonell, and T. M. Mitchell (Eds.), *Machine Learning: An Artificial Intelligence Approach.* Redwood City CA: Morgan Kaufmann.

Quinlan, J. R. (1986). Induction of decision trees. *Machine Learning 1*(1), 81–106.

Quinlan, R. J. (1993). *C4.5 Programs for Machine Learning.* Morgan Kaufmann.

Redmond, M. (1990). Distributed Cases for Case-Based Reasoning; Facilitating Use of Multiple Cases. In *Proceedings of the Annual National Conference on Artificial Intelligence AAAI-90*, Boston, Massachusetts, USA, pp. 304–309. AAAI: Morgan Kaufmann Publishers.

Reinartz, T., I. Iglezakis, and T. Roth-Berghofer (2001). On quality measures for case-base maintenance. *Computational Intelligence – Special Issue on Maintaining CBR Systems 17*(2).

Ricci, F. and L. Senter (1998). Structured cases, trees and efficient retrieval. See Smyth and Cunningham (1998).

Richter, M. (1997). A note on fuzzy set theory and case based reasoning. Technical report, International Computer Science Institute, University of California.

Richter, M. M. (1992a). Classification and learning of similarity measures. In Opitz, Lausen, and Klar (Eds.), *Studies in Clasification, Data Analysis and Knowledge Organisation (Proceedings der Jahrestagung der Gesellschaft für Klassifikation)*. Springer Verlag.

Richter, M. M. (1992b). *Prinzipien der Künstlichen Intelligenz*. Stuttgart, Germany: B. G. Teubner.

Richter, M. M. (1994). On the Notion of Similarity in Case-Basd reasoning. In G. d. Riccia (Ed.), *Proc. Invitational Workshop on Uncertainty Reasoning*, Udine, Italy.

Richter, M. M. (1995). The knowledge contained in similarity measures. Invited Talk on the ICCBR-95.

Richter, M. M. and K.-D. Althoff (1999). *Similarity and Utility in Non-Numerical Domains*, pp. 403 – 413. Physika-Verlag.

Richter, M. M. and S. Schmitt (2001). Kundenmodellierung und Dialogführung: Eine Herausforderung für eCRM. In *Festschrift anläßlich des 60. Geburttages von Prof. Bliemel*.

Roddick, J. (1995). Survey of schema versioning issues for database systems. *Info, SW Technology 37*(3).

Rombach, H. D. and M. Verlage (1995). Directions in software process research. In M. V. Zelkowitz (Ed.), *Advances in Computers, Vol. 41*, pp. 1–61. Academic Press.

Rosewitz, M. and U. Timm (1998). Editor für elektronische Produktberatung. *Wirtschaftsinformatik 40*, 21–28.

Ruttkay, Z. (1994). Fuzzy constraint satisfaction. In *IEEE International Conference on Fuzzy Systems*, Volume 2, Orlando, pp. 1263–1268. IEEE.

Sacerdoti, E. (1974). Planning in a hierarchy of abstraction spaces. *Artificial Intelligence 5*, 115–135.

Salzberg, S. (1991). A nearest hyperrectangle learning method. *Machine Learning 6*, 277–309.

Sanders, K., B. Kettler, and J. Hendler (1997). The case for graph-structured representations. See Leake and Plaza (1997).

Schaaf, J. W. (1995). Fish and Sink: an anytime-algorithm to retrieve adequate cases. See Aamodt and Veloso (1995), pp. 538–547.

Schaaf, J. W. (1996). Fish and shrink: a next step towards efficient case retrieval in large scaled case bases. See Smith and Faltings (1996), pp. 362 376.

Schaaf, J. W. (1998). *Über die Suche nach situationsgerechten Fällen im Case-Based Reasoning*. DISKI 179. Infix.

Schmitt, S. simVar: A similarity-influenced question selection criterion for e-sales dialogs. *Artificial Intelligence Review*. Forthcoming.

Schmitt, S. and R. Bergmann (1999a). Applying case-based reasoning technology for product selection and customization in electronic commerce environments. In *12th Bled Electronic Commerce Conference*.

Schmitt, S. and R. Bergmann (1999b). Product customization in an electronic commerce environment using adaptation operators. In *7th German Workshop on Case-Based Reasoning*.

Schmitt, S. and R. Bergmann (2001). A formal approach to dialogs with online customers. In *14th Bled Electronic Commerce Conference*.

Schmitt, S., P. Dopichaj, and P. Dominguez-Marin (2002). Entropy-based vs. similarity-influenced: Attribute selection methods for dialogs tested on different electronic commerce domains. In *Proceedings of the European Conference on Case-Based Reasoning (ECCBR-02)*. Springer.

Schmitt, S., D. Jerusalem, and T. Nett (2000). An acquisition framework to implement questioning strategies for query building for CBR systems. See Göker (2000).

Schmitt, S., R. Maximini, G. Landeck, and J. Hohwiller (2000). A product customization module based on adaptation operators for CBR systems in e-commerce environments. See Blanzieri and Portinale (2000).

Schulz, S. (1999). CBR-works: A state-of-the-art shell for case-based applications. See Melis (1999).

Schumacher, J. (1998). Design and implemantation of a knowledge-intensive approach to product configuration in electronic commerce applications. Diplomarbeit, Universität Kaiserslautern.

Schumacher, J. and R. Bergmann (2000). An effective approach for similarity-based retrieval on top of relational databases. See Blanzieri and Portinale (2000).

Schumacher, J. and R. Traphöner (2000). Knowledge modelling. Technical report, Deliverable D3.4 of the WEBSELL Project.

Secchi, P. (Ed.) (1999). *Proceedings of Alerts and Lessons Learned: An Effective Way to Prevent Failures and Problems*, Noordwijk, The Netherlands. European Space Agency.

Seidl, T. (1998). *Adaptable Similarity Search in 3-D Database Systems*. Informatik. München, Germany: Herbert Utz Verlag.

Seidl, T. and H.-P. Kriegel (1997). Efficient user-adaptable similarity search in large multimedia databases. In *Proceedings of the 23rd International Conference on Very Large Databases*.

Sellis, T., N. Roussopoulos, and C. Faloutsos (1987). The r+-tree: A dynamic index for multi-dimensional objects. In *Proceedings of the 13th International Conference on Very Large Databases*, pp. 507–518.

Shannon, C. E. (1948). *The mathematical theory of communication*. Urbana: University of Illinois Press.

Shaw, M. (1990). Prospects for an engineering discipline of software. *IEEE Software 7*, 15–24.

Shaw, M. and B. Gaines (1996). Requirements acquisition. http://ksi.cpsc.ucalgary.ca/articles/SE/SeqAcq/.

Shimazu, H. (1998). A textual case-based reasoning system using XML on the world-wide web. See Smyth and Cunningham (1998).

Smith, I. and B. Faltings (Eds.) (1996). *Advances in Case-Based Reasoning*, Lecture Notes in Artificial Intelligence, 1186. Springer Verlag.

Smyth, B. (1996). *Case-Based Resign.* Ph. D. thesis, Trinity College Dublin.

Smyth, B. and P. Cotter (1999). Surfing the digital wave, generating personalized TV listings using collaborative, case-based recommendation. See Althoff et al. (1999).

Smyth, B. and P. Cotter (2000). A personalized television listings service. *Communications of the ACM 43*(8), 107–111.

Smyth, B. and P. Cunningham (1992). Déjà Vu: a hierarchical case-based reasoning system for software design. In B. Neumann (Ed.), *ECAI 92: 10th European Conference on Artificial Intelligence, August 1992, Vienna*, pp. 587–589. Chichester: Wiley.

Smyth, B. and P. Cunningham (1996). The utility problem analysed: A case-based reasoning perspective. See Smith and Faltings (1996).

Smyth, B. and P. Cunningham (Eds.) (1998). *Advances in Case-Based Reasoning (EWCBR'98)*, Lecture Notes in Artificial Intelligence (LNAI). Springer Verlag.

Smyth, B. and M. T. Keane (1993). Retrieving adaptable cases: The role of adaptation knowledge in case retrieval. See Wess et al. (1993), pp. 209–220.

Smyth, B. and M. T. Keane (1995). Remembering to forget. In C. S. Mellish (Ed.), *Proceedings of the 14th International Conference on Artificial Intelligence IJCAI-95*, pp. 377–382.

Smyth, B. and M. T. Keane (1996). Using adaptation knowledge to retrieve and adapt design cases. *Journal of Knowledge Based Systems 9*, 127–135.

Smyth, B. and E. McKenna (1996). Building compact competent case-bases. See Althoff et al. (1999).

Software Quality Institute. SPICE. http://www-sqi.cit.gu.edu.au/spice/.

Stahl, A. (2000). Recursive case-based reasoning and its application for product configuration in e-commerce environments. Master's thesis, University of Kaiserslautern.

Stahl, A. (2001). Learning feature weights by using case order feedback. In D. Aha and I. Watson (Eds.), *Proceedings of the 4th International Conference on Case-Based Reasoning.*

Stahl, A., B. Bergmann, and S. Schmitt (2000). A customization approach for structured products in electronic shops. In *13th Bled Electronic Commerce Conference.*

Stahl, A. and R. Bergmann (2000). Applying recursive CBR for the customization of structured products in an electronic shop. See Blanzieri and Portinale (2000).

Standish, T. (1984). An essay on software reuse. *IEEE Transactions on Software Engineering 10*(5), 494 – 497.

Stewart, T. (1997). *Intellectual Capital: The New Wealth of Organizations.* New York: Doubleday.

Stolpmann, M. and S. Wess (1999). *Optimierung der Kundenbeziehung mit CBR Systemen.* Addison Wesley Longmann (Business and Computing).

Strube, G., A. Enzinger, D. Janetzko, and M. Knauff (1995). Knowledge engineering for CBR systems from a cognitive science perspective. See Aamodt and Veloso (1995), pp. 548–558.

Strube, G. and D. Janetzko (1990). Episodisches Wissen und fallbasiertes Schließen. *Schweizerische Zeitschrift für Psychologie 49*, 211–221.

Studer, R., A. Abecker, and S. Decker (1999). Informatik-Methoden für das Wissensmanagement. In *Festschrift Zum 60. Geburtstag Von Prof. Dr. Wolffried Stucky.* Teubner.

Sycara, K. and D. Navinchandra (1991). Influences: A thematic abstraction for the creative reuse of multiple cases. See Bareiss (1991), pp. 133–144.

Tambe, M. and A. Newell (1988). Some chunks are expensive. In *Proceedings of the 5th International Conference on Machine Learning*, pp. 451–458.

Tan, M. (1993). Cost-sensitive learning of classification knowledge and its applications in robotics. *Machine Learning 13*, 7–33.

Tautz, C. (2000). *Customizing Software Engineering Experience Management Systems to Organizational Needs.* Ph. D. thesis, University of Kaiserslautern.

Tautz, C. and K.-D. Althoff (1997). Using case-based reasoning for reusing software knowledge. See Leake and Plaza (1997), pp. 156–165.

tec:inno GmbH (1999). CBR-works 4.0 reference manual.

The Knowledge Management Forum (1996). What is knowledge management. http://www.km-forum.org/what_is.html.

Thomas, C. (1993). Design, implementation and evaluation of an adaptive user interface. *Knowledge-Based Systems 6*, 230–238.

Thomas, D. and P. Moorby (1991). *The Verilog Hardware Description Language.* Kluwer Academic Publishers.

Thomas, H., R. Foil, and J. Dacus (1997). New technology bliss and pain in a large customer service center. See Leake and Plaza (1997), pp. 166–177.

Turney, P. (2000). Types of cost in inductive concept learning. In *Workshop on Cost-Sensitive Learning at the Seventeenth International Conference on Machine Learning (WCSL at ICML-2000).*

Tversky, A. (1977). Features of similarity. *Psychological Review 84*, 327–352.

Ullman, J. R. (1976). An algorithm for subgraph isomorphism. *Journal of the Association for Computing Machinery. 23*(1), 31 – 42.

v. Neumann, J. and O. Morgenstern (1944). *Theory of games and economic behavior.* John Wiley and Sons, Inc.

Van de Velde, W. (1994). *An Overview of CommonKADS.* IOS Press.

Veloso, M. M. (1994). *Planning and Learning by Analogical Reasoning.* Number 886 in Lecture Notes in Computer Science. Berlin: Springer.

Vollrath, I. (1998). Reuse of complex electronic designs - requirements analysis for a CBR application. See Smyth and Cunningham (1998).

Vollrath, I. (2000). Handling vague and qualitative criteria in case-based reasoning applications. See Göker (2000).

Vollrath, I. and P. Oehler (1998). READEE – A Similarity-Based Reuse Assistant. In *Design, Automation and Test in Europe Conference (DATE'98), University Booth Demonstration Abstracts.*

Vollrath, I., W. Wilke, and R. Bergmann (1998). Case-based reasoning support for online catalog sales. *IEEE Internet Computing 2*(4), 47–54.

Voß, A. (1994, August). The need for knowledge acquisition in case-based reasoning – some experiences from an architectural domain. In A. G. Cohn (Ed.), *ECAI'94*, Amsterdam, pp. 463 – 467. Wiley, Chichester.

Voß, A. (1996, August). Towards a methodology for case adaptation. In W. Wahlster (Ed.), *ECAI'96, 12th European Conference on Artificial Intelligence, Aug. 1996, Budapest*, pp. 147–151. John Wiley and Sons, Chichester.

Voß, A. (1997). Case reusing systems – survey, framework and guidelines. *The Knowledge Engineering Review 12*(1), in print.

Voß, A., B. Bartsch-Spörl, L. Hovestadt, K. P. Jantke, U. Petersohn, and G. Strube (1996). FABEL. *KI – Künstliche Intelligenz 10*(3), 70–76.

Wagner, R. A. and M. J. Fischer (1974). The string-to-string correction problem. *Journal of the Association for Computing Machinery 23*(1), 168–173.

Wahlmann, T. (1999). Implementierung einer skalierbaren diskreten Kosinustransformation in VHLD. Master's thesis, University of Siegen.

Wang, Y., N. Inuzuka, and N. Ishii (1994). A method of similarity metrics using fuzzy integration. In *Proceedings of the 3rd Pacific Rim International Conference on AI*, pp. 1028 – 1034.

Waszkiewicz, P., P. Cunningham, and C. Byrne (1999). Case-based user profiling in a personal travel assistant. See Kay (1999).

Weber, R., D. Aha, and I. Becerra-Fernandez (2000). Categorizing intelligent lesson learned systems. In D. Aha and R. Weber (Eds.), *Intelligent Lessons Learned Systems: Papers from the 2000 Workshop (Technical Report WS-00-03).* AAAI Press.

Wess, S. (1993). PATDEX – Ein Ansatz zur wissensbasierten und inkrementellen Verbesserung von Ähnlichkeitsbewertungen in der fallbasierten Diagnostik. In F. Puppe and Guenter (Eds.), *Proceedings XPS-93*, Hamburg. Springer-Verlag.

Wess, S. (1995). *Fallbasiertes Problemlösen in wissensbasierten Systemen zur Entscheidungsunterstützung und Diagnostik.* Ph. D. thesis, Universität Kaiserslautern. Available as DISKI 126, infix Verlag.

Wess, S., K.-D. Althoff, and G. Derwand (1993). Using kd-trees to improve the retrieval step in case-based reasoning. See Wess et al. (1993), pp. 167–181.

Wess, S., K.-D. Althoff, and M. M. Richter (Eds.) (1993). *Topics in Case-Based Reasoning. Proc. of the First European Workshop on Case-Based Reasoning (EWCBR-93)*, Lecture Notes in Artificial Intelligence, 837. Springer Verlag.

Wetter, T. (1984). *Ein modallogisch beschriebenes Expertensystem, ausgeführt am Beispiel von Ohrenerkankungen.* Ph. D. thesis, RWTH Aachen.

Wettschereck, D. and D. W. Aha (1995). Weighting features. See Aamodt and Veloso (1995), pp. 347–358.

Wiig, K. (1997). Knowledge management: Where did it come from and where will it go? *Expert Systems with Applications 14.*

Wilke, W. (1999). *Knowledge Management for Intelligent Sales Support in Electronic Commerce.* DISKI 213. Infix Verlag.

Wilke, W. and R. Bergmann (1996a). Considering decision cost during learning of feature weights. See Smith and Faltings (1996), pp. 460–472.

Wilke, W. and R. Bergmann (1996b). Incremental Adaptation with the INRECA-System. In *ECAI 1996 Workshop on Adaptation in Case-Based Reasoning.*

Wilke, W. and R. Bergmann (1998). Techniques and knowledge used for adaptation during case-based problem solving. In *Proceedings of the 11th International Conference on Industrial and Engineering Applications of Artificial Intelligence and Expert Systems.* Wiley.

Wilke, W., M. Lenz, and S. Wess (1998). Case-based reasoning for electronic commerce. In H.-D. Burkhard, B. Bartsch-Spörl, M. Lenz, and S. Wess (Eds.), *Case-Based Reasoning Technology: From Foundations to Applications*, Number 1400, Chapter 4, pp. 91–114. Springer.

Wilke, W., B. Smyth, and P. Cunningham (1998). Using configuration techniques for adaptation. In M. Lenz, B.-S. B., H.-D. Burkhard, and S. Wess (Eds.), *Case-Based Reasoning Technology: From Foundations to Applications.*, Chapter 6, pp. 139–167. Springer.

Wilke, W., I. Vollrath, K.-D. Althoff, and R. Bergmann (1997). A Framework for Learning Adaptation Knowledge Based on Knowledge Light Approaches. See Bergmann and Wilke (1997), pp. 235–242.

Wilkins, D. (1988). *Practical Planning: Extending the classical AI planning paradigm.* Morgan Kaufmann.

Wilson, D. and D. Leake (2001). Maintaining case-based reasoners: Dimensions and directions. *Computational Intelligence – Special Issue on Maintaining CBR Systems 17(2).*

Winograd, T. (1975). Frame representations and the declarative/procedural controversy. In D. G. Bobrow and A. M. Collins (Eds.), *Representation and Understanding: Studies in Cognitive Science*, pp. 185–210. New York: Academic Press.

Wolf, T., S. Decker, and A. Abecker (1999). Unterstützung des Wissensmanagements durch Informations- und Kommunikationstechnologie. In A.-W. Scheer and M. Nüttgens (Eds.), *Electronic Business Engineering / 4. Internationale Tagung Wirtschaftsinformatik*, pp. 746–766. Physica-Verlag.

Wong, J. H. Y., K. Ng, and H. Leung (1996). A stochastic approach to solving fuzzy constraint satisfaction problems. In *Lecture Notes in Computer Science*, Volume 1118, pp. 568–569. Springer.

Yokoyama, T. (1990). An object-oriented and constraint-based knowledge representation system for design object modeling. In *Proceedings of the Sixth Conference on Artificial Intelligence Applications*, pp. 146–150. IEEE, Los Alamitos, CA.

Zalta, E. N. Stanford encyclopedia of philosophy. http://plato.stanford.edu/.

Zito-Wolf, R. and R. Alterman (1992). Multicases: A case-based representation for procedural knowledge. In *Proceedings of the Fourteenth Annual Conference of the Cognitive Science Society*, pp. 331–336. Lawrence Erlbaum.

Index

Lecture Notes in Artificial Intelligence (LNAI)

Lecture Notes in Computer Science